Understanding Oracle APEX 5 Application Development

Second Edition

Edward Sciore

〈IOUG〉
Independent oracle users group

Apress®

Understanding Oracle APEX 5 Application Development

ISBN-13 (pbk): 978-1-4842-0990-5

ISBN-13 (electronic): 978-1-4842-0989-9

Managing Director: Welmoed Spahr
Lead Editor: Jonathan Gennick
Technical Reviewer: Darl Kuhn
Editorial Board: Steve Anglin, Mark Beckner, Gary Cornell, Louise Corrigan, Jim DeWolf,
    Jonathan Gennick, Robert Hutchinson, Michelle Lowman, James Markham,
    Susan McDermott, Matthew Moodie, Jeffrey Pepper, Douglas Pundick, Ben Renow-Clarke,
    Gwenan Spearing, Matt Wade, Steve Weiss
Coordinating Editor: Jill Balzano
Copy Editor: Nancy Sixsmith
Compositor: SPi Global
Indexer: SPi Global
Artist: SPi Global
Cover Designer: Anna Ishchenko

Distributed to the book trade worldwide by Springer Science+Business Media New York,
233 Spring Street, 6th Floor, New York, NY 10013. Phone 1-800-SPRINGER, fax (201) 348-4505,
e-mail orders-ny@springer-sbm.com, or visit www.springeronline.com. Apress Media, LLC is a
California LLC and the sole member (owner) is Springer Science + Business Media Finance
Inc (SSBM Finance Inc). SSBM Finance Inc is a **Delaware** corporation.

For information on translations, please e-mail rights@apress.com, or visit www.apress.com.

Apress and friends of ED books may be purchased in bulk for academic, corporate, or promotional use. eBook versions and licenses are also available for most titles. For more information, reference our Special Bulk Sales–eBook Licensing web page at www.apress.com/bulk-sales.

Any source code or other supplementary material referenced by the author in this text is available to readers at www.apress.com. For detailed information about how to locate your book's source code, go to www.apress.com/source-code/.

Contents at a Glance

About IOUG Press

IOUG Press is a joint effort by the ***Independent Oracle Users Group (the IOUG)*** and ***Apress*** to deliver some of the highest-quality content possible on Oracle Database and related topics. The IOUG is the world's leading, independent organization for professional users of Oracle products. Apress is a leading, independent technical publisher known for developing high-quality, no-fluff content for serious technology professionals. The IOUG and Apress have joined forces in IOUG Press to provide the best content and publishing opportunities to working professionals who use Oracle products.

Our shared goals include:

- Developing content with excellence
- Helping working professionals to succeed
- Providing authoring and reviewing opportunities
- Networking and raising the profiles of authors and readers

To learn more about Apress, visit our website at **www.apress.com**. Follow the link for IOUG Press to see the great content that is now available on a wide range of topics that matter to those in Oracle's technology sphere.

Visit **www.ioug.org** to learn more about the Independent Oracle Users Group and its mission. Consider joining if you haven't already. Review the many benefits at www.ioug.org/join. Become a member. Get involved with peers. Boost your career.

www.ioug.org/join

Apress®

Contents

About the Author

Edward Sciore is an associate professor in the computer science department at Boston College. He has been teaching college students for more than 35 years. His research specialty is database systems, and he thoroughly enjoys teaching the wonders of database technology to captive students.

About the Technical Reviewer

Darl Kuhn is a DBA/developer working for Oracle. He teaches Oracle classes at Regis University in Denver, Colorado, and is an active member of the Rocky Mountain Oracle Users Group. Darl enjoys sharing knowledge, and it has led to several book projects over the years.

Acknowledgments

First and foremost, I would like to thank the APEX user community. Numerous people routinely and generously share their APEX knowledge by writing blogs, creating demonstration APEX sites, and answering all kinds of questions on the APEX web forums. I learned much from them. This book is my attempt to give something back.

I also want to thank my Apress editors, Jonathan Gennick and Jill Balzano. Jonathan convinced me to write the book, and provided guidance and encouragement every step of the way. Jill was always supportive, and smoothed out the inevitable bumps in the road.

I also want to acknowledge the support of my two children, Leah and Aaron. Aaron's name can also be found somewhere in Chapter 10.

Most importantly, I want to acknowledge my wife Amy. She listened to my ideas, helped me resolve technical issues, worked through the APEX examples, and pointed out passages in the book that needed clarification. She was a relentless proofreader. I could have written the book without her, but it would not have been anywhere near as good. Thanks.

Introduction

Application Express (otherwise known as APEX) is a web application that is tightly coupled to an Oracle database. It has several uses: you can use its SQL Workshop tool to query the database, modify its contents, or change its structure; you can use its Application Builder tool to create your own web applications that interact with the database; and you can run the web applications created by you and others.

The application builder is especially interesting because it provides a simple, nontraditional way to build web pages. You do not specify code for the page directly; instead, you choose from a set of built-in templates. There is a template for the overall page and templates for each kind of component that you want to put on the page (such as reports, buttons, and so on). Each template has a set of properties, whose values determine where each component is located on the page, what it looks like, and how it behaves. You create a page simply by choosing templates for the components you want and assigning values to their properties.

The APEX application builder saves the property values for each component in a private database. When a browser requests one of your application's pages, the APEX server extracts the property values relevant to that page from its database, constructs the HTML code corresponding to those values, and returns that code to the browser. This process is called *rendering* the page, and APEX is called an *HTML generator*.

The advantage of using an HTML generator such as APEX is that you can build web pages without any knowledge of HTML (or CSS, JavaScript, or PHP). Moreover, because APEX is tightly coupled to an Oracle database, it automatically handles the intricacies of database interaction. APEX makes it possible to easily create good-looking, highly functional, and database-aware pages with only a rudimentary knowledge of SQL.

Why This Book?

Designing a page with APEX seems straightforward — all you have to do is choose the components you want and then assign the appropriate values to their properties. Choosing components is straightforward, but assigning property values is not. A page and its components have many properties, and you have to know the purpose of those properties to know what values to assign. These properties range from the essential (such as the *source query* of a report) to the obscure (such as the *static ID* of a report). Some properties (such as the *HTML expression* of a report column) are hooks that allow you to insert customized HTML or JavaScript code into the generated web page.

The purpose of this book is to gently lead you through the cornucopia of properties. To this end, the book develops a demo web application that illustrates various APEX techniques for building typical web-page functionality. The pages of this application start out simply and gradually increase their level of sophistication. With each page,

I introduce a few new properties, discuss their purpose, and illustrate their usefulness. By the end of the book, you will have been so immersed in the world of APEX properties that you should feel confident enough to tackle any web site project of your own. And if your project requires even more sophistication than appears here, you should be comfortable enough to use properties that are not covered, perhaps by looking at the documentation, examining the numerous prepackaged applications provided by Oracle, checking a web forum, or even figuring it out on your own.

Another way to build web pages in APEX is to rely on wizards. APEX provides wizards to generate common components, such as report pages, data entry forms, and tabular forms. Each wizard asks you a series of questions (such as What is the name of the page? What table do you want to display? Should the page have an entry in the navigation menu?) and then uses your responses to generate appropriate components having appropriate properties. The advantage, of course, is that you don't need to know anything about properties. The disadvantage is that wizards tend to produce "one size fits all" pages, in terms of both their appearance and their functionality.

Wizards can take you only so far. If you want any kind of control over the look, feel, and behavior of your page, you need to get involved with its properties. This book provides the guidance you need.

Demo Application

As this book explains each part of the APEX application builder, it guides you through the development of a small application. I encourage you to build your own version of the application as you follow along. You can run my version of the application by going to the URL apex.oracle.com/pls/apex/f?p=87059:1. You can also download the source code for the application from the Apress web site.

Unlike demo applications in many books, this application does not "do" anything particularly interesting. Instead, each page is constructed to illustrate one or more techniques. Some of the pages have similar functionality, in order to illustrate the trade-offs between different implementation techniques.

The demo application uses the DEPT and EMP database tables provided with every APEX workspace. The DEPT table lists the departments of a company, and the EMP table lists the employees in those departments. Their columns are as follows:

```
DEPT(DeptNo, DName, Loc)
EMP (EmpNo, EName, Job, Mgr, HireDate, Sal, Comm, DeptNo)
```

The key of DEPT is DeptNo, and the key of EMP is EmpNo. Each table has a built-in sequence for generating unique values for these keys, as well as an associated insertion trigger. If you insert a record into one of the tables and omit a value for the key, the trigger will automatically generate a key value from the appropriate sequence.

The demo application makes one modification to these tables: the EMP table has the additional column OffSite of type char(1). An employee will have the value 'N' for this column if the employee works in the department office, and 'Y' if the employee works offsite. For your reference, here is the SQL code to add the new column.

```
alter table EMP
add OffSite char(1);
```

After altering the table, you will need to assign an Offsite value for each existing employee. In my demo, the employees SCOTT, ALLEN, WARD, and TURNER work offsite; the others work onsite. Chapter 1 discusses the APEX tools needed to make these database modifications.

Required Background

This book is for people who are comfortable using a database system and want to learn how to write nontrivial web applications in APEX. Many of the techniques used to write APEX pages involve skills in the following database and web-design languages and technologies.

SQL

The most important skill you need is the ability to write SQL queries. All data access in APEX is performed via SQL statements, and the value of many properties involves SQL in some way. The more fluent you are in SQL, the more sophisticated your reports and forms can be. This book assumes that you are comfortable with SQL. For the most part, the demo application uses relatively simple SQL statements, but occasionally I include something more complex (such as an outer join or nested query) to illustrate what is possible.

HTML

This book also assumes that you are familiar with basic HTML — in particular, how tags such as <p>, <b>, <a>, and <img> can be used to format text and display images. Advanced features such as JavaScript and CSS are ignored.

PL/SQL

APEX uses PL/SQL to specify behavior. PL/SQL is Oracle's programming language; its main feature is an embedded SQL syntax that makes it easy to write procedures that interact with the database. Prior knowledge of PL/SQL is a plus, but not necessary. This book introduces PL/SQL in Chapter 7 and uses only basic features of the language.

APEX

Finally, this book does not require you to have prior experience with APEX. Although it is possible to follow the book without actually using APEX, doing so seems rather pointless. So you should get an APEX account. The easiest and best way to get an account is by going to the apex.oracle.com site. Because I created my demo application from there, you should see the same screens that appear in this book.

Distinguishing Screens from Pages

APEX is a web application that is used to create other web applications. Thus APEX has a home page, and its various tools have their own sets of pages. Throughout this book, I describe how to use APEX to build a page of an application. This can lead to some strange sentences, such as "Clicking the Run button from the application's APEX home page runs its home page." To avoid such confusion, I denote all APEX pages as "screens." The previous sentence becomes "Clicking the Run button from the application's home screen runs its home page," which is less awkward and hopefully less confusing.

CHAPTER 1

▀ ▀ ▀

The SQL Workshop

Congratulations! You are on the brink of learning how to build APEX web applications. But before you can begin, you need an APEX account. There are several ways to obtain an account: you can register for a free account through the apex.oracle.com web site; you might be given an account to an APEX server at your job; or you can even install an APEX server yourself and create your own account to it.

No matter the circumstance, your account will have an associated URL. Invoking the URL from your browser takes you to a login screen. Figure 1-1 shows the login screen used by the apex.oracle.com server.

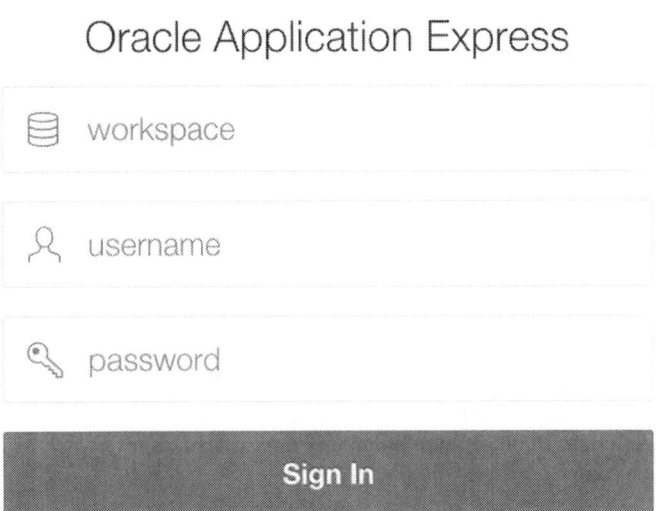

Figure 1-1. APEX login screen

Entering your credentials then takes you to the APEX home screen, the top of which is shown in Figure 1-2.

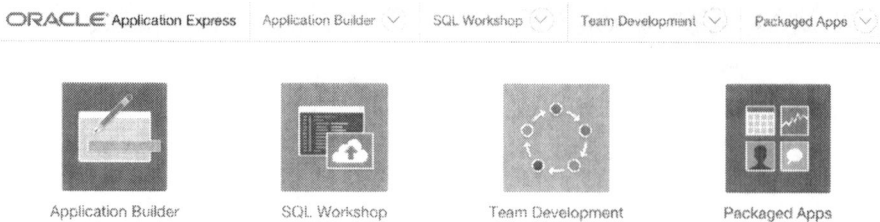

Figure 1-2. *APEX home screen*

The APEX development environment contains several tools. Of primary importance is the application builder tool, which will be covered in depth starting in Chapter 2. We begin here by looking at two tools from the APEX SQL Workshop: the object browser, and the SQL command tool. These tools allow you to directly manipulate the database — the object browser gives you a graphical user interface, and the SQL command tool lets you submit SQL statements and PL/SQL code blocks for execution.

Although the SQL Workshop tools are not essential for application development, using them can make your life much easier. Here are five ways that they can help an application developer:

- *To remind you of the database structure.* For example, a typical application involves several tables, each of which can have numerous columns. It is often impractical to memorize the details of each one. When building a page that references a table, you can use these tools to help refresh your memory.

- *To modify the structure of the database.* For example, these tools are the easiest way to execute the alter table command given in the introduction.

- *To modify the contents of the database.* For example, you might want to insert or modify records to test the behavior of a page or to reset the database after testing the page.

- *To examine the contents of the database.* After running a page, you can verify that the database updated correctly.

- *To debug an SQL statement or PL/SQL block.* By executing code in the SQL command tool first, you can verify that it produces the expected result before you actually assign it as the value of some property on a page.

To get to the SQL Workshop, click the SQL Workshop button on the APEX home screen. The resulting screen is shown in Figure 1-3. From this screen, you can then click the Object Browser or SQL Commands button to get to the desired tool.

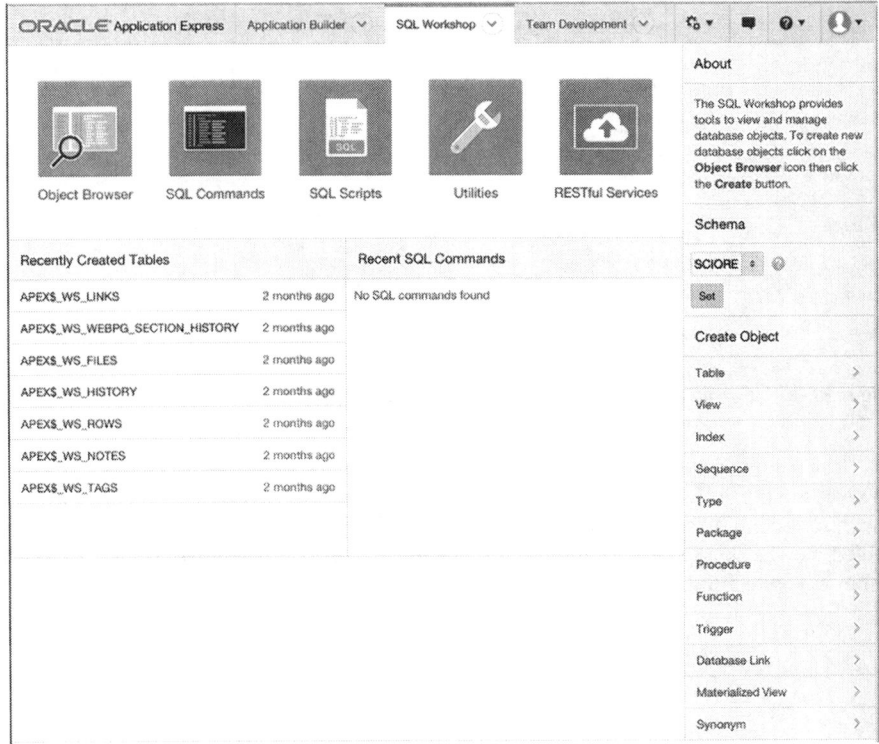

Figure 1-3. *SQL Workshop home screen*

Object Browser

The object browser lets you interact with a database quickly and easily. From it, you can examine the description of each table — that is, the types and properties of its columns, and its constraints, indexes, and triggers — as well as its contents. You can also use the object browser to make simple changes to the description or contents of a table.

The home screen for the object browser displays a list of table names along its left side. Clicking a table name displays information about that table. For example, the screen for the EMP table appears in Figure 1-4.

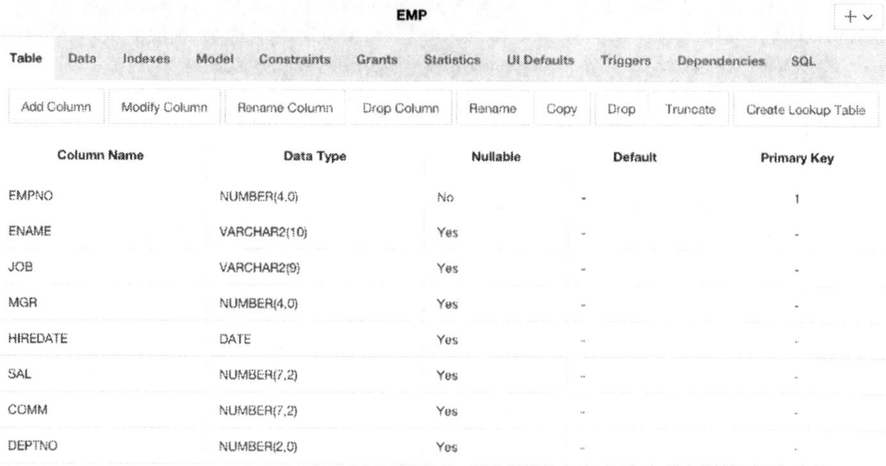

EMP					

Table Data Indexes Model Constraints Grants Statistics UI Defaults Triggers Dependencies SQL

Add Column Modify Column Rename Column Drop Column Rename Copy Drop Truncate Create Lookup Table

Column Name	Data Type	Nullable	Default	Primary Key
EMPNO	NUMBER(4,0)	No	-	1
ENAME	VARCHAR2(10)	Yes	-	-
JOB	VARCHAR2(9)	Yes	-	-
MGR	NUMBER(4,0)	Yes	-	-
HIREDATE	DATE	Yes	-	-
SAL	NUMBER(7,2)	Yes	-	-
COMM	NUMBER(7,2)	Yes	-	-
DEPTNO	NUMBER(2,0)	Yes	-	-

Figure 1-4. *Viewing the EMP table from the object browser*

The center of the screen displays information about each column of the table. Above this information is a series of buttons that let you modify it. As an example, recall that the introduction discussed the need for an Offsite column; let's add that column to the table now. Clicking the Add Column button displays a form to fill in the details of the new column. Figure 1-5 shows how I filled in this form.

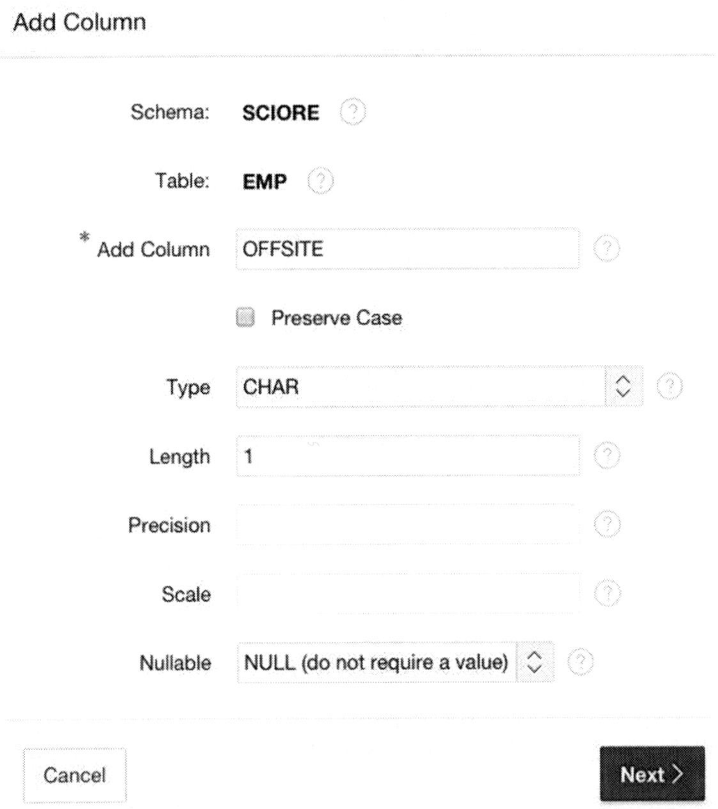

Add Column

Schema:	**SCIORE** ⓘ
Table:	**EMP** ⓘ
* Add Column	OFFSITE ⓘ
	☐ Preserve Case
Type	CHAR ↕ ⓘ
Length	1 ⓘ
Precision	ⓘ
Scale	ⓘ
Nullable	NULL (do not require a value) ↕ ⓘ

Cancel   Next >

Figure 1-5. *Adding a new column to EMP*

Clicking the Next button takes you to a confirmation screen; from there, click Finish to complete the action. The EMP screen should now display the new column.

Figure 1-4 shows a tab bar above the row of buttons, with the Table tab currently selected. This tab displays column information for the table, as you have seen. The other tabs show you other kinds of information, and provide appropriate ways to view and modify that information. For example, clicking the Triggers tab displays the current triggers for the table. Clicking the name of a trigger displays additional detail about that trigger (including a button for examining its SQL code). For another example, the SQL tab displays the SQL code that defines the table.

Finally, consider the Data tab, which displays the contents of the table. The top of this table appears in Figure 1-6. Note that there is a button to insert a new row and an edit link for each row.

Figure 1-6. *Viewing the contents of EMP*

Clicking a row's edit link displays a form for modifying it. Figure 1-7 shows this form when you click the link for employee 7698. Clicking the Apply Changes button performs any modifications that may have been made to the column values; clicking the Delete button deletes the record.

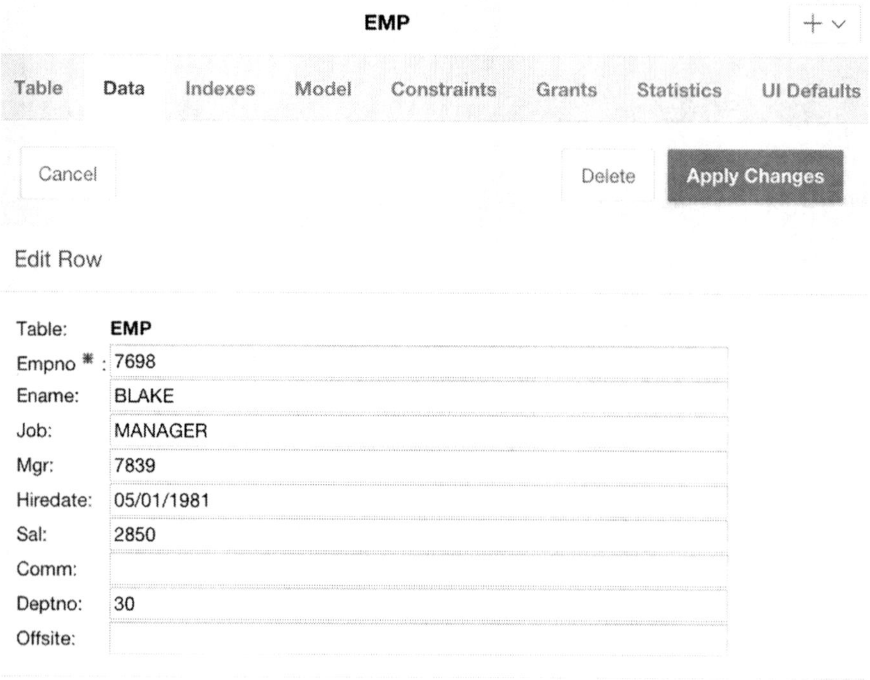

Figure 1-7. *Editing the contents of employee 7698*

If you look at the contents of the EMP table in Figure 1-6, you see that the values for the Offsite column are all null. If you want, you can proceed to edit each record, setting the column value to **'Y'** or **'N'** as desired. However, given the tediousness of this approach, it is easier to use the SQL command tool, which is discussed in the next section.

SQL Command Tool

Most of the actions that you can perform in the object browser correspond to one or more SQL statements. In effect, the object browser is merely a convenient way to formulate and execute the simpler SQL statements. If you want to perform more complex activities, use the SQL command tool.

The command tool divides the screen into two sections. You type an SQL statement or PL/SQL block into the top section, and the result appears at the bottom. Figure 1-8 shows the screen after executing the SQL statement `select * from EMP`.

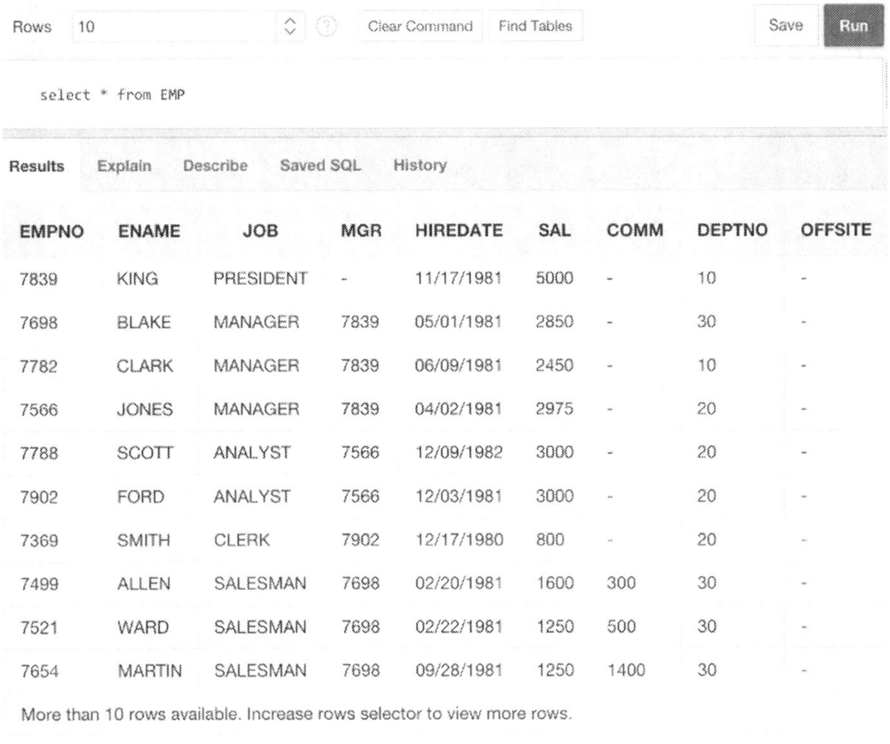

| Rows | 10 | | | Clear Command | Find Tables | | | Save | Run |

```
select * from EMP
```

Results   Explain   Describe   Saved SQL   History

EMPNO	ENAME	JOB	MGR	HIREDATE	SAL	COMM	DEPTNO	OFFSITE
7839	KING	PRESIDENT	-	11/17/1981	5000	-	10	-
7698	BLAKE	MANAGER	7839	05/01/1981	2850	-	30	-
7782	CLARK	MANAGER	7839	06/09/1981	2450	-	10	-
7566	JONES	MANAGER	7839	04/02/1981	2975	-	20	-
7788	SCOTT	ANALYST	7566	12/09/1982	3000	-	20	-
7902	FORD	ANALYST	7566	12/03/1981	3000	-	20	-
7369	SMITH	CLERK	7902	12/17/1980	800	-	20	-
7499	ALLEN	SALESMAN	7698	02/20/1981	1600	300	30	-
7521	WARD	SALESMAN	7698	02/22/1981	1250	500	30	-
7654	MARTIN	SALESMAN	7698	09/28/1981	1250	1400	30	-

More than 10 rows available. Increase rows selector to view more rows.

Figure 1-8. *Using the SQL command tool*

Only 10 of the 14 employee records are displayed, due to the Rows select list located above the query. By default, its value is set to 10; if you want more rows displayed, you must first select a larger number. This feature is intentional. By forcing you to explicitly specify the output size of your query, APEX protects you from yourself. Suppose, for example, that you execute a multi-table query in which you wrote the join conditions incorrectly (or forgot them entirely). The resulting output could easily have billions of records that, if not truncated, would cause your APEX session to be unusable.

To the right of the Rows select list is a Find Tables button, which is useful if you need to be reminded about the tables and their columns. Clicking this button displays a window similar to the object browser. You can scroll through the available tables; selecting a table shows its column information. Figure 1-9 shows the result of using the Table Finder window to display the DEPT columns.

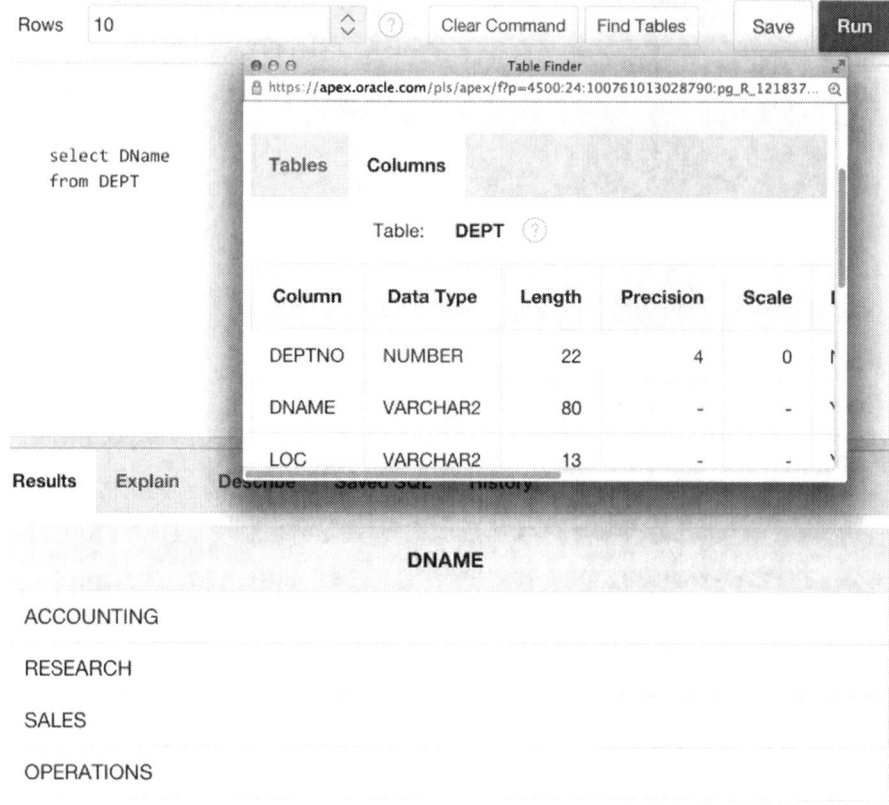

***Figure 1-9.** Using the Table Finder window*

Figure 1-8 points out the need to modify the Offsite values for the EMP records. In the introduction, I suggested that all employees work onsite except SCOTT, ALLEN, WARD, and TURNER. The easy way to handle this is to execute two update commands: the first one sets everybody's Offsite value to 'N', and the second sets the four chosen records to 'Y'. You can either run each statement individually in the command tool or combine them into a single PL/SQL block and execute it. The code for the latter option appears in Listing 1-1.

Listing 1-1. A PL/SQL Block to Assign Offsite Values

```
begin
    update EMP
    set OffSite = 'N';

    update EMP
    set OffSite = 'Y'
    where EName in ('SCOTT', 'ALLEN', 'WARD', 'TURNER');
end;
```

Summary

This chapter examined the object browser and SQL command tools in the APEX SQL Workshop. Both tools allow you to view and modify the database, but via very different interfaces. The object browser provides a visual interface, in which you perform tasks by clicking buttons and filling out forms. The SQL command tool provides a command-based interface, in which you perform tasks by executing SQL statements.

The object browser is ideal for performing common and simple tasks. As its name implies, the object browser is also well-suited for exploring the database. The point-and-click interface makes it easy to discover the various tables in the database and explore their columns. The object browser also does not require familiarity with SQL, so it is especially suitable for casual users.

The SQL command tool, on the other hand, assumes that the user is both familiar with the database structure and proficient in SQL. The command tool is therefore suitable for experienced users of the database. If you know the appropriate SQL, you can perform many tasks much more easily from the SQL command tool than from the object browser.

CHAPTER 2

■ ■ ■

Applications and Pages

This chapter begins an examination of the APEX application builder. You will learn about the basic tools for creating applications and pages — notably, the Create Application wizard and Create Page wizard — and use them to build a multi-page application that can be run from any browser. You will also see how to use the APEX page designer to modify the properties of the pages in your application. Although these pages will have no content to speak of, the techniques in this chapter provide the basis for the content-creation techniques of subsequent chapters.

Creating an Application

To use the application builder, you need to get to its home screen. You can either click the Application Builder tab in the APEX menu bar, or click the large Application Builder button from the APEX home screen of Figure 1-2.

The application builder's home screen displays an icon for each application in your workspace. It is likely that your APEX account has the preinstalled application called Sample Database Application; if so, your application builder home screen looks like Figure 2-1.

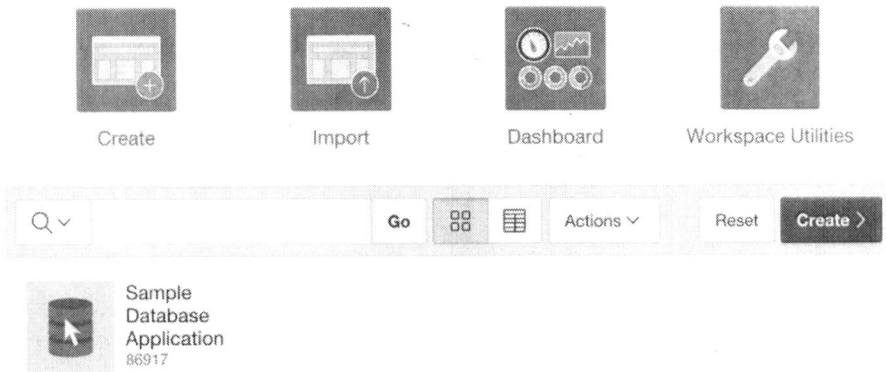

Figure 2-1. Application builder home screen

Let's create a new application. There are two relevant buttons on the application builder's home screen: a large Create button at the top left and a smaller Create button on the far right of the search bar. Clicking either button brings up a wizard to help you specify the required property values. Properties having a red asterisk are most critical because you must supply a non-blank value for them. The other properties can usually be left with their default values.

The first screen of the wizard asks you to select an application type. Your application will be a desktop application, so select Desktop. The next screen, shown in Figure 2-2, assigns default values for some properties.

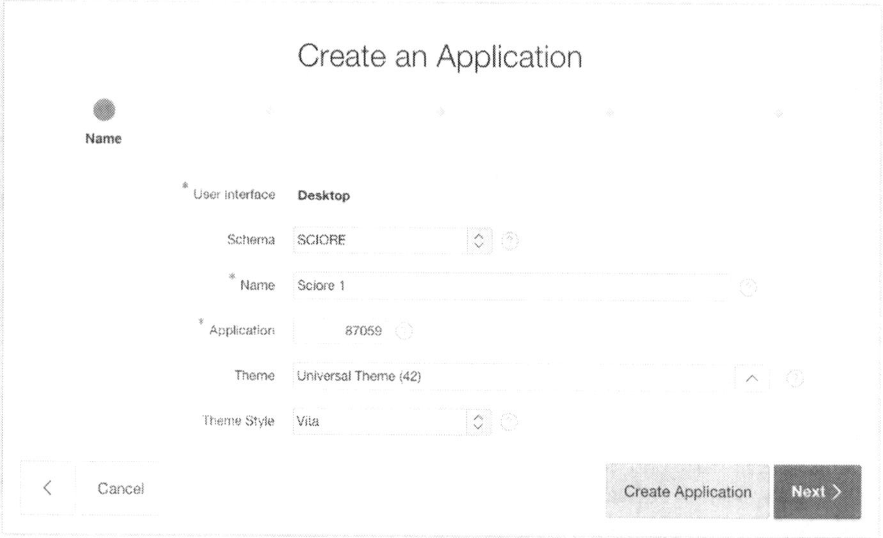

Figure 2-2. *Second screen of the Create Application Wizard*

You should rename the application to something more appropriate, such as **Employee Demo**. You should also consider changing the theme. If you click the up arrow of the theme's text box, the wizard will display a list of the available themes. I kept Universal Theme as my theme, but changed the theme style to Vita-Slate.

You now have the option of either creating the application, thereby accepting default values for its remaining properties, or continuing through more specification screens. Because this is your first time through the wizard, you should check out your options; so click the Next button to continue.

The third wizard screen is for specifying the application's initial pages. By default, a new application contains only a home page. You can click the Add Page button to specify additional pages, and you can click the "x" on the right of a page listing to delete it. Although this screen can be useful for experienced developers, it is not necessary — you can easily add and delete pages after the application has been created. It is simplest to create your application with just a home page, so leave the listing as-is and click Next.

The fourth wizard screen asks about copying the shared components from an existing application. You don't have anything to copy, so select No and click Next to continue.

The fifth screen asks you to specify an authentication scheme and some date/time preferences. The authentication scheme determines how people log in to your application. For the moment, choose the No Authentication scheme, which eliminates logins altogether. You will revisit this choice in Chapter 12, where the various authentication options are examined in detail. As for the date/time specifications, feel free to leave them blank. APEX will use the default values specified by your system administrator, which are usually sufficient.

The final wizard screen asks you to confirm your choices. If you have second thoughts about any of your choices, you can always use the back (<) button to return to a previous screen.

Editing Application Properties

The application builder home screen displays an icon for each application you create. Clicking an icon takes you to the home screen for that application, which displays an icon for each of the application's pages. If you created your application as directed previously, its home screen should display an icon for the home page, as shown in Figure 2-3. If you specified a different form of authentication, you will also see an icon for a Login page.

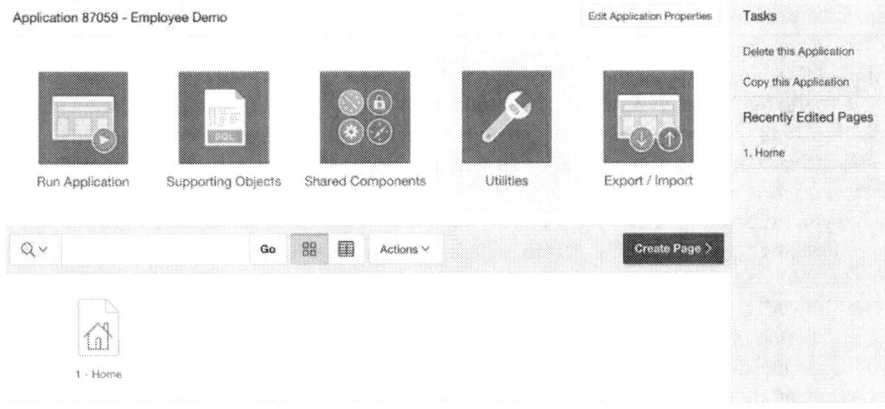

Figure 2-3. *Home screen of a newly created application*

Each application has numerous properties that can be used to customize it. Clicking the Edit Application Properties button at the top right of the home screen displays a screen of properties, the top of which is shown in Figure 2-4.

Definition   Security   Globalization   User Interface

Application 87059

Cancel   Delete   **Apply Changes**

Show All   Name   Properties   Availability   Error Handling   Global Notifi...   Substitutions   Build Options

Name

Application	**87059** ⑦
* Name	Employee Demo ⑦
Application Alias	F_87059 ⑦
* Version	release 1.0 ⑦
Application Group	- Unassigned - ⑦

Figure 2-4. *Editing an application's properties*

The screen organizes the application's properties into *sections* for manageability. Figure 2-4 displays the Name section and its five properties. The first property, Application, holds the ID assigned to that application and cannot be modified. The other properties are modifiable; simply type the desired value into the text box (or select a value from the select list in the case of Application Group) and click the Apply Changes button. For us, the only interesting property is Name, which lets you change the application name.

To the right of each property is a small question mark icon. Clicking that icon displays help text for that property, which is especially useful when a property is unfamiliar to you and you want to understand its purpose. As an experiment, click the help icon for each of the properties in the Name section and see whether their purpose is what you expected.

Looking again at Figure 2-4, notice the row of tabs above the Name section. The first tab is labeled Show All, and is currently selected; the others are labeled by section names. The Show All tab displays the properties of all sections in a single screen. Clicking one of the section tabs displays the properties for that section. Again, clicking the help icon for the properties in each section is a useful exercise, if only to get a sense of what kind of customization is possible. Most of the properties will seem obscure because you have not delved very deeply into APEX. Certainly none of them (apart from Name) is interesting at this point.

Your application has still more properties. Look at the four links at the top of Figure 2-4, labeled Definition, Security, Globalization, and User Interface. Note that Definition is selected, meaning that you have so far seen only the definition properties. Click the other three links to get a quick look at the other properties. The security properties govern various security restrictions, and are the subject of Chapter 12. The globalization properties allow you to modify the time/date settings, in case you neglected to do so when you created the application. And the user interface properties govern certain page display issues. Here, the Logo section is of interest — it lets you manage the logo that appears at the top left of each page of the application. By default, the logo is the name of the application, but you can specify any desired text or even an image. For example, the APEX screens have an image-based Oracle logo. We will return to this property in Chapter 3.

Deleting an Application

There are two ways to delete an application. At the right of the application's home screen (refer to Figure 2-3), there is a task labeled Delete This Application; clicking the link performs the deletion. Alternatively, on the application's global properties screen (refer to Figure 2-4), there is a Delete button on the left of the Apply Changes button, which appears when the Definition properties are shown.

Running an Application Page

A web application is a collection of web pages. By *running a page*, you are asking APEX to render it in your browser. The term *running an application* is shorthand for running its home page. There are two ways to run a page: from within APEX (as a developer) and from outside of APEX (as a user). Each is considered in the following sections.

Running a Page from within APEX

The easiest way to run an application from within APEX is to click the big Run Application button on the top left of the application's home screen (refer to Figure 2-3). Alternatively, you can go to the application builder's home screen and roll the cursor over the icon for the application; the icon will change to display two smaller buttons, as shown in Figure 2-5. Clicking the arrow button runs that application.

Figure 2-5. *Rolling the mouse over the Employee Demo icon*

To run an arbitrary page of an application, you must open the page designer for that page. (The page designer will be discussed later in this chapter, but you can find a screenshot of it in Figure 2-10.) Click the blue arrow button on the top right of the designer to run the page.

If you run your newly created application, APEX will display its home page, as shown in Figure 2-6. This page has the logo Employee Demo in the navigation bar along the top, a breadcrumb labeled Home in the gray region below it, and a single entry (also labeled Home) in the navigation menu along the left side of the page. Clicking the three-line icon at the top left toggles the visibility of this menu. Your browser's tab or title bar should also be titled Home. The page has no other content because, of course, you have not yet specified any.

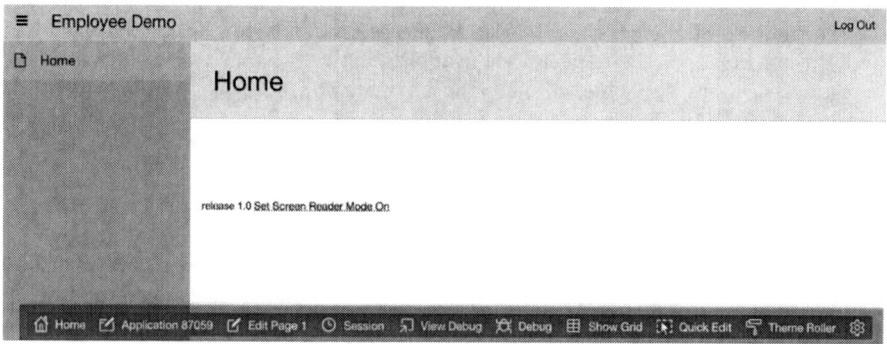

Figure 2-6. *Newly created home page run from within APEX*

Figure 2-6 also shows a row of buttons along the bottom of the page. These buttons, known as the *developer toolbar*, appear whenever you run a page from within APEX. Three buttons are particularly useful for building and debugging your application. The Edit Page button takes you to the page designer for the current page so that you can edit it. The Application button takes you to the home page for the current application so that you can work on a different page. And the Session button pops up a window that displays the current state of the application so that you can verify that it is behaving correctly. This latter topic will be discussed in Chapter 6.

Running a Page from Outside of APEX

The APEX Create Application wizard assigns an ID number to each new application. You can see from Figure 2-2 that my Employee Demo application was assigned the ID 87059. This number is displayed throughout the application builder; for example, it appears in the screens of Figures 2-3 through 2-6. APEX also assigns an ID number to every page of an application. By default, the home page has an ID of 1.

To run a page from outside of APEX, you need its URL. This URL consists of some characters that identify the APEX server, followed by the application ID and page ID. For example, the URL for my Employee Demo home page is

```
http://apex.oracle.com/pls/apex/f?p=87059:1.
```

Up through the characters f?p=, this URL is the same for every APEX application hosted by the apex.oracle.com server. The characters following the equals sign are the application ID and page ID, separated by a colon. If you omit the page ID from the URL, APEX assumes that you mean page 1.

If you are the owner of the application and are logged in to APEX when you submit this URL, then the developer toolbar will be displayed at the bottom of the screen just as if you had run the application from within APEX. Otherwise, you will see the page without it, exactly as a regular user does.

Creating a New Page

There are several ways to create a new page for your application, but the most direct way is to click the Create Page button on the application's home screen (refer to Figure 2-3). Doing so brings up the Create Page wizard, which you should use to create a second page in your application.

The first screen of the wizard, shown in Figure 2-7, asks you to choose the page type. For now, I suggest that you create only blank pages; the other page types are shortcuts intended for experienced developers (or clueless beginners). For example, a Report page is simply a blank page containing a report region.

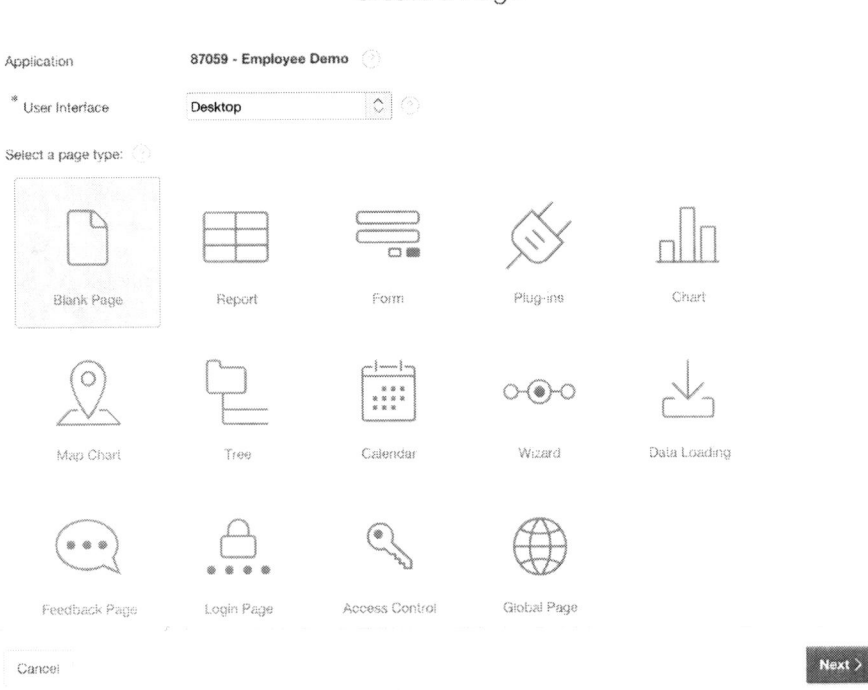

Figure 2-7. *First screen of the Create Page wizard*

The second wizard screen asks for the name, number, and mode of the page; see Figure 2-8. Feel free to use the page number suggested by the wizard. Enter **Region Practice** for the page name, and set the mode to Normal. (Other modes will be discussed in the "Property Editor" section.) The Breadcrumb property specifies whether the page should display a breadcrumb. Breadcrumbs will be discussed in Chapter 4; for now, set the Breadcrumb property to Don't Use Breadcrumbs.

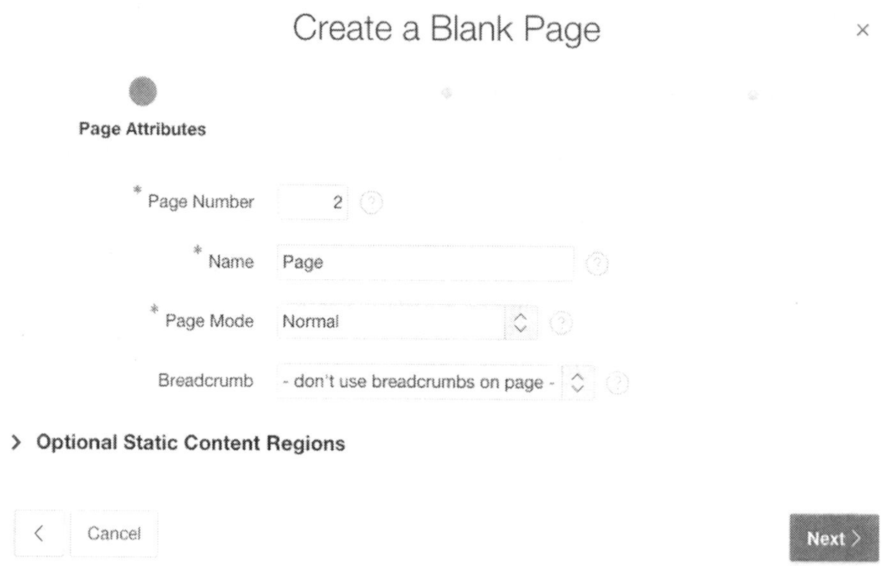

Figure 2-8. *Second screen of the Create Page wizard*

Figure 2-9 shows the third wizard screen, which asks you to specify whether the page should have a navigation menu entry. Selecting the Create A New Navigation Menu Entry option causes the screen to display items for specifying the name of the entry and its parent. These options will be discussed in more detail in Chapter 4; for now, use the values shown in the figure.

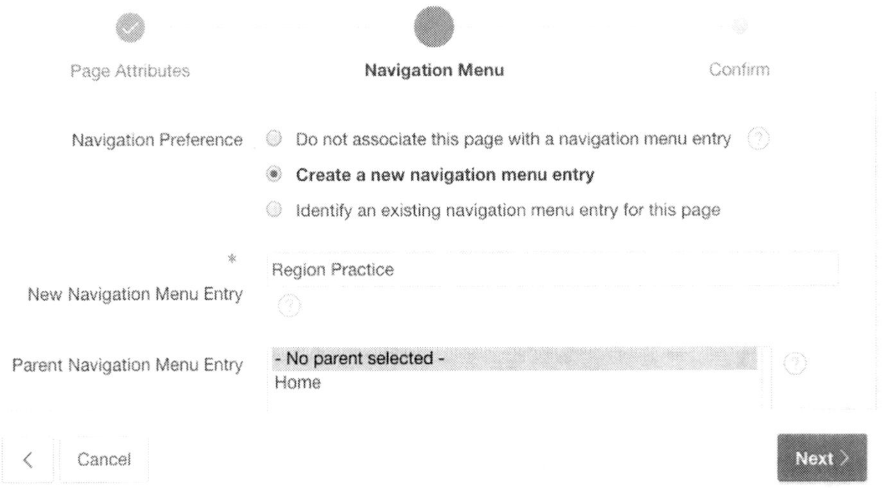

Page Attributes   **Navigation Menu**   Confirm

Navigation Preference   ○ Do not associate this page with a navigation menu entry ⑦
    ◉ **Create a new navigation menu entry**
    ○ Identify an existing navigation menu entry for this page

*
New Navigation Menu Entry   Region Practice

Parent Navigation Menu Entry   - No parent selected -
    Home

⟨ Cancel   Next ⟩

Figure 2-9. *Third screen of the Create Page wizard*

The fourth wizard screen asks for confirmation. When you click the Finish button, APEX will bring you to the page designer for your new page. But before you delve into the page designer and its use, you should take a look at the page you just created.

Return to your application's home screen (refer to Figure 2-3), either by clicking the link on the page designer breadcrumb, or by clicking the Application Builder tab and then selecting the icon for your application. Note that the application's home screen now contains two page icons. Run the home page of your application and observe that the navigation menu now has two entries. Click the Region Practice entry to see your new page. Note that this page has even less content than the home page, because it is missing the breadcrumb. Also note that you can move between the pages by clicking their navigation menu entries.

Page Designer

The page designer is the part of the application builder where you manage the properties and content of your pages. The page designer is new to APEX 5; in previous versions of APEX, each page component had its own edit screen. Although each individual edit screen was relatively easy to use, moving among them was tedious, inefficient, and error-prone. The purpose of the page designer is to improve productivity by having everything in one place.

As a consequence, however, the page designer is extremely dense and can be daunting for beginners. In this book you will learn about the different parts of the page designer gradually, on an as-needed basis. Each time a new APEX feature is introduced, you will also see how it relates to the page designer. This section introduces the basic functionality of the page designer.

To get to the page designer for a page, begin at the application's home screen and click the icon for the desired page. Figure 2-10 shows the top of the page designer screen for your home page.

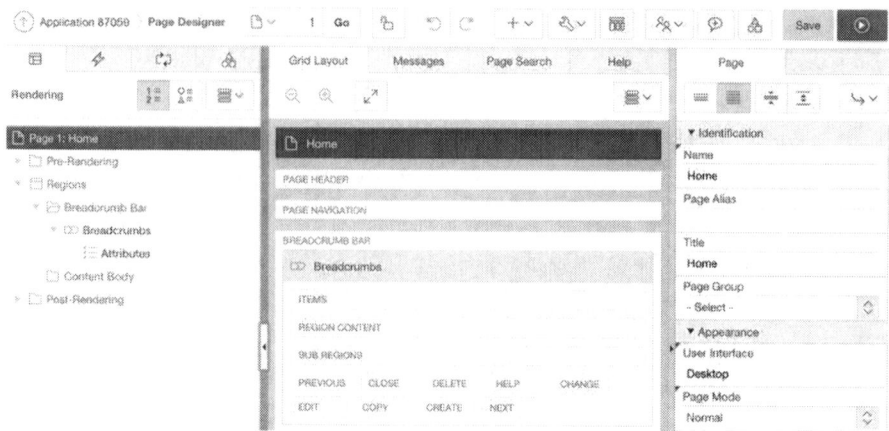

Figure 2-10. *Page designer for the home page*

At the top of the page designer, to the right of the breadcrumb, is a toolbar that consists of several buttons. Here are some immediately useful ones:

- The undo and redo buttons (to the right of the lock) restore the page to a previous state in the typical way.

- The utilities button (labeled with a wrench) has a menu item that lets you delete the page.

- The save button saves your changes to the page.

- The run button (on the right of the save button) runs the page.

The structure of the page designer supports an iterative page development methodology. The idea is to edit the contents of a page from within the page designer, save the changes, and run the page. After examining the output, you then return to the page designer and repeat the process until the page is satisfactory.

Below the toolbar are three vertical panels that form the heart of the page designer. The left panel specifies the components on the page. The right panel specifies the properties of a selected component, and is called the *property editor*. The middle panel combines several utility functions. It currently displays a visual representation of the page layout. You can change the size of the middle panel by dragging its left and right borders, and you can click on the tabs at the top of the panel to select the other utility functions.

A page's components are categorized into four sections: Rendering, Dynamic Actions, Processing, and Page Shared Components. The page designer will display only one of these sections at a time. You choose the section you want by clicking one of the four icons at the top of the left panel. This book focuses only on the Rendering and Processing sections, and begins with the Rendering section. The Processing section will be introduced in Chapter 7.

APEX uses the components in the Rendering section when it renders the page. The properties of these components determine the content and appearance of the page. You can view these components as a tree, organized either by processing order or by component type.

By default, the rendering tree is organized by processing order, as can be seen in Figure 2-10. For readability, this tree is reprinted in Figure 2-11. The components in this tree are grouped according to when they are rendered. The tree has a folder for each of the three rendering stages:

- the pre-rendering stage, in which preliminary computations are performed;

- the main rendering stage, in which each region and its components are laid out;

- the post-rendering stage, in which any final computations occur.

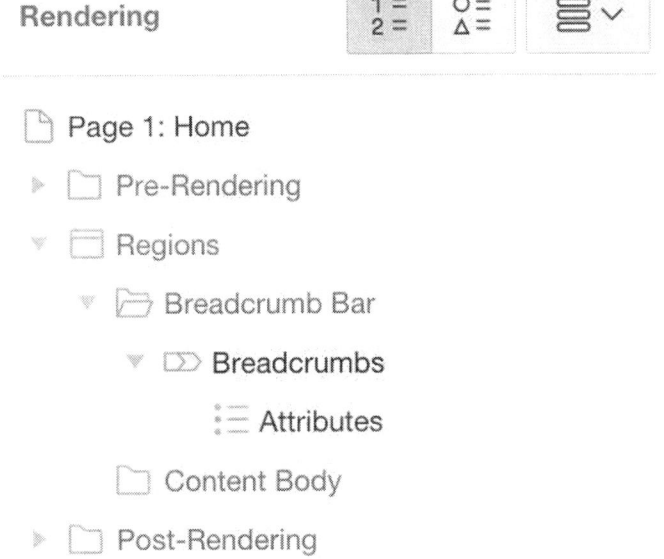

Figure 2-11. *Displaying the page components according to processing order*

The main rendering stage is the most important. The rendering tree for this stage has a node named Regions; this node has a child for each position on the page. Figure 2-11 shows two page positions, named Breadcrumb Bar and Content Body. The Breadcrumb Bar position contains a region named Breadcrumbs, which in turn has a sub-component named Attributes.

The other form of the rendering tree is organized by component type, and appears in Figure 2-12. This tree has a folder for each component type. Since your page currently has no components other than the breadcrumb region, its Regions folder looks the same as in the earlier tree. The difference between the trees will become apparent when you add other components to the page. As an example, consider a page containing some buttons. In the representation of Figure 2-12, the entry for each button will be added to the Buttons folder. In the representation of Figure 2-11, each region will have its own Buttons folder.

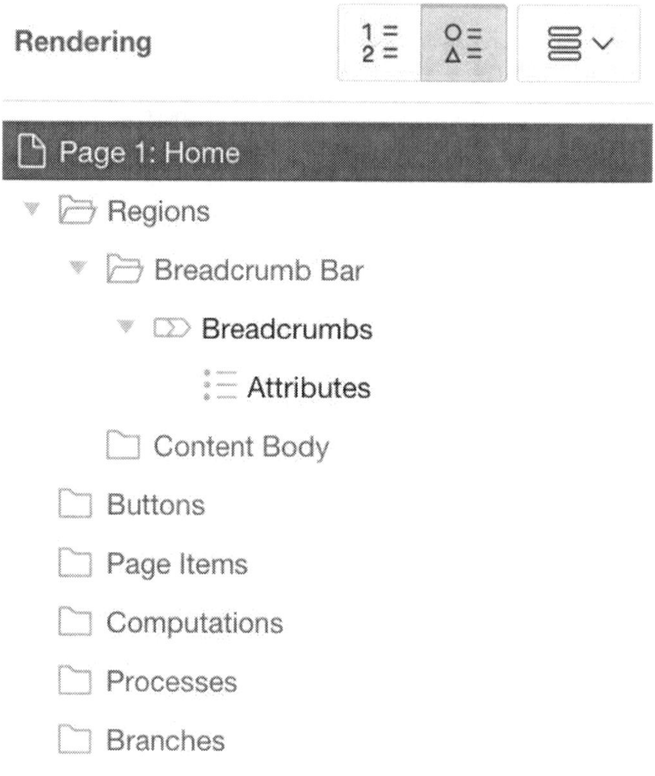

Rendering

▼ 🗀 Page 1: Home

   ▼ 🗁 Regions

      ▼ 🗀 Breadcrumb Bar

         ▼ ⊃ Breadcrumbs

            ≔ Attributes

        🗀 Content Body

   🗀 Buttons

   🗀 Page Items

   🗀 Computations

   🗀 Processes

   🗀 Branches

Figure 2-12. *Displaying the page components according to component type*

It is easy to switch between these two rendering trees. Note the three buttons to the right of the Rendering label in Figure 2-11 and Figure 2-12. The first two buttons toggle between the rendering trees. The left button displays them according to their processing order, and the middle button displays them according to their type. In general, the choice of which tree to use is a matter of personal preference. If a page has a large number of regions and components, then grouping by processing order is often easier to manage. But when you are learning to use APEX and the pages are simple, grouping by component type is simpler. Consequently, this book displays rendering trees by component type.

You manipulate a rendering tree of either type as follows. Each non-leaf node in the tree (except the root) has a collapse/expand arrow to its left. Clicking an arrow expands the node to show its children; clicking it again collapses the node to hide the children. You can also right-click a node to recursively collapse or expand the node's subtree. For example, right-clicking the root and selecting Expand All Below displays the entire tree. The tree of Figure 2-12 is fully expanded; that of Figure 2-11 is not.

A node represented by a non-folder icon denotes a page component. Folder icon nodes have no content of their own; in a sense, they serve only as a structural framework in which to place other components. For example, you can see from Figure 2-12 that the rendering tree of the home page has three components: the root, the Breadcrumbs region, and the Breadcrumbs region attributes.

Property Editor

Recall that the property editor is the right panel of the page designer. Its role is to display the properties of whatever component is selected in the left panel.

For example, go to the page designer for the home page and click the root component of the Rendering section. The right panel will then display the page-level properties for that page. Figure 2-13 shows the top portion of the property editor for the home page. Note the four buttons underneath the word *Page*. These buttons determine which properties are displayed. Clicking the leftmost button displays only the commonly used properties; clicking the button to its right displays all properties. The last two buttons are to collapse/expand the displayed properties. Clicking the collapse button displays just the headers of each section; clicking the expand button also displays their properties.

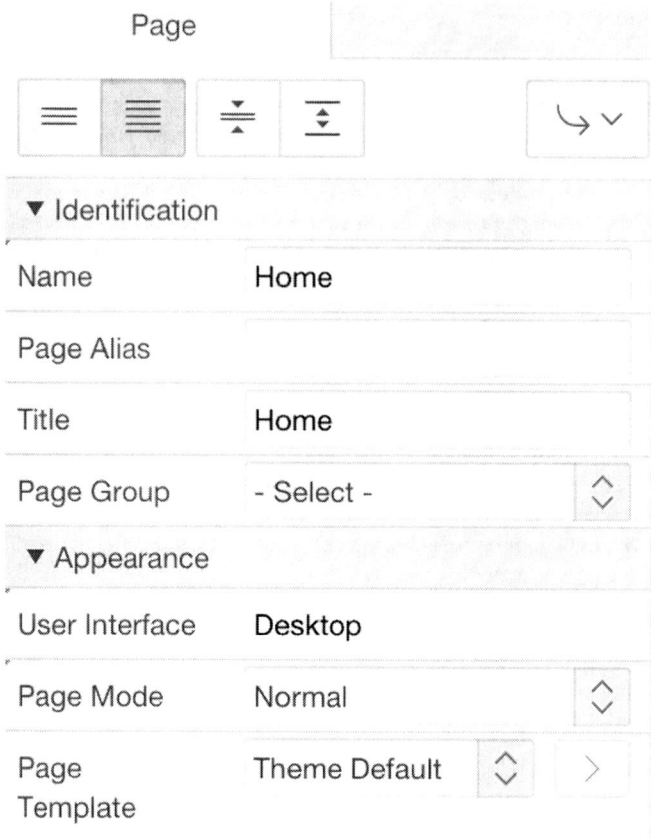

Figure 2-13. *The property editor for the home page*

Figure 2-13 shows properties for the page's Identification and Appearance sections. There are three properties worth mentioning at this point: Name, Title, and Page Mode.

The Name property identifies the page from within the application builder. You give a page a name when you create it, and you can change the name if you decide on a better one later on.

The Title property identifies the page to a user. Browsers typically display the page title in a browser tab. The property currently has the value Home. For fun, change its value to "This is my home page", re-run the page, and observe the change in the browser tab.

The Page Mode property specifies how the page is to be used. There are three possible values: Normal, Modal, and Non-Modal.

Most pages in a web application are normal. A browser displays a normal page by simply replacing whatever page was previously there. The history of a tab (or window) can be thought of as the sequence of accesses to normal pages.

A non-modal page opens in a new browser window. Such pages are typically used as auxiliary pages, peripheral to the primary flow of normal pages. You saw an example of a non-modal page when you examined the SQL command tool in Chapter 1. Its home page, shown in Figure 1-8, is a normal page. But when you click its Find Tables button, the Table Finder window pops up, as shown in Figure 1-9. The content of that window is a non-modal page. You can keep it open for as long as you want, move it around on the screen however you like, and transfer control between it and the current normal page whenever you want.

A modal page corresponds to a dialog box. It opens on top of the current normal page, and will not let the user do anything else until it is closed. An example of a modal page appears in the application builder's Create Page wizard, shown in Figures 2-7 through 2-9. Although you cannot tell from those figures, the wizard screens appear on top of the application's home screen. All components of the underlying screen (such as buttons, links, and tabs) are disabled until the user exits the wizard.

As a side note, observe that not all wizards in APEX are modal. Consider the Create Application wizard screens, one of which appeared in Figure 2-2. These screens are normal pages that masquerade as modal dialog boxes. You can tell this in two ways: they do not sit on top of a previous normal page, and you can escape from the wizard at any point by clicking a menu bar tab.

It is good practice to try out the different page modes. Go to the page designer for the Region Practice page and set its page mode to Modal. You cannot run the page directly (because a modal page can be displayed only on top of another page), so instead run the Home page and then click the Region Practice menu entry. You should observe the modal nature of the page. Then re-edit the page in the page designer, set the page mode to Non-Modal, and repeat the experiment. Observe that the page still cannot be run directly. And when you run the Home page and click the Region Practice menu entry, the Region Practice page will open in a new independent browser window. When you are done, set the page's mode back to Normal.

Accessing Built-in Help

So far, you have seen two different ways to edit properties: the Application Properties screen of Figure 2-4 (for editing the properties of an application) and the property editor in Figure 2-10 (for editing the properties of a specified page). One interesting difference between these two interfaces is the way they provide built-in help. To read the help text for an application property, you click the question mark icon to its right. To read the help text for a page property, you use the Help section of the page designer.

The top of the middle panel of the page designer has four tabs: Grid Layout, Messages, Page Search, and Help. Selecting the Help tab causes the middle panel to display help text for a chosen property of the property editor. As you move from one property to the next in the property editor, the middle panel displays the help text for that property.

Summary

In this chapter, you began your journey through the APEX application builder. You saw how to create an application, populate it with pages, and run them from a browser. You also saw how to use the APEX page designer to view and change the properties of a page.

So far, the pages in your application are devoid of content. The remaining chapters of this book examine the different types of content you can add to your pages. Chapter 3 introduces regions.

CHAPTER 3

■ ■ ■

Regions

A page's content is divided into rectangular areas called *regions*. Consider, for example, the APEX SQL Workshop home screen shown in Chapter 1 (refer to Figure 1-3). This screen has six regions. Five of the regions have titles: Recently Created Tables, Recent SQL Commands, About, Schema, and Create Object. The sixth region, which contains the five large buttons, is untitled.

Each region has a *type* that denotes what kind of content it can contain. The regions in Figure 1-3 belong to three different region types:

- The Recently Created Tables and Recent SQL Commands regions contain reports and are of the type Classic Report.

- The Create Object region contains a list of links and is of type List.

- The About region contains HTML text and is of type Static Content. The Schema and untitled regions are also of type Static Content and their content is empty.

A region can also contain *controls*—that is, items and buttons. In Figure 1-3, the Schema region contains a select list item and a button, and the untitled region contains five large buttons. Because APEX considers a region's controls to be distinct from its content, any region, regardless of type, can contain controls. This chapter focuses on a region's content; controls will be discussed in Chapters 5 and 6.

APEX supports many different region types. This chapter covers four fundamental types: Static Content, Classic Report, Interactive Report, and Chart. Subsequent chapters introduce other region types: Breadcrumb and List in Chapter 4, Region Display Selector in Chapter 6, Tabular Form in Chapter 10, and Classic Report (based on Function) in Chapter 11.

Creating and Deleting Regions

To create a new region for a page, go to the page designer for that page, right-click the Regions node of its rendering tree, and select Create Region. APEX will then add a region component (named New) to the rendering tree as a child of the Content Body folder. This component will also have a child of its own, named Attributes. For example, Figure 3-1 displays the rendering tree for a new region in the Region Practice page. (This figure displays the rendering tree ordered by component type, as discussed in Chapter 2.)

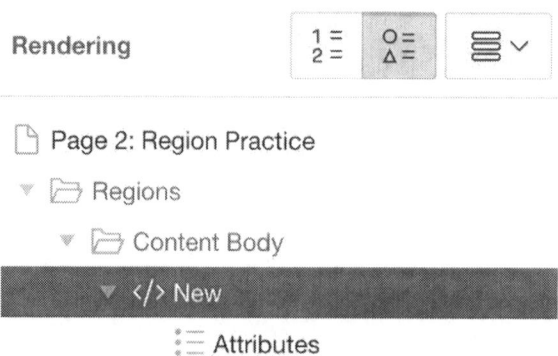

Figure 3-1. *The Region Practice rendering tree contains a new region*

It might seem strange that APEX uses two components in the rendering tree to represent a single region. The reason is that the properties of these components have separate concerns. In particular, the region component (here labeled New) contains the properties common to all regions, whereas the Attributes component contains the properties specific to the region's type. The type-independent properties will be discussed in the next section, with the type-specific properties following.

If you want to delete a region, simply right-click its component in the rendering tree and select Delete. For example, you really don't need the breadcrumb region that came with the home page. Go to the page designer for that page, find the Breadcrumb region in the rendering tree, and delete it.

Type-Independent Region Properties

To edit the type-independent properties of a region, select its region component in the rendering tree; the properties will appear in the property editor. For example, Figure 3-2 shows the property editor corresponding to the New region of Figure 3-1. This figure shows only the commonly used properties, and only the Identification and Source sections have been expanded. Each section will be considered in turn (except for Condition, which is postponed until Chapter 6).

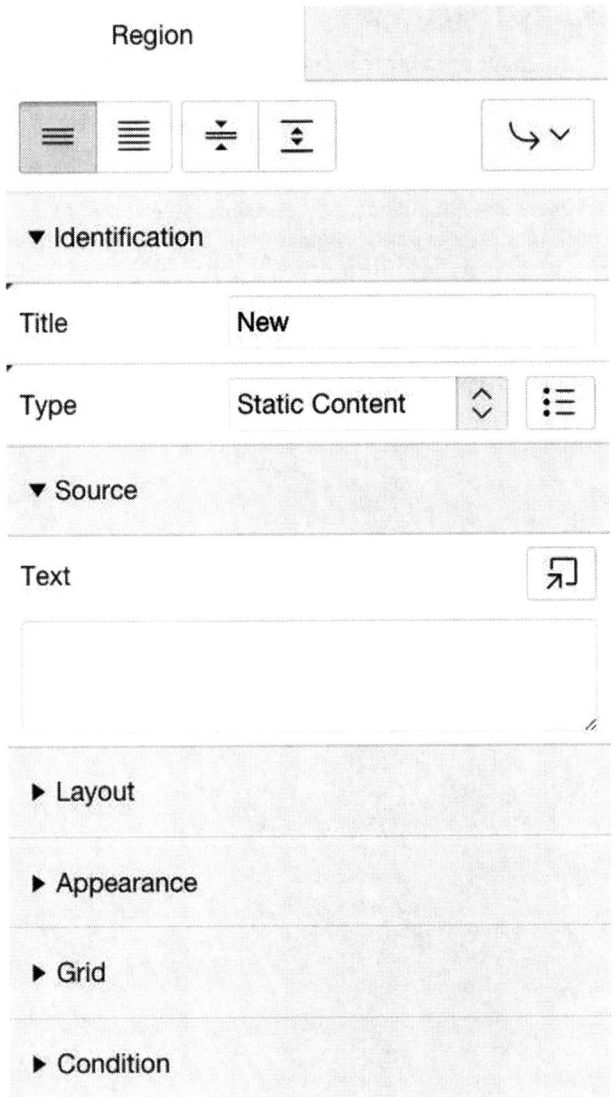

Figure 3-2. Identification and Source properties for a new region

Identification and Source Sections

Every region has a title, which is the value of its Title property. A title serves two purposes. First, it identifies the region so that the page developer can keep track of which region is which. Second, it can be displayed in the region when the page is rendered. Recall from Figure 1-3 that all but one of the regions on that page displayed their titles.

A new region is assigned the title New by default. The first thing you should do after creating a region is to assign it a more meaningful title. APEX accepts HTML formatting tags here. For example, go to the page designer for the Region Practice page, select the New region in the rendering tree, and change its Title property to this:

```
<i>My First Region</i>
```

Then create two more regions on the page with this title:

```
<b>My Second Region</b>
```

and this title:

```
<span style="color:red">My Third Region</span>
```

Save and run the page, which should look like Figure 3-3. Note that the region titles are in italics, bold, and red, respectively.

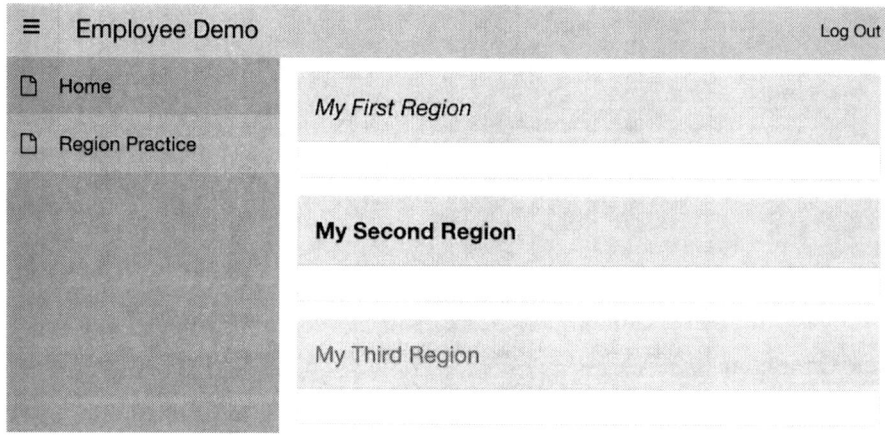

Figure 3-3. *Three regions on the Region Practice page*

A region's Type property lets you select the region's type from a drop-down list of possible types. The Text property (from the Source section) lets you enter the text that specifies the region's content. Figure 3-2 shows that by default, a new region is assigned the type Static Content having an empty source text.

A common region type is `Classic Report`, whose source text is an SQL query. Each time the page is rendered, APEX will evaluate the query and display the result table within the region.

As an example, modify the `Region Practice` page as follows. Add some source text to `My First Region` and `My Second Region`. I went for something simple, namely `This is my first region` and `This is my second region`. Then change the type of `My Third Region` to `Classic Report`, having the source `select * from DEPT`. Notice that when you change the type to `Classic Report`, the Text property is outlined in red, and an error message appears. The reason is that a classic report region must have a non-empty source, and the page designer will not let you rest until you specify one.

Figure 3-4 displays the result of running the revised page.

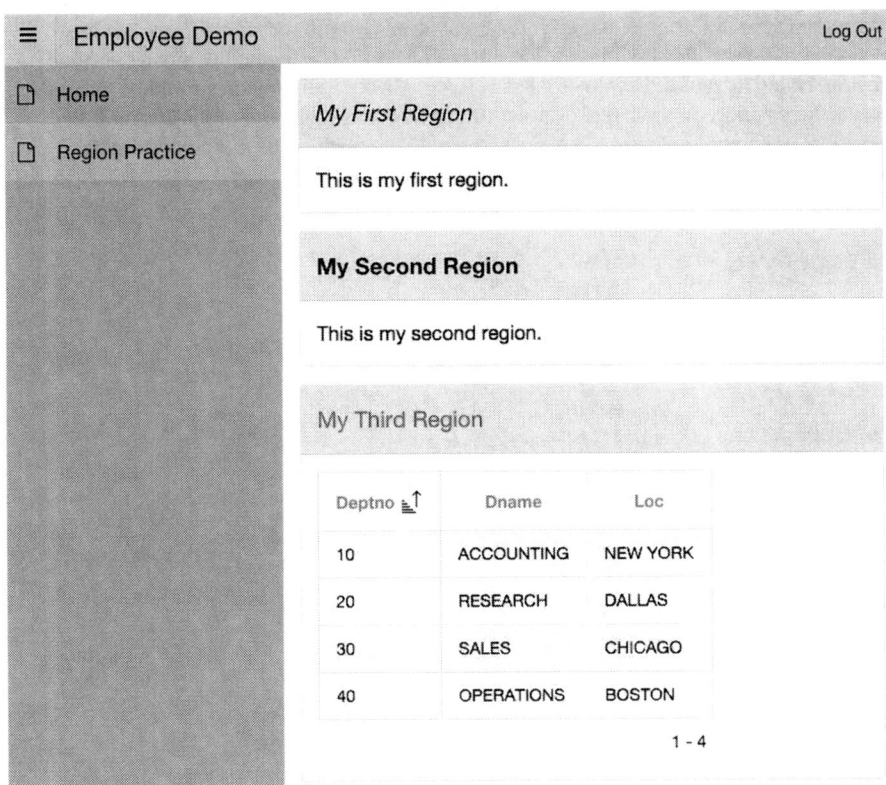

Figure 3-4. *Changing the type and source of the Region Practice regions*

Layout Section

The Layout section contains properties that specify the position of a region on its page. It has three properties, as shown in Figure 3-5.

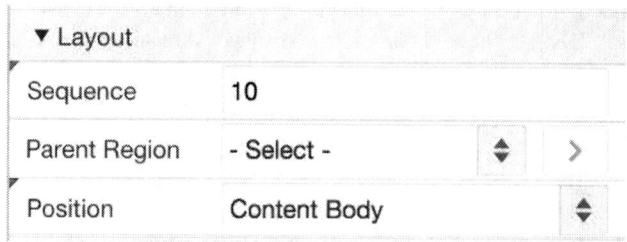

Figure 3-5. *Layout section of the Property Editor*

The Parent Region and Position properties provide two different ways to specify the region's location on the page. Only one of these two properties can have a value. A value for Parent Region means that the region should be located within a specified region, called its *parent*. A value for Position means that the region should be located at a specific position on the page. By default, a new region is located in the Content Body position, as shown in Figure 3-5. You can change the position by selecting from the drop-down list shown in Figure 3-6.

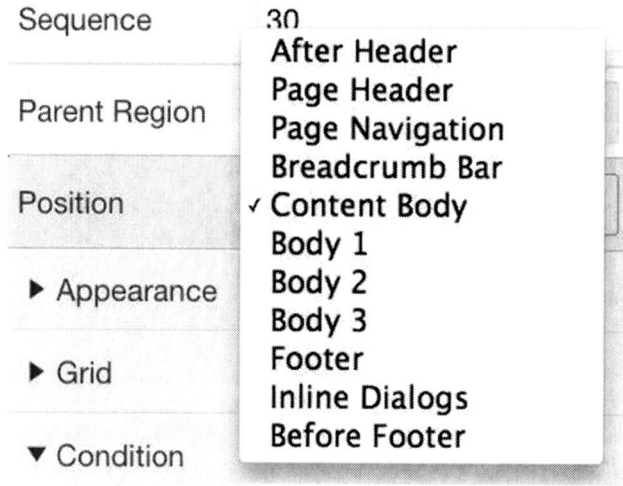

Figure 3-6. *Possible region positions*

These positions are listed in the order they appear on the page, from top to bottom. Most positions have specific purposes. For example, the Content Body position is the primary location for general-purpose regions, the Page Navigation position is intended for the navigation menu along the left side of the page, and the Breadcrumb Bar is for breadcrumb regions.

> ■ **Note** Some of these positions (namely, After Header, Body 1, Body 2, Body 3, Footer, and Before Footer) are *legacy* positions. That is, they exist only to support applications written with older versions of APEX. New applications should not use them.

The set of possible region positions is determined by the page's *template*. When a page is created, it is assigned the default template defined by the application's theme. For example, the default page template for the Universal theme is called Standard.

It is possible to change a page's template. Select the component for the page in the rendering tree, and look at its properties. Note the Page Template property in the Appearance section. At the moment, the template is set to Theme Default. You can change the template by clicking the property's select list. Figure 3-7 shows the options.

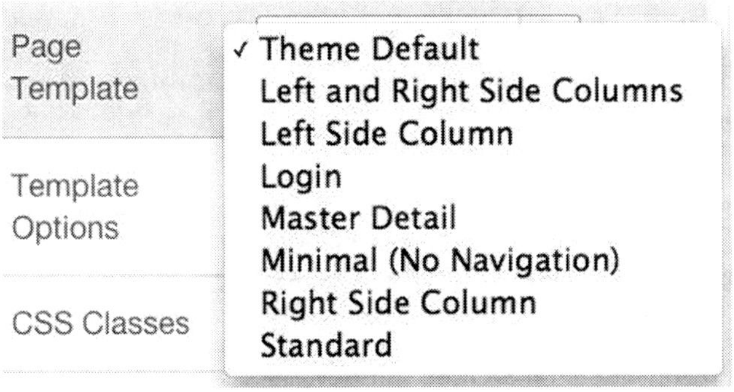

Page	✓ Theme Default
Template	Left and Right Side Columns
	Left Side Column
Template	Login
Options	Master Detail
	Minimal (No Navigation)
CSS Classes	Right Side Column
	Standard

Figure 3-7. *Page template options*

Go to the property editor for the Region Practice page and change its template to Right Side Column. Then choose a region (say, My Second Region) and re-examine its list of Position values; you will discover that in addition to the values in Figure 3-6, there is also the Right Column value. Set the position of My Second Region to Right Column and re-run the page. That region should now appear as a right sidebar, as shown in Figure 3-8. (I added more text to the source of the second region to make it more sidebar-like.) Note that the sidebar region has an associated three-bar icon at its top left. Clicking the icon toggles between displaying the sidebar and hiding it.

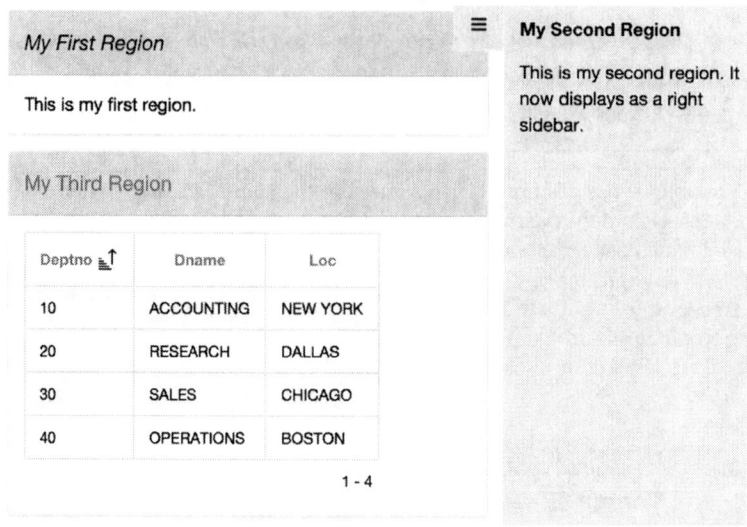

Figure 3-8. *Page containing a sidebar region*

If two regions are located in the same position on a page, the value of their Sequence property (refer to Figure 3-5) determines the order in which they are placed in that position. Regions are assigned sequence numbers in the order in which they were created, but you can change that order by simply assigning different sequence numbers. For example, the My First Region and My Third Region regions are both located in the Content Body position, with sequence numbers of 10 and 30, respectively. If you change the sequence number of My Third Region to 5, the rendered page will look similar to Figure 3-8, except that My Third Region will appear above My First Region.

Grid Section

Although it is good to experiment with placing regions in various positions on the page, most regions on a page are usually located in the same position (in particular, Content Body). In this case, the properties of the Grid section determine the relative location of the regions within that position.

The regions in a position are organized in a grid; each region is assigned to a row and column of that grid. APEX positions the regions according to their sequence number. The first region is placed in the first column of the first row of the grid. Each subsequent region is then placed in one of the following ways:

- in the same row and column as the previous region (in which case it is displayed beneath the previous region);
- in the next column of the current row;
- in the first column of a new row

Figure 3-9 displays the Grid section of the property editor. Each of the previous three options arise from appropriately selecting Yes or No for the Start New Row and New Column properties of each region. For example, the values in Figure 3-9 specify a region that is placed in a new column of the same row.

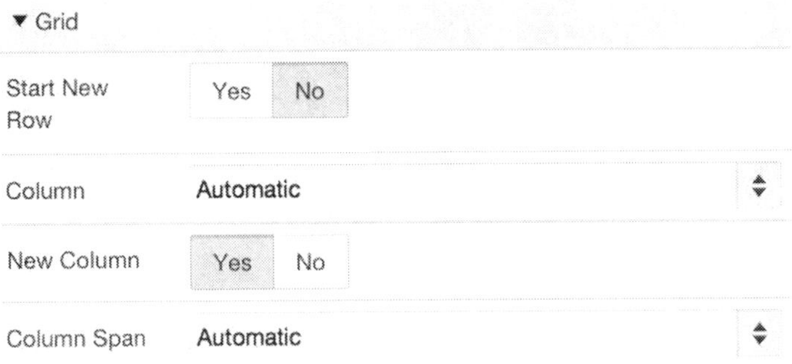

Figure 3-9. *Grid section of the property editor*

After assigning each region to a row and column, APEX then considers how to locate the regions within the position. To do so, APEX uses the values of the Column and Column Span properties (shown in Figure 3-9) to determine the offset and width of each region in a row.

The Column property specifies the offset of the region within its row. APEX divides the width of a position into 12 "grid points"; the value of Column is a number from 1 to 12, denoting one of those points. A value of 1 specifies that the region begins at the far left of the position; a value of 7 specifies that the region begins in the position's center. The Column Span property specifies the width of the column. Its value is also a number from 1 to 12, denoting the width in grid points.

For example, Figure 3-10 shows yet another configuration of the Region Practice regions; let's examine how to change the layout of Figure 3-8 to Figure 3-10. Begin by changing the page template back to Theme Default, moving My Second Region back to the Content Body position with the others, and changing the sequence number of My Third Region to be the smallest. Set their Grid properties as follows:

- My Third Region starts a new row, its Column value is 3, and Column Span value is 8. That is, its width is two-thirds the size of the position and centered.

- My First Region starts a new row, its Column value is 1, and the Column Span value is 4. Thus its width is one-third the size of the position and left-justified.

- My Second Region does not start a new row. Its Column value is 9, and the Column Span value is 4. Thus its width is also one-third the size of the position, but right-justified.

35

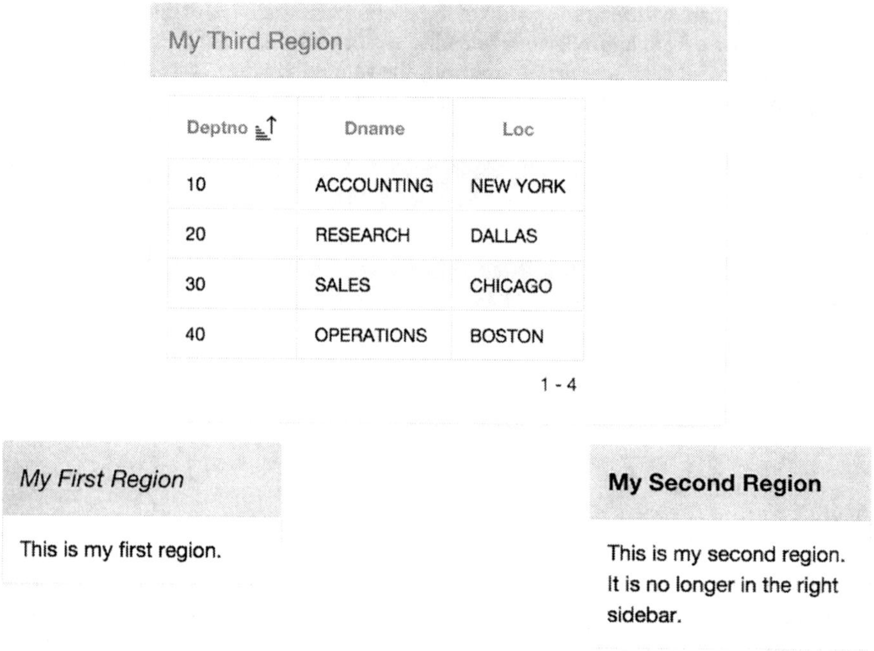

My Third Region

Deptno ↕↑	Dname	Loc
10	ACCOUNTING	NEW YORK
20	RESEARCH	DALLAS
30	SALES	CHICAGO
40	OPERATIONS	BOSTON

1 - 4

My First Region

This is my first region.

My Second Region

This is my second region. It is no longer in the right sidebar.

Figure 3-10. Another way to display the Region Practice regions

If you do not need such fine control over the placement of the regions in a row, you can assign the Automatic value to their Column and Column Span properties (refer to Figure 3-9). In this case, APEX will place the regions in the row so that they have equal widths and expand to fill the entire position.

Appearance Section

A region's Template property (in the Appearance section) lets you specify its look and feel. Figure 3-11 shows the various values for this property.

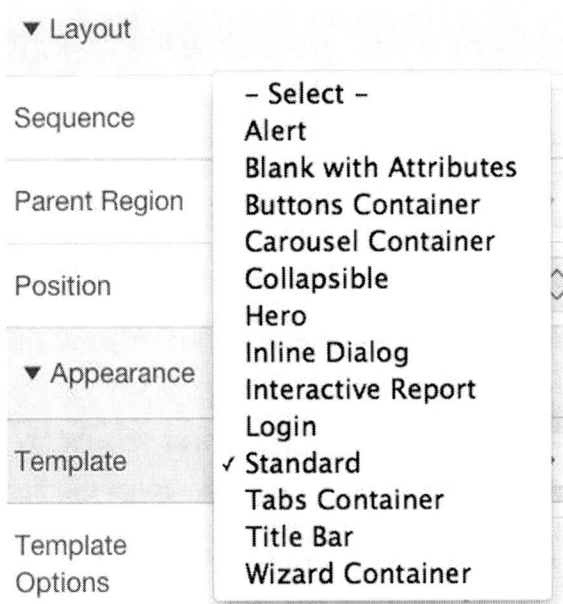

Figure 3-11. *Options for the Template property*

The Standard template, which is the most common, displays the region's title in a shaded border across the top. Many of the other templates have special purposes, such as Alert, Inline Dialog, Login, Title Bar, and Wizard Container.

The Collapsible template is similar to Standard, with the addition of a small button in the top-left corner. Clicking the button toggles between hiding the body of the region and displaying it. Regions using the Button Region or Blank Region template are untitled; the main difference between them is that a button region has a border, whereas a blank region does not.

Drag and Drop

Turn your attention to the middle panel of the page designer. Recall from Figure 2-10 that the section contains four tabs: Grid Layout, Messages, Page Search, and Help. The Help tab was discussed at the end of Chapter 2 — when that tab is chosen, the middle panel displays help text for the currently selected property in the property editor.

Let's now examine the Grid Layout tab. Clicking this tab causes the middle panel to display a stylized representation of the page's content. There is an area corresponding to each region position, and each area contains a representation of the regions assigned to that position.

For example, consider the Region Practice page as it appears in Figure 3-10; its grid layout is shown in Figure 3-12. From it, you can see the three regions in the Content Body position, displayed in approximately the same way that they will be when the page is rendered.

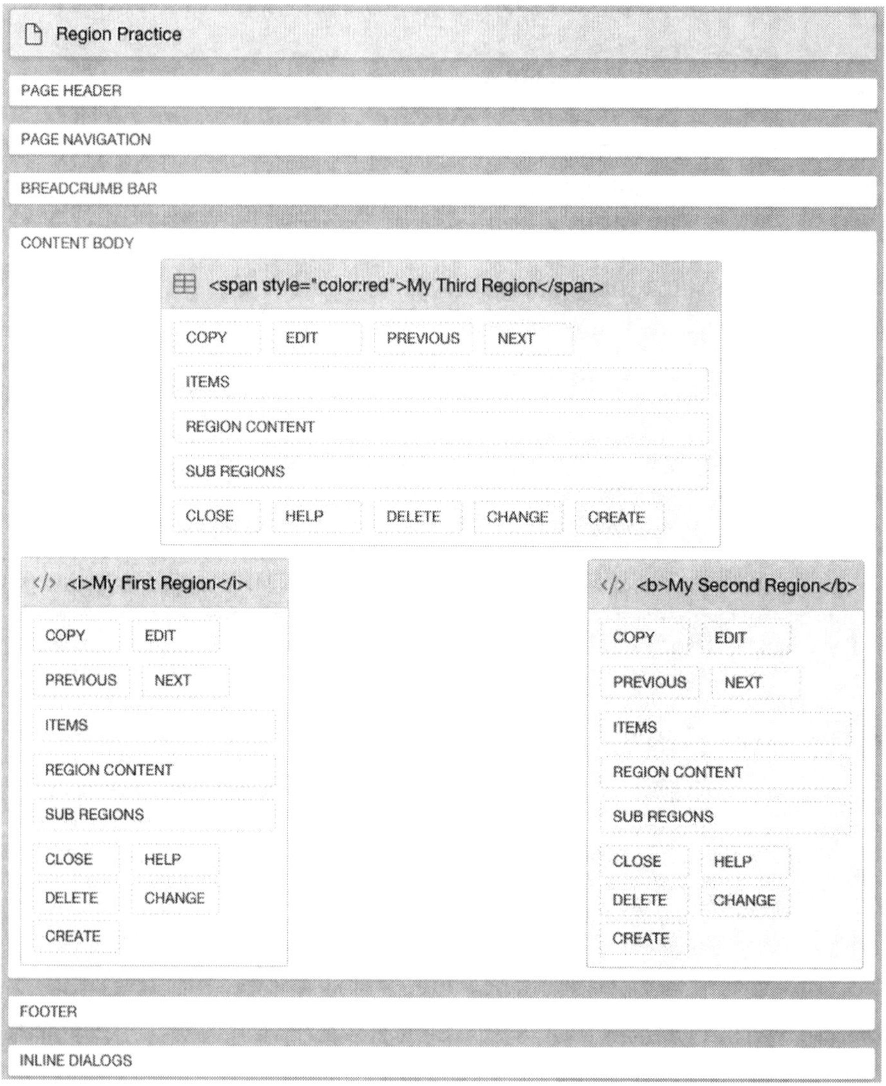

Figure 3-12. Grid Layout area

The grid layout gives you a visual approximation of the layout of the rendered page, while you are designing it. When you change the `Position` and `Grid` property values of a region, the grid layout will change accordingly.

If you click the title bar of a region in the grid layout, the properties for that region appear in the property editor. You can also drag a region to another location on the grid layout. As you drag, the available positions are highlighted in yellow, and drop-off spots within those regions are indicated by an outlined rectangle. You can drop a region to an empty position; to the `Sub Regions` section of another region (so that the region is now a child of the other region); or above, below, left, or right of another region (to add the region to that position's grid). As you do so, you will see that the region's `Layout` and `Grid` properties change correspondingly.

There is an area at the bottom-middle section of the page designer, below the grid layout, known as the *gallery*. This area is minimized by default. To expose it, click the handle at the bottom middle of the grid layout. You can use this area to create page components via drag and drop. In particular, clicking the gallery's `Regions` button will cause it to display an icon for each possible region type, as shown in Figure 3-13. To create a region of a specific type, click its icon and drag it to the desired position on the grid layout.

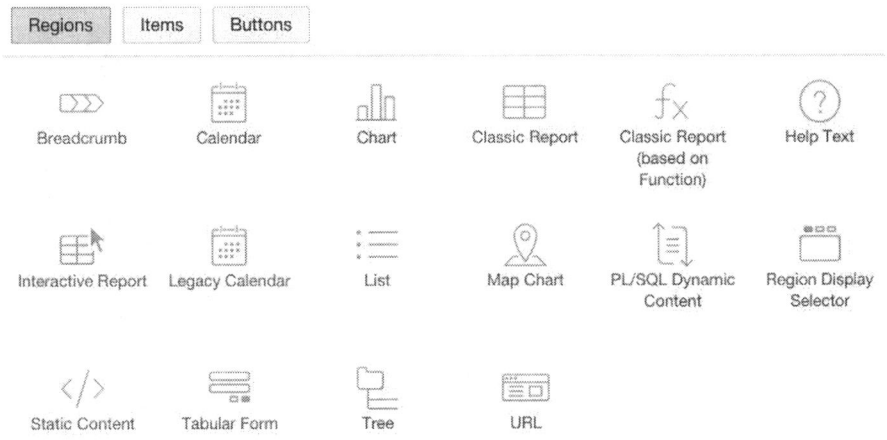

Figure 3-13. *Region gallery*

This use of the gallery is a convenient way to create a region, with the added benefit that APEX assigns appropriate values to its type and location properties for you. But once it has been created, such a region becomes the same as any other region. In particular, a region's properties (including its type and location) can be modified at any time, without restriction, regardless of how it was created.

Static Content Regions

A *static content region* can display text or formatted HTML code. APEX contains several examples of static regions. For example, consider again the SQL Workshop home screen (refer to Figure 1-3). The region titled About on the right side of the page is a static content region whose source is the displayed text. The source contains HTML tags that cause Object Browser and Create to be displayed in bold.

You can do similar things to your demo application. Let's beef up the home page to contain four static content regions. Figure 3-14 shows what the page will look like. The goal of this section is to learn the concepts needed to create this page.

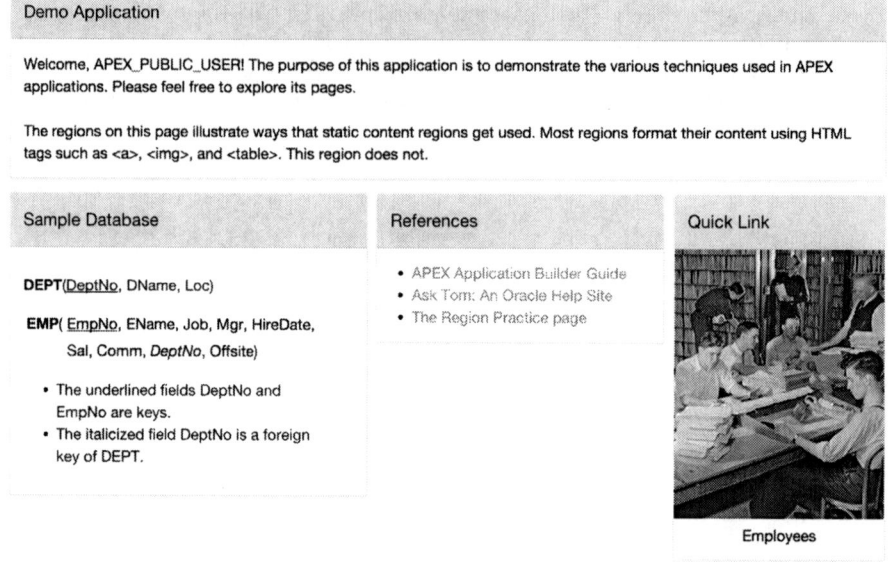

Figure 3-14. *Home page with four static content regions (photo courtesy of Library of Congress, Prints & Photographs Division, LC-H261-4562)*

The first step is to create and position the regions on the page before you assign any content to them. To do so, perform the following tasks:

1. Go to the page designer for the home page and create four new regions. These regions will by default have the type Static Content, which is what you want.

2. Assign the titles Demo Application, Sample Database, References, and Quick Link to the regions, in that order.

3. Place the regions in the Content Body position, and use their Grid values to specify their placement on the page. In particular, the Demo Application and Sample Database regions start new rows, and the other two regions start new columns; all four regions use automatic column positioning.

At this point, you can run your home page and verify that it has the intended structure. The page should look like Figure 3-15.

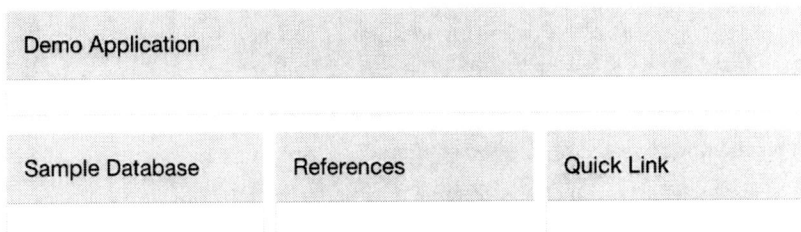

Figure 3-15. *Structure of the home page*

The next step is to add content to these regions. The following sections address the relevant issues.

Formatted vs. Unformatted Text

The source of a static content region is the text to be displayed. APEX can interpret this text in two ways: as the characters exactly as written, or as HTML code to be formatted. The property that specifies this option is called Output As, and it appears in the Settings section of the region's Attributes component in the page rendering tree. Figure 3-16 shows this section with the two possible values of the Output As property.

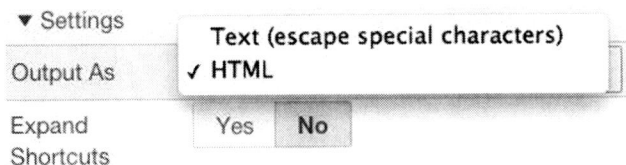

Figure 3-16. *Type-specific properties for a static content region*

An Output As value of HTML specifies that the region's source contains HTML code. APEX will send this code as-is to the browser when it renders the page, so that the browser can format the source accordingly.

On the other hand, a value of Text (escape special characters) specifies that the source should be displayed exactly as it appears. In this case, APEX needs to transform the text so that there are no HTML tags for the browser to execute. It does so by replacing certain characters (such as < and >) with different characters that happen to print the same (such as < and >). This transformation is called *escaping* the characters. The result is text that looks like HTML code, but really is not.

41

The Sample Database region of Figure 3-14 illustrates several kinds of formatting:

- The description of the EMP and DEPT tables makes use of the bold, italic, and underline tags.

- To get the fields of EMP to line up in two rows, you can use a borderless table having two columns: the first row consists of "EMP(" in one column and the fields in the second column, and the second row consists of nothing in the first column and the remaining fields in the second column.

- The bullet list is implemented as an unordered list in HTML, and each bullet point is a list item.

Consequently, the region's Output As property needs to be set to HTML. The source code for the region is given in Listing 3-1.

Listing 3-1. Source of the Sample Database Region

```
<p>
<b>DEPT</b>(<u>DeptNo</u>, DName, Loc)
</p><p>
<table border=0>
<tr>
      <td><b>EMP</b>(</td>
      <td><u>EmpNo</u>, EName, Job, Mgr, HireDate, </td>
</tr>
<tr>
    <td> </td>
      <td>Sal, Comm, <i>DeptNo</i>, Offsite) </td>
</tr>
</table>
</p>
<ul>
<li> The underlined fields DeptNo and EmpNo are keys.
<li> The italicized field DeptNo is a foreign key of DEPT.
</ul>
```

Now consider the Demo Application region. Its content is unformatted, and in fact contains HTML tags that should not be formatted. So the Output As property for this region should be Text (escape special characters). Its source appears in Listing 3-2.

Listing 3-2. Source of the Demo Application Region

```
Welcome, &APP_USER.! The purpose of this application is to demonstrate the various
techniques used in APEX applications. Please feel free to explore its pages.

The regions on this page illustrate ways that static content regions get
used. Most regions format their content using HTML tags such as <a>, <img>,
and <table>. This region does not.
```

The beginning of this listing makes reference to "&APP_USER.". This string is called a *substitution string*, and APEX interprets it as the name of the user. This topic is addressed next.

Substitution Strings

The APEX server has several built-in variables that hold information of interest. Here are three useful ones:

- The variable APP_USER holds the username of whoever is currently logged in. If the application does not require users to log in, the value of the variable is APEX_PUBLIC_USER.

- The variable APP_ID holds the ID of the current application.

- The variable APP_SESSION holds the ID of the current session.

To refer to the value of a variable from within HTML text, you prepend the character & and append the period character (.) to the variable name. Such an expression is called a *substitution string*. In other words, the substitution string for a variable named X is written "&X.". When the APEX server renders a page, it textually replaces the substitution string by the value of its variable.

For example, the substitution string &APP_USER. appears in the source of the Demo Application region. When the APEX server renders the page, it textually replaces the substitution string with the value of the variable APP_USER, which in this case is APEX_PUBLIC_USER.

Referring to APEX pages

The References region contains a bullet list of three entries. The first two entries contain links to external web pages; the third entry is a link to the application's Region Practice page. The source of the region appears in Listing 3-3.

Listing 3-3. Source of the References Region

```
<ul>
<li><a href="https://docs.oracle.com/cd/E59726_01/doc.50/e39147/toc.htm">
     APEX Application Builder Guide </a></li>
<li><a href="http://asktom.oracle.com/pls/apex/f?p=100:1">
     Ask Tom: An Oracle Help Site </a></li>
<li><a href="f?p=&APP_ID.:2:&APP_SESSION.">
     The Region Practice page</a></li>
</ul>
```

The HTML <a> tag specifies a link; its argument is the URL of the target location. The first link in the listing is a typical link, which refers to a page on an external website. The second link refers to a page of another APEX application — in particular, page 1 of application 100 on the APEX server at asktom.oracle.com. Note how the link uses the "f?p=" notation, as described in Chapter 2.

The third link in the listing refers to page 2 of the current application; thus it can be written as a relative reference. It uses the built-in variables APP_ID and APP_SESSION to refer to the current application ID and session ID. The tag looks like this:

```
<a href="f?p=&APP_ID.:2:&APP_SESSION.">
```

The concept of a session will be covered in Chapter 6. For the moment, it suffices to know that APEX uses a session identifier to indicate related page accesses. By passing the current session ID into the URL, you ensure that the current session will continue when the link is followed. Note that the second link in the region did not include a session identifier. This was appropriate, since the link was beginning a new session with the Ask Tom application.

Referring to Local Images

An HTML <img> tag displays an image; its argument is the URL of the image file. If the URL is a reference to a file on another web server, an absolute URL works fine. However, if you want to store an image file on the APEX web server then you should use a relative URL. The format of this URL is determined as follows.

The first thing to do is upload the file to the server. Go to the home screen of your application, click the Shared Components button, and find the Files section as shown in Figure 3-17.

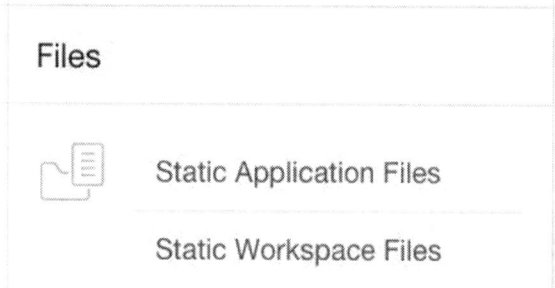

Figure 3-17. *Files section of the Shared Components screen*

You have two options to choose from: Static Application Files or Static Workspace Files. The difference between them is one of visibility. An application file can be referenced from a specific application only, whereas a workspace file can be accessed by any application in the workspace. Whichever option you choose, you will be taken to a screen that lets you choose your file. Click the Upload button to upload it.

To display your image file using an HTML <img> tag, you must specify its location on the server. However, APEX will not tell you where it stored your image files; instead, it provides you with built-in variables. There are two variables, WORKSPACE_IMAGES and APP_IMAGES, whose values hold the path to the location in which your workspace images and application images are stored. You use substitution strings to access the value of these variables. For example, I uploaded the employee photograph to a file named employees.jpg and saved it in APEX as an application file. You should do the same with a picture of your choice. The HTML tag to display this file is this:

```
<img src="&APP_IMAGES.employees.jpg">
```

Note the two different uses of the period character in this tag. The first one is part of the substitution string notation and will be replaced by the path to the image directory when the page is rendered; the second one is part of the filename.

With this in mind, take a look at the source of the Quick Link region in Listing 3-4.

Listing 3-4. Source of the Quick Link Region

```
<div align=center>
<a href="f?p=&APP_ID.:3:&APP_SESSION.">
<img src="&APP_IMAGES.employees.jpg">
</a><br>
Employees
</div>
```

You can see that the region uses the <img> tag to display the employees.jpg image, and then uses <a> and </a> tags to wrap this image in a link. Consequently, clicking the image takes the user to page 3 of the application (which means that the link will be nonfunctional until the next section, in which page 3 is created).

Chapter 2 discussed the possibility of using an image as the application's logo. To demonstrate this, I used a Word Art program to create a stylized image of the words "Employee Demo", saved it in the file Logo.jpg, and uploaded it as an APEX application file. I then configured the application's User Interface properties as shown in Figure 3-18.

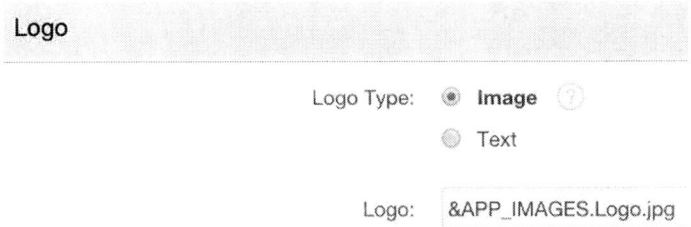

Figure 3-18. Demo application's Logo properties

The resulting logo appears in Figure 3-19.

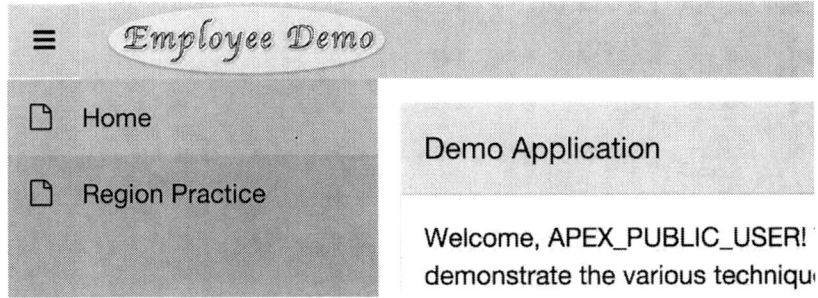

Figure 3-19. Logo corresponding to Figure 3-18

Classic Report Regions

You had a brief encounter with a classic report region earlier in this chapter, when you created a report in the Region Practice page having the source query select * from DEPT. This section examines classic reports in more detail. Figure 3-20 displays page 3 of the demo application, titled Classic Reports.

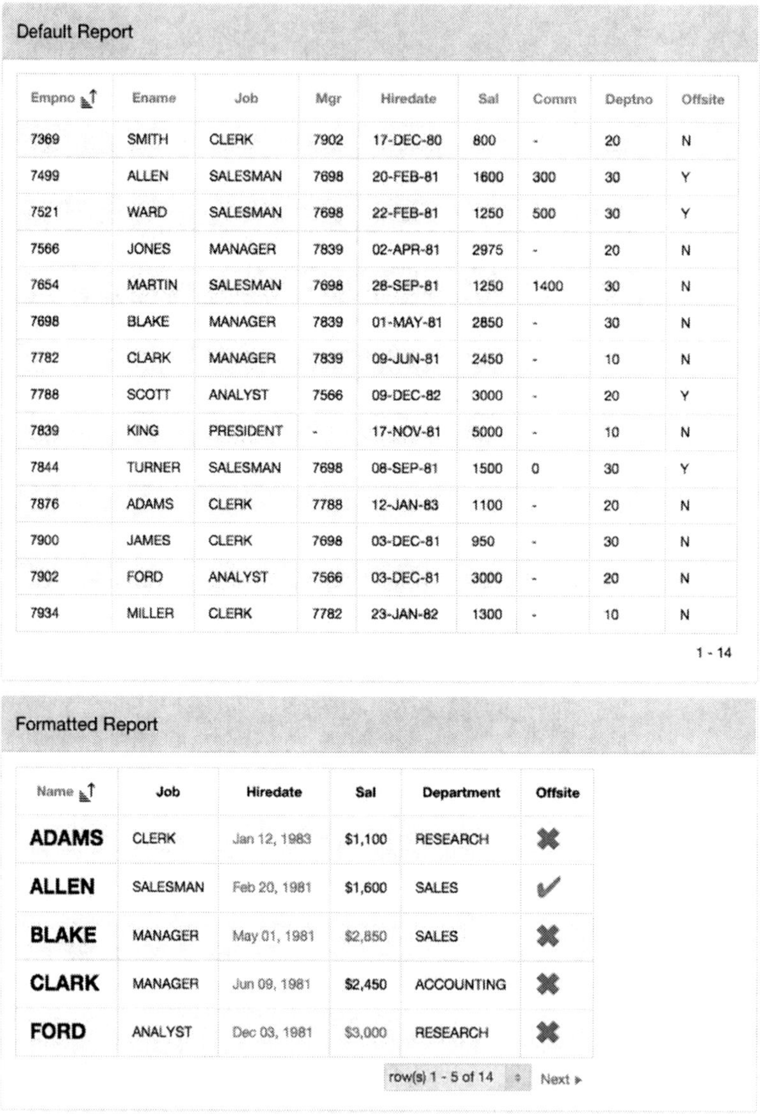

Default Report

Empno ↑	Ename	Job	Mgr	Hiredate	Sal	Comm	Deptno	Offsite
7369	SMITH	CLERK	7902	17-DEC-80	800	-	20	N
7499	ALLEN	SALESMAN	7698	20-FEB-81	1600	300	30	Y
7521	WARD	SALESMAN	7698	22-FEB-81	1250	500	30	Y
7566	JONES	MANAGER	7839	02-APR-81	2975	-	20	N
7654	MARTIN	SALESMAN	7698	28-SEP-81	1250	1400	30	N
7698	BLAKE	MANAGER	7839	01-MAY-81	2850	-	30	N
7782	CLARK	MANAGER	7839	09-JUN-81	2450	-	10	N
7788	SCOTT	ANALYST	7566	09-DEC-82	3000	-	20	Y
7839	KING	PRESIDENT	-	17-NOV-81	5000	-	10	N
7844	TURNER	SALESMAN	7698	08-SEP-81	1500	0	30	Y
7876	ADAMS	CLERK	7788	12-JAN-83	1100	-	20	N
7900	JAMES	CLERK	7698	03-DEC-81	950	-	30	N
7902	FORD	ANALYST	7566	03-DEC-81	3000	-	20	N
7934	MILLER	CLERK	7782	23-JAN-82	1300	-	10	N

1 - 14

Formatted Report

Name ↑	Job	Hiredate	Sal	Department	Offsite
ADAMS	CLERK	Jan 12, 1983	$1,100	RESEARCH	✖
ALLEN	SALESMAN	Feb 20, 1981	$1,600	SALES	✔
BLAKE	MANAGER	May 01, 1981	$2,850	SALES	✖
CLARK	MANAGER	Jun 09, 1981	$2,450	ACCOUNTING	✖
FORD	ANALYST	Dec 03, 1981	$3,000	RESEARCH	✖

row(s) 1 - 5 of 14   Next ▶

Figure 3-20. *Two ways to display an employee report*

The report at the top is the default report created from the source query select * from EMP. The formatted report below it differs in the following ways:

- The columns Empno, Mgr, and Comm are not displayed.
- The columns Ename and Deptno have been renamed.
- The records are sorted by employee name and cannot be sorted otherwise.
- Employee names are accentuated by writing them in a larger font and in bold.
- Hire dates, which are formatted differently, are links.
- Salary values are formatted as currency and aligned right, and values over $2,500 are colored red.
- Department values are shown as department names instead of department numbers.
- Values for the Offsite column are displayed as images instead of text.
- Fewer rows are displayed at a time, with pagination controls.

In this section, you will see how to use the type-specific properties of the report region (together with some additions to the SQL source code) to build the formatted report.

Begin by creating a new page containing two classic report regions, each having the source select * from EMP. Follow these steps:

1. Create a new blank page named Classic Reports, numbered page 3. Create a navigation menu entry for the page, also named Classic Reports.

2. Go to the page editor for this page and create two new regions. Title the regions Default Report and Formatted Report, and place them in the Content Body position of the page.

3. Set the type of each region to be Classic Report having the source query select * from EMP.

4. Configure the Grid properties so that the Formatted Report region starts a new row. (Or if you prefer to see the reports side by side, set the grid properties so that the formatted report does not start a new row.)

Figure 3-21 depicts the top of the resulting rendering tree, showing the components for the Default Report region. Note that APEX assigned several components to each report: a component (labeled with the region name) that contains the type-independent properties, a component (labeled Attributes) that contains report-specific properties, and a component for each column of the report, that contains the column-specific properties. The following sections examine these column-specific and report-specific properties.

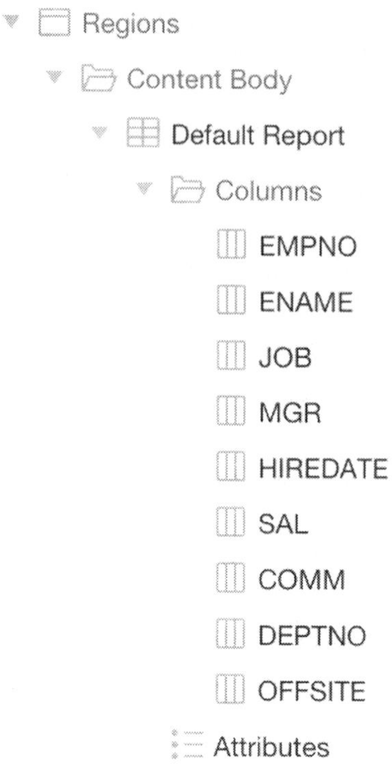

▼ ☐ Regions

   ▼ 🗁 Content Body

      ▼ ⊞ Default Report

         ▼ 🗁 Columns

              ⫼ EMPNO

              ⫼ ENAME

              ⫼ JOB

              ⫼ MGR

              ⫼ HIREDATE

              ⫼ SAL

              ⫼ COMM

              ⫼ DEPTNO

              ⫼ OFFSITE

         ⸬ Attributes

Figure 3-21. *Rendering tree for a Classic Report region on EMP*

Column-Specific Properties

When you select a column from the rendering tree, the property editor shows you its column-specific properties. Figure 3-22 displays the relevant properties for the EMPNO column of the default report.

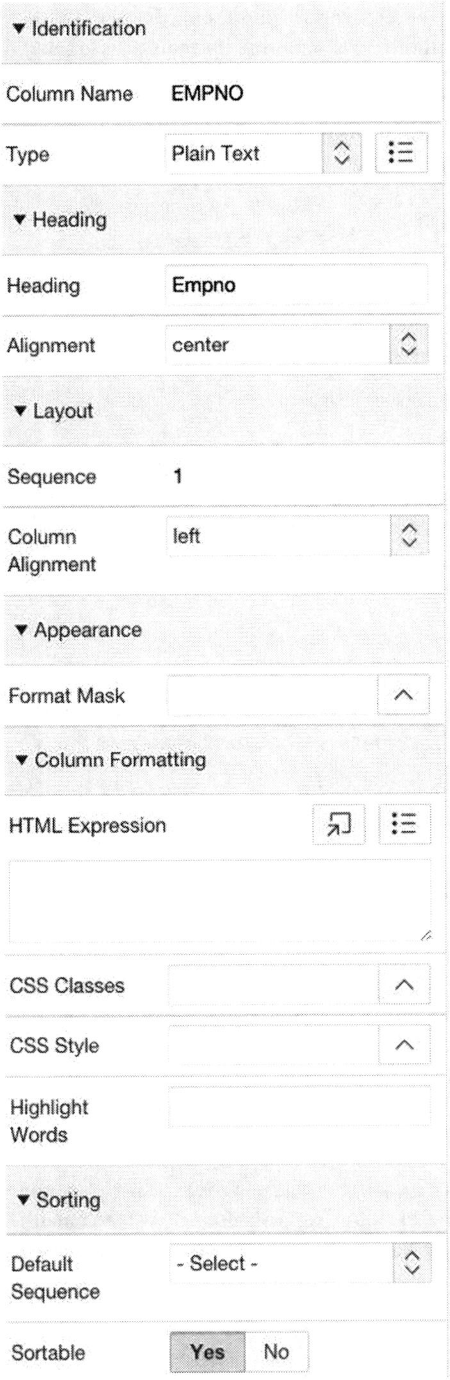

▼ Identification

Column Name	**EMPNO**
Type	Plain Text

▼ Heading

Heading	**Empno**
Alignment	center

▼ Layout

Sequence	**1**
Column Alignment	left

▼ Appearance

Format Mask	

▼ Column Formatting

HTML Expression	
CSS Classes	
CSS Style	
Highlight Words	

▼ Sorting

Default Sequence	- Select -
Sortable	Yes No

Figure 3-22. *Column-specific properties of the EMPNO column*

The properties in the first three sections are relatively straightforward. For example, Figure 3-22 tells you the following things about the EMPNO column: its heading is labeled Empno and is aligned center, it appears first in the report, and its values are aligned left and are displayed normally (that is, in "plain text").

The following sub-sections show how to use the properties of Figure 3-22 to construct the Formatted Report region of Figure 3-20.

Column Visibility

Recall that the EMPNO, MGR, and COMM columns are not part of the Formatted Report region. You can achieve this in APEX by setting their Type property (in the Identification section) to the value Hidden Column.

Column Headers

A column's Name property identifies the column within the application builder; its value comes from the SQL query. A column's Heading property is the value that is displayed in the report. The formatted report contains modified headings for the ENAME and DEPTNO columns. In general, the value for Heading can include HTML code, which means that the header can contain formatted text or even an image.

Column Alignment

By default, column values are aligned to the left. You can specify a different alignment by changing the column's Column Alignment in its Layout section. The alignment of the SAL column in the formatted report is set to right.

Sort Order

If a report's source query has an order by clause, the records are sorted in that order and cannot be altered by the user. But if there is no such clause, then APEX allows the user to interactively sort the report on any column. You can see this in the Default Report region in Figure 3-20. The column headings of the default report are links — clicking a link sorts the region on that column, and repeated clicking of that link toggles between ascending and descending sort order.

The sortability of a column is determined by the properties in its Sorting section. If the Sortable property has the value Yes, the column heading has a sort link; otherwise, the heading has no link. In the formatted report, all the columns except ENAME have their Sortable property set to No.

Assigning a value to the Default Sequence property implies that Sortable is Yes, and allows you to sort by more than one column. For example, suppose that you set the default sequence of JOB to 1 and ENAME to 2. Clicking the header for JOB will cause the records to be sorted by job, and all records having the same job will be sorted by their EName values.

Computed Display Values

Consider the DEPTNO column of the formatted report (which has the heading Department). Note that its values come from the DEPT table, even though the source of the report mentions only the EMP table. How can this be?

The answer is that the values in the column have not changed; they are still department numbers. However, you can set up a correspondence between department names and numbers, and tell APEX to display the name corresponding to a given department number. This correspondence between the result value (the department number) and its display value (the department name) is called a *list of values*.

Formally, a list of values is a two-column table. The first column holds the display values, and the second column holds the corresponding result values. One useful way to specify a list of values is to use an SQL query. For example, the query for the DEPTNO column is simply this:

```
select DName, DeptNo
from DEPT
```

To tell APEX to use a list of values when displaying a column, change the column's type to Plain Text (based on List of Values). When this type is selected, the property editor displays a List of Values section in which you can enter the SQL query. Figure 3-23 shows the relevant properties for the formatted DEPTNO column.

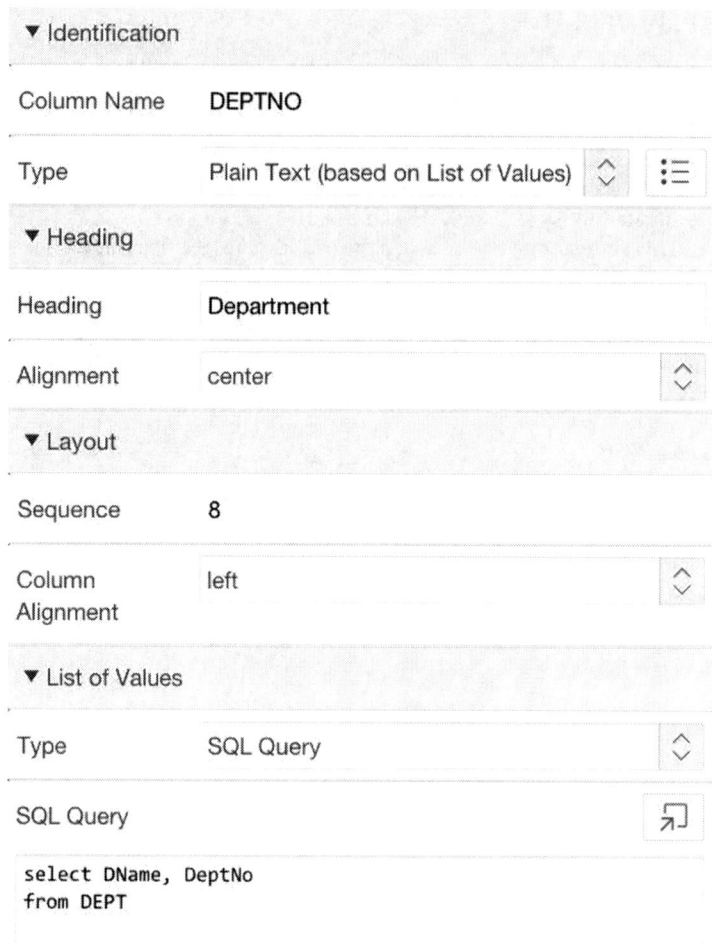

Figure 3-23. *Formatting a column using a list of values*

Format Masks

You occasionally might want to display a number as a string having a particular format. For example, you might use a comma to separate every three digits, you might have a prescribed number of digits to the right of the decimal point, or you might prefix the number with a currency character. Date values can also be written in different formats. In each case, you can use a *format mask* to express your desired format.

A column's Format Mask property is in its Appearance section (refer to Figure 3-22). Clicking the up-arrow displays a list of common formats; selecting a format places its mask in the property's text box. If you are not familiar with the Oracle format mask syntax, you can get a reasonable understanding by examining the various masks. For example,

9 denotes an optional digit, 0 a required digit, G a thousands' separator, D the decimal point, and so on. Such an understanding makes it possible to modify the mask to fit your needs.

For example, to get the mask for the SAL column, I chose the currency format from the format list, which produced the mask FML999G999G999G999G990D00. However, because the database stores salary values in whole dollars, I did not want to display the decimal point and the two digits to its right. So I removed the D00 from the end of the mask.

The mask for HIREDATE was created similarly. An examination of the various date format masks shows that DD denotes the day, Mon the three-character abbreviation of the month, and YYYY the four-digit year. I combined these elements to create my desired format mask, which is Mon DD, YYYY.

For a complete description of format mask syntax, search the Oracle SQL documentation for "format models".

Wrapping Values in HTML Expressions

The Column Formatting section of Figure 3-22 allows you to format the column's values by means of HTML expressions. Consider, for example, the formatting for ENAME in Figure 3-20. The values are bold and in a large font. The HTML expression for the employee named ADAMS is the following:

```
<span style="font-size:150%;font-weight:bold">ADAMS</span>
```

If you assigned this expression to the column's HTML Expression property, the report would display ADAMS, large and in bold, for each employee. This is almost what you want; you just need a way to get APEX to display the name of each employee. APEX uses the following convention: for a column named X, the term #X# denotes the value of X in the current row. Thus you should replace ADAMS in the preceding expression by #ENAME#, resulting in the expression

```
<span style="font-size:150%;font-weight:bold">#ENAME#</span>
```

This expression uses a common idiom — you place the column value within HTML span tags that indicate the formatting style for the value. The CSS Style property makes use of this idiom, so that you only have to specify the style. That is, the above expression is equivalent to placing the following in the CSS Style property:

```
font-size:150%;font-weight:bold
```

The HTML Expression property can do more than simply format the column value. You can also use it to add text to a value or to combine multiple values. For example, Figure 3-24 shows a modification to the Formatted Report region in which the ENAME and JOB values have been combined. Two steps are needed to perform the modification: set the type of JOB to Hidden Column, and then set the HTML expression of ENAME to this:

```
<span style="font-size:150%;font-weight:bold">#ENAME#</span> the #JOB#
```

53

Formatted Report				
Name ⬆	Hiredate	Sal	Department	Offsite
ADAMS the CLERK	Jan 12, 1983	$1,100	RESEARCH	✖
ALLEN the SALESMAN	Feb 20, 1981	$1,600	SALES	✔
BLAKE the MANAGER	May 01, 1981	$2,850	SALES	✖
CLARK the MANAGER	Jun 09, 1981	$2,450	ACCOUNTING	✖
FORD the ANALYST	Dec 03, 1981	$3,000	RESEARCH	✖

row(s) 1 - 5 of 14 ⬍   Next ▶

Figure 3-24. *Combining the values of two columns*

Conditional Formatting

You can also use the HTML Expression property to format SAL values in a particular color. For example, the following expression makes all salary values red:

```
<span style="color:red">#SAL#</span>
```

But how do you make it so that only some of the values are colored red? HTML by itself cannot perform calculations, so you must rely on SQL to do it for you. The idea is to have the SQL source query compute a new column, whose value is the color of the salary value. The following query does the job:

```
select e.*,
    case when e.Sal>2500 then 'red' else 'black' end as SalColor
from EMP e
```

You can then format the SAL column by assigning the following code to its HTML Expression property:

```
<span style="color:#SALCOLOR#">#SAL#</span>
```

You can apply the same technique to the OFFSITE column. In the formatted report, an Offsite value shows an image of a green check mark if its value is 'Y' and a red check mark otherwise. Assume that these two images have been saved to APEX as the application files checkgreen.jpg and checkred.jpg. Then a value of 'Y' should be formatted as the following HTML expression:

```
<img src="&APP_IMAGES.checkgreen.jpg">
```

The value of 'N' should be formatted as follows:

```
<img src="&APP_IMAGES.checkred.jpg">
```

The way to distinguish between these two file names is to extend the SQL source query so that it computes a new column, named OffsiteImage, whose value is either 'checkgreen.jpg' or 'checkred.jpg'. The SQL query now looks like this (new code is in bold):

```
select e.*,
    case when e.Sal>2500 then 'red' else 'black' end as SalColor,
    case when e.Offsite = 'Y' then 'checkgreen.jpg'
        else 'checkred.jpg' end as OffsiteImage
from EMP e
```

The value of the HTML Expression property for the OFFSITE column can then be written as follows:

```
<img src="&APP_IMAGES.#OFFSITEIMAGE#">
```

Of course, these computed columns will also need to be formatted. The typical choice is to set their Type property to Hidden Column.

Values as Links

The HireDate values in Figure 3-20 are formatted as links. In particular, clicking a date (say, Feb 20, 1981) redirects the browser to the URL http://www.infoplease.com/year/1981.html.

That is, clicking a hire date redirects to a web page giving the current events of the year the employee was hired. Recall that the HTML code to define a link has two parts: the target URL and the link text. The link text is simply the HireDate value. The target URL is the same for all values, except for the year of hire. The way to obtain this value is to once again modify the SQL source query; this time, the query should create a new column that extracts the year from the hire date. The query now becomes the following (new code is in bold):

```
select e.*,
    case when e.Sal>2500 then 'red' else 'black' end as SalColor,
    case when e.Offsite = 'Y' then 'checkgreen.jpg'
        else 'checkred.jpg' end as OffsiteImage,
    extract(year from e.HireDate) as HireYear
from EMP e
```

You can then specify the link by assigning the following code to the HTML Expression property for the Offsite column:

```
<a href="http://www.infoplease.com/year/#HIREYEAR#.html"
   target="_blank">#HIREDATE#</a>
```

Note that the second argument to the <a> tag is target="_blank". This argument causes the target page to open in a new browser tab, which in this case seems reasonable.

Although this technique works, a better way to format a column as a link is to set its Type property to Link. Doing so causes the property editor to display a Link section. This section has the property Target, whose initial value is No Link Defined. Clicking that box opens a Link Builder page, in which you specify whether the target is a page of an APEX application or an arbitrary URL. Select URL, enter the target URL into the text box that appears, and click the OK button to return to the property editor. You can then enter the appropriate values for Link Text and Link Attributes, as shown in Figure 3-25. Note that you need to enter the "http://" portion of the URL in the link builder, even though the Target property does not display it.

▼ Link	
Target	infoplease.com/year/#HIREYEAR#.html
Link Text	#HIREDATE#
Link Attributes	target="_blank"

Figure 3-25. *Link properties for the HireDate column*

Report-Specific Properties

A classic report's report-specific properties handle issues such as pagination and record grouping. Recall that these properties are associated with the region's Attributes component in the rendering tree. Figure 3-26 shows the Layout and Pagination sections for the Formatted Report region.

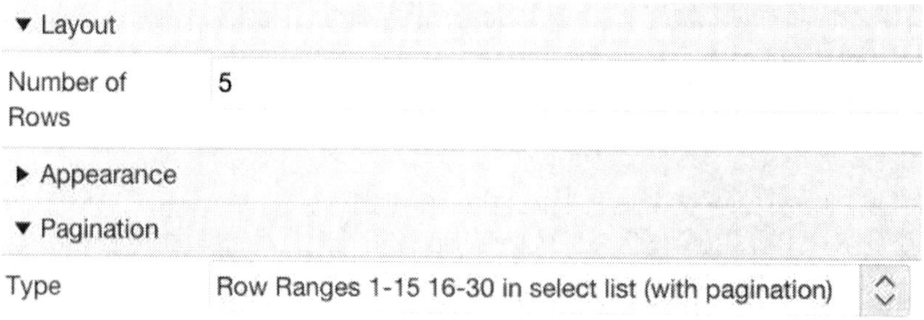

▼ Layout	
Number of Rows	5
▶ Appearance	
▼ Pagination	
Type	Row Ranges 1-15 16-30 in select list (with pagination)

Figure 3-26. *Type-specific properties of a classic report region*

The Number of Rows property specifies how many rows of the report to display at a time. By default, the value is 15, but it was changed to 5 in the Formatted Report region. The pagination Type property allows you to select the format of the pagination controls. Figure 3-27 shows the possible values.

	No Pagination (Show All Rows)
▼ Pagination	Row Ranges X to Y (no pagination)
	Row Ranges X to Y of Z (no pagination)
	Row Ranges X to Y of Z (with pagination)
	Row Ranges 1–15 16–30 (with set pagination)
Type	✓ Row Ranges 1–15 16–30 in select list (with pagination)
	Search Engine 1,2,3,4 (set based pagination)
Display	Use Externally Created Pagination Buttons
Position	Row Ranges X to Y (with next and previous links)

Figure 3-27. *Pagination control values*

These possibilities are fairly straightforward. The option selected in the figure was used for the Formatted Report region in Figure 3-20. The best way to understand the other options is to try each one on your report to see its effect.

When developing a report, one issue to keep in mind is that APEX examines pagination properties only once per session. This means that if you run a page containing a classic report, then change a pagination value from the property editor, and then re-run the page, the pagination changes will not be reflected in the report. In order to see pagination changes, you must either start a new session or tell APEX to "reset pagination". One way to start a new session is to log out of APEX and log back in again. Another way is to run the page by entering a URL with a session ID of 0. For example:

```
apex.oracle.com/pls/apex/f?p=87059:3:0
```

To tell APEX to reset pagination without changing the session, you pass the current session ID as the third argument to the URL, and pass the value RP as the sixth argument. For example:

```
apex.oracle.com/pls/apex/f?p=87059:3:102741688116062:::RP
```

Using the Source Query for Formatting

Although the previous sections have focused on how to use APEX to format the rows of a source query, it is important to realize that you can get many of these same features by using a more precise source query. Here are some examples for the Formatted Report demo region.

Instead of hiding a column, it might be more appropriate to simply not include it in the query. In particular, the columns EmpNo, Mgr, and Comm serve no purpose in the formatted report and are better off being left out of its source query entirely. On the other hand, the columns SalColor, OffsiteImage, and HireYear are needed for the formatting of other columns, so they must appear in the source query and therefore must be of type Hidden Column. Another example is the report of Figure 3-24, in which the Job column needs to be available but hidden, because its value is needed to help format the EName column.

Instead of changing a column's heading in the property editor, you could change the column's name in the source query. An example is the EName column, which was renamed as Name. The alternative is to use the AS keyword in the source query, like this:

```
select EName as Name, ...
from EMP
```

If you don't want the user to be able to change the sort order of the records interactively, it is easier to specify the sort order in the source query than to set the sortability property of each column individually.

Instead of using a list of values to format the DeptNo column, you can modify the source query to be a join of the EMP and DEPT tables like this:

```
select e.EName as Name, ..., d.DName, ...
from EMP e join DEPT d
on e.DeptNo = d.DeptNo
```

In this case, it is hard to say which of these two approaches is better than the other. The list of values approach requires that APEX search the list of values for each row of the report, which is potentially more expensive than simply doing the join in one shot. On the other hand, the list of values approach is simpler, and more directly conveys the intent of the designer.

The rule of thumb is that the source query should specify *what* you want displayed, whereas the column properties should specify *how* you want them displayed. In some cases (such as hidden columns), this distinction is clear. In others (such as using a list of values), it is less so.

Chart Regions

A *chart* is a visual way to display data points. A data point consists of two values: the X-coordinate, called the *label*, and the Y-coordinate, called the *value*. As an example, let's build a page named Charts, which will be page 4 of the application. This page contains two chart regions, and is shown in Figure 3-28.

Employee Count per Job

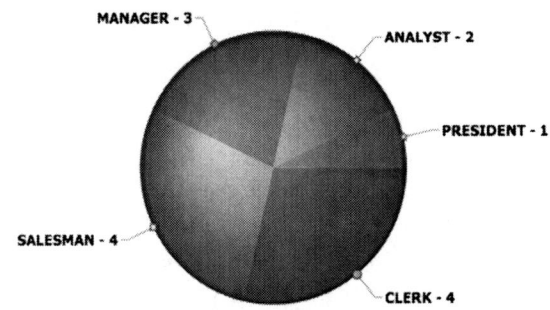

Max and Min Salary per Job

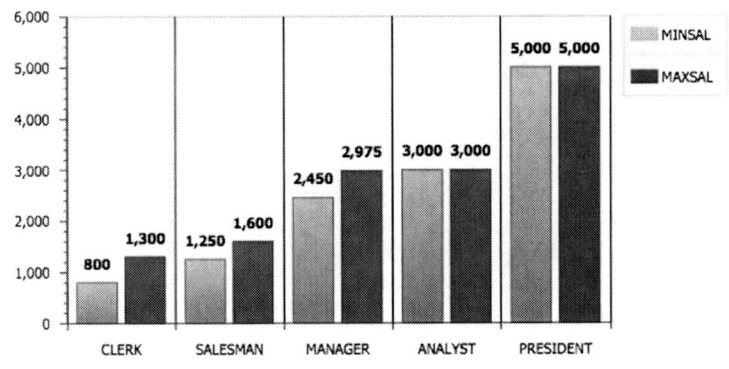

Figure 3-28. The Charts page

The pie chart consists of five data points, one for each job. The label of each point is the name of the job, and the value is the number of employees having that job. That chart displays a section of the pie for each label in proportion to its value. For example, two of the fourteen employees are analysts, so the size of the ANALYST section is two-fourteenth the size of the pie.

The column chart consists of ten data points, giving the minimum and maximum salaries of employees at each job. These points are organized into two *series* of five points each.

Creating a Chart Region

To build this page, begin by creating a new page named Charts and two regions of type Chart. Name the first region Employee Count per Job and the second region Max and Min Salary per Job. Figure 3-29 shows the rendering tree for these regions.

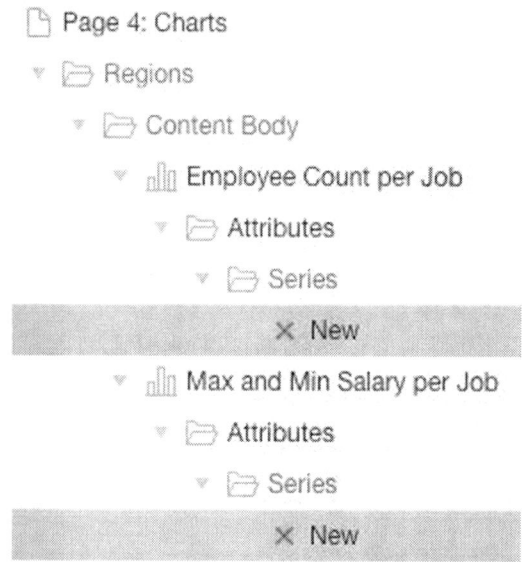

Figure 3-29. *Rendering tree for the two chart regions*

From this figure, you can see that a chart has three kinds of properties: the type-independent properties (denoted by the chart name), the chart-specific properties (denoted by Attributes), and the properties specific to each series (denoted by Series). By default, a chart is created with one series (named New), but you can rename the series and add others.

In Figure 3-29, the component for a new series is flagged with a red X, which denotes an error. In this case, the error occurs because each series does not yet have a source query. This issue will now be addressed.

A Chart's Source Query

The source of a chart needs to specify its data points, and an SQL query works well for this purpose. Each type of chart has slightly different needs, so the structures of their source queries vary slightly. Pie charts and column charts have a similar structure: the first column is a URL, the second column denotes the names of the labels, and the remaining columns denote the values for each series.

A pie chart can have only one series, so its source query must have three columns. For example, the Employee Count per Job chart has the following source query:

```
select null, Job, count(*) as EmpCount
from EMP
group by Job
order by EmpCount desc
```

Ignoring the first column for the moment, the query has one row for each job, with that row containing the name of the job and the number of employees having that job. The job names form the labels along the X-axis of the chart, and the counts form the corresponding Y-axis values.

If a column chart has N series, then its source query will have N+2 columns. For example, the Max and Min Salary per Job chart has two series, so its source query has four columns. The second column specifies the X-axis labels, which again are the various jobs; and the third and fourth columns specify the two series of Y-axis values, which are the minimum and maximum salary per job. The source query is as follows:

```
select null, Job, min(Sal) as MinSal, max(Sal) as MaxSal
from EMP
group by Job
order by MinSal
```

The first column for both these queries is null. In general, however, it is a URL, and its purpose is to enable a user to "drill down" through the chart. When a user clicks on the chart, APEX redirects to the URL associated with that label. For example, clicking a segment of the pie chart would redirect to the URL associated with that segment, which might display a report listing those employees having the specified job.

Constructing a useful URL involves the ability to access and manipulate the session state, so the discussion of links and chart drill-down will be postponed until Chapter 6. Until then, the value of a chart's URL column will be null, which means that the chart will not respond to user clicks.

Chart-Specific Properties

The chart-specific properties are concerned with the appearance of the chart. To access these properties, you select the chart's Attributes component in the rendering tree. Figure 3-30 shows the most common properties, configured with the values for the pie chart.

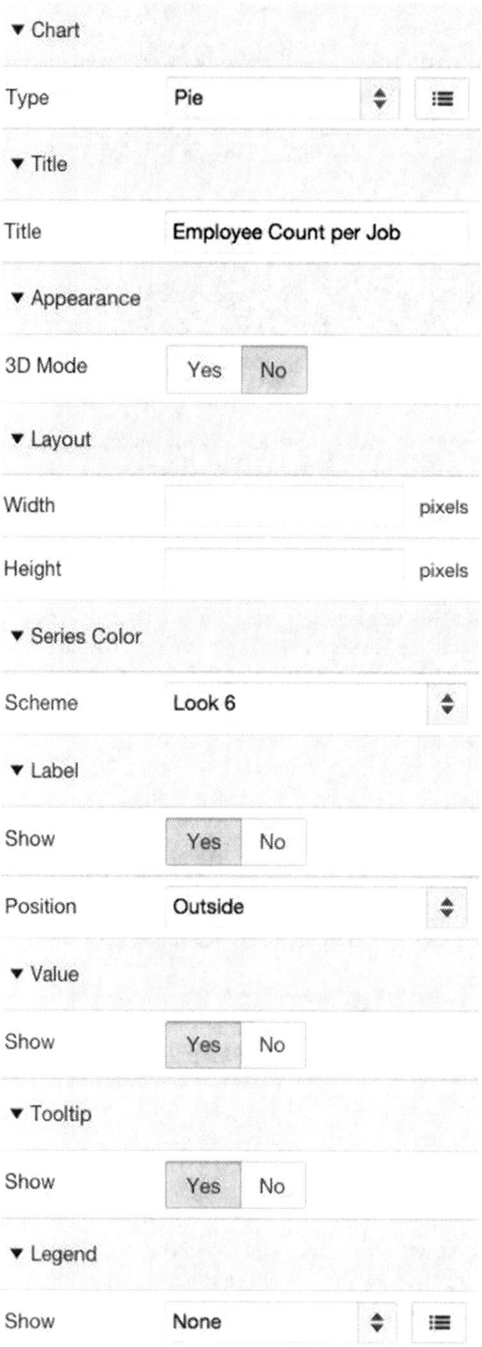

▼ Chart

| Type | Pie | ⇕ | ☰ |

▼ Title

| Title | Employee Count per Job |

▼ Appearance

| 3D Mode | Yes | No |

▼ Layout

| Width | | pixels |
| Height | | pixels |

▼ Series Color

| Scheme | Look 6 | ⇕ |

▼ Label

| Show | Yes | No |
| Position | Outside | ⇕ |

▼ Value

| Show | Yes | No |

▼ Tooltip

| Show | Yes | No |

▼ Legend

| Show | None | ⇕ | ☰ |

Figure 3-30. *Common chart properties*

The Type property specifies the chart type. As you might expect, there are several chart types to pick from. The top region of Figure 3-28 is of type Pie, and the bottom region is of type Column.

The value of the Title property gets displayed above the chart. I chose to display the title for demonstration purposes, but as you can see from Figure 3-28, the region title often works better than a chart title.

By default, a chart region expands to fill the browser window. You can use the Layout properties to specify an exact size, if desired.

The Series Color properties let you change the chart's color palette.

If the Label and Value properties are set, those values are displayed with the chart. Both charts in Figure 3-28 display labels and values.

The Legend properties let you choose whether to display a legend, and if so, where to display it. A *legend* identifies each series on the chart, so it is needed only when a chart has multiple series. In Figure 3-28, the column chart contains a legend, but not the pie chart.

Series-Specific Properties

You access a chart's series-specific properties by selecting the desired series in the rendering tree. Figure 3-31 shows some of these properties for the column chart of Figure 3-28.

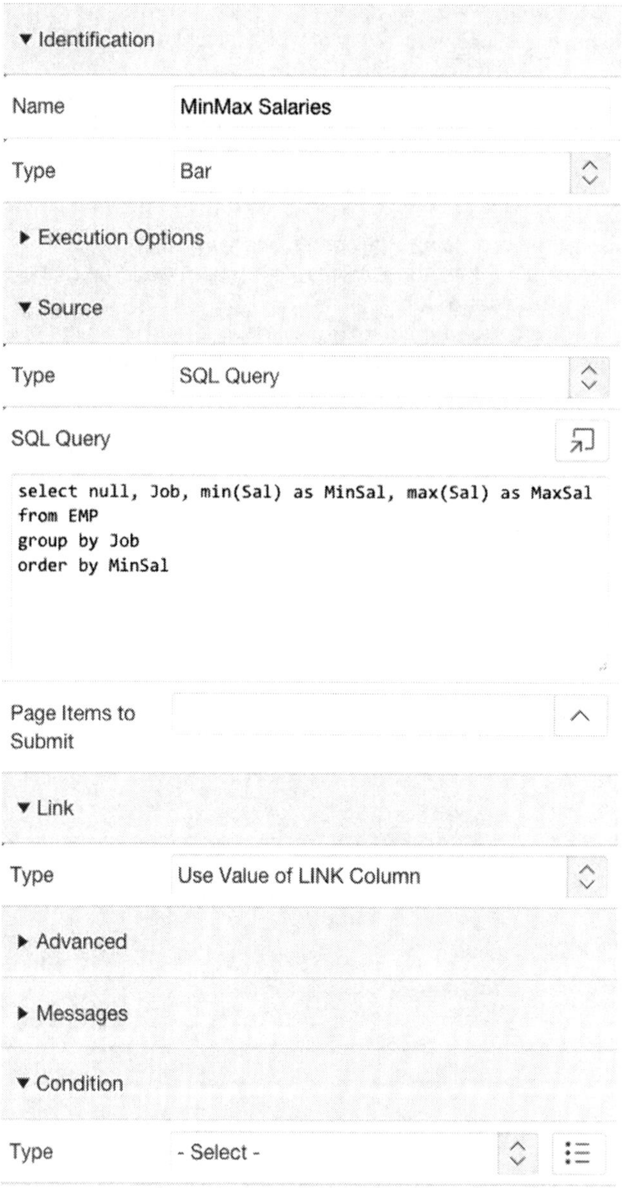

▼ Identification

Name	**MinMax Salaries**
Type	Bar

▶ Execution Options

▼ Source

Type	SQL Query

SQL Query

```
select null, Job, min(Sal) as MinSal, max(Sal) as MaxSal
from EMP
group by Job
order by MinSal
```

Page Items to Submit	

▼ Link

Type	Use Value of LINK Column

▶ Advanced

▶ Messages

▼ Condition

Type	- Select -

Figure 3-31. *Series properties of the bar chart*

The most important property is SQL Query, in which you enter the source query. Typically, a single source query is sufficient to define all the series. In general, you need to create multiple Series components (each with its own source query) only if they have different display characteristics. For example, the Condition property causes that series to be displayed or hidden independently of the other series, depending on the value of its condition. That property is blank in Figure 3-31, indicating that the series will always be displayed. In Chapter 6 you will examine some interesting ways to use this property.

The best way to understand charts and their properties is to experiment. Edit the two charts by changing their properties in various ways. For example, move the legend and title around, change the color scheme and background, include labels or values on the chart, and so on.

Interactive Report Regions

The previous sections have examined how you can use properties to format classic reports and charts. In doing so, you are in effect customizing your reports and charts for presentation to the user. An *interactive report* enables users to perform some of this customization themselves, as they view the page.

Figure 3-32 displays a vanilla, unformatted, interactive report region. To create it, I created a new blank page named Interactive Reports, which is page 5 of the application. I then created a new region within it named Employees, of type Interactive Report, and having the source query select * from EMP.

Q ∨				**Go**	Actions ∨			

Empno	Ename	Job	Mgr	Hiredate	Sal	Comm	Deptno	Offsite
7839	KING	PRESIDENT	-	17-NOV-81	5000	-	10	N
7698	BLAKE	MANAGER	7839	01-MAY-81	2850	-	30	N
7782	CLARK	MANAGER	7839	09-JUN-81	2450	-	10	N
7566	JONES	MANAGER	7839	02-APR-81	2975	-	20	N
7788	SCOTT	ANALYST	7566	09-DEC-82	3000	-	20	Y
7902	FORD	ANALYST	7566	03-DEC-81	3000	-	20	N
7369	SMITH	CLERK	7902	17-DEC-80	800	-	20	N
7499	ALLEN	SALESMAN	7698	20-FEB-81	1600	300	30	Y
7654	MARTIN	SALESMAN	7698	28-SEP-81	1250	1400	30	N
7844	TURNER	SALESMAN	7698	08-SEP-81	1500	0	30	Y
7876	ADAMS	CLERK	7788	12-JAN-83	1100	-	20	N
7900	JAMES	CLERK	7698	03-DEC-81	950	-	30	N
7934	MILLER	CLERK	7782	23-JAN-82	1300	-	10	N
7521	WARD	SALESMAN	7698	22-FEB-81	1250	500	30	Y

1 - 14

Figure 3-32. Interactive report region on the EMP table

Note that an interactive report region has a default template that is different from the other report types you have seen. Those regions used the Standard template, whereas Figure 3-32 uses the Interactive Report template. The most obvious difference is that an Interactive Report template does not display its title across the top.

■ **Note** As always, you can change a region's template from its Appearance section in the property editor.

Apart from its region template, Figure 3-32 looks a lot like a classic report region. In fact, all the properties of classic report regions also apply to interactive report regions—you can specify the region's position on the page, its source query, and the format of each column. If you want, you can configure this region so that it looks exactly like the formatted report of Figure 3-20. For now, it will remain unformatted to better focus on the customization that is specific to interactive reports.

The one new feature in Figure 3-32 is the row of items above the report, which is called the *search bar*. The search bar lets users interactively customize the report, by filtering its rows, hiding columns, sorting, creating charts, and performing simple calculations on its values. Although not shown in the figure, an interactive report can also display a *link column* that allows users to examine the report's records individually.

The following sections address issues surrounding the search bar and link column — in particular, how they are used, and how an application designer can configure their properties.

Using the Search Bar

The search bar contains four items: the magnifying glass, text box, Go button, and Actions button. The first three items let a user filter the rows of the report. The user enters a search string in the box, clicks the magnifying glass to choose the column to search (All Columns can also be chosen), and clicks Go. The records not containing the search text will be filtered from the report.

For example, entering 82 in the text box and selecting the column Hiredate has the effect of filtering for all employees hired in 1982. Figure 3-33 shows the resulting region.

Empno	Ename	Job	Mgr	Hiredate	Sal	Comm	Deptno	Offsite
7788	SCOTT	ANALYST	7566	09-DEC-82	3000	-	20	Y
7934	MILLER	CLERK	7782	23-JAN-82	1300	-	10	N

Figure 3-33. Result of filtering the report of Figure 3-32

Note that the region now has a row below the search bar that describes the filter. You can click the check box on the left to enable/disable it, or you can click the X on the right to permanently remove it.

It is possible to have multiple concurrent filters. For example, to find employees hired in 1982 who work offsite, you would need to add another filter for the Offsite column. The result is shown in Figure 3-34.

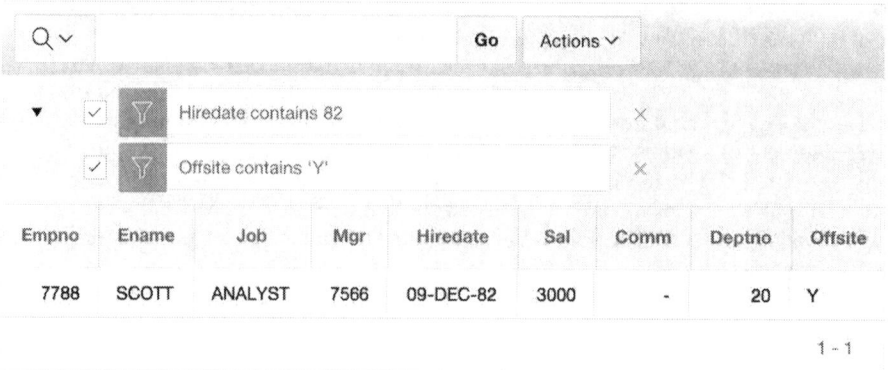

Figure 3-34. *Adding a second filter to the report of Figure 3-33*

In general, a user can explore the contents of a report by creating multiple filters and selectively enabling various subsets of them.

The Actions button allows a user to further customize the report. Clicking the button displays a menu of possible operations. This menu appears in Figure 3-35, showing the submenu for the Format action. The following sections describe the more useful of these operations.

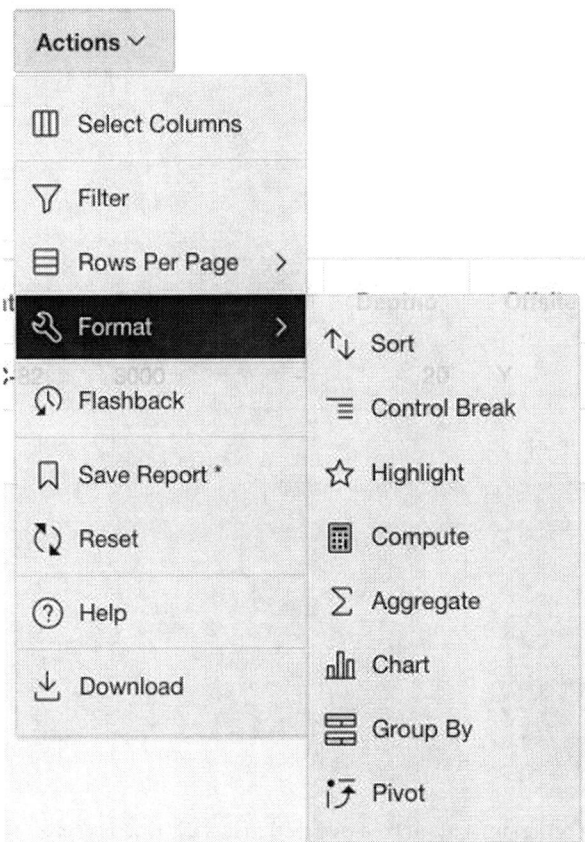

Figure 3-35. *Actions menu*

Select Columns

Choosing the Select Columns operation brings up a modal dialog box that lets the user choose the columns to be displayed in the report and in what order; see Figure 3-36.

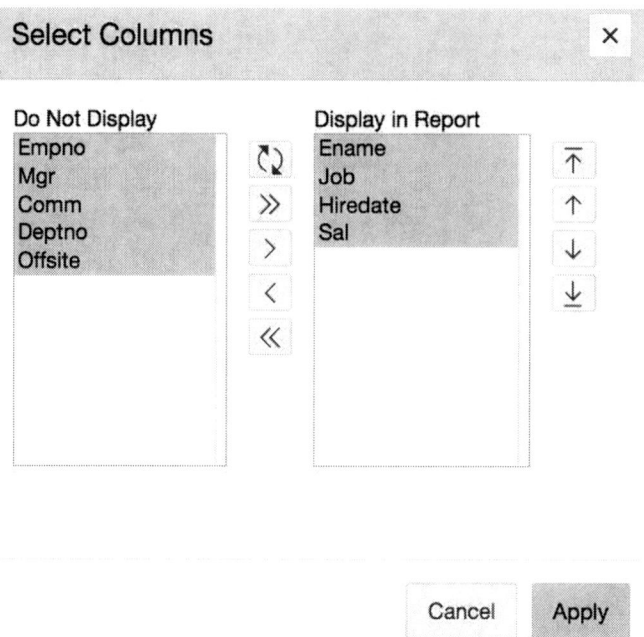

Figure 3-36. Select Columns dialog box

Filter

Choosing the Filter operation brings up a modal dialog box that lets the user create a filter; see Figure 3-37. It produces filters just like the filters you created for Figures 3-33 and 3-34. The difference is that these earlier filters could check only for text containment, whereas this dialog box allows for many kinds of operations. For example, the filter specified in Figure 3-37 is Job != 'CLERK'.

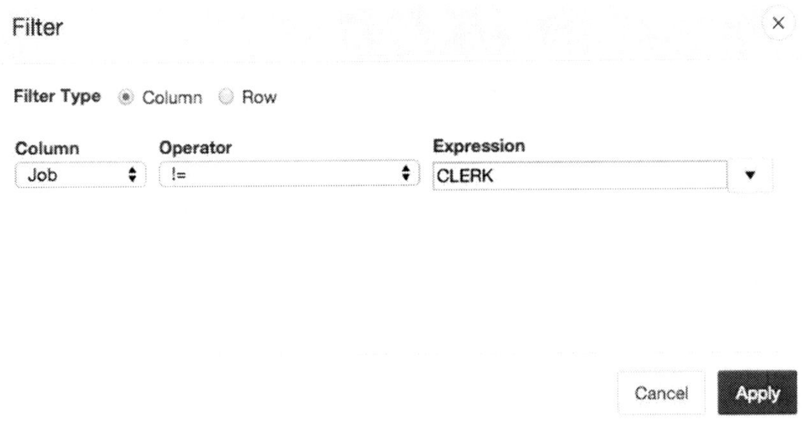

Filter   ⊗

Filter Type ⦿ Column ○ Row

Column   **Operator**   **Expression**
[Job   ⬍]   [!=   ⬍]   [CLERK   ▾]

Cancel   **Apply**

Figure 3-37. Filter dialog box

Rows Per Page

The Rows Per Page operation allows the user to change the report pagination at will. Clicking the menu item displays a submenu, in which the user can choose from a list of possible rows per page.

Sort

Choosing the Sort operation brings up a modal dialog box that lets the user choose the desired sort order; see Figure 3-38. The user selects the column(s) to be sorted and whether the sort direction is ascending or descending. The figure shows the menu to select a sort column. Note that the user can sort on both visible and hidden columns.

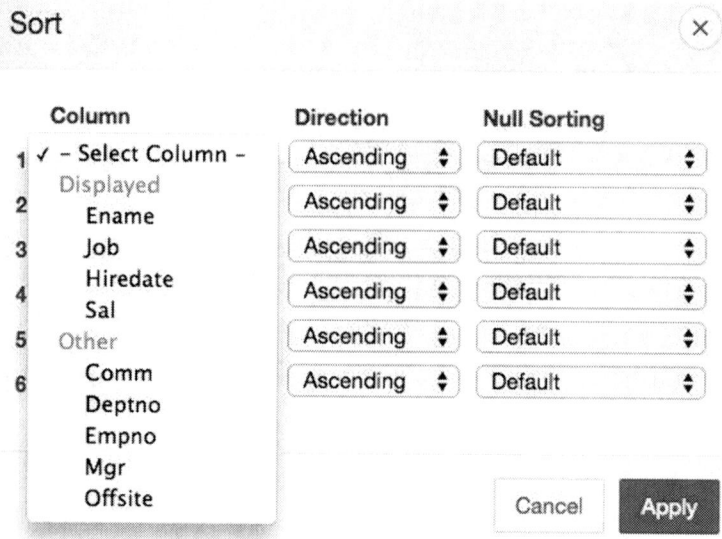

Figure 3-38. *Sort dialog box*

Highlight

The Highlight operation allows the user to highlight rows or cells that satisfy a specified criterion. Recall that the formatted classic report of Figure 3-20 displayed high salary values in red. This is a form of highlighting. The Highlight operation allows the user to express this and other forms of highlighting easily.

   Choosing the Highlight option brings up the modal dialog box of Figure 3-39. The Highlight Condition values specify the values of interest. If the value of Highlight Type is Cell, those values are highlighted; if it is Row, the row containing those values are highlighted. Highlighting can involve the background color, text color, or both. The figure shows the highlighting corresponding to Figure 3-20.

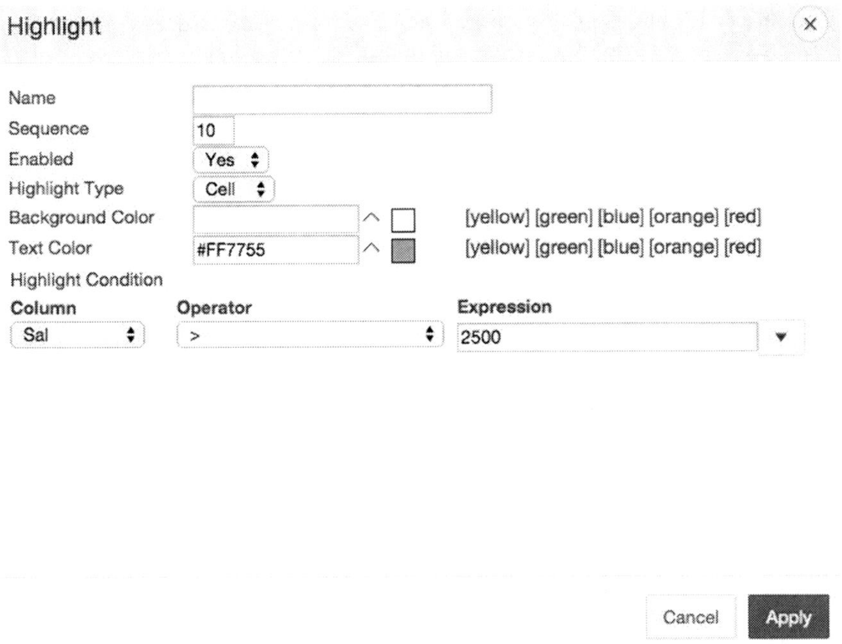

Highlight   ⊗

Name	
Sequence	10
Enabled	Yes ↕
Highlight Type	Cell ↕
Background Color	∧ ☐ [yellow] [green] [blue] [orange] [red]
Text Color	#FF7755 ∧ ▨ [yellow] [green] [blue] [orange] [red]
Highlight Condition	

Column	Operator	Expression
Sal ↕	> ↕	2500 ▼

                                             Cancel   **Apply**

Figure 3-39. *Highlight dialog box*

Chart

Choosing the Chart operation brings up a modal dialog box that lets the user create charts based on the data in the report; see Figure 3-40.

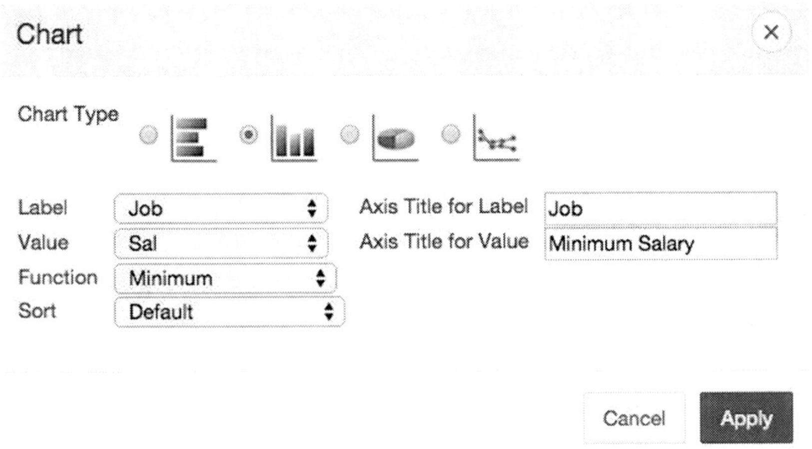

Chart   ⊗

Chart Type   ○ ≣   ⊙ ᴸᴵᴵ   ○ ◖   ○ ⤳

Label	Job ↕	Axis Title for Label	Job
Value	Sal ↕	Axis Title for Value	Minimum Salary
Function	Minimum ↕		
Sort	Default ↕		

                                             Cancel   **Apply**

Figure 3-40. *Chart dialog box*

73

From this dialog box, a user can create a single-series chart that aggregates over a single column. The figure specifies a bar chart that gives the minimum salary per job, similar to the bar chart shown in Figure 3-28. The resulting chart appears in Figure 3-41.

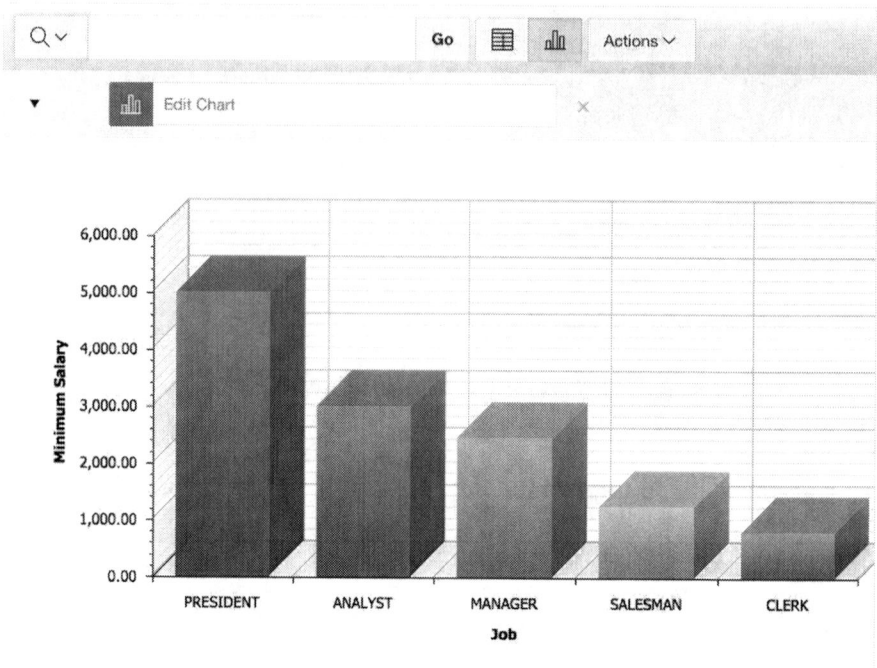

Figure 3-41. *Interactive chart*

There are two things worth noting in this figure. First, many aspects of the chart are not customizable. For example, a chart can have only a single series and will always be formatted in 3D mode. Second, the search bar has been extended to include two report/chart buttons to the left of the Action button. The user can use these buttons to toggle between the interactive report and its chart.

Configuring the Search Bar

Clearly the search bar has a lot of functionality. However, some of that functionality might not be appropriate in a particular application, so an interactive report has properties that allow the application developer to limit this functionality. This section examines those properties.

Figure 3-42 shows the rendering tree for the Interactive Reports page and its interactive report region Employees. Note that this tree has the same structure as a classic report (refer to Figure 3-21): the Attributes component contains the report-specific properties, and the Columns folder contains the properties for each column.

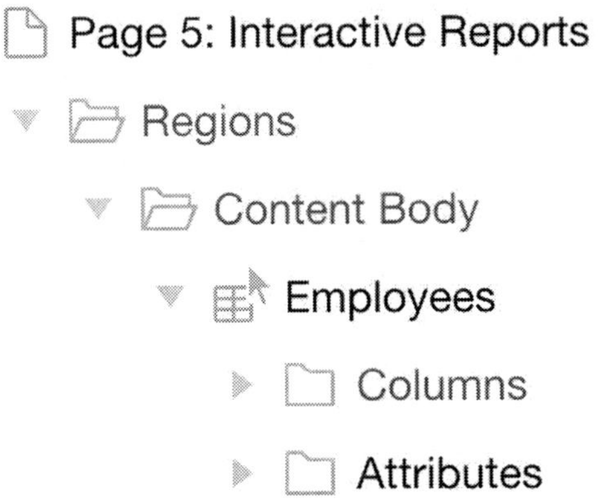

📄 Page 5: Interactive Reports

▼ 🗁 Regions

   ▼ 🗁 Content Body

      ▼ 🗗 Employees

         ▶ 🗋 Columns

         ▶ 🗋 Attributes

Figure 3-42. Rendering tree for the Interactive Reports page

The property editor for the Attributes component contains two relevant sections: Search Bar and Actions Menu. Figure 3-43 shows the first two properties of the Search Bar section. These properties let you selectively display different portions of the search area. In particular, a No value for the Include Search Bar property completely disables the bar; a No value for Search Field enables only the Action button.

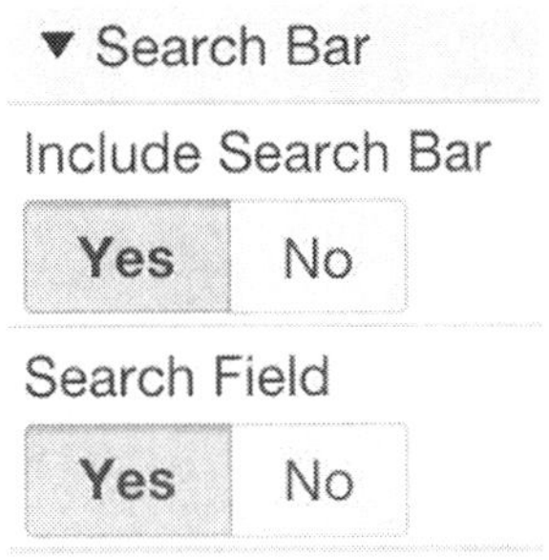

▼ Search Bar

Include Search Bar

| **Yes** | No |

Search Field

| **Yes** | No |

Figure 3-43. Properties to configure the search area

Figure 3-44 shows the first several properties of the Actions Menu section. These properties let you specify which operations are displayed in the menu. (Not all the properties are shown due to lack of space.)

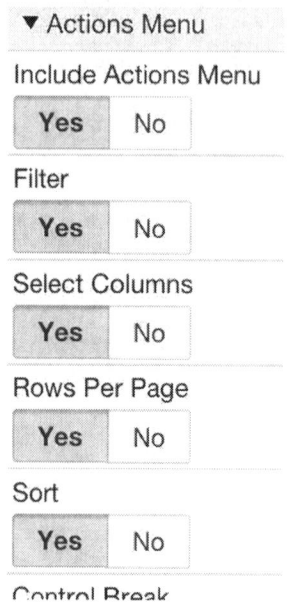

Figure 3-44. *Some properties of the Actions Menu section*

Finally, each column of an interactive report has properties for configuring its specific capabilities. These properties appear in the Enable Users To section and are shown in Figure 3-45. (Again, not all properties are shown because of lack of space and the fact that the omitted properties are just more of the same.)

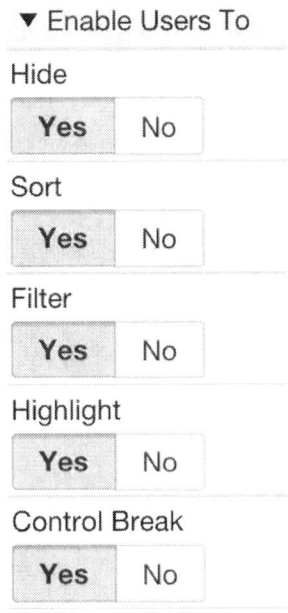

Figure 3-45. *Some properties of a column's Enable Users To section*

Link Column

An interactive report can have a special column whose value is a link. This link can be configured to display the report in *single row view*. That is, when a user clicks a link for a row, the report changes to show the values of only that row; it also displays navigation buttons for the user to move to the next or previous record, and a button to return to the original report. Figure 3-46 shows the interactive report with the link column displayed. Figure 3-47 shows the single row view of the report after the link for BLAKE is clicked. Note that this single row view displays all the columns, not just the ones displayed in the report.

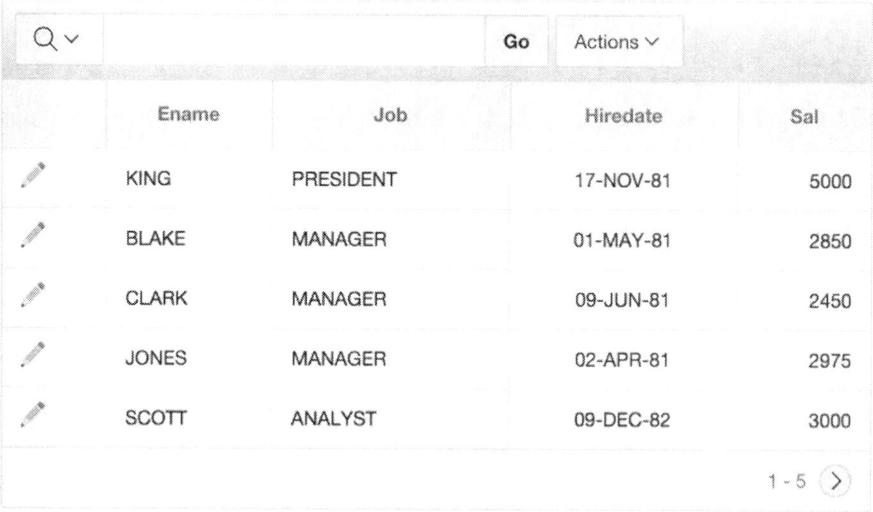

	Ename	Job	Hiredate	Sal
	KING	PRESIDENT	17-NOV-81	5000
	BLAKE	MANAGER	01-MAY-81	2850
	CLARK	MANAGER	09-JUN-81	2450
	JONES	MANAGER	02-APR-81	2975
	SCOTT	ANALYST	09-DEC-82	3000

1 - 5 >

Figure 3-46. Interactive report with its link column

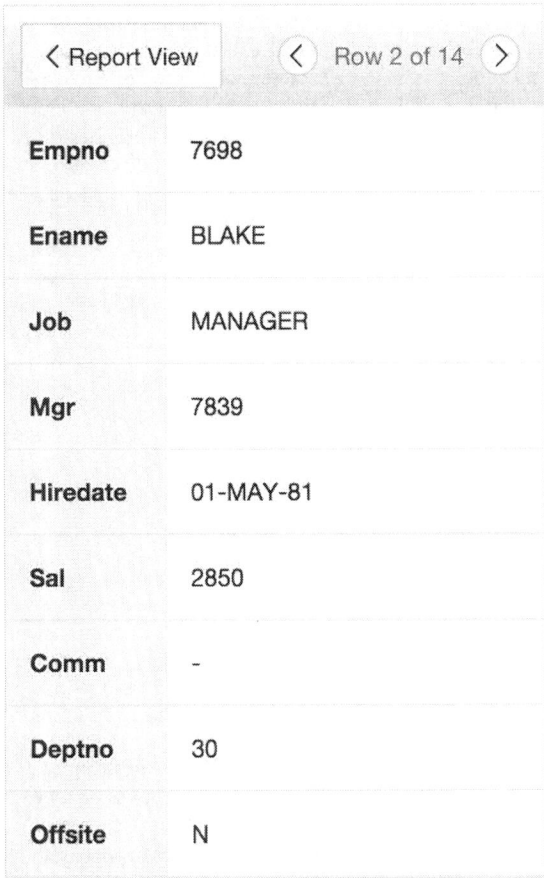

Figure 3-47. Interactive report in single row view

The property editor for the region's Attributes component displays two sections—Link and Single Row View—that let you enable the link column and configure its behavior. The properties for the Link section appear in Figure 3-48.

▼ Link

Link Column	Link to Single Row View	⬍
Uniquely Identify Rows by	ROWID	⬍

Figure 3-48. Properties to enable single record view

79

To enable the link column, set the value of the Link Column property to Link to Single Row View. (You can also set it to link to an arbitrary URL, but this choice is less interesting.) You then have to specify which row is to be selected when the link is clicked. The value ROWID says to use the row that was clicked, which is the most natural.

Figure 3-49 shows the Single Row View section. The interesting property here is Only Displayed Columns: a value of Yes specifies that the single row view should display the same columns as the report; a value of No specifies that it should display all the columns.

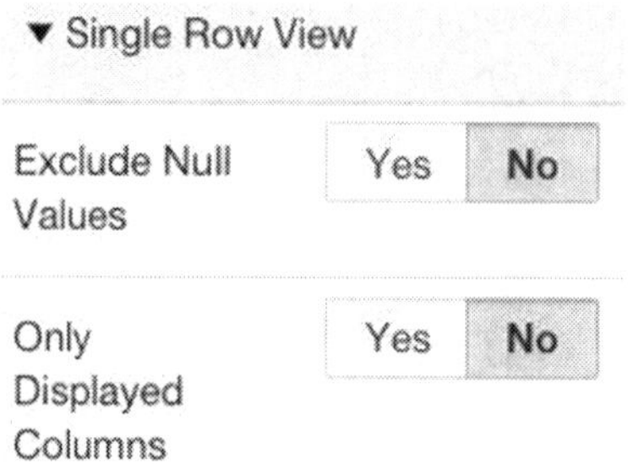

▼ Single Row View

| Exclude Null Values | Yes | **No** |
| Only Displayed Columns | Yes | **No** |

Figure 3-49. *Single Row View properties*

Summary

This chapter focused on the design and use of APEX regions. You began by examining different ways to create a region, the properties needed to specify its location on a page, and its look and feel. You then explored four common region types: Static Content, Classic Report, Chart, and Interactive Report. You looked at how regions of each type are used and how to take advantage of their type-specific properties to format them effectively.

A static content region is used primarily to display HTML code. You examined the APEX-specific nuances associated with relative references — in particular, how to refer to an image stored on the APEX server and how to link to a page of the current application. These relative references relied on the value of certain APEX built-in variables, such as APP_IMAGES and APP_ID. You saw how to use *substitution strings* to access the value of these variables.

A classic report region displays the output of an SQL query. You saw how to use APEX properties to customize the way the region is displayed. Of particular interest is a column's HTML Expression property, which lets you format a column value by wrapping it in an HTML expression. You also saw how to perform conditional formatting by modifying the report's source query.

A chart region displays a chart. You saw how to use an SQL query to specify the content of the chart and how to take advantage of properties to configure the way the chart looks.

An interactive report region displays a report, similar to a classic report region. The interactive report differs in two ways. First, its search bar enables users to customize the report interactively. Second, its link column allows users to view the report in single-record mode. You examined the functionality provided by these features and compared them with what is possible using classic report and chart regions. You also saw how an application developer can enable only parts of this functionality by setting the properties of the interactive report region, as desired.

CHAPTER 4

Navigation

Web application users need to easily navigate through the application's pages. You have already encountered three navigational features in your use of APEX: links, breadcrumbs, and the navigation menu. This chapter examines these features in detail, and shows you different ways to use them in your applications.

Lists

In common parlance, a *list* is simply a collection of things. In APEX, however, a list is a collection of links. A list is a useful navigation tool, for the obvious reason that clicking a link takes you to a new page.

For a good example of an APEX list, consider again the SQL Workshop home screen from Chapter 1 (refer to Figure 1-3). Its Create Object region is a list that enables quick access to the various object–creation wizard pages. That list has an entry for each kind of SQL object, with its link taking you to the creation wizard for that object.

For another example, recall the References region of your demo application's home page, as shown in Figure 3-14 of Chapter 3. This region is also a list with links that take you to selected web pages.

Perhaps the most notable example of a list is the navigation menu. Each of its entries is a link that takes you to the specified page of the application.

The APEX *list manager* lets you view, edit, and create lists. To get to the list manager, begin at the application's home screen and click the large Shared Components button at the top of the page. Search for the Navigation section and then click Lists. You will be taken to the main screen of the list manager, which is shown in Figure 4-1.

	Lists	List Details	Unused		Conditional Entries		Utilization		History	

Q ∨			Go	88	⊞	Actions ∨	Reset	Copy	Create >

Name ↕	Type	Entries	References	Entries Updated	List Updated	Navigation Bar	Navigation Menu
Desktop Navigation Bar	Static	1	0	-	-	Yes	No
Desktop Navigation Menu	Static	5	0	44 hours ago	44 hours ago	No	Yes

Figure 4-1. List manager

The figure shows that the application already has two lists: Desktop Navigation Bar and Desktop Navigation Menu. APEX treats these lists in a special way — their respective entries are displayed in the navigation bar (which runs across the top of the page) and the navigation menu (which runs down the left side of the page). The following sections explain how to use the list manager.

Viewing List Details

Clicking the name of a list (or selecting the List Details link at the top of the screen) brings you to the List Details screen. Figure 4-2 shows this screen for the Desktop Navigation Menu list.

Lists	List Details	Unused	Conditional Entries	Utilization	History

List	Desktop Navigation Menu ⇕ ⑦		Reset	Grid Edit	Edit List	Create List Entry >

Q ∨		Go	Actions ∨

Sequence ↕	Name	Parent Entry	Target	Conditional	Updated
10	Home	-	f? p=&APP_ID.:1:&APP_SESSION.::&DEBUG.:	-	-
20	Region Practice	-	f?p=&APP_ID.:2:&SESSION.::&DEBUG.	-	3 weeks ago
30	Classic Reports	-	f?p=&APP_ID.:3:&SESSION.::&DEBUG.	-	2 weeks ago
40	Charts	-	f?p=&APP_ID.:4:&SESSION.::&DEBUG.	-	63 seconds ago
50	Interactive Reports	-	f?p=&APP_ID.:5:&SESSION.::&DEBUG.	-	12 seconds ago

Figure 4-2. Details of the Desktop Navigation Menu list

The screen displays information about each entry in the selected list. The most relevant values are Sequence, Name, and Target.

- The sequence numbers determine the order in which the entries appear in the list.

- The name of an entry specifies how it is displayed in the list.

- The target of an entry is the URL that is called when the link is clicked.

Note in the figure that each target URL refers to a page of the current application, using the syntax described in Chapter 2. One new aspect of that syntax is the string "&DEBUG.", which appears as the fifth argument to each URL. This portion of the URL specifies that the application should continue to use the current debug mode (which is an issue of minor concern, and is ignored in this book).

Editing List Entries

The name of each list entry in the List Details screen is a link. Clicking the link for an entry takes you to a List Entry screen, in which you can edit these values. Figure 4-3 shows a portion of this screen that results from clicking the Classic Reports entry.

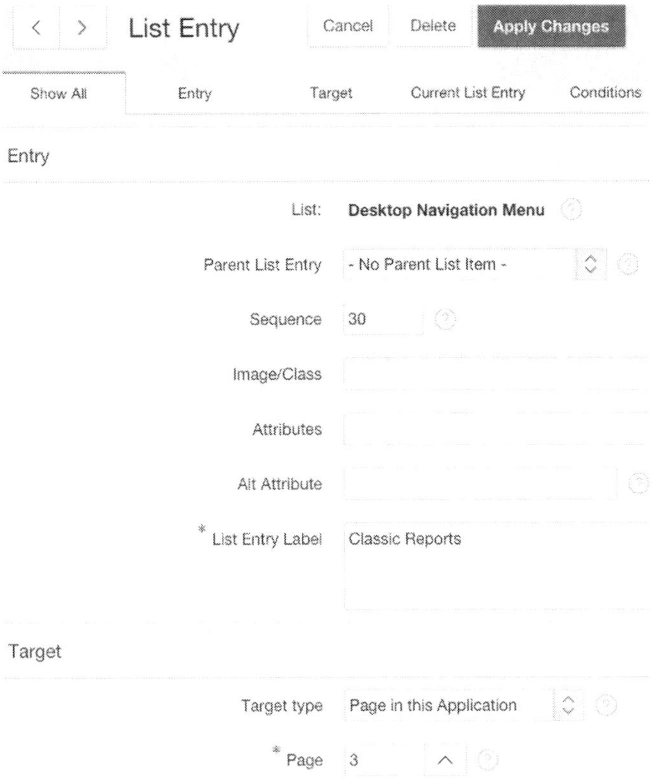

Figure 4-3. *Part of the List Entry screen*

The relevant properties here are Sequence, List Entry Label, and Page. As an experiment, change the values of these properties — for example, set Sequence to 60 and List Entry Label to Employee Reports. Then run the application. Notice that the navigation menu now looks like Figure 4-4. In particular, the entry formerly titled Classic Reports is now titled Employee Reports and appears last.

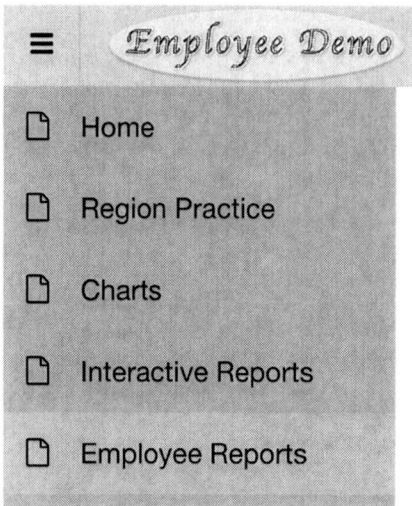

Figure 4-4. *Modified navigation menu*

Creating New List Entries

Now turn your attention to the Desktop Navigation Bar list. The navigation bar in an APEX application runs across the top of each page. By default, the left side of the navigation bar displays the logo, and the right side displays a link labeled Log Out (which you can see in Figure 2-6 of Chapter 2). The general intent of the navigation bar is to provide quick links to common tasks. For example, the logo is actually a link to the home page, and the logout link calls a procedure that logs out the user. Navigation bars typically contain links for displaying a site map, online help, or contact information.

Let's modify the navigation bar to have two new entries: a link to this book's web page and a link to a Contact Info page. To do so, go to the List Details screen for the Desktop Navigation Bar list; this screen is shown in Figure 4-5. Note that the list currently contains a single entry that corresponds to the logout link.

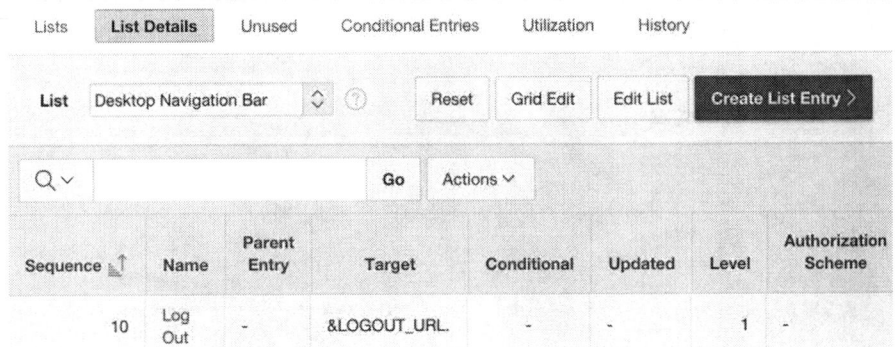

Figure 4-5. *Details of the Desktop Navigation Bar list*

To create additional entries, click the Create List Entry button. The List Entry screen is then displayed, as shown in Figure 4-6. Note that this screen is essentially the same as Figure 4-3, except that its buttons are for entry creation instead of update.

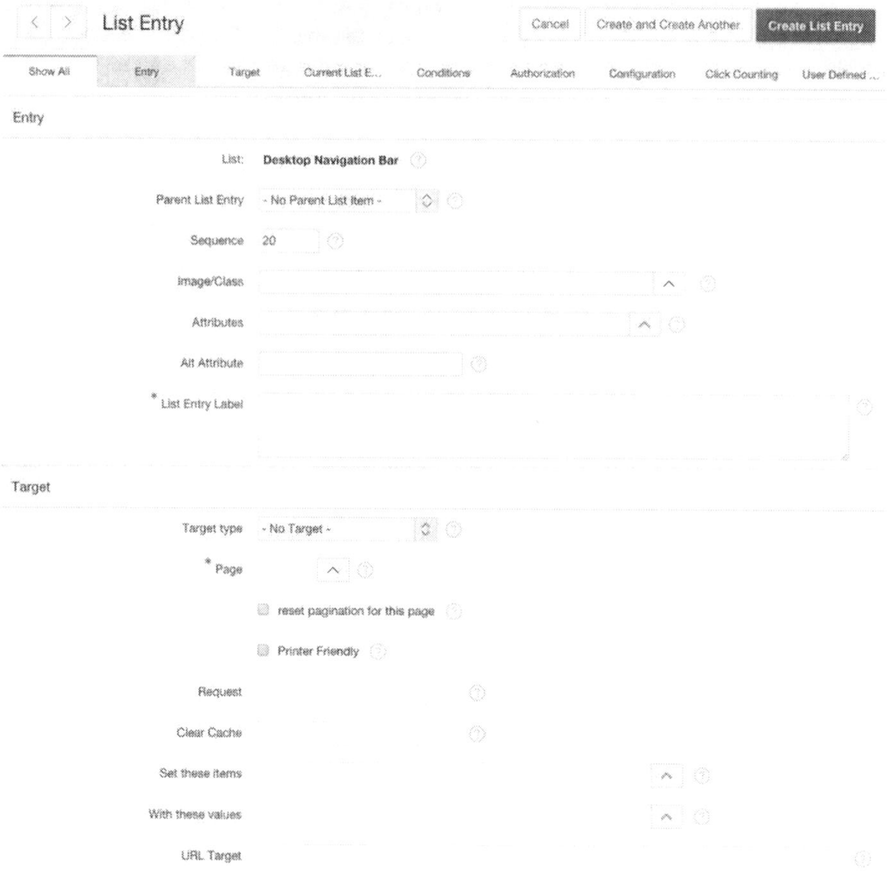

Figure 4-6. *List Entry screen for creating a list entry*

To create the link to this book's web page, you only have to enter a value for the property List Entry Label (I entered Get the Book), set the target, and click Create List Entry. Here, the target is a URL, so you set the Target type property to URL and its URL Target property to http://www.apress.com/9781484209905.

While you're at it, you might as well create the link to the Contact Info page now, even though the page does not yet exist. Assuming that it will be page 6, create a new list entry and set its List Entry Label to Contact Us, its Target type to Page in this Application, and its Page value to 6.

Now create the Contact Info page. You can, of course, design the page any way you want. But for simplicity you could create a blank page containing a single Static Content region whose source is a simple text message. The result for my application is shown in Figure 4-7. For variety, I set the Template property of the region to the value Alert. The screenshot was taken immediately after clicking the Contact Us link on the navigation bar. Note that this page does not need an entry in the navigation menu because it has an entry in the navigation bar.

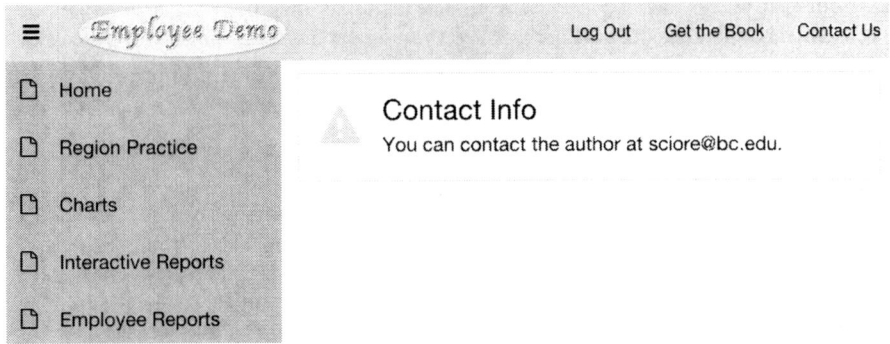

Figure 4-7. *Using the Contact Us link on the navigation bar*

Creating a New List

Let's create a list to hold the three links of the References region on the home page. Return to the list manager screen of Figure 4-1. Clicking the Create button brings up the APEX list creation wizard. This wizard has four screens. On the first screen, choose to create the list From Scratch. On the second screen, give the list a name (say, References), and set its type to Static.

The third screen gives you the opportunity to create menu entries by entering their label and URL. You can create the entries there, or you can wait and create each entry individually, as shown in the previous section. I find it quicker to create the entries now. For your reference, the URLs for these entries appeared in Listing 3-3 in Chapter 3, and also appear in Figure 4-8 below.

Lists	**List Details**	Unused	Conditional Entries	Utilization	History

| List | References |

| Q ∨ | | | Go | Actions ∨ |

Sequence ↑	Name	Parent Entry	Target
10	APEX Application Builder Guide	-	https://docs.oracle.com/cd/E59726_01/doc.50/e39147/toc.htm
20	Ask Tom: An Oracle Help Site	-	http://asktom.oracle.com/pls/apex/f?p=100:1
30	The Region Practice page	-	f?p=&APP_ID.:2:&APP_SESSION.

Figure 4-8. *Entries for the References list*

The final screen asks if you want to create a region for the list. Because you have not yet learned about list regions, select No. When you finish, the list manager will display an entry for the new list. Clicking its link should produce the screen shown in Figure 4-8.

Modifying the Navigation Interface

By default, the Desktop Navigation Menu list is displayed down the left side of the page, and the Desktop Navigation Bar list is displayed along the top. You can change these defaults by modifying the application's properties.

Chapter 2 discussed how to examine an application's properties. To review: go to the application's home screen (refer to Figure 2-3 in Chapter 2) and click the Edit Application Properties button at the top right. You are taken to the application's property screen (refer to Figure 2-4 in Chapter 2), which has four tabs: Definition, Security, Globalization, and User Interface. Selecting the User Interface tab displays the user interface properties, the top of which is shown in Figure 4-9.

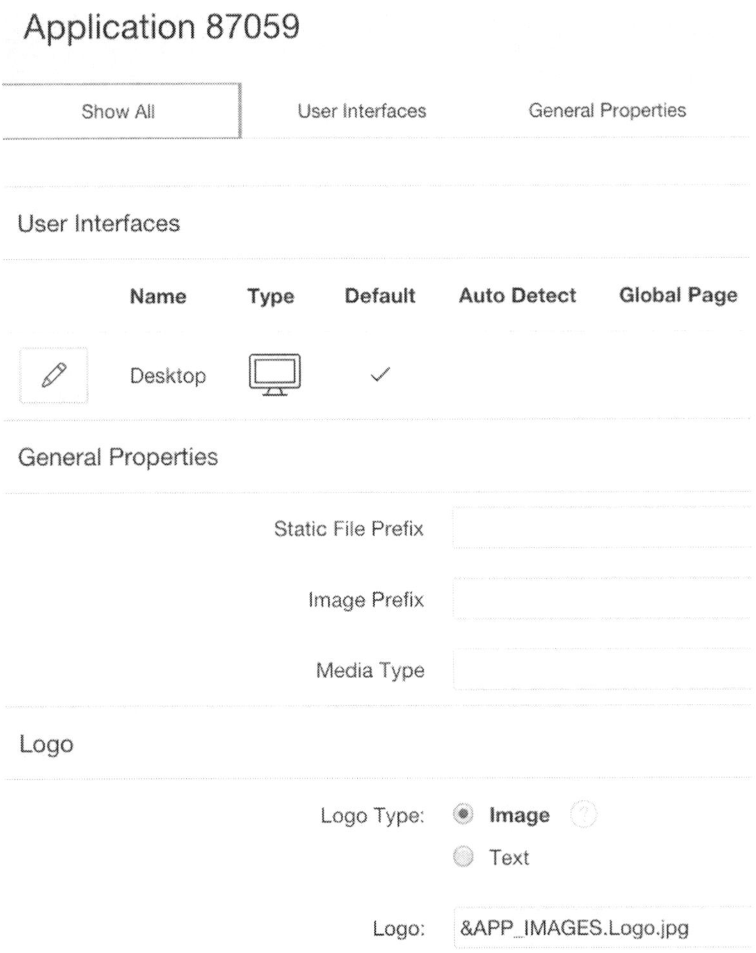

Application 87059

Show All	User Interfaces	General Properties

User Interfaces

	Name	Type	Default	Auto Detect	Global Page
✎	Desktop	🖥	✓		

General Properties

Static File Prefix	
Image Prefix	
Media Type	

Logo

Logo Type:	● **Image** ⓘ
	○ Text
Logo:	&APP_IMAGES.Logo.jpg

Figure 4-9. *Some user interface properties*

You might remember the Logo properties from Chapter 3 (refer to Figure 3-18). Right now, however, you are interested in the User Interfaces section. Clicking the Desktop pencil icon brings up the User Interface Details screen. Its Navigation Menu and Navigation Bar sections appear in Figure 4-10. Their properties allow you to configure the navigation menu and navigation bar.

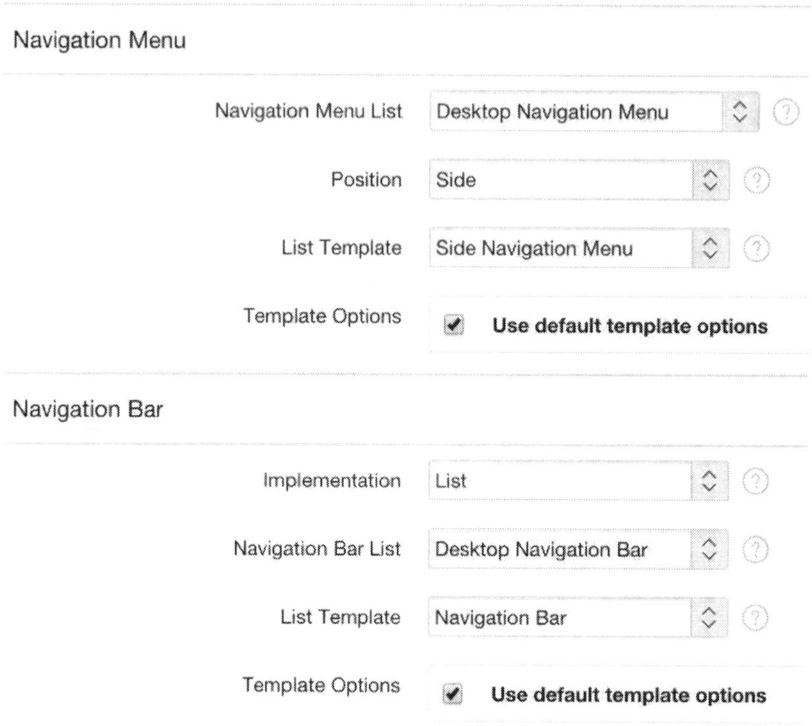

Navigation Menu

Navigation Menu List	Desktop Navigation Menu ⌃⌄ ⑦
Position	Side ⌃⌄ ⑦
List Template	Side Navigation Menu ⌃⌄ ⑦
Template Options	☑ **Use default template options**

Navigation Bar

Implementation	List ⌃⌄ ⑦
Navigation Bar List	Desktop Navigation Bar ⌃⌄ ⑦
List Template	Navigation Bar ⌃⌄ ⑦
Template Options	☑ **Use default template options**

Figure 4-10. *Application's Navigation Menu and Navigation Bar properties*

Configuring the Navigation Menu

The Navigation Menu List property lets you specify the list that will appear as the navigation menu. You can choose from any existing list. For example, choosing the References list results in the navigation menu shown in Figure 4-11.

Figure 4-11. *References list is now the navigation menu*

You can also choose the value -Select Navigation Menu List- as the navigation menu. Doing so sets the Navigation Menu List property to null, which causes APEX to not render the navigation menu area at all.

The Position property can have the value Side or Top. Choosing Top tells APEX to render the navigation menu along the top of the page, below the navigation bar. The List Template property must be coordinated with the chosen position. If the navigation menu goes along the top of the page, its template should be Top Navigation Menu. The result is shown in Figure 4-12.

Figure 4-12. *Navigation menu now appears along the top*

Configuring the Navigation Bar

The Navigation Bar List property lets you specify the list that will appear in the navigation bar. As with the navigation menu, it can be any list, although it cannot be null. For example, Figure 4-13 shows the result of placing the Desktop Navigation Menu list in the navigation bar.

Figure 4-13. *Navigation menu now appears in the navigation bar*

In this view, the navigation menu appears as links aligned to the right side of the navigation bar. An alternative is to set the navigation bar's List Template property to Top Navigation Menu, which displays the menu entries as tabs, aligned to the left. This option is shown in Figure 4-14. If you do use this implementation of the navigation menu, note that since the logo is a link to the home page, the Home entry in the navigation menu is now redundant and can be removed.

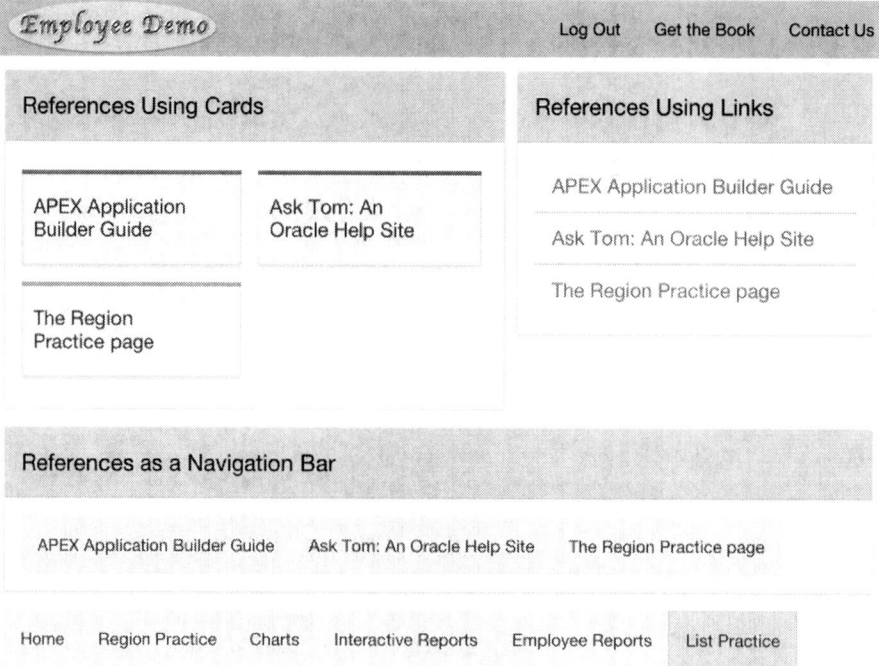

Figure 4-14. *Navigation bar serves as the navigation menu*

List Regions

For the contents of a list to be visible on a page, the list must be assigned to a location on that page. The navigation bar and navigation menu locations are predefined. If you want a list to appear anywhere else, you must place it in a region that you create. The region should be of type List, and its source should be the name of the list.

As an example, Figure 4-15 shows the List Practice page, which is page 7 of the demo application. This page contains four regions, all of type List. The top three regions display the References list (in different ways), and the bottom region displays the Desktop Navigation Menu list.

Figure 4-15. *List Practice page*

To build this page, you should create a new page and add four new regions to it. I titled these regions References Using Cards, References Using Links, References as a Navigation Bar, and Navigation Menu. The second region begins a new column of the same row; the other regions begin new rows.

Set the type of each region to List. The source of a List region is a list, so you need to specify the desired list for each region. The property editor lets you choose from the existing lists; see Figure 4-16. Select Desktop Navigation Menu for the Navigation Menu region and References for the other three regions.

Figure 4-16. *Selecting the source of a list region*

At this point, you have the list regions you want, but they are all formatted as links. This is appropriate for the References Using Links region, but the other regions need to be different. To change the way a list is displayed, you must change its template. A region of type List has a property called List Template, which is accessed by selecting its Attributes component in the rendering tree. The possible values for this property appear in Figure 4-17.

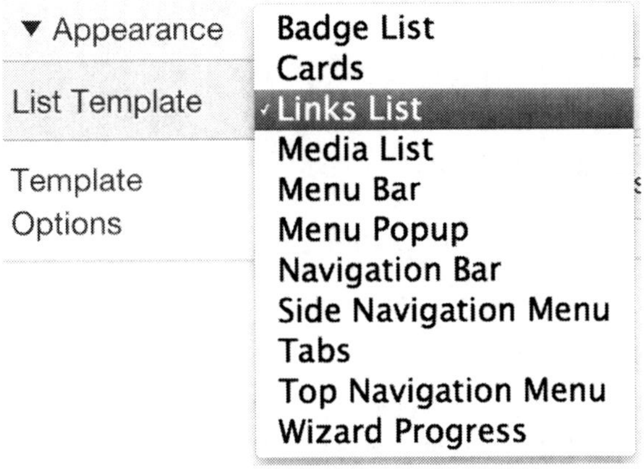

Figure 4-17. *Possible list template values*

To produce the page shown in Figure 4-15, you will need to set the template of the References Using Cards region to Cards, and the templates of both the References as a Navigation Bar and Navigation Menu regions to Navigation Bar. For fun, you also might want to experiment with assigning other templates to these regions, such as Badge List, Media List, and Tabs.

For further customization, several list templates have options that can be set via the Template Options property. For example, the References Using Cards region uses the options Style=Compact, Layout=2 Columns, Body Text=Hidden, and Color Accents=Use Theme Colors. In general, the best way to understand the purpose of the various template options is to experiment with them on your regions.

In addition to choosing a list template, recall that you can also customize a region by choosing a region template. (Figure 3-11 in Chapter 3 showed the possible templates.) The top three regions of Figure 4-15 use the Standard template, which displays the region name in a gray header. The bottom region uses the Tabs Container template. This template displays its contents with no additional border; in fact, it looks a lot like a menu bar. This region demonstrates how you can use a list region to mimic a menu bar that appears somewhere other than the default places on the page.

Another feature of Figure 4-15 is that it does not display the navigation menu area. You saw in the previous section how to hide the navigation menu on all pages of an application by setting the global property Navigation Menu List to null. But what if you want to hide the menu on just a single page? The answer is to use the Navigation Menu properties of the page, as shown in Figure 4-18.

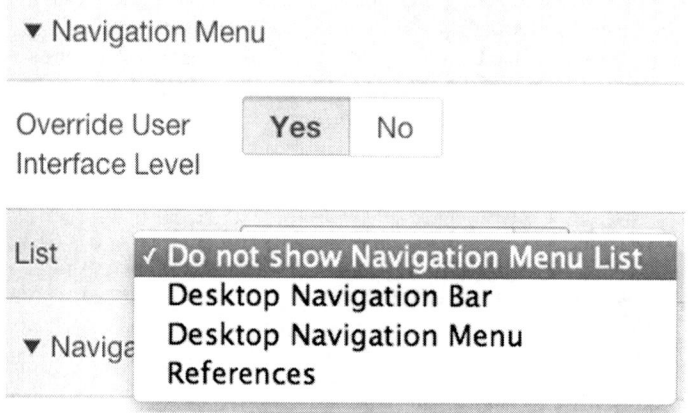

Figure 4-18. *Configuring the navigation menu for a single page*

Setting the Override User Interface Level property to Yes displays the List property. You can then choose the list that will be the navigation menu for the page, or you can choose to not specify the navigation menu.

Storing links in a list and displaying them in a list region is an important technique; it is far superior to manually formatting the links in HTML, as you did on the References region of the home page. One reason is that the template of a list region takes responsibility for formatting the list entries; you just need to choose the template you want. In other words, a list region separates the content (the source list) from the formatting (the list template). Writing HTML code to implement a list is not only tedious, but it also intermixes content and formatting. Any decision to change the format of the entries requires you to rewrite the HTML.

A second advantage of using a list region is that it will automatically be updated as the list changes. This is especially important for regions that display the Desktop Navigation Menu list. For example, whenever you create a navigation menu entry for a new page, the Navigation Menu region of Figure 4-15 will adjust accordingly.

Hierarchical Lists

The demo application currently has six entries in its Desktop Navigation Menu list. Because there are so few entries, it is reasonable to simply display them linearly along the side (or top) of the page. However, as the number of entries grows, a long linear list becomes unwieldy. The common solution is to display the entries *hierarchically*.

The APEX navigation bar is a case in point (refer to Figure 1-3 in Chapter 1). Its first tab (containing the logo) corresponds to the APEX home screen; the other tabs correspond to sections of APEX. Each section tab has a primary target page, which acts as the home screen for that section. Clicking the main portion of a section tab takes you to that page. Each section tab also has a circled down-arrow; clicking it displays a pull-down list of secondary tabs for that section. The result is a functional but clean interface, with the secondary tabs hidden until needed.

In a hierarchical list, each list entry can have a *parent* entry. A list entry without a parent defines a hierarchy and is called the *root* of that hierarchy. A hierarchy can have several levels, in the sense that the parent of an entry may also have a parent. For example, Figure 4-19 shows the Application Builder entry of the APEX navigation bar. One of its children, Workspace Utilities, has its own children.

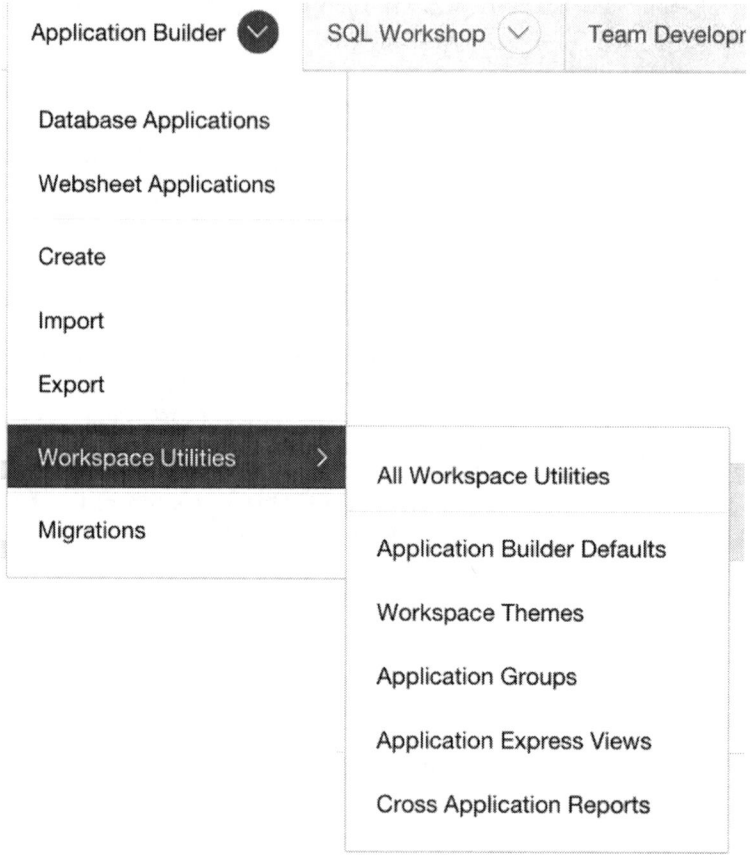

Figure 4-19. Application Builder entry in the APEX navigation bar

Let's restructure the Desktop Navigation Menu list of the demo application to consist of the home page plus two hierarchies:

- a Regions hierarchy that contains the pages Region Practice, Classic Reports, Charts, and Interactive Reports;

- a Lists hierarchy that contains the page List Practice.

Each hierarchy corresponds to a chapter of the book — the Regions hierarchy contains the pages developed in Chapter 3, and the Lists hierarchy contains the page from Chapter 4. As the book progresses I shall keep to this convention, creating a new hierarchy for the pages developed in each chapter.

Before you begin to create the hierarchies, you need to consider how you will configure their root entries. Clearly, you should assign the value null to each Parent List Entry property, denoting that it is a root. However, what values should you give to its Target properties?

There are three reasonable strategies: create a dedicated "home screen" to be the target; set the target to be the same as the target of one of its children; or set the target to be null. APEX adopts the first strategy — there is a home screen for the application builder, one for the SQL workshop, and so on. Adopting the second strategy has the effect of making the chosen target be the default page for that section. And adopting the third strategy makes it impossible to choose the parent, thereby forcing the user to select one of the children. This book shall follow the convention that a root having a single child will have that child be its target, whereas a root having several children will have a null target.

To create this hierarchical list, begin at the List Details screen for the Desktop Navigation Menu (refer to Figure 4-2). Create two new list entries to be the roots of the two hierarchies, and set their target pages according to the above convention: the target of the Regions entry should be null, and the target of the Lists entry should be the List Practice page.

You now need to set the parents of the five child entries. The straightforward way is to go to the List Entry screen for each entry (refer to Figure 4-3), and modify its Parent List Entry property. However, the List Details screen has a wizard to expedite this process. Click the link titled Reparent List Entries Within this List at the right side of the List Details screen. The link brings you to a Reparent List Entries screen, from which you can quickly specify the children of a given parent entry.

Figure 4-20 and Figure 4-21 show screenshots of the resulting navigation menu, corresponding to the two different ways of positioning the navigation menu. In Figure 4-20 the menu is positioned at the top; in Figure 4-21, it is positioned at the side. The screenshots were taken after a user clicked the arrow of the Regions entry and moved the mouse over the Interactive Reports entry.

Figure 4-20. *Hierarchical navigation menu, from the top*

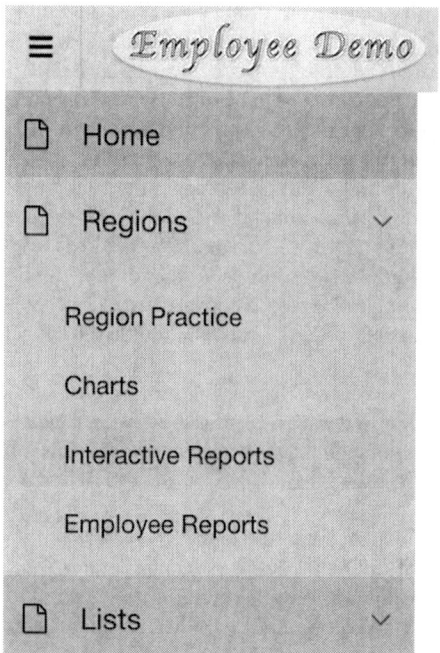

Figure 4-21. *Hierarchical navigation menu, from the side*

In general, these hierarchical menu entries behave as follows. Clicking the arrow portion of a parent entry expands it to show its children. If the parent entry has a target, then clicking its main portion redirects to its target page. If the entry has no target, then clicking its main portion will either show its children (if the menu is across the top) or do nothing (if the menu is along the side).

Each time you create a new page, you could use the above techniques to add an entry for it to the Desktop Navigation Menu list. However, it is often more convenient to add a new entry into the list as the page is created. Consider the third screen of the create page wizard, shown in Figure 4-22.

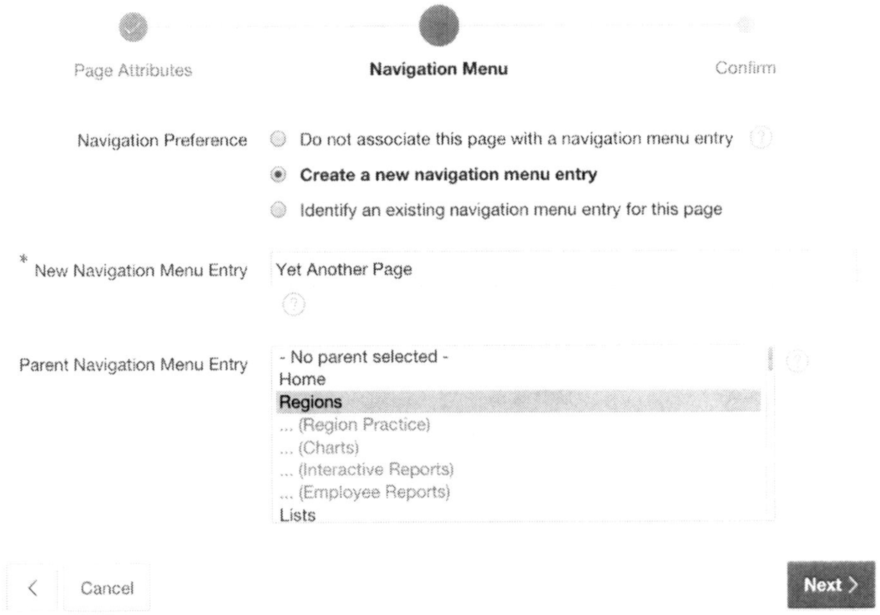

Figure 4-22. *Specifying the menu hierarchy during page creation*

The select list labeled `Parent Navigation Menu Entry` displays every entry in the navigation menu list. The default value is `No parent selected`, which causes the new menu entry to be a root. If you want the new entry to be a child of another entry, you must specify a parent. Ideally, you should be able to just select the entry you want from the list. However, some of the entries are grayed-out, and are not selectable. In particular, the selectable entries are the ones that either are already parents or are "potential parents" in the sense that they have no target. Most of the time, the parent you want will be selectable. But if you want your new entry to be a child of one of the grayed-out entries, you must do so via the list manager.

Page Hierarchy

A large web application contains too many pages for all of them to be in the navigation menu. Instead, the navigation menu contains the application's *landing pages* — those pages that denote the start of the most prominent tasks.

Typically, the set of all pages in an application also has a hierarchical structure. An explicit rendering of this page hierarchy is called a *site map*. As an example, consider the page hierarchy for an APEX site. The root of the hierarchy is the APEX home page. The children of the root correspond to the various sections of the application, such as the application builder, the SQL workshop, and the team development tools. Each section has a "home page" that heads a subtree containing the pages of its section.

Figure 4-23 lists a portion of the page hierarchy corresponding to the APEX application builder. Due to space limitations, the figure shows only some of the many pages in the `Application` subtree.

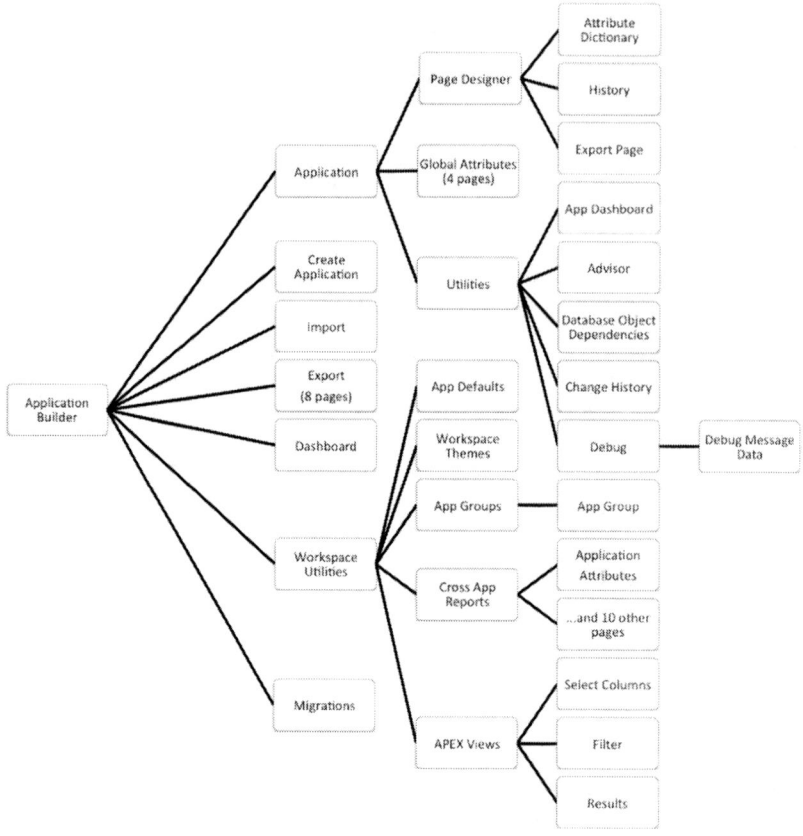

Figure 4-23. *Application builder's page hierarchy*

It is worthwhile to compare this page hierarchy with the application builder's navigation menu entries. Those entries cover most (but not all) of the pages at the first three levels of the tree. Prominently missing from the navigation menu are entries corresponding to the Application subtree; these pages are instead accessed from icons and buttons on the application builder home page.

Breadcrumbs

You can describe the location of any page in an application by giving the sequence of pages in the path between it and the home page in the page hierarchy. For example, the location of the Application Attributes page is

```
Application Builder > Workspace Utilities > Cross Application Reports >
Application Attributes
```

This path is known as a *breadcrumb*. Not all APEX screens display their breadcrumbs, but if they do, they display them below the tab bar. Note that the first entry in an APEX breadcrumb is displayed as a circled up-arrow, which denotes the root page of the hierarchy.

As an exercise, navigate to other pages on the APEX site and notice their breadcrumbs. In fact, see if you can find all of the pages listed in Figure 4-23. Note that a breadcrumb is clickable. Clicking on any portion of its path takes you to that corresponding page.

The navigation menu and breadcrumb are complementary navigation tools. The menu is the same for all pages and its entries encompass the entire functionality of the application. By looking at the menu, a user can determine the appropriate starting page for any desired action. On the other hand, a page's breadcrumb is specific to that page and provides context about where the page is located within the page hierarchy. For example, suppose that you are looking at the application builder's Application Attributes page. Its breadcrumb tells you that the page is one of the cross-application reports. That information might cause you to click the breadcrumb to explore other cross-application reports.

In APEX, the entire page hierarchy is called a *breadcrumb object*. A breadcrumb object is essentially the same as a hierarchical list — it contains an entry for each page in the hierarchy, with each entry (except the root) having a parent.

APEX automatically creates a breadcrumb object (named Breadcrumb) with each application. The APEX *breadcrumb manager* lets you create and edit this object. To get to the breadcrumb manager, begin at the application's home screen and select the Shared Components button at the top of the page. Search for the Navigation section, click Breadcrumbs, and then click the Breadcrumb icon. You will be taken to the breadcrumb manager for that breadcrumb object. Figure 4-24 shows the initial breadcrumb manager for my demo application.

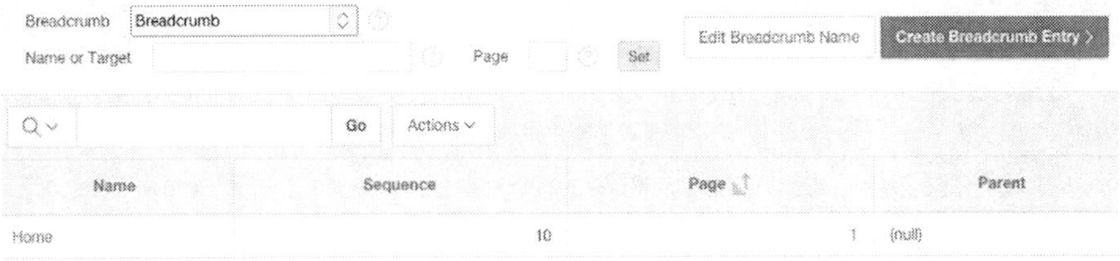

Figure 4-24. Breadcrumb manager

The figure shows that there is only one breadcrumb entry, which corresponds to the home page. This entry was created automatically when I created the application. Note that the entry still exists, even though I deleted the breadcrumb region from the home page.

When I created the other pages, I told the wizard to not create a breadcrumb entry for the new page. Instead, I can create the breadcrumb entries now, using the breadcrumb manager. Click the Create Breadcrumb Entry button. Figure 4-25 shows the resulting screen.

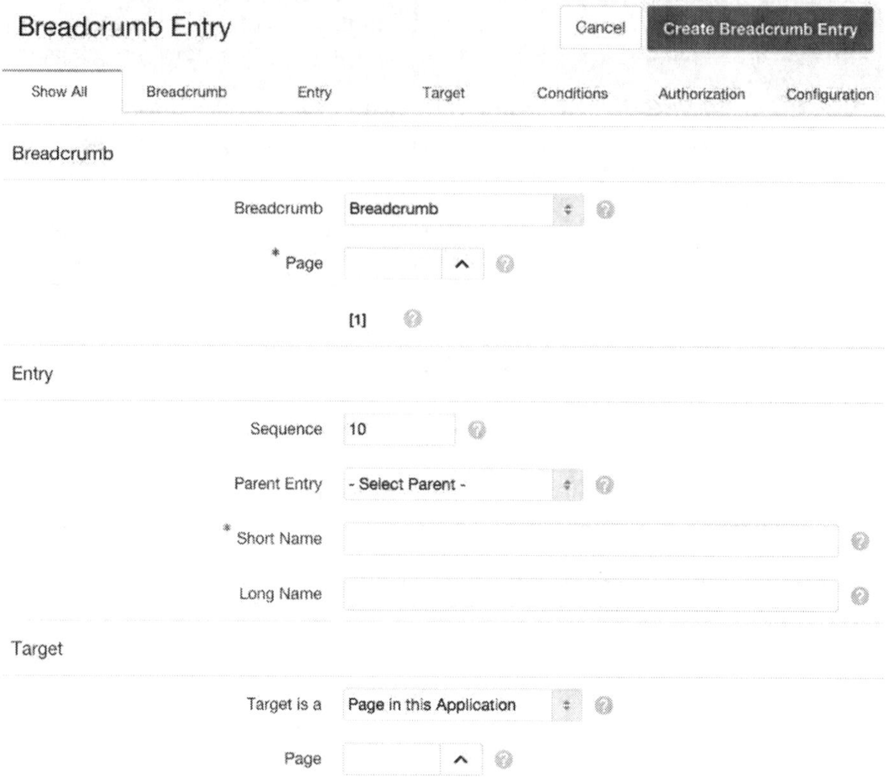

Figure 4-25. *Breadcrumb Entry screen*

This screen lets you specify the page and its parent, as well as information about how the breadcrumb will be displayed on the page. In particular:

- The Page property (in the Breadcrumb section) specifies the page.

- The Parent Entry property specifies the parent.

- The Short Name property specifies how the page will be displayed on the breadcrumb. Choosing the page's name is often reasonable.

- The Page property (in the Target section) specifies what happens when a user clicks that breadcrumb entry. It typically has the same value as the earlier Page property.

For example, suppose that you want to create an entry for page 7, which is the List Practice page, and that you want the entry to be a child of the home page. You thus enter 7 for the Breadcrumb Page and Target Page properties, 1 for the Parent Entry property, and List Practice for the Short Name property.

If you choose to create a breadcrumb during page creation, your task is a bit simpler. Figure 4-26 shows the second screen of the create page wizard, had you chosen to create a breadcrumb for the List Practice page when you created it. You only need to enter values for the Parent Entry and Entry Name items.

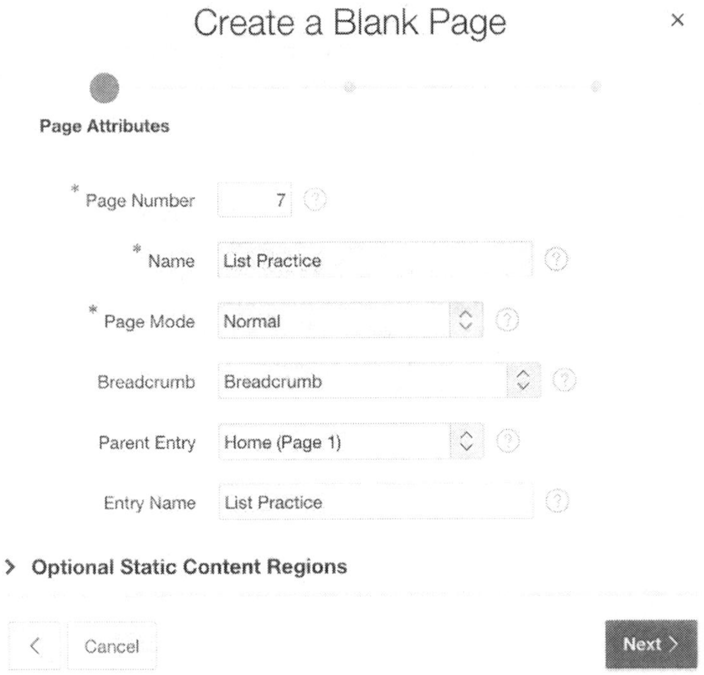

Create a Blank Page   ×

Page Attributes

* Page Number	7	
* Name	List Practice	
* Page Mode	Normal	
Breadcrumb	Breadcrumb	
Parent Entry	Home (Page 1)	
Entry Name	List Practice	

> **Optional Static Content Regions**

< Cancel   Next >

Figure 4-26. Creating a breadcrumb entry during page creation

Breadcrumb Regions

If you want a page to display its breadcrumb object, you must create a region for it. The Breadcrumb region type is designed for this purpose. Although you can place a breadcrumb region anywhere on the page, it naturally goes in the Breadcrumb Bar position, which renders immediately below the navigation bar. In general, you need to follow these steps to add a breadcrumb region to a page.

- Add a new region to the page.
- Set the type of the region to be Breadcrumb.
- Set the source of the region to be the Breadcrumb object.
- Assign the region to the Breadcrumb Bar position.
- Set the region template to Blank Region with Attributes, so that it will display without a border or title.

Use these steps to add a breadcrumb region to the List Practice page. Figure 4-27 shows the navigation bar and breadcrumb region of the resulting page. Note that unlike a list region, a breadcrumb region does not display its entire source object. Instead, it only displays the breadcrumb corresponding to the current page.

Figure 4-27. *Breadcrumb object in a breadcrumb region*

If the Short Name property of a breadcrumb entry contains HTML code, the breadcrumb region will use that code to format the entry. For example, many sites use an image for the home page in a breadcrumb — APEX screens represent home as a circled up-arrow; other sites use the image of a house. You can easily implement this idea in your demo application. I created an image of a star as an APEX application file named starsymbol.jpg. I then set the Short Name of the Home breadcrumb entry to the following HTML expression:

```
<img src="&APP_IMAGES.starsymbol.jpg">
```

The image will appear in the breadcrumb, as shown in Figure 4-28. And like all breadcrumb entries, the image will be clickable.

Figure 4-28. *The Home breadcrumb entry as an image*

Global Page

As you have seen, you should display a list or a breadcrumb object by placing it in a region on a page. This technique provides for considerable flexibility — each page can display the list or breadcrumb in a different location and with a different template. However, you often don't want this much flexibility. Suppose instead that you want every page to display a list or breadcrumb exactly the same way. The easiest way to enforce this uniformity is to use the *global page*.

The global page is a special page whose contents are included in every other page of the application. If you place the breadcrumb region of Figure 4-27 or the Navigation Menu region of Figure 4-15 in the global page, those regions will appear uniformly on all pages of the application. You create the global page from the page creation wizard, as shown at the bottom of Figure 4-29. By convention, the global page has page number 0.

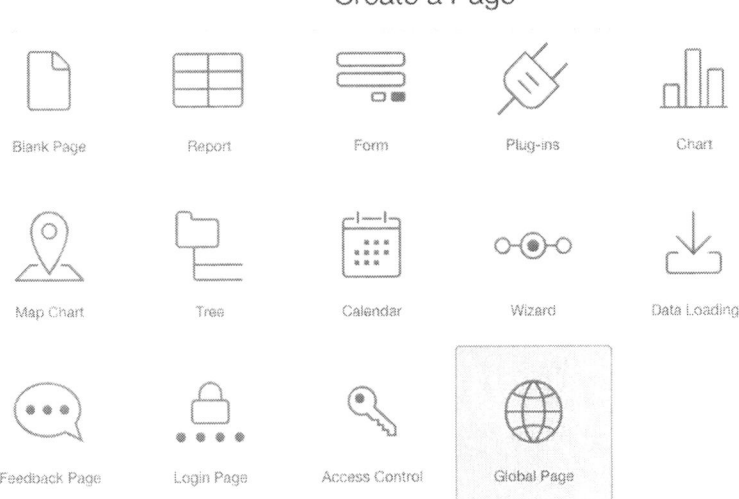

Figure 4-29. *Creating the global page*

One of the nice things about a breadcrumb region is that APEX will render it only if the page has a breadcrumb. So even if you put the breadcrumb region in the global page, it will appear only on those pages that actually have a breadcrumb.

Summary

The dominant navigational tool in APEX is the list of links, otherwise known as a *list*. The entries of the built-in Desktop Navigation Bar list are displayed in the application's navigation bar, and the entries of the Desktop Navigation Menu list appear in the application's navigation menu. The list manager allows you to edit the contents of these lists, and the application's User Interface properties allow you to customize their location, style, and contents.

You can also use the list manager to create lists of your own. You can display a list on a page by placing it in a region of type List. Each list region has a Template property, which lets you customize how the list is displayed.

A list can be hierarchical, in the sense that a list entry can be the parent of one or more sub-entries. This hierarchy provides a structure to the list entries. This structure is especially useful for the navigation menu list because it allows the menu to contain a large number of entries without overwhelming the user.

Another navigational tool is the *breadcrumb*. To define a breadcrumb for a page, you must first understand how the page fits within the hierarchy of all application pages. A page's breadcrumb is the path in the hierarchy from that page to the root. To display a breadcrumb on a page, you must place it in a region of type Breadcrumb. It is common to place the breadcrumb region in the application's global page (page 0) so that it appears in the same place on every page.

CHAPTER 5

Items and Buttons

This book has so far focused on how the application can display information to users. In this chapter and the next, you will examine constructs that allow users to send information back to the application. These constructs, which are *items* and *buttons*, are known as *form controls* because they typically appear in web forms.

There are many types of items, which look and behave quite differently from each other. However, they all can be understood as variations of a few basic concepts. The purpose of this chapter is to explore these concepts and examine how they are embodied in the different item types.

Items

An *item* is an element of a web page that holds a value. Each item belongs to an *item type*, such as a text field, checkbox, or select list. Each item type provides a different way to display its value and let a user modify that value.

You have already encountered several item types from your use of the application builder. For example, consider the List Entry screen of Chapter 4 (refer to Figure 4-3). The figure shows nine items: one display-only item (for List), two select lists (for Parent List Entry and Target Type), two text fields (for Sequence and Alt Attribute), three pop-up lists (for Image, Attributes, and Page), and a text area (for List Entry Label). In general, each time you enter a value into an application builder screen, you do so via an item.

APEX supports 19 different item types. These item types can be grouped into three categories: *text-based* items let users specify a value by typing it, *list-based* items let users specify a value by choosing it from a list, and *display-based* items prevent users from specifying values. Figure 4-3 in Chapter 4 contains examples of all three item categories. These categories and their item types will be discussed throughout this chapter.

Item Sampler Page

The running example for this chapter will be the Item Sampler page shown in Figure 5-1. This page will be page 8 of the demo application.

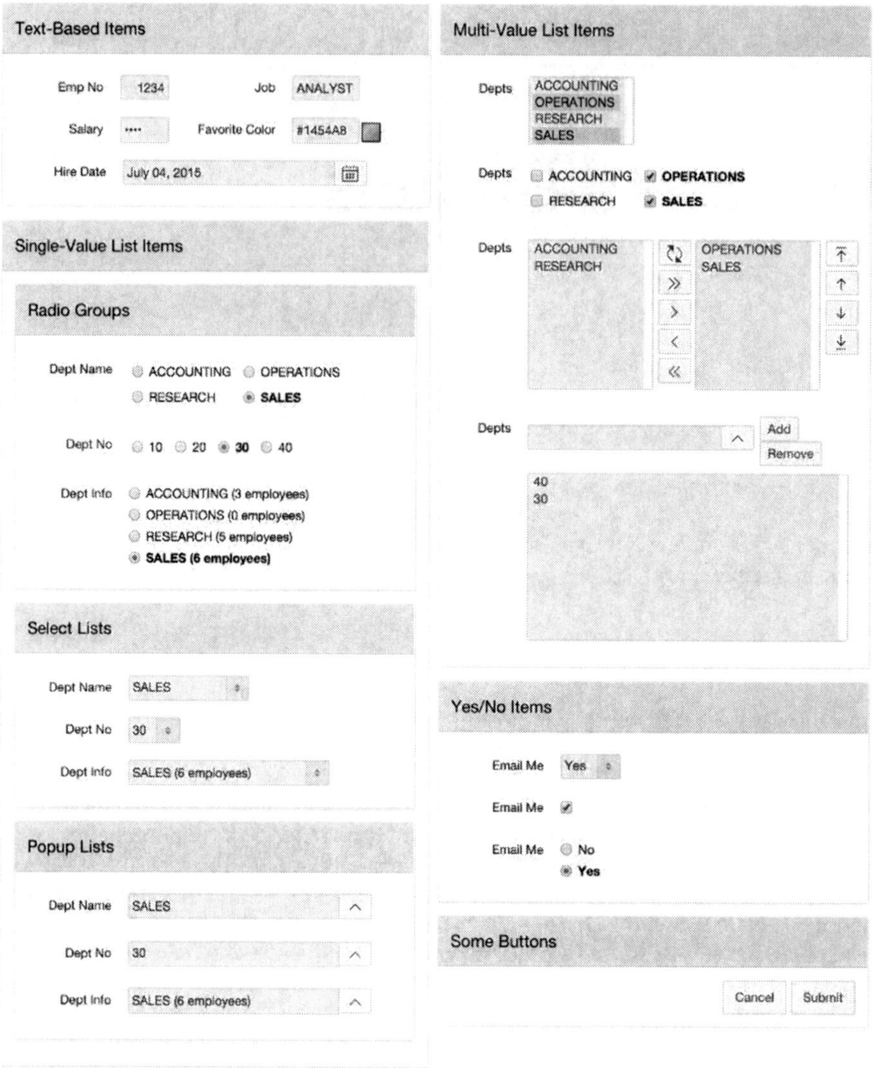

Figure 5-1. *Item Sampler demo page*

As a first step in building this page, create a blank page and eight static content regions. Use the Parent Region and Grid properties of each region to locate them on the page, in this order:

- Text-Based Items begins a new row.

- Single-Value List Items is in the same row and column, which causes it to be placed underneath Text-Based Items.

- Radio Groups, Select Lists, and Popup Lists have the Single-Value List Items region as their parent. They each begin a new row.

- Multi-Value List Items begins a new column of the same row.

- Yes/No Items and Some Buttons are in the same row and column.

As a result, the regions form a single row of two columns. Figure 5-2 shows the resulting empty regions.

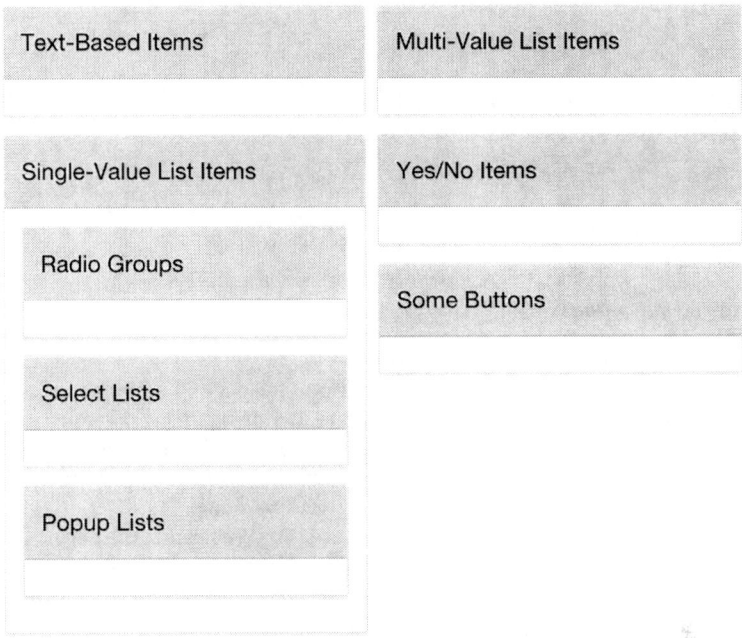

Figure 5-2. *Structure of the Item Sampler page*

Creating and Deleting Items

An item must be placed in a region. To create an item for a region, right-click the region's entry in its rendering tree and select Create Page Item. APEX will create a new item and place an entry for it within the Page Items folder of the rendering tree. For example, Figure 5-3 shows the Page Items folder after a new item is created in the Text-Based Items region.

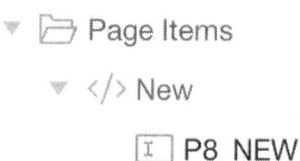

Figure 5-3. *Rendering tree with a new item*

When a new item is created, APEX assigns default values to its Name and Type properties. These properties appear in the Identification section of the property editor, as shown in Figure 5-4.

▼ Identification

Name	P8_NEW
Type	Text Field ⌃⌄

Figure 5-4. *Item's identification section*

The name of the new item is P8_NEW. The prefix denotes the page containing the item, which in this case is page 8. The suffix is an arbitrary identifying string that must be in capital letters. Although you should rename the suffix to be more meaningful, you should keep the prefix. The APEX community strongly suggests using the page number as the prefix of an item's name, and there is no reason not to follow along.

An alternative way to create an item is to use drag and drop. Recall that the page designer has a gallery section, located at the bottom of its middle panel. The gallery has an icon for each item type, as shown in Figure 5-5. You can create a new item by dragging one of these icons to your chosen region of the page.

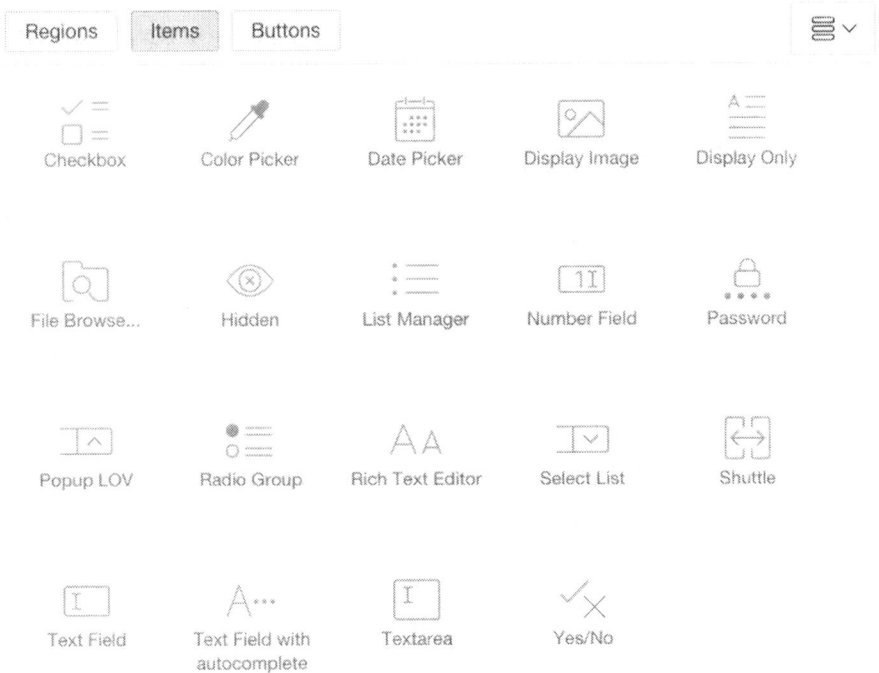

Figure 5-5. *Item gallery*

Each item has an associated *label*, which is the string that you want displayed with the item. The Label property (in the Label section of the property editor) holds the string, and the Template property (in the Appearance section) determines the label format. Figure 5-6 shows the five possible values for the Template property. The value Hidden hides the label; the value Optional displays the label normally; and the value Required formats the label with a red asterisk (which is APEX's way of distinguishing items that require the user to enter a value), but does not enforce this requirement. The Optional-Above and Required-Above values are similar, but they place the label above the item instead of to its left.

▼ Appearance

Template

Template
Options

– Select –
Hidden
Optional
Optional – Above
Required
Required – Above

Figure 5-6. *Item's Template property*

113

To delete an item, right-click its entry in the rendering tree and select the Delete option.

You should now create all 21 items of the Item Sampler page, placing them in the appropriate regions with the appropriate labels. In particular, the Text-Based Items region has five items, the Single-Value Items regions have three items each, the Multi-Value Items region has four items, and the Yes/No Items region has three items. The type of each item is not yet important; you can leave them as text fields for now. The next task is to position the items within their region.

Positioning an Item

APEX displays a region's items in rows, either at the top or bottom of the region. The region's Item Display Position property (in its Appearance section) lets you specify whether its items appear above or below its content. Note that this property is irrelevant for the Item Sampler page because its regions have no other content.

The Grid and Layout sections of each item determine the position of that item within its region. APEX places the items into the table from left to right, according to the value of their Sequence property (in the Layout section), moving to a new row whenever its Start New Row property (in the Grid section) has the value Yes.

APEX positions the items within a region similarly to how it positions regions within a page. The width of the region is divided into 12 grid points. Each item (including its label) has a starting grid point and a width in grid points. The location of the right side of the label also has a specified grid point. For example, suppose that a text field item has the Grid values shown in Figure 5-7. These values specify that the item will span the six grid points from grid point 3 to grid point 8, and that its label ends (and the input box begins) at grid point 5.

▼ Grid

Start New Row

| Yes | No |

Column

3

Column Span

6

Label Column Span

2

Figure 5-7. *Item's Grid section*

By default, the Column and Column Span properties of an item have the value Automatic, which tells APEX to distribute the items in the row as evenly as possible. The Label Column Span property of an item has the default value of Page Template, which lets the page determine the span of the label.

Consider the Item Sampler page shown in Figure 5-1. In the Text-Based Items region, the items labeled Emp No and Salary begin at grid point 1 and have a span of 5 grid points; the Job and Favorite Color items begin at grid point 6 and have a span of 7. The Hire Date item takes up the entire row — it begins at grid point 1 and has a span of 12. In the Multi-Value Items region, the items have default values for Column and Column Span, but have a Label Column Span of 2. The items of the other regions all have default Grid values. Figure 5-8 shows the result of making these positioning changes to the demo page.

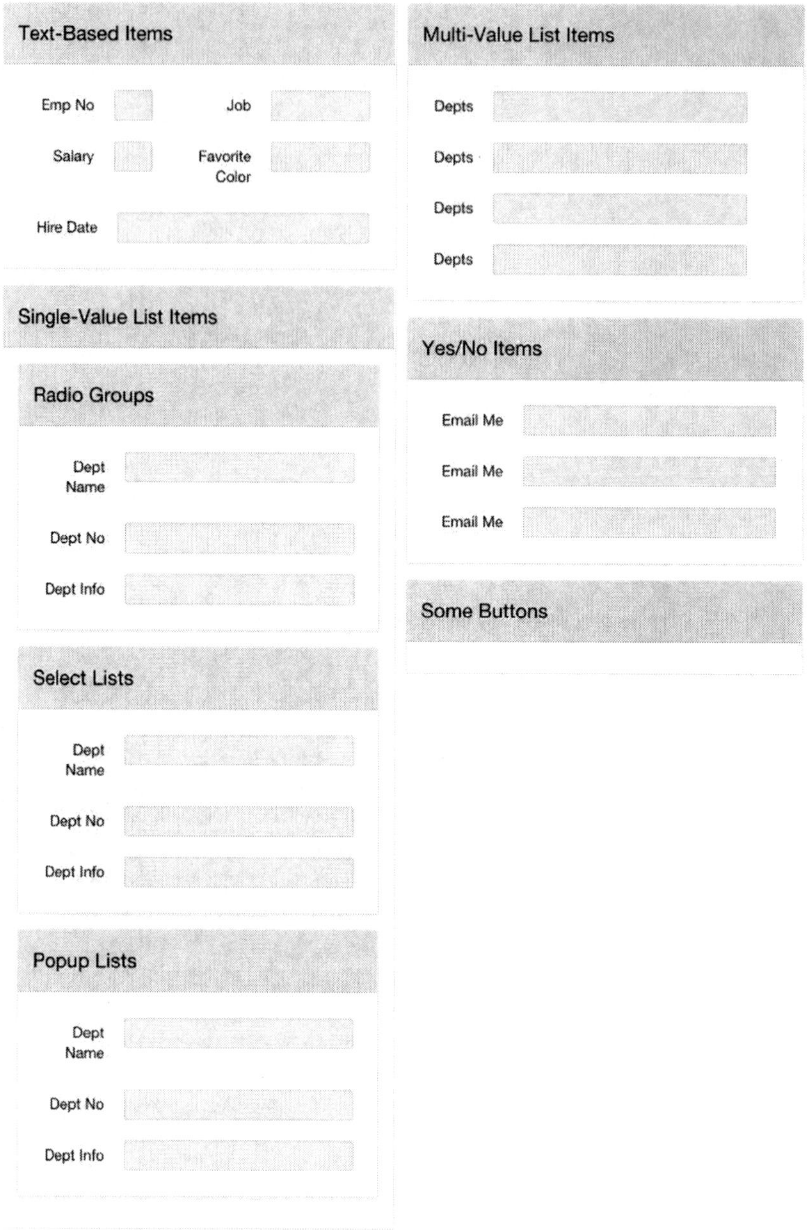

Text-Based Items

Emp No   [ ]   Job   [ ]

Salary   [ ]   Favorite   [ ]
                   Color

Hire Date   [ ]

Single-Value List Items

Radio Groups

Dept   [ ]
Name

Dept No   [ ]

Dept Info   [ ]

Select Lists

Dept   [ ]
Name

Dept No   [ ]

Dept Info   [ ]

Popup Lists

Dept   [ ]
Name

Dept No   [ ]

Dept Info   [ ]

Multi-Value List Items

Depts   [ ]

Depts   [ ]

Depts   [ ]

Depts   [ ]

Yes/No Items

Email Me   [ ]

Email Me   [ ]

Email Me   [ ]

Some Buttons

Figure 5-8. *Adding items to the page in Figure 5-2*

This page now has the proper structure, but the items still have the default type Text Field. This situation is addressed next.

Text-Based Items

A text-based item is characterized by its input box, into which a user can type a value. APEX supplies several kinds of text-based items, most of which are shown in the Text-Based Items region of Figure 5-1.

Three important properties common to all text-based items are Width, Format Mask (in the Appearance section), and Maximum Length (in the Validation section). The Width property specifies the size of the input box in characters. In Figure 5-1, the items labeled Emp No and Salary have widths of 6, Job and Favorite Color have widths of 8, and Hire Date has the default width of 30.

The Format Mask property works the same way as in reports. The value of the property is an expression that describes how the item value gets displayed. In Figure 5-1, the Hire Date item has a format mask of Month DD, YYYY.

The Maximum Length property specifies the maximum number of characters that a user can type into the input box. If a user enters a value that is larger than the width of the input box, then APEX will scroll the value within the box. By default, the maximum length is blank, denoting no maximum. A good design rule is to define a maximum length for all text-based items. In Chapter 12, you will see how an item with no maximum length (or an unreasonably large one) can contribute to serious security loopholes.

The various text-based item types will now be considered. The Settings section contains properties specific to each type.

Text Fields

Text Field is the simplest item type, in that there is no restriction on what values can be entered in the input box. The value of the item is whatever the user types into the input box.

Number Fields

The Emp No item in Figure 5-1 is a number field; it differs from a text field in that its value can only be numeric. The Settings section of a number field item has several number-specific properties. In particular, the Minimum Value and Maximum Value properties allow you to restrict the allowable item values in the obvious way. The Number Alignment property allows you to specify the alignment of the number within the input box. Figure 5-9 shows these properties for Emp No.

▼ Settings

Minimum Value

0

Maximum Value

9999

Number Alignment

Right ⌄⌃

Figure 5-9. *Properties relevant to number fields*

Password Items

The Salary item in Figure 5-1 is a password field, which differs from a text field in that its value is not displayed on the page. Instead, its characters are replaced by circles when the value is being entered, and are invisible when the value is obtained from the server.

Text Fields with Autocomplete

A text field with autocomplete is a text field with an associated list of suggested values. As a user types a value into the input box, the page displays a menu of matching values. If the user clicks a displayed value, that value is entered into the input box automatically. For example, the item labeled Job in Figure 5-1 is a text field with autocomplete. Its associated list consists of the five current job titles. When the user typed *a*, the job title ANALYST was displayed (because it was the only job beginning with *a*); the user then clicked that title without the need for further typing.

Autocomplete fields make it easy for a user to enter the most common values, but do not require the user to pick from those values. Even after selecting a suggested value from the list, the user is free to alter that value via continued typing.

An autocomplete field has a List of Values section in which you can specify the list of suggested values. Figure 5-10 shows this section for Job.

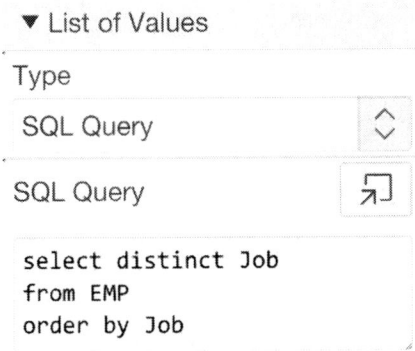

Figure 5-10. Specifying the autocompletion list

There are two ways to specify the list. Figure 5-10 uses the first way, which is an SQL query. The query contains one column, and the list is defined by the values in each output row. This method of expressing the list is *dynamic* because the list changes as the job titles in the database change.

An alternative way to specify the list of values is to use a *static expression*. In APEX, a static expression consists of STATIC: followed by a comma-separated list of values. For example, if you want users to be able to pick from a fixed set of four jobs, you can use the following static expression:

STATIC:CLERK,ANALYST,SALESMAN,MANAGER

Note the lack of spaces in this expression. If the typed characters match more than one value on the list, APEX will display them in sorted order. If you want the values displayed in the order in which they appear in the expression, use STATIC2 instead of STATIC.

Another relevant autocompletion property is Search, which appears in the Settings section. This property has four possible values, as shown in Figure 5-11. These values cover two issues: whether the text typed by the user is case-sensitive, and whether the text typed by the user can match anywhere within a suggested value or must it match only from the beginning of the string. The figure shows that the item labeled Job was configured to be case-insensitive and to match from the beginning only.

Figure 5-11. *Possible Search values for an autocomplete item*

Color Pickers

Colors on the computer are typically represented by their red, green, and blue component values, with each component having a value from 0 to 255. For example in Figure 5-1, the value chosen for the Favorite Color item has (red, green, blue) component values of (20, 84, 168). That color is mostly blue, with some green and a little red.

These component values can be represented compactly as a hexadecimal number. Because a two-digit hexadecimal number can represent 256 different values, a six-digit number can represent every possible color. In Figure 5-1, that color is represented by the number #1454A8. Note that 14 is the hexadecimal value of 20, 54 is the hexadecimal value of 84, and A8 is the hexadecimal value of 168.

An APEX color picker item lets a user type the value of the color if it is known. Or the user can click the color wheel to choose the desired color, and APEX will place the corresponding numeric value in the input box.

Date Pickers

The Hire Date item in Figure 5-1 is an example of a date picker. Date picker items consist of an input box and a calendar icon. As with all text-based items, the user is free to type the desired date into the input box. But the user can also click the icon to bring up a calendar and then navigate the calendar to select a date, which causes the textual representation of the date to appear in the input box.

The properties relevant to date pickers appear in the Settings section, and are shown in Figure 5-12.

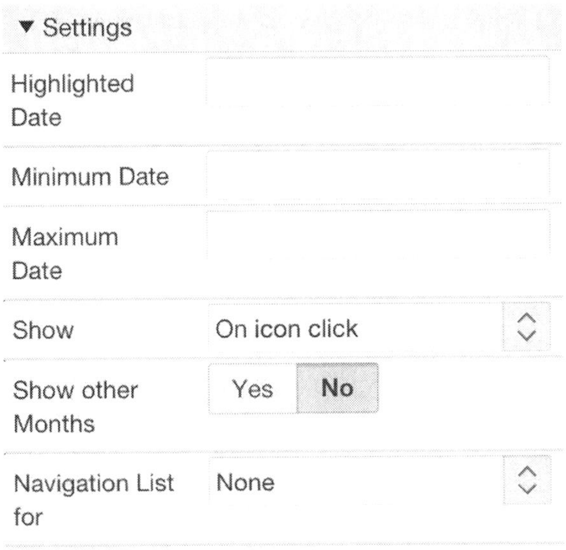

▼ Settings	
Highlighted Date	
Minimum Date	
Maximum Date	
Show	On icon click ⌄
Show other Months	Yes **No**
Navigation List for	None ⌄

Figure 5-12. *Properties relevant to Date Picker items*

The properties `Highlighted Date`, `Minimum Date`, and `Maximum Date` have straightforward meanings. The property `Show` allows you to configure the display of the calendar. The calendar can be shown when the icon is clicked (as in the figure), shown on mouse rollover, or always displayed on the page. The `Navigation List for` property allows you to configure the calendar for quicker access to dates. By default, the calendar has buttons to navigate only to the previous and next months. You can set the property so that there are also menus for moving directly to a specified month or year.

List-Based Items

Unlike a text-based item, a list-based item does not have an input box. Instead, a list-based item presents the user with a list of possibilities to choose from. Moreover, the value that a user chooses is not necessarily the value assigned to the item. That is, the item presents a list of *display values* to the user; when the user selects a display value, a corresponding *result value* is assigned to the item.

For example, consider the three child regions of `Single-Value List Items` in Figure 5-1. Each region is devoted to one of the three common list-based item types — radio groups, select lists, and pop-up lists — and contains three items of that type. Although you cannot tell from the figure, all nine of these items have the same set of possible result values: the set {10, 20, 30, 40} of department numbers. In fact, the selections shown in the figure are such that every item has the same value: 30.

These nine items have identical functionality: a user selects a department, and the corresponding department number is assigned to the item. The items differ only in what their display values are and how they present those values to the user.

Let's consider first the radio groups. In a radio group, all of the display values appear on the page, and the user selects a desired value by clicking it. Each radio group in the Radio Groups region has a different list of display values: the first group displays the list of department names, the second displays the list of department numbers, and the third displays each department name with the count of its employees in parentheses.

Now consider the select lists. When a user clicks a select list, a menu of display values appears. The display values in the first select list are identical to those of the first radio group, and similarly for the other two select lists.

Finally, consider the pop-up lists. When a user clicks the arrow to the right of the item, a menu of display values appears for the user to pick from. The display values are the same as in the other two regions.

The most important issue is how to specify the display values and result values for a list-based item. In APEX, the values can either be specified dynamically, via an SQL query, or statically, via explicit values. All nine items in the Single-Value List Items region are specified dynamically, so the discussion begins with them.

Dynamic List–Based Items

An SQL query to specify the correspondence between display values and result values must have two columns: the first column gives the display values, and the second column gives the result values. The names of these columns are not important. For an example, consider the first radio group in the Radio Groups region. The query for this item should have department names in its first column and department numbers in its second column. The following query does the trick:

```
select DName, DeptNo
from DEPT
order by DName
```

The first select list and first pop-up list have the same display values and result values as this radio group, so those items are specified by the exact same query.

Suppose that the display values and result values of an item are the same. This situation occurs in the second item of the Radio Groups, Select Lists, and Popup Lists regions, as their display and result values are both department numbers. If you wrote their SQL query in the straightforward way then the two column names would be identical, which is illegal in SQL. To make the query legal, you need to rename at least one of its columns. The query should look something like this:

```
select DeptNo as DisplayVal, DeptNo as ResultVal
from DEPT
order by DisplayVal
```

▨ **Note** The names of the columns can be anything; SQL requires only that they be different from each other.

The third item of each subregion demonstrates that the display values can be arbitrarily complex. Here is the query:

```
select d.DName || ' (' || count(e.EmpNo) || ' employees)' as DisplayVal,
       d.DeptNo as ResultVal
from DEPT d left join EMP e on d.DeptNo = e.DeptNo
group by d.DeptNo, d.DName
order by DisplayVal
```

The left join of the query ensures that all departments are included, even those with no employees.

As an aside, recall that you also used an SQL query to specify the suggestion list of a Text field with autocomplete item. Unlike list-based queries, however, autocomplete queries have only one column because their display and result values are always the same.

Static List-Based Items

When you use a query to specify the values of a list-based item, APEX will execute that query each time it renders the page. If you know that the output of the query will never change, you can use a static expression to avoid the call to the database.

Recall that the values of a STATIC expression are displayed in alphabetical order, whereas the values of a STATIC2 expression are displayed in the order given. For a list-based item, each option consists of a display and result value separated by a semicolon. For example, the following expression is a static specification of the first radio group of the Item Sampler page:

```
STATIC:ACCOUNTING;10,OPERATIONS;40,RESEARCH;20,SALES;30
```

If the display value and result value are the same, they need not be repeated, and you can use the same syntax as with autocomplete items. For example, the following expression is a static specification of the second radio group of the Item Sampler page:

```
STATIC:10,20,30,40
```

Static expressions are most commonly used for items that have a fixed set of choices, such as Yes/No, Male/Female, and so on.

Properties for List–Based Items

Each list-based item has a List of Values section for specifying its values. The properties of this section are shown in Figure 5-13.

▼ List of Values		
Type	SQL Query	⌄
SQL Query		⬏
select DName, DeptNo from DEPT order by DName		
Display Extra Values	Yes **No**	
Display Null Value	Yes **No**	

Figure 5-13. *List of Values section for list-based items*

The Type property specifies whether the list is defined via an SQL query or a static expression. For an SQL query, there is a property SQL Query for entering the query, as shown in Figure 5-13. For a static expression, there is instead the Static Values property. The property Display Null Value makes it possible for a user to choose a null value instead of one of the list items. If you set this property to Yes, additional properties appear on the screen for you to specify the display value for this new entry (such as I don't know) and its actual value (usually blank, indicating null). In Figure 5-1, all the list-based items have their Display Null Value property set to No.

■ **Note**   The Display Extra Values property will be discussed later, in the section "Initial Item Values".

The Settings section for a radio button item also has the property Number of Columns. This property determines the placement of the radio buttons on the page. In Figure 5-1, you can see that the first radio group has two columns, the second group has four columns, and the third group has one column.

Multi-Value List Items

A list-based item allows a user to choose only one value from its list. A *multi-value list item* lets a user choose multiple values from its list. The Multi-Value List Items region of the Item Sampler page contains four types of multi-valued item. In Figure 5-1, each of these items has the operations and sales departments chosen.

Multi-value list items are configured the same way as single-value items. In particular, they use an SQL query or static expression to indicate their display values and result values. For example, the SQL query for each of the four items in the region is this:

```
select DName, DeptNo
from DEPT
order by DName
```

The main issue is how to assign a single value to the item that has multiple display values selected. APEX uses the convention that the value of a multi-value item is a string that contains the selected result values separated by colons. If no display values are selected, the item's value is null. For example, the items in the Multi-Value List Items region of Figure 5-1 all have the value 40:30.

Let's examine these four item types. The first item is a select list; that is, the same item type as in the Single-Value List region. To specify that the item is to be a multi-value select list, you set its Allow Multi Selection property (in the Settings section) to Yes. The value of its Height property (in the Appearance section) determines how many menu rows to display. All other properties are configured the same. Note that the two kinds of select list look and behave differently. The multi-value select list displays the entire menu on the page at all times, instead of on demand. A user can choose additional menu items by holding the control or command key while clicking, depending on the operating system.

The second item in the region is a checkbox group. Checkbox properties are configured exactly the same as for radio groups. Checkboxes behave differently from radio groups in that multiple checkboxes can be selected, and clicking a box toggles its value.

The third item is a shuttle list, which is very similar to a multi-value select list and is configured the same way. The difference between them is that a multi-value select list denotes selected values by highlighting them, whereas a shuttle has separate menus for the selected and unselected values. A user can double-click a value to move it between the two menus.

The fourth item is a list manager, which is a cross between an autocompletion text box and a pop-up list. Similar to autocompletion, a user can enter any value into the input box and click the Add button to add it to the selected-value list. Alternatively, the user can click the pop-up arrow to bring up a menu of values to choose from, with the selected value getting added to the input box. It is important to note, however, that although the pop-up list shows display values, it places result values in the input box. Thus Figure 5-1 shows that the department numbers 30 and 40 are selected, even though the pop-up list displays department names.

Yes/No Items

A web page often needs to request yes/no information from users. The Yes/No Items region of the Item Sampler page illustrates three different ways to perform this task. The region contains three list-based items, each denoting whether the user wants to be contacted.

The first item has the type Yes/No. It appears as a select list on desktop applications and a toggle on mobile applications. By default, its display and result values are set to Yes and No. You can change these defaults by going to the Settings property (in the Settings section) and selecting the value Custom.

The second item is a checkbox. The checkbox belongs to a checkbox group having just one member and does not have a visible display value. Its list of values can be defined by the static expression

STATIC:;Yes

This expression specifies that there is one member in the list, which has an empty display value and the result value Yes. The value of the item is thus Yes if the box is selected and (as with all multi-value items) it is null if not selected.

The third item is a radio group. Its values are defined by the static expression

STATIC:No,Yes

Its display and result values are identical to the Yes/No item.

Display-Based Items

There are two other item types that are extremely useful but do not appear in the Item Sampler page: Display Only items, and Hidden items. These items differ from the others you have seen in that there is no way for a user to assign a value to them; their values can be assigned only by the APEX server.

A display-only item has a label and a textual value, similar to a text field; the difference is that the value is not in an input box and is not editable. For example, refer again to the List Entry screen of Figure 4-3 in Chapter 4; you can see that the field labeled List is display only.

A hidden item is not visible, and users have no idea that they exist. They are typically used to hold the value of one operation, so that another operation can use it. You will see examples of this technique in Chapter 6.

Initial Item Values

When APEX renders a page, it assigns an initial value to each item on the page. If the item is text-based, APEX places that value inside that item's input box; if the item is list-based, APEX uses that value to determine the corresponding initial display value.

APEX determines this initial value in one of two ways: it can evaluate a *source expression*, or it can use a value previously stored in the session state. Because the concept of session state has not yet been covered, assume for now that session state values are always null.

You specify an item's initial value in its Source section of the property editor. Figure 5-14 shows the two important properties of this section, with their default values.

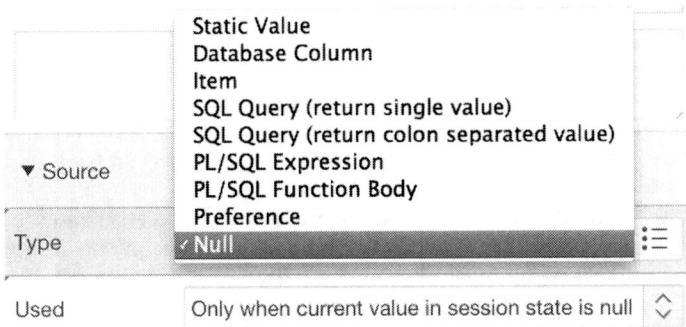

Figure 5-14. *Item's source properties*

The Type property specifies the type of the source expression, and Figure 5-14 shows all of the possible values. The three common choices are Null (which is the default), Static Value, and SQL Query (return single value). Choosing a type other than Null will cause the property editor to display an area for entering the source expression.

The Used property specifies when the source expression is applicable. The default choice, shown in Figure 5-14, is to use the session state if it is not null, and the source expression otherwise. The other choice, not shown in the figure, is to always use the source expression.

If you use an SQL query as the source type, that query must return a single row and column; the initial value of the item is the value returned by the query. For example, consider again the text-based items of the Item Sampler page. Suppose that you want the initial value of the Emp No item to be the employee number of the president. You set its source type value to be SQL Query (return single value) and its source expression to be the following query:

```
select EmpNo
from EMP
where Job = 'PRESIDENT'
```

For another example, suppose that you want the initial value of each list-based item in the Item Sampler page to be the department that is first alphabetically (with the lowest department number breaking the tie if there are multiple departments having the same name). You can assign the following source expression to each item:

```
select min(DeptNo)
from DEPT
where DName in (select min(DName) from DEPT)
```

A source expression whose type is Static Value is typically a constant. For example, suppose instead that you want the initial value of the list-based items in Figure 5-1 to be the sales department. Simply set the source expression for each item to be 30. If you want the initial value of the multi-value list items to be both the operations and sales departments, set the source expression of those items to be 30:40.

One issue that arises with list-based items is how they should respond to an initial value that is not one of their specified result values. For example, suppose that you assign the static value 85 to be the source of the list-valued items. What should the items display, given that there is no department numbered 85? There are two options: accept the value and add it (temporarily) to the list, or reject the value and display an arbitrary value from the list. This choice is specified by the Display Extra Values property in the List of Values section, which appeared in Figure 5-13. In most cases, it makes no sense to display a value that is not a valid selection option, so the value of Display Extra Values should usually be set to No.

Buttons

A button performs an *action* when clicked. An APEX button has two fundamental actions: it can redirect or it can submit. The term *redirect* simply means to move to another web page. In this respect, the button acts like an HTML link. The term *submit* means to have the web server process the current page. This processing can involve setting the session state and performing operations on the database, as well as moving to another page. These issues will be covered in Chapters 6 through 9.

As an example, let's populate the Some Buttons region of the Item Sampler page. This region has two buttons: the Cancel button with the action Redirect to page 8, and the Submit button with the action Submit.

There are two ways to create a button in a region. The first way is to right-click the region's entry in the rendering tree and select the Create Button operation. APEX will create an entry for the button in the Buttons folder of the rendering tree. Alternatively, you can drag a button icon from the page designer gallery to the region (in a way similar to dragging items). Figure 5-15 shows the Buttons folder of the rendering tree after the two buttons are created.

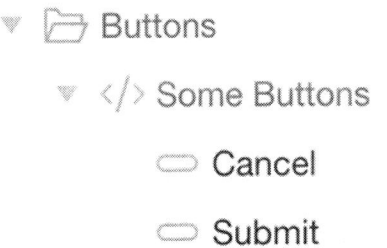

Figure 5-15. *Rendering tree with two buttons*

To configure a button, you need to specify four things: its name, label, action, and position. The button's name and label are specified in the Identification section. The name of the button is an internal value that APEX uses to identify the button and cannot have spaces. The button's label is an arbitrary string that is displayed with the button when the page is rendered.

The button's action is specified in its Behavior section. The Action property has five possible values, which are shown in Figure 5-16. The most common options are Submit Page and Redirect to Page in this Application. The Target property, which is applicable to redirect actions, lets you specify the target page.

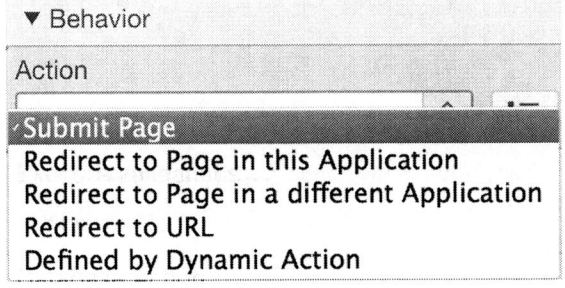

Figure 5-16. *Possible button actions*

The position of a button is determined by its Button Position property in the Layout section. Figure 5-17 shows the possible values.

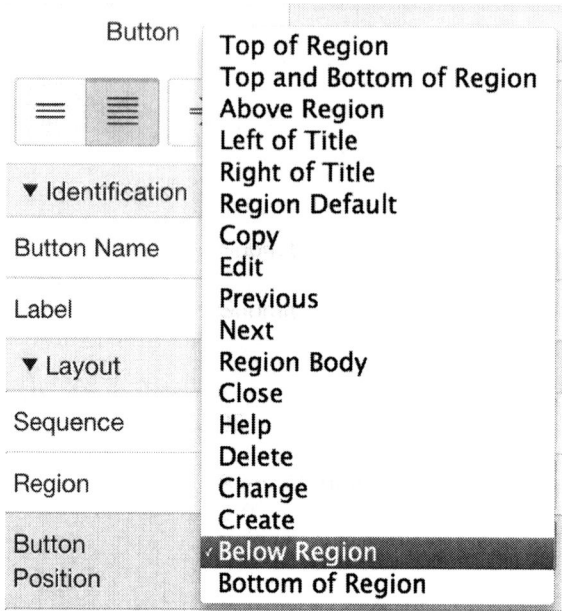

Figure 5-17. Possible button positions

Although there are a lot of possible positions, they actually can be grouped into four basic categories:

- On the region's title bar
- At the top or bottom of the region
- At specific locations in the region
- In the region body

Use the values Left of Title and Right of Title to position a button in the region's title bar. If several buttons are in the same position, their relative position is determined by their sequence numbers.

Use the values Top, Bottom, Top and Bottom, Above Region, and Below Region to display buttons at the top or bottom of the region. When you choose one of these values, the property editor displays the Horizontal Alignment property, which lets you specify that the button should appear at the left or right side of the region. The buttons in Figure 5-1 are positioned at the top of the region, aligned to the right.

Many page templates have specially designated positions for certain buttons. Their purpose is to ensure that buttons common to multiple regions are located in the same place in those regions. The button positions Copy, Edit, Previous, Next, Close, Help, Delete, Change, and Create correspond to these special-purpose buttons.

Finally, consider the Region Body position. This position is different from the others because the button is placed with the region's items. When you select this value, a Grid section appears for you to specify the position of the button relative to the other items in the region. Moreover, the entry for the button shows up in the rendering tree in the Page Items folder.

Summary

An item is a page element that holds a value. There are many item types, which differ in the way in which they display their value on the page and how they help users specify the value. Of primary importance is the distinction between text-based items and list-based items.

A text-based item displays its value in an input box, and users can specify a value by typing it into the input box. The text-based item types support the entry of unusual values (such as colors and dates), aid in data entry (such as autocompletion), and restrict allowable values (such as number fields).

A list-based item forces a user to choose from a given list of values. This list can be defined dynamically, via an SQL query, or statically via explicit values. In every case, there is a distinction between the display values (the values presented to the user) and the result values (the value that is actually held by the item). The various list-based item types differ primarily in how they present the display values on the page.

The purpose of an item is to allow a user to send a value to the server. Chapters 6 and 7 will examine this issue and provide examples that show typical uses of items in web applications.

CHAPTER 6

Session State

A user's interaction with an application is called a *session*. A session can encompass several page requests. For example in an e-commerce application, a session can involve browsing the products for sale, adding some of them to a shopping cart, entering payment and shipping information, and finalizing the transaction.

During a session, the user assigns values to page items, perhaps over several pages, and sends these values to the server for processing. The item values for a given session comprise what is called its *session state*. In this chapter you will examine the various ways that an application can modify and access the session state, and look at some common page design techniques that make use of this state.

Session IDs

Sessions can be tricky to implement, primarily because browser requests are anonymous. There is no built-in way for a server to know whether two browser requests are part of the same session. APEX solves this problem by assigning an identifier to each session. A browser request indicates its session by adding the session's ID to the request.

Recall that an APEX URL consists of the f?p= string followed by a colon-delimited string of values. The first two values are the application ID and page ID; the third value is the session ID. To see session IDs in action, log in to APEX and browse a bit. Look at the URL associated with each screen you visit. You should discover that every URL has the same session ID value. Now log out of APEX. When you log back in, APEX will assign a new session ID to the interaction. The URL of each screen you visit will now have this new session ID.

You can also observe the session IDs in your own applications. Log out of APEX and run your demo application. APEX will assign a session ID that will appear in the URL of each page. You can request a new session by submitting a request having a session ID of 0. (Actually, any random ID value will do.) For example, I can view the home page of my demo application in a new session by submitting the URL:

```
apex.oracle.com/pls/apex/f?p=87059:1:0
```

When the page loads, the URL will contain a new session ID.

Submit vs. Redirect

Suppose that you modify the value of an item on a web page, such as by selecting a radio button or typing into a text field. Your browser will display this change directly, without having to ask the server to re-render the page. Consequently, the server will know nothing about the change you made to the item, and thus cannot use the new value.

If you want your application to know about the values of the items on a page, you must first upload those values to the server. This operation is called *submit*. The server holds a variable for each item of each page of the application. When you submit a page, the value of each item on that page is saved in the corresponding variable. In effect, the submit operation synchronizes the session state with the current page.

Recall that the action of a button is either submit or redirect. Both actions cause the APEX server to render a target page and send it to the browser. For redirect, you specify the target page as part of the redirect action. For submit, you specify the target page via a separate *branch* component — if no branches are specified, the current page is reloaded. Branches are discussed in Chapter 9, so for now you can assume that a submit operation always reloads the current page.

The primary difference between submit and redirect is that submit uploads the page's item values to the server, whereas redirect does not. If a user changes the value of some items on a page and then does a redirect, those changes will be lost — even if the redirect is to the same page.

To see an example of this difference, consider the Item Sampler demo page from Chapter 5 (refer to Figure 5-1). Recall from Chapter 5 that the initial value of an item is determined by its Source properties. The default is to use the session state value if it is not null. This means that if you assign a non-null value to an item and submit, then that value will become the item's initial value when the page is reloaded. You can verify this fact by changing some of the values on the page and clicking the Cancel button. Because that button does a redirect, your changes are lost. Now modify those values again and click the Submit button. The item values remain as chosen because the submit operation wrote those changes to the session state and then retrieved them when the page was reloaded. If you navigate to a different page and come back, the values will still be there.

Recall that when you run a page from within APEX, several buttons appear on the bottom of the screen. The button labeled Session shows you the current session state. Clicking it opens a window that displays all items and their current session values. This window is very useful when debugging pages. In the example, open the session window and look at the session state. Then change some items and submit. Open the session window again, and verify that the item values have changed.

It is important to understand that specifying an initial value of an item will affect the value of the item in the browser, but will never, ever change its value in the session state. You can run some experiments on the Item Sampler page to verify this fact. Go to the property editor, set the source of the Job item to be the static expression CLERK, and have it be used Always, replacing any existing value in session state. Run the page, change the item's value to ANALYST, and click the Submit button, checking the session state at each step. The session state value stays blank until the page is submitted, at which point it becomes ANALYST. The browser, however, will show CLERK when the page is rendered. Now go back to the property editor and change the Source Used property of the item to be Only when current value in session state is null and repeat the experiment. (Start by setting the value of the item to blank and clicking the Submit button to clear the session state.) You should observe that the session state values behave the same as before. The browser, however, will display CLERK when the page is rendered until you submit a new value, after which it will display that value.

Using an Item to Submit a Page

The primary way to submit a page is to use a button. However, certain item types can also perform a submit. The Settings section of a text field or password field has the property Submit when Enter pressed. Setting this property to Yes causes the item to submit the page when the user presses the Enter key.

The Settings section of a select list or radio group has the property Page Action on Selection. This property is shown in Figure 6-1 for a select list. The default value of the property is None. If you set it to Submit Page, then the page will be submitted each time a user changes the value of the item.

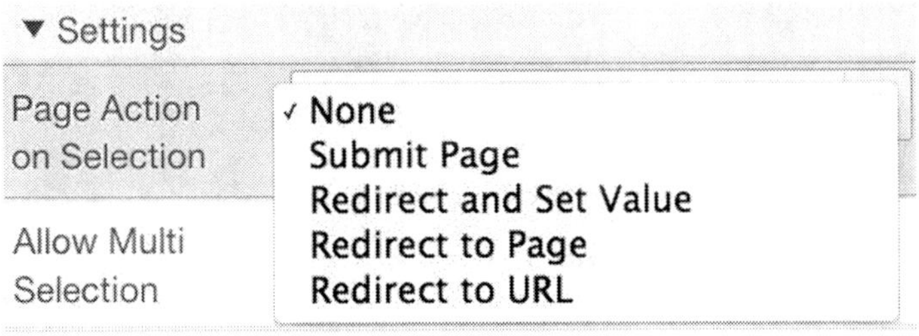

Figure 6-1. *Possible actions for a select list*

The figure also shows three other values for this property. These values correspond to different forms of redirect. The Redirect and Set Value option saves the value of that item in the session state and then redirects to the same page. That is, it behaves like submit, but for just one item instead of all items on the page.

The Redirect to Page and Redirect to URL options have different intents. The Redirect to Page action causes the item to act as a navigation list — its values are interpreted as page numbers, and selecting a value causes APEX to redirect to that page. For example, consider a select list having the following value definition:

STATIC:Home;1,Employees;3,Item Sampler;8

This item displays the three options (Home, Employees, Item Sampler); choosing an option redirects to the corresponding page number. The Redirect to URL option is similar, except that the item values are assumed to be URLs. Neither of these two options changes the session state.

Setting Session State During a Redirect

Now consider the redirect action of a button. Even though that action does not submit the page, it nevertheless can modify the session state.

When you set the action of a button to Redirect to Page in this Application, the Target property appears in the property editor. Clicking the property's input box brings up the Link Builder wizard page shown in Figure 6-2.

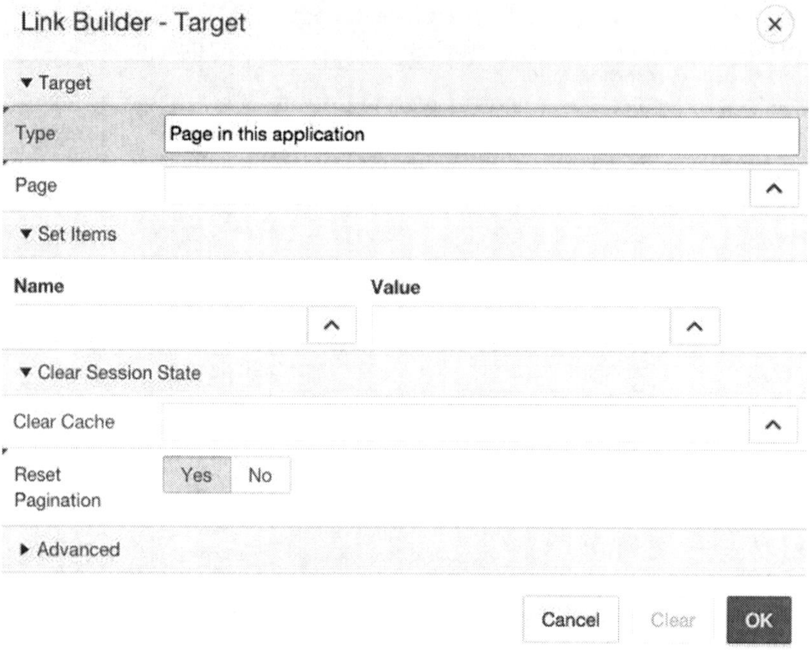

Figure 6-2. Link Builder wizard page

In addition to setting the Page property to the desired target, you can use the Set Items section to set the value of as many items as you want. Enter the item name in the Name box and its desired session state value in the Value box. Each time you fill up a row, another row appears, thus allowing you to enter arbitrarily many name/value pairs.

For example, consider again the Item Sampler page from Chapter 5 (refer to Figure 5-1). Suppose that you want the Cancel button to set the value of the items Emp No to 9999 and Job to CLERK, and to clear the value in Salary. Assuming that those three items have the names P8_EMPNO, P8_JOB, and P8_SALARY, the Set Items section of the link builder would look like Figure 6-3.

▼ Set Items			
Name		Value	
P8_EMPNO	∧	9999	∧
P8_JOB	∧	CLERK	∧
P8_SALARY	∧		∧

Figure 6-3. *Specifying item values upon redirect*

Suppose that you want the Cancel button to clear the session state of all items in the page. APEX calls this *clearing the cache* and provides the Clear Cache property in the link builder to do so. For example in Figure 6-2, typing 3,4,8 into the Clear Cache input box will clear the session state for all items on pages 3, 4, and 8. If you have also specified items in the Set Items section, APEX will assign values to those items after clearing the cache.

Note that this way of modifying the session state is totally unlike the submit action because it does not (and cannot) use values displayed in the browser. That is, a redirect can set the session state value of an item to a constant or computed value, but it cannot set it to a browser value entered by the user.

Referring to a Session State Variable

Now that you know how to set the value of a session state variable, you need to know how to get a page to access that value. There are two primary techniques. If you want to reference the variable from within SQL code, prepend a colon in front of the item name. Such a reference is called a *bind variable*. If you want to reference an item from within an HTML expression, prepend an ampersand in front of the item name and append a period at its end. This latter reference, which is called a *substitution string*, was introduced in Chapter 3.

For example, consider the item named P8_EMPNO on the Item Sampler page. To refer to it as a substitution string, write "&P8_EMPNO." To refer to it as a bind variable, write ":P8_EMPNO".

So far, you have seen several uses for SQL queries, such as the source of a report or chart, the initial value of an item, and the definition of the values of a list-based item. You have also seen several uses for HTML expressions, such as the title of a page or region, the label of an item, and a static expression. The remaining sections of this chapter give examples of how you can greatly increase the functionality of your pages by using item references within these SQL queries and HTML expressions.

Customized Reports

A *customized report* is a report whose contents are affected by the values of one or more items. A user enters values for some items on the page and clicks a Submit button. The page then displays a report based on those input values. In this section, you will build three customized report pages to illustrate this technique.

Filter by Job and Department Page

The first page, which is titled Filter by Job and Department, is page 9 of the demo and appears in Figure 6-4. The idea is that a user chooses values for the Job and Dept items and clicks the Submit button. The report then shows the employees who have the selected job and are in the selected department. For example, Figure 6-4 shows the clerks who work in the research department.

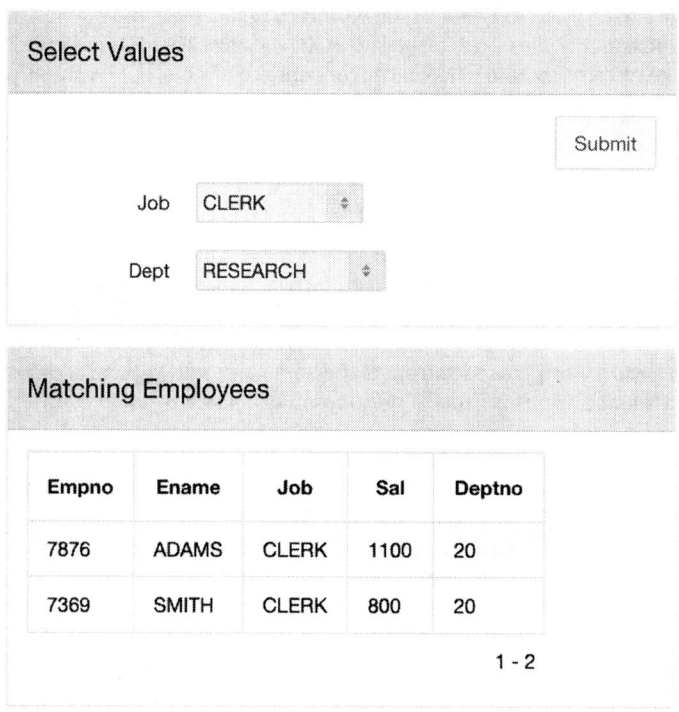

Figure 6-4. Filter by Job and Department page

This page has two regions: Select Values and Matching Employees. The Select Values region is a static content region that contains two select lists, P9_JOB and P9_DEPTNO, both of whose values are defined by SQL queries. The query for P9_JOB is as follows:

```
select distinct Job as DisplayVal, Job as ResultVal
from EMP
order by DisplayVal
```

The query for P9_DEPTNO is as follows:

```
select DName, DeptNo
from DEPT
order by DName
```

The action of the button is submit.

The Matching Employees region is a report region. For the report to display the EMP records having the selected job and department number, its source query needs to reference the value of the two items. The following query does the trick; note how it uses bind variable syntax to refer to the two items.

```
select EmpNo, EName, Job, Sal, DeptNo
from EMP
where Job = :P9_JOB  and  DeptNo = :P9_DEPTNO
order by EName
```

You can improve the functionality of this region by allowing a user to select a null value for P9_JOB or P9_DEPTNO. The intent is that a null value for P9_JOB (or P9_DEPTNO) should mean that the query will not use that item for filtering. For example, if both items were null, the report would display all employees. To enable this functionality, revise the source query to explicitly test for null item values, as follows:

```
select EmpNo, EName, Job, Sal, DeptNo
from EMP
where (:P9_JOB is null  or  Job = :P9_JOB)
and   (:P9_DEPTNO is null  or  DeptNo = :P9_DEPTNO)
order by EName
```

Filter by Possible Department Page

The second custom report page, titled Filter by Possible Department, is page 10 of the demo and appears in Figure 6-5. This page has a structure similar to the previous one. The top region is used for input — the user selects departments from a checkbox item and clicks the Submit button. The bottom region displays a report of the employees in the selected departments. For example, the ACCOUNTING and RESEARCH boxes are checked in Figure 6-5, which means that the report lists those employees in either the accounting or research departments. If no boxes are checked, the report will display no records.

139

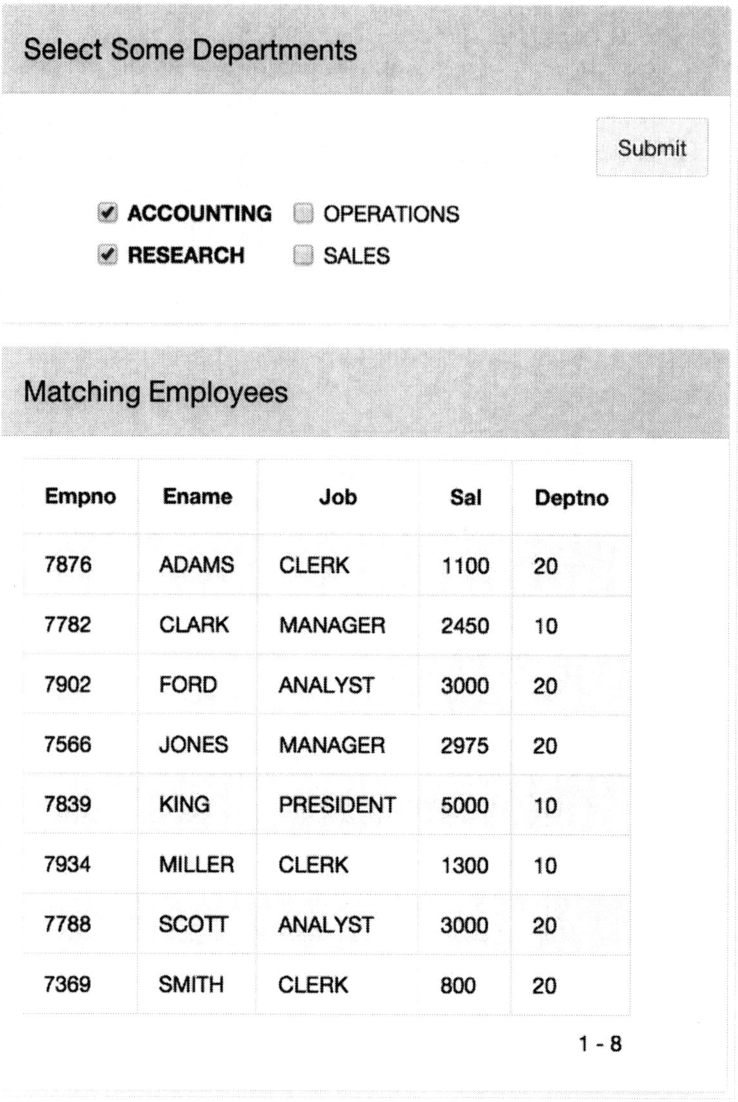

Figure 6-5. *Filter by Possible Department page*

The Select Some Departments region is a static content region containing a checkbox item and a button. The checkbox item is named P10_DEPTNO, its label is blank, and its values are defined by the query

```
select DName, DeptNo
from DEPT
order by DName
```

Recall that the value of a multi-value item is a string containing the selected checkbox values separated by colons. For example, the value of P10_DEPTNO in Figure 6-4 is 10:30. If all four departments were checked, the value would be 10:40:20:30. (The order of the selected values in the string is based on the sort order of the item's LOV query, which in this case is by department name.)

The Matching Employees region is a classic report. The task is to come up with a source query for the report that will filter the records based on this item value. One approach is to test each EMP record to see if its DeptNo value is a substring of P10_DEPTNO. This approach leads to the following query, which almost works:

```
select EmpNo, EName, Job, Sal, DeptNo
from EMP
where InStr(:P10_DEPTNO,  DeptNo) > 0
order by EName
```

The InStr function tests whether the second argument is a substring of the first one. If so, it returns the character position of the match; otherwise, it returns 0. Thus the query returns those EMP records whose DeptNo value appears somewhere in the item. This query is almost what you want, but not quite. For example, suppose that the value of the item is 10:30. The EMP records having a DeptNo value of 10 and 30 will match, and those having a value of 20 and 40 will not match. This is correct, but look at what happens if a new department is created with the department number 3. The employees in this department will match, which is incorrect.

The solution is to not only test for the DeptNo value but to also test for the colons on either side of it. To handle the first and last components of the item value, add a colon to either side of it as well. The query thus becomes this:

```
select EmpNo, EName, Job, Sal, DeptNo
from EMP
where InStr( ':' || :P10_DEPTNO || ':',    ':' || DeptNo || ':' ) > 0
order by EName
```

▓ **Note**   Many people (including me) have difficulty coming to terms with all the colons in this InStr function call; if you feel the same, try working on an example. In particular, note the two different uses of the colon: the colon outside of quotes denotes a bind variable, whereas a colon inside the quotes is a delimiter character.

Filter by Salary Range Page

The final customized report page, titled Filter by Salary Range, is page 11 of the demo and appears in Figure 6-6. A user enters the minimum and maximum salary values and clicks the Submit button. The page then customizes an employees-per-job chart that considers only those employees in the specified salary range.

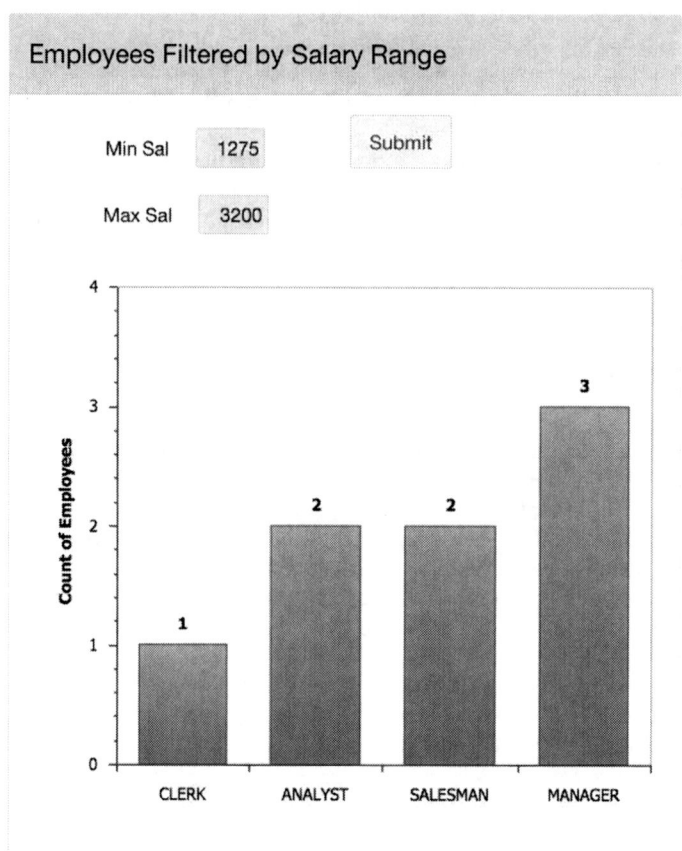

Figure 6-6. *Filter by Salary Range page*

This page contains a single chart region. The region's Item Display Position property (in its Appearance section) has the value Above Contents, which is why the two items and Submit button are located above the chart. The two items, named P11_MINSAL and P11_MAXSAL, are number fields having a Width value of 5. The button's position is Region Body, which causes it to be placed among the items. In this case, its sequence number is between that of P11_MINSAL and P11_MAXSAL, and its Grid properties are configured to begin a new column in the same row.

Of course, this page customizes a chart, not a report, but the technique is exactly the same. Recall from Chapter 3 that the source query for this chart will have three output fields: a URL value, which for your purposes is null; a label, which here is the value of Job; and the series value, which here is the count of records for that job. To customize the chart to consider employees only in the specified salary range, simply add that restriction to the where-clause of the query. The source query becomes this:

```
select null as URL, Job, count(*) as EmpCount
from EMP
where (:P11_MINSAL is null  or  :P11_MINSAL <= Sal)
and   (:P11_MAXSAL is null  or  :P11_MAXSAL >= Sal)
group by Job
order by EmpCount
```

As with the Filter by Job and Department page, this query ensures that a null item value will not contribute to the filter.

Master-Detail Reports

A *master-detail report* is a set of two reports. These reports are *linked*, in the sense that each record of the detail report has an associated record in the master report. A user interacts with the reports by choosing one of the master records; the detail report responds by displaying just the detail records associated with the chosen master record.

In this section you will build a master-detail page titled Employees by Department, which is page 12 of the demo application. Its master report contains one record for each department. Clicking a department record causes the detail report to display the list of employees in that department. Figure 6-7 shows the page after clicking the link for the research department.

Departments

Dname	Loc	Empcount	Deptno
ACCOUNTING	NEW YORK	3	Click for details
OPERATIONS	BOSTON	0	Click for details
RESEARCH	DALLAS	5	Click for details
SALES	CHICAGO	6	Click for details

1 - 4

Employee Details

Empno	Ename	Job	Sal
7876	ADAMS	CLERK	1100
7902	FORD	ANALYST	3000
7566	JONES	MANAGER	2975
7788	SCOTT	ANALYST	3000
7369	SMITH	CLERK	800

1 - 5

Figure 6-7. Employees by Department page

Consider how to implement this page. The main issue is that the master report needs to let the detail report know which record was selected. The standard technique is to use a hidden item, whose value is the key of the selected record. Let's name this item P12_DEPTNO. The master report will assign to P12_DEPTNO the DeptNo value of the selected record. The detail report will then use this value to customize itself.

Implementing the customized detail report is straightforward and has the following source query:

```
select EmpNo, EName, Job, Sal
from EMP
where DeptNo = :P12_DEPTNO
order by EName
```

The hard part is implementing the master report. You have three questions to answer: What is the source query of the report? How do you get its fourth column to display a link? And how do you assign the appropriate value to P12_DEPTNO?

The master report has four columns. The first three are the department name, location, and employee count; the fourth contains the link to the detail table. Because the purpose of the link is to select a department number, it makes sense for the value of that column to be DeptNo. You therefore have the following source query (which is a right-join so that the master report can display departments having no employees):

```
select d.DName,  d.Loc,  count(e.EmpNo) as EmpCount,  d.DeptNo
from EMP e  right join  DEPT d
on  e.DeptNo = d.DeptNo
group by d.DeptNo, d.DName, d.Loc
order by DName
```

Chapter 3 described how to specify a link for a report column. To review: Go to the page designer and click the DeptNo column in the rendering tree. Set the type of the column to Link. Find the Link section in the property editor (refer to Figure 3-25 in Chapter 3) and set the link text to Click for details. Clicking the Target box will take you to the Link Builder page, in which you can set the target to page 12 (the current page).

Wait a minute. A redirect to the current page doesn't do anything, so what is the point of the link? Its real purpose is to change the session state. Recall that the link builder also has a Set Items section, in which you can set the hidden item P12_DEPTNO to the selected department number. Recall from Chapter 3 that you can refer to the value of column X in the current record by writing #X#. Thus you should set P12_DEPTNO to #DEPTNO#. See Figure 6-8.

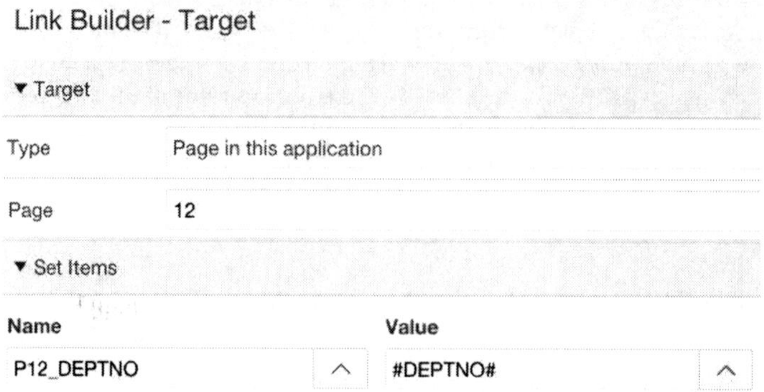

Link Builder - Target

▼ Target	
Type	Page in this application
Page	12

▼ Set Items

Name		Value	
P12_DEPTNO	∧	#DEPTNO#	∧

Figure 6-8. *Configuring the master report's column link*

Finally, you have to actually create the item P12_DEPTNO. You know that it should be a hidden type, but where should it be placed? Because the item is hidden, it doesn't really matter which region on the page it goes in. I chose to place it in the master region because that is where its value is assigned.

Chart Drill-Down

The next page, Employees by Job, is page 13 of the demo application and is shown in Figure 6-9. The page has two regions: a pie chart and an employee report. The chart gives the employee count per job. Clicking a pie segment customizes the report so that it displays only the employees having that job. Figure 6-9 shows the page after clicking the CLERK slice.

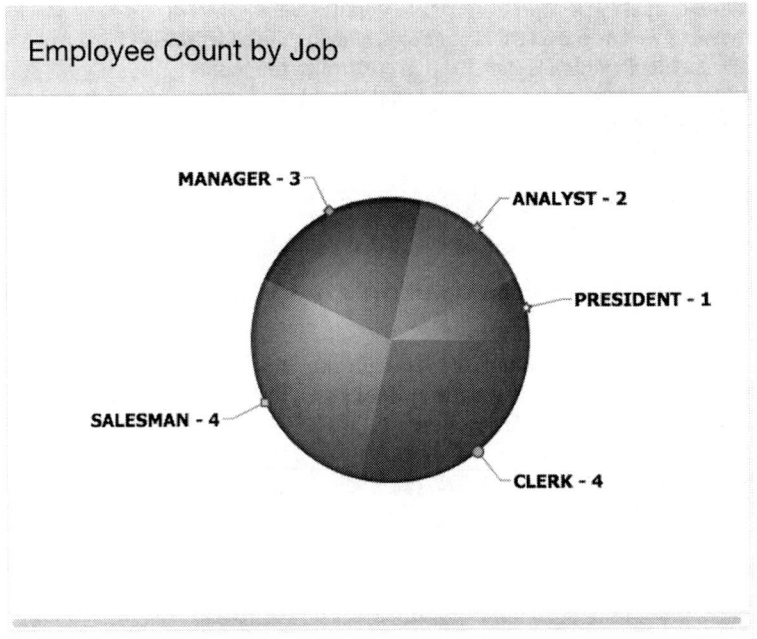

Figure 6-9. Employees by Job page

This technique of clicking a chart to see more detail is called *chart drill-down*, which works for bar charts as well as pie charts. In general, clicking the chart selects a category value (APEX calls it a *label*), which is then used to customize the report.

Chart drill-down is very similar to master-detail. The chart is the master, and the report is the detail. In fact, the implementation strategy is essentially the same as for master-detail reports:

1. Create a hidden item, here called P13_JOB.

2. Create the detail report customized by that item.

3. Create the chart, configuring it to assign the selected job to the hidden item when clicked.

The source query for the detail report is essentially the same as in Employees by Department. The only difference is that the query does a join so that the report can display the department name. The SQL code is as follows:

```
select e.EmpNo, e.EName, d.DName, e.Sal
from EMP e join DEPT d
on     e.DeptNo = d.DeptNo
where e.Job = :P13_JOB
order by EName
```

Recall from Chapter 3 that a pie chart is specified by an SQL query having three columns. The following query creates a pie section for each job, whose value is the number of employees having that job:

```
select null as URL, Job, count(*) as EmpCount
from EMP
group by Job
order by EmpCount desc
```

The only remaining issue is how to specify the chart's behavior when it is clicked. This behavior is determined by the Link properties of the chart's series (see Figure 6-10).

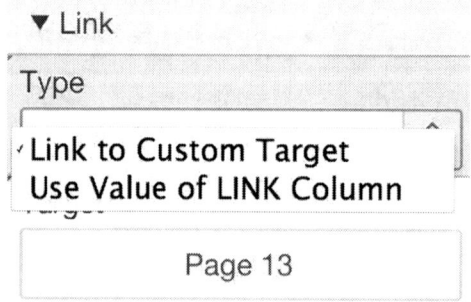

Figure 6-10. Chart's Link properties

The Type property has two possible values. The first value, Link to Custom Target, lets you use the Link Builder wizard to specify the target page. Figure 6-11 shows the wizard as it was configured for the chart. You use the same technique that you used for the master report of Figure 6-8: choose the target to be the current page and set the value of the hidden item. The only difference is how you refer to the selected value. When you referenced that value from a report, you used the name of the column. To reference the value from a chart, use the keyword LABEL.

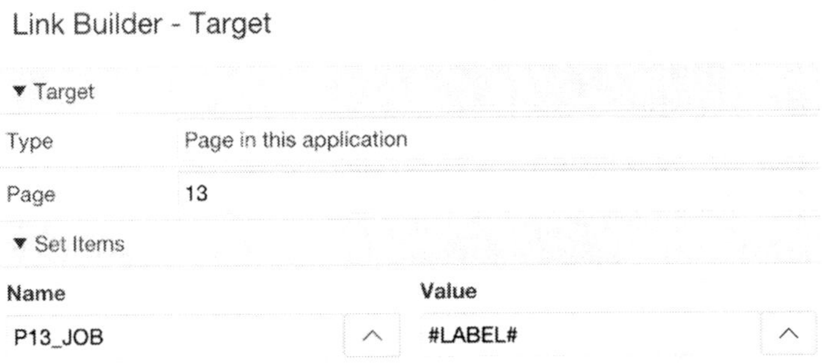

Link Builder - Target

▼ Target	
Type	Page in this application
Page	13

▼ Set Items		
Name		**Value**
P13_JOB	∧	#LABEL# ∧

Figure 6-11. *Configuring a chart for drill-down*

Instead of using the link builder to configure the target, you can use the chart's source query by choosing the Use Value of LINK Column option (refer to Figure 6-10). This option says that the URL of the target page is in the first column of the source query. If the first column is null (as it was in Chapter 3), then there is no target, and clicking the chart does nothing.

Let's see how to create the URL for the chart's target page. Run your Employees by Job page and click a slice of the pie chart (say, CLERK). Note the URL that appears in your browser's address bar. Mine is this:

```
apex.oracle.com/pls/apex/f?p=87059:13:13460846598074::NO:RP:P13_JOB:CLERK
```

This is the URL that you need the source query to generate. Actually, you can use a relative reference, which lets you omit the portion of the URL before the f?p= string. Following that string are several values, separated by colons. The first value is the application ID, the second is the target page, and the third is the session ID. The fourth, fifth, and sixth values are not relevant to you, and can be omitted. (FYI: the value NO says not to enter debug mode, and the RP says to reset pagination.) The last two values set the page items; in this case, they set the hidden item P13_JOB to CLERK.

You therefore need to modify the source query of the chart so that its first column computes a similar URL. The query looks like this:

```
select 'f?p=' || :APP_ID || ':13:' || :APP_SESSION || ':::::P13_JOB:' || Job
        as URL,
      Job,  count(*) as EmpCount
from EMP
group by Job
order by EmpCount desc
```

Note that the URL is broken into pieces that are then concatenated. The built-in variables APP_ID and APP_SESSION hold the current application ID and session ID. You reference these variables using the bind variable notation because you are in an SQL query.

Clearly, this way of constructing the target URL is much more difficult than using the link builder. In fact, that is why the link builder exists. The only reason to construct the URL explicitly is when the link builder doesn't do what you need.

For an example, suppose that you want to configure the chart so that the target is page 1 if the user clicks PRESIDENT, and page 3 otherwise. The link builder is of no use here because it cannot handle conditional targets. Instead, the query needs to construct the URL explicitly, as follows.

```
select case when Job='PRESIDENT'
            then 'f?p=' || :APP_ID || ':1:' || :APP_SESSION
            else 'f?p=' || :APP_ID || ':3:' || :APP_SESSION  end as URL,
       Job,  count(*) as EmpCount
from EMP
group by Job
order by EmpCount desc
```

Customized Titles and Labels

In Chapter 3, you saw how to use HTML tags to format a region title. In fact, you can use HTML tags to format any property whose value is displayed on the page, such as page and region titles, item labels, and button text. Moreover, these properties can also be customized by item values.

For example, looking back at the master-detail and chart drill-down pages, you can see a small problem: the detail reports do not tell you which master record (or chart slice) was selected. A good solution to this problem is to customize the title of the detail region. For example, Figure 6-12 shows the revised detail region for the Employees by Department page. Note that the region title contains the selected department name.

Employee Details: RESEARCH department

Empno	Ename	Job	Sal
7876	ADAMS	CLERK	1100
7902	FORD	ANALYST	3000
7566	JONES	MANAGER	2975
7788	SCOTT	ANALYST	3000
7369	SMITH	CLERK	800

1 - 5

Figure 6-12. *Employees by Department detail report with a customized title bar*

Similarly, Figure 6-13 shows the revised detail region for the Employees by Job page. Its title bar shows the selected job.

Employee Details: CLERK

Empno	Ename	Dname	Sal
7876	ADAMS	RESEARCH	1100
7900	JAMES	SALES	950
7934	MILLER	ACCOUNTING	1300
7369	SMITH	RESEARCH	800

1 - 4

Figure 6-13. *Employees by Job detail report with a customized title bar*

The technique for implementing these title bars is relatively straightforward. In Figure 6-13, the region's `Title` property simply has the following expression:

`Employee Details: &P13_JOB.`

Note that you use the substitution string notation because this is an HTML expression. Similarly in Figure 6-12, the region's `Title` property has the following expression:

`Employee Details: &P12_DNAME. department`

There is just one glitch to this second expression: the page currently has no item named `P12_DNAME`. For this expression to make sense, you have to create the item and assign the selected department name to it. Fortunately, you know how to do these things. First, create `P12_DNAME` as a hidden item. Then go back to the master report, enter the link builder for the `DeptNo` column, and add a row to the `Set Items` property. See Figure 6-14.

Link Builder - Target

▼ Target		
Type	Page in this application	
Page	12	

▼ Set Items				
Name			**Value**	
P12_DEPTNO	∧		#DEPTNO#	∧
P12_DNAME	∧		#DNAME#|	∧

Figure 6-14. Setting two hidden item values in the link builder

Cascading Lists

The next task is to build a page that enables a user to choose an employee name from a select list, and then displays a report containing information about that employee. This page, titled `Cascading Lists`, is page 14 of the demo application and appears in Figure 6-15. The page has two regions, each of which gives a solution to this problem.

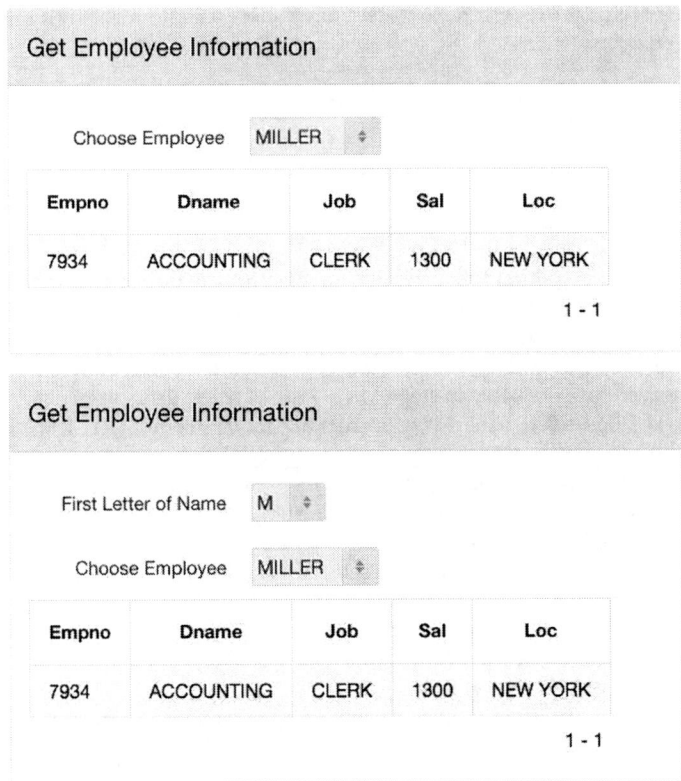

Figure 6-15. Cascading lists

The top region has a single item, named P14_EMPNO. This item is a select list that displays the names of all employees and has employee numbers as the result values. That is, its list of values query is this:

```
select EName, EmpNo
from EMP
order by EName
```

The top region has no button. Instead, the select list has the action Redirect and Set Page, which means that choosing an employee name from the select list causes the item's value to be changed in the session state.

The type of the top region is Classic Report. Its source query is customized by the value of P14_EMPNO, as follows:

```
select e.EmpNo, d.DName, e.Job, e.Sal, d.Loc
from EMP e join DEPT d
on    e.DeptNo = d.DeptNo
where e.EmpNo = :P14_EMPNO
order by EmpNo
```

If you try out this region, you should discover that it is easy to scan through the list of names, due to the small number of employees. Suppose, however, that the EMP table were large, with thousands of employees to pick from. Scrolling through the select list would be awkward and time-consuming, even if the names were sorted. A common solution to this problem is to let the user choose the name in steps, via a series of select lists.

The bottom region of Figure 6-15 uses two select lists to choose an employee. The first select list displays the first letter of each employee name, and the second one displays the names of employees whose names begin with that letter.

This technique is called a *cascading list*, in which the display values of the second select list change according to the value selected for the first one. This technique can be extended to multiple select lists — the values of each select list except the first change according to the values chosen for the select lists previous to it. The advantage of this approach is that a user can scroll through several small select lists instead of one large one.

The two select lists in the bottom region are named P14_FIRST_LETTER and P14_EMPNO_CASCADE. They are defined as follows.

The select list P14_FIRST_LETTER is not dependent on any other items, so its query is straightforward:

```
select FirstLetter as DisplayVal, FirstLetter as ResultVal
from  (select distinct substr(EName, 1, 1) as FirstLetter
        from EMP)
order by DisplayVal
```

The list P14_EMPNO_CASCADE is dependent on the value of P14_FIRST_LETTER, resulting in the following query:

```
select EName, EmpNo
from EMP
where substr(EName, 1, 1) = :P14_FIRST_LETTER
order by EName
```

As before, you set the action of P14_EMPNO_CASCADE to Redirect and Set Page, so that choosing a name from the select list customizes the employee report.

The one issue that has not been addressed is how to configure the select lists so that choosing from the first one causes the contents of the second one to be regenerated. There are two approaches you can take.

The first approach is to set the action of the first select list to be Redirect and Set Value. In this case, selecting a first letter will cause the selected value of P14_FIRST_LETTER to be saved on the server, which will cause the values of P14_EMPNO_CASCADE to be recomputed.

The other approach is to use the Cascading LOV Parent Item(s) property of a list-based item, which appears in its List of Values section. In this approach, you set the action of the first select list to None and the Cascading LOV Parent Item(s) property of the second select list to P14_FIRST_LETTER. Specifying an LOV parent item means that when the parent list is modified, its value is added to the session state, and the child's list values are recomputed, but without having to reload the entire page. (Instead, APEX uses JavaScript and Ajax to update only the select list.) It is the most efficient way to implement cascading.

Conditional Rendering

Throughout your use of the application builder, you have come across numerous situations in which choosing a particular value in the property editor caused the editor to suddenly display another section of properties. The Link Builder page shown in Figure 6-2 is such an example — choosing the target type Page in this application causes the Set Items section to appear. And if you change its value back to URL, those items disappear. What's going on here?

Although it looks like the items are getting created and deleted on the spot, they are not; instead, those items always exist. When you select the value Page in this application in the link builder, APEX displays the additional items; when you select the value URL, APEX hides them. This ability to dynamically show or hide an item is called *conditional rendering*.

Conditional rendering can be defined for items, buttons, and regions. Each one has a Condition section in its property editor, which lets you choose a condition type from a select list. Although there are many condition types, the focus here is on the type SQL expression. The value of this type is an SQL expression that returns true/false. The value of the condition is the value of the expression.

For an example, let's return to the master-detail page of Figure 6-7. Note that the detail report region will be empty until a value from the master report has been chosen. Suppose that you don't want the page to display an empty report region. You can use conditional rendering, displaying the region only when the item P12_DEPTNO is not null. Its conditional SQL expression is this:

```
:P12_DEPTNO is not null
```

For another example, consider the Display Table page shown in Figure 6-16, which will be page 15 of the demo application. The Select Table region contains a radio group. This group has three options, indicating whether the page should also display a report of the EMP table, a report of the DEPT table, or both reports. The radio group has the action Redirect and Set Value, so selecting a radio button immediately causes APEX to display the selected report(s).

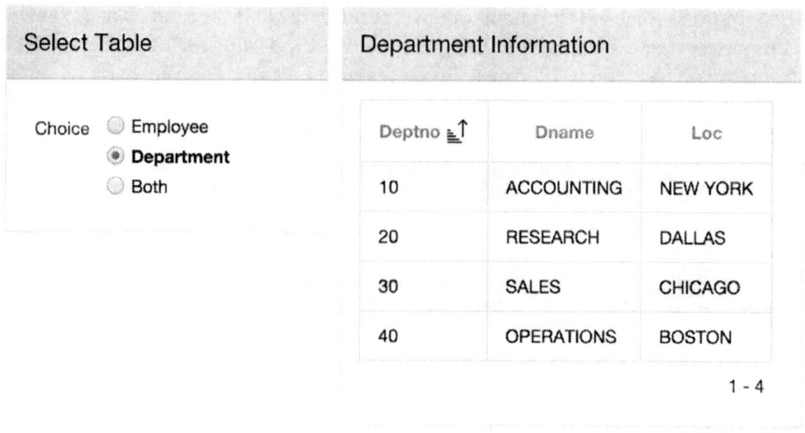

Figure 6-16. *Conditional region rendering*

Implementing the Select Table region is straightforward. Its radio group item is named P15_CHOICE, and is defined by the following expression:

STATIC2:Employee,Department,Both

The page contains two other regions, both of which are of type Classic Report. The Employee Info region has the following source:

select * from EMP

and the Department Info region has the following source:

select * from DEPT

Both of these regions are displayed conditionally, depending on the value of P15_CHOICE. The condition for Employee Info is the following SQL expression:

:P15_CHOICE = 'Employee' or :P15_CHOICE = 'Both'

and the condition for Department Info is the following SQL expression:

:P15_CHOICE = 'Department' or :P15_CHOICE = 'Both'

For a third example of conditional rendering, consider the navigation bar. In Chapter 4, you saw how to change its contents by modifying the list Desktop Navigation Bar. By default, that list has the entry Log Out, which is displayed regardless of whether the user has logged in. A reasonable approach is to use conditional rendering to display the list entry only when the user has logged in.

To do so, go to the list manager and find the List Details page for Desktop Navigation Bar. Clicking the Log Out entry brings you to its List Entry page. Find the Conditions section, choose SQL Expression for the condition type, and set the expression to this:

```
:APP_USER <> 'APEX_PUBLIC_USER'
```

Figure 6-17 shows the resulting List Entry page with its Conditions section.

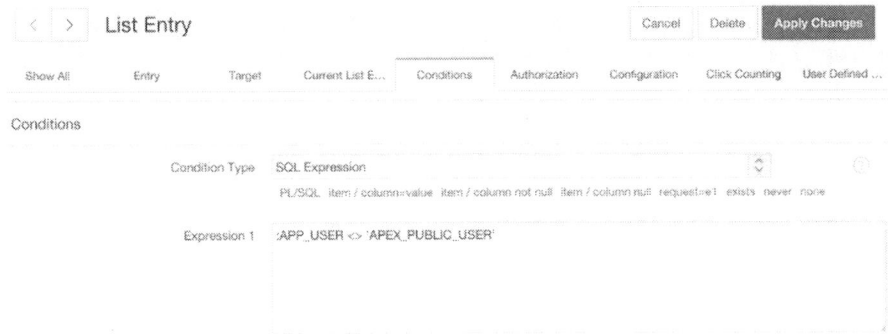

Figure 6-17. *Making the Log Out navigation link conditional*

Region Display Selectors

Figure 6-17 illustrates something interesting about the List Entry page: it has a tab bar under the title, with tabs labeled Show All, Entry, Target, and so on. This bar is a *region display selector*. If you click the Show All tab, the page displays all its sections; if you click any of the other tabs, the page displays only the chosen section. Figure 6-17 shows the page after clicking the Conditions tab.

You can add a region display selector to your pages. Let's build a page similar to the Display Table page of Figure 6-16, but using a region display selector instead of a radio group. This page, titled Select Region, will be page 16 of the demo application. Figure 6-18 shows the page with the Department Information tab selected.

This page consists of two classic report regions, one for each of the EMP and DEPT tables. Above it is a Region Display Selector region. To create the display selector region, create a region in the page designer and then change its type to Region Display Selector. Unlike every other region you have encountered, this region has no source; its sole purpose is to display a tab bar for the regions of the page.

The region display selector in Figure 6-18 is placed in the Content Body position with a small sequence number so that it appears first. Its template is Buttons Container, which formats the region without a title.

Show All	Employee Information	Department Information

Department Information

Deptno ↑	Dname	Loc
10	ACCOUNTING	NEW YORK
20	RESEARCH	DALLAS
30	SALES	CHICAGO
40	OPERATIONS	BOSTON

1 - 4

Figure 6-18. *Using a region display selector region*

The region display selector need not have a tab for every region on the page. Each page has a property in its Advanced section named Region Display Selector, whose value is either Yes or No. Setting the value to No excludes that region from having a tab in the display selector and causes the region to always display.

Summary

The server maintains data about each user session; this data is called the *session state*. In this chapter, you saw how the session state gets modified and examined ways that an application developer can make use of it.

The session state maintains a variable for each item in the application. These variable values can get modified as the result of a submit or redirect action. When a page is submitted, the values of all items on the page will be updated in the session state. When a page redirects to a target page, the redirect operation can assign values to specific items. In particular, when you configure a button, link, or chart to redirect, the property editor will display the Link Builder wizard, which has a section for specifying session state values.

One common use of session state is to allow a user to customize a report. The idea is that the user specifies some values, and those values affect which of the report records are displayed. You saw examples of several ways that a user could specify those values:

- The user can enter the values directly into items on the page.

- The user can select a record from a master report.

- The user can select a value by doing chart drill-down.

This chapter also considered additional uses of session state, such as *cascading lists*, in which the value chosen for one select list determines the values displayed by another; and *conditional rendering*, in which the value of an item determines whether a region should be visible or hidden.

Session state is an immensely important aspect of APEX. Most of the examples in the rest of the book will make use of the techniques mentioned here.

CHAPTER 7

■ ■ ■

Processes

As you have seen, it is possible to write highly functional web pages using only items, reports, and charts. But to implement anything more complex, you have to be able to perform calculations and interact with the database more generally. The notion of a *process* addresses both issues. This chapter examines some typical situations that require the use of processes, and introduces the basics of PL/SQL so that you can write your own code to implement these processes. It also examines the pitfalls you might encounter with writing PL/SQL code, such as the possibility of lost updates. Finally, the chapter discusses the built-in processes and forms provided by APEX. You will learn how to make use of them in your pages, what their limitations are, and how to customize them to achieve the functionality you want.

Stages of a Submit Action

Recall that the left panel of the page designer contains four sections. So far, this book has focused on the Rendering section; it is now time to move to the Processing section. To get to this section, click the third icon from the left at the top of the panel. As with the Rendering section, the Processing section can be displayed in two ways — by processing order, or component type. Figure 7-1 shows the Processing section displayed by component type.

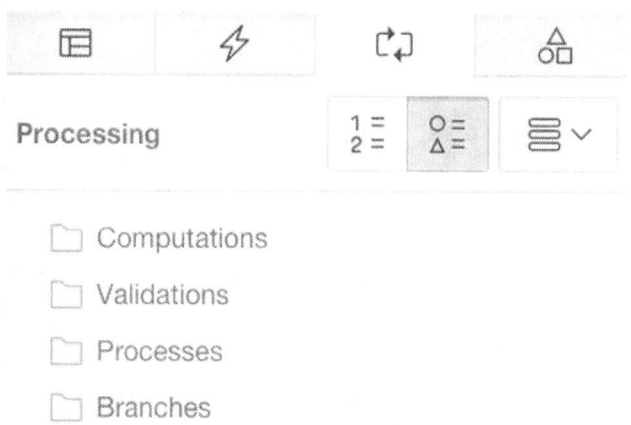

Figure 7-1. Processing section of the page designer, organized by component

The four folders in the figure contain the four types of component that can be associated with a submit action. Each component type corresponds to a different kind of activity. APEX executes these activities during the following stages:

- During the *computation* stage, the server computes additional session state values in preparation for the main processing activity. Such computations are not generally needed, and many web applications do not make use of this stage. It will not be considered in this book.

- During the *validation* stage, the server runs validation checks to ensure that the submit action has been called with appropriate data. The server will abort further processing if it detects a problem. Validation is the subject of Chapter 8.

- During the *processing* stage, the server executes the processes that have been associated with the submit request. The definition and use of these processes is the subject of this chapter.

- During the *branching* stage, the server decides which page to return to the browser. Branching is the subject of Chapter 9.

Note the three buttons to the right of the Processing label in Figure 7-1. The middle button is selected, which tells the page designer to organize these components according to their type. For most applications, this display method is sufficient and appropriate.

If you want more control over when a component executes, click the left button, which will display the components according to the server's processing order (see Figure 7-2). This display gives you more flexibility — for example, you can create a process that executes during the computation stage or a branch that executes during any of the stages. The benefits of such flexibility are beyond the scope of this book. The AJAX Callback folder contains processes that are used to enhance dynamic actions; the uses of these processes are also beyond the scope of this book.

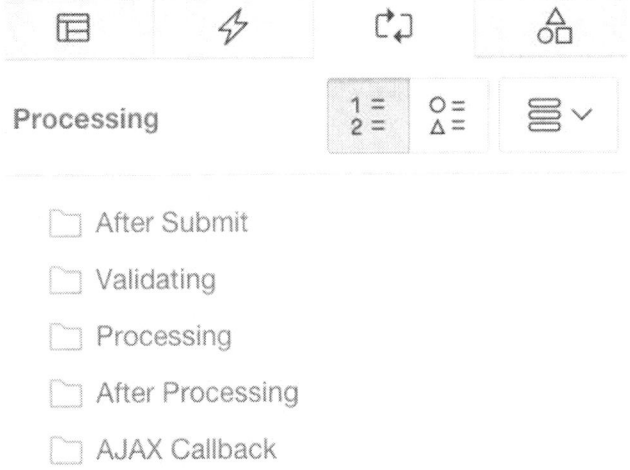

Figure 7-2. Processing section of the page designer, organized by processing order

The rightmost of the three buttons is an actions menu. To create a new component, select the folder of the desired component and click this menu button. Alternatively, right-clicking the folder of a component shows you the same menu.

PL/SQL Processes

To create a new process, right-click the Processing folder in the page designer and select Create Process. The application builder will create a process of type PL/SQL Code, titled New.

APEX has many built-in process types, which are given by the Type property's select list; see Figure 7-3. Most of these process types facilitate their own special kind of action, such as sending e-mail or clearing the session state. The exception is the PL/SQL Code type, which lets you write your own general-purpose actions. This section introduces PL/SQL processes.

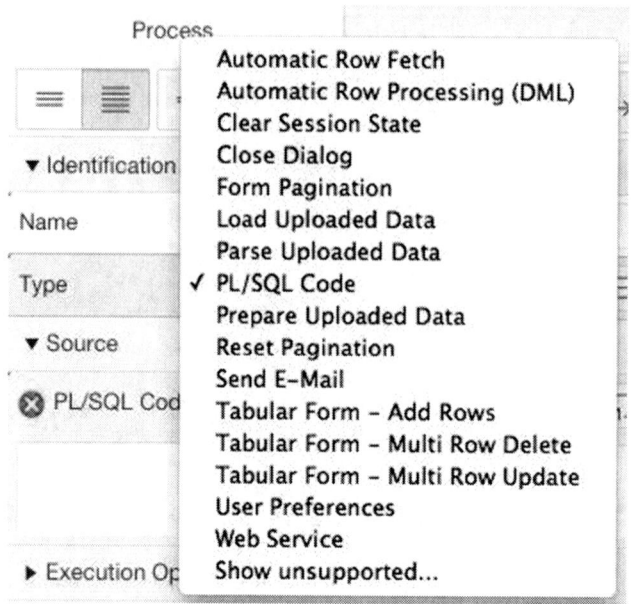

Figure 7-3. *Process types*

You specify the behavior of a process by assigning values to the properties in its Source section. The source of a PL/SQL process is a block of code written in PL/SQL, Oracle's database programming language. You can see the Source section in Figure 7-3, with the text area for its PL/SQL Code property partially obscured. That property is displaying an error icon because no code has yet been specified.

In its most basic form, a PL/SQL block consists of one or more statements surrounded by the keywords begin and end. For example, Listing 7-1 shows the simplest possible PL/SQL block. Performing it executes the null statement, which (as you might imagine) does absolutely nothing.

Listing 7-1. Simplest PL/SQL Block

```
begin
    null;
end;
```

Note the semicolons. Each statement must be followed by a semicolon, as must the end keyword. If you forget to do this (and you probably will at some point), APEX will display an error message. When in doubt, check for forgotten semicolons.

A process has two properties that specify when it should execute. The first property, called Point, is located in the Execution Options section. The value of this property indicates the stage when the process executes. If you created the process by clicking the Processing folder, the Point property will have the value Processing, meaning that it will execute during a submit operation. This is the most common execution point for a process. Other processing points will be considered later in this chapter.

164

By default, a process will execute whenever a submit action occurs on its page. This is rarely what you want. Most often, a process is associated with a particular button, and should execute only when that button is pressed. For example, consider the data entry page shown in Figure 7-4. The next section discusses this page in detail; for now, note that the page has four buttons. If the `Delete` button is pressed, you want a deletion process to execute; if the `Insert` button is pressed, you want the insertion process to execute, and so on.

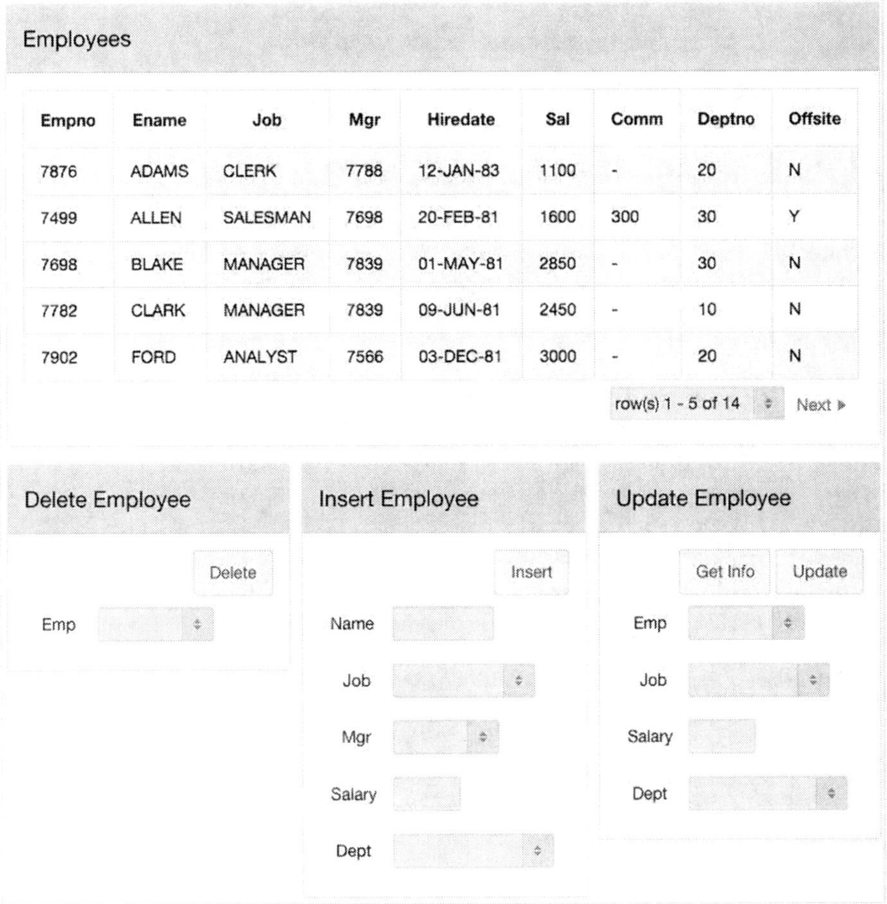
Employees
Empno Ename Job Mgr Hiredate Sal Comm Deptno Offsite
7876 ADAMS CLERK 7788 12-JAN-83 1100 - 20 N
7499 ALLEN SALESMAN 7698 20-FEB-81 1600 300 30 Y
7698 BLAKE MANAGER 7839 01-MAY-81 2850 - 30 N
7782 CLARK MANAGER 7839 09-JUN-81 2450 - 10 N
7902 FORD ANALYST 7566 03-DEC-81 3000 - 20 N
row(s) 1 - 5 of 14
Next
Delete Employee
Delete
Emp
Insert Employee
Insert
Name
Job
Mgr
Salary
Dept
Update Employee
Get Info
Update
Emp
Job
Salary
Dept

***Figure 7-4.** Employee data entry page*

Each process has a `When Button Pressed` property, located in its `Condition` section. This property specifies the correspondence between the process and its button. The process will execute only when the specified button is pressed. The property presents you with a select list of all buttons on the page, and you choose the one you want. Figure 7-5 shows the choices for the page of Figure 7-4.

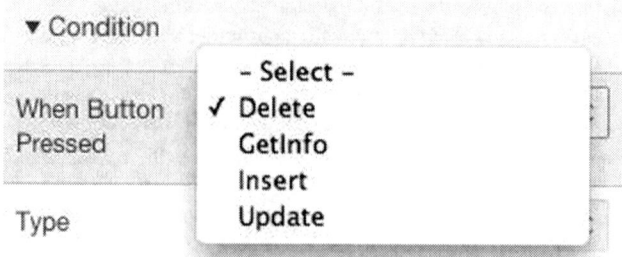

Figure 7-5. *When Button Pressed property*

PL/SQL to Access the Database

One of the most common uses of a PL/SQL process is to access the database. As an example, let's build the page from Figure 7-4; this page will be titled Employee Data Entry and will be page 17 of the demo application. This page has regions to delete a specified employee, insert a new employee and update the columns of a specified employee. Above these regions is a classic report region that displays the employee table ordered by EName, so you can see the effect of your modifications.

A PL/SQL process to change the database can be remarkably short and simple. An SQL data modification command can be used as a PL/SQL statement, which means that a process that modifies the database often consists of just that one statement.

Delete Employee Region

The Delete Employee region contains a select list and a submit button. The select list is named P17_DELETE_EMPNO, whose values are defined by the query:

```
select EName, EmpNo
from EMP
order by EName
```

A user chooses an employee from the list and then clicks the Delete button to submit the page. Listing 7-2 shows the PL/SQL process associated with this button.

Listing 7-2. PL/SQL Code for the Delete Button

```
begin
    delete from EMP
    where EmpNo = :P17_DELETE_EMPNO;
end;
```

Note that the PL/SQL code uses bind variable syntax to reference items.

Insert Employee Region

The Insert Employee region contains five items and a submit button. The items correspond to columns of the EMP table, and have the names P17_INSERT_ENAME, P17_INSERT_JOB, and so on. Item P17_INSERT_ENAME is a text field, and P17_INSERT_SALARY is a number field. The other three items are select lists, whose values are defined via the following queries.

The values of P17_INSERT_JOB are defined by the query:

```
select distinct Job as DisplayVal, Job as ResultVal
from EMP
order by DisplayVal
```

The values of P17_INSERT_MANAGER are defined by the query:

```
select EName, EmpNo
from EMP
where Job = 'MANAGER'
order by EName
```

The values of P17_INSERT_DEPT are defined by the query:

```
select DName, DeptNo
from DEPT
order by DName
```

A user enters values for the items and clicks the Insert button. The process associated with the button will then insert a new record into the EMP table, using the specified values for five of the columns and computing values for the other four columns, as follows:

- EmpNo gets the next value in the sequence, as determined by the built-in insertion trigger.

- HireDate gets the current date.

- Comm gets 0.

- Offsite gets 'N'.

The PL/SQL code for this process also consists of a single SQL command, and appears in Listing 7-3.

Listing 7-3. PL/SQL Code for the Insert Button

```
begin
    insert into EMP (EName, Job, Mgr, Sal, DeptNo, HireDate, Comm, Offsite)
    values (:P17_INSERT_ENAME,
            :P17_INSERT_JOB,
            :P17_INSERT_MANAGER,
```

```
        :P17_INSERT_SALARY,
        :P17_INSERT_DEPT,
        current_date,  0,  'N');
end;
```

Update Employee Region

The Update Employee region has four items and two submit buttons. The items are named P17_UPDATE_EMPNO, P17_UPDATE_JOB, and so on. The select list values are defined as in the other regions.

Two steps are required to use this region. First, a user selects the desired employee from P17_UPDATE_EMPNO and clicks the Get Info button. The process associated with this button populates the items P17_UPDATE_JOB, P17_UPDATE_SALARY, and P17_UPDATE_DEPT with the corresponding values from that employee's EMP record. The user then changes those items as desired. When the user clicks the UPDATE button, the process associated with that button updates the record with the new values.

This region has two PL/SQL processes, one for each button. The process for the Update button contains a single SQL command, as shown in Listing 7-4.

Listing 7-4. PL/SQL Code for the Update Button

```
begin
    update EMP
    set Job    = :P17_UPDATE_JOB,
        Sal    = :P17_UPDATE_SALARY,
        DeptNo = :P17_UPDATE_DEPT
    where EmpNo = :P17_UPDATE_EMPNO;
end;
```

The process for the Get Info button differs from the other processes in that it reads from the database instead of writing to it. The technique is to write an SQL query that places its output into items on the page. The PL/SQL code in Listing 7-5 does just that.

Listing 7-5. PL/SQL Code for the Get Info Button

```
begin
    select Job, Sal, DeptNo
    into :P17_UPDATE_JOB, :P17_UPDATE_SALARY, :P17_UPDATE_DEPT
    from EMP
    where EmpNo = :P17_UPDATE_EMPNO;
end;
```

The critical part of the query is the clause beginning with the keyword into. This clause indicates that the query's three output values will be placed into the three specified items. In other words, the into-clause turns an SQL query into a PL/SQL statement that extracts values from the database and assigns them to items. Note that the into-clause makes sense only if the SQL query returns exactly one row. A PL/SQL process that executes a multi-row SQL query needs to do something totally different, as you will see later.

PL/SQL to Compute Values

This section considers the programming-language aspects of PL/SQL. At its heart, PL/SQL is a traditional programming language with variables, assignment statements, conditionals, and loops. In this regard, it is not much different from C, Java, Python, and similar languages. If you have experience with any of these languages, you should find that the most difficult part of writing PL/SQL code is figuring out the appropriate syntax.

As an example, let's build the Sales Commission page shown in Figure 7-6, which will be page 18 of the demo application.

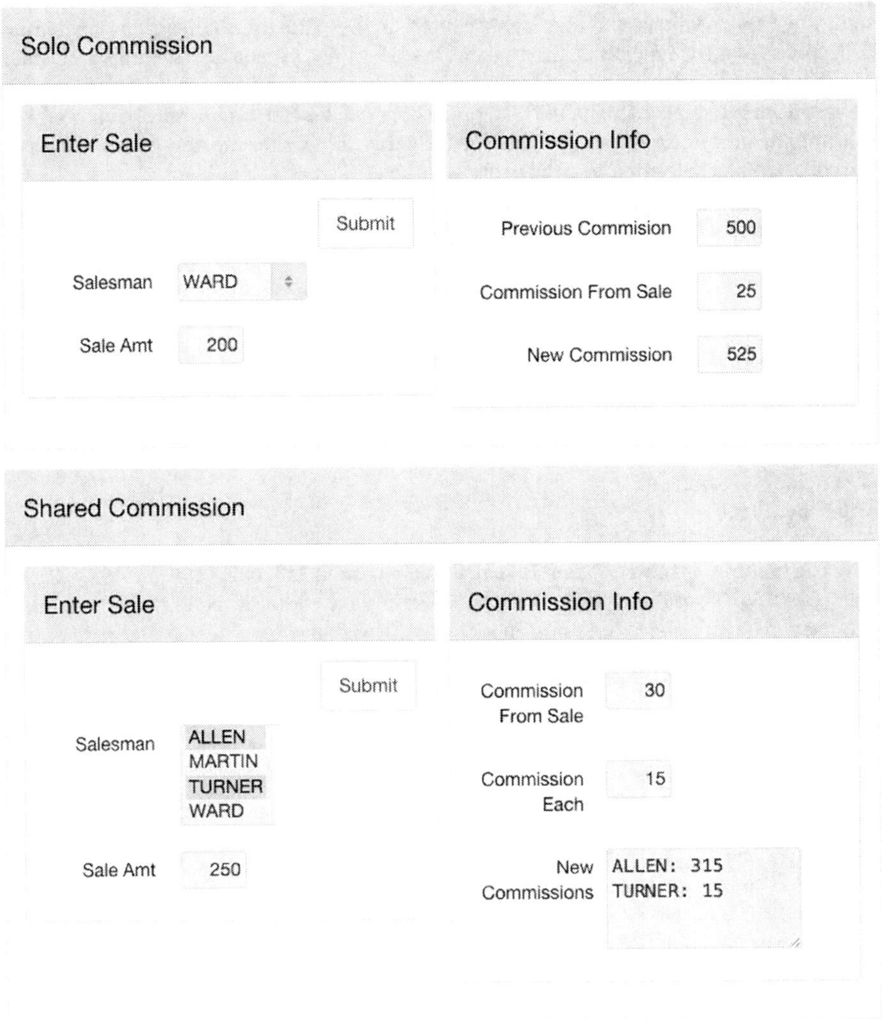

Figure 7-6. Page to calculate sales commissions

This page will get used each time a salesman makes a sale. Assume that salesmen receive 15 percent commission on the first $100 of a sale, and 10 percent on the remaining amount; if several salesmen collaborate on a sale, they split the commission equally. The page has two outer regions. The top region, titled Solo Commission, is used for entering an individual sale. The bottom region, titled Shared Commission, is used for entering a collaborative sale.

The Solo Commission region works as follows. A user selects the salesman's name and enters the amount of the sale into the Enter Sale region. Clicking the Submit button submits the page and causes a PL/SQL process to execute. This process does several things: It calculates the commission based on the sale amount, retrieves the salesman's previous commission from the EMP table, calculates the new commission amount by summing the two values, and places those three values in the three corresponding items of the Commission Info region. It also updates the EMP table with the new commission value.

The Shared Commission region works similarly, except that several salesmen can be chosen from the select list. The PL/SQL process calculates the total commission on the sale and the prorated amount, updates the EMP table, and writes the new commissions for the collaborating salesmen into the text area.

This section considers the implementation of the Solo Commission region. (The Shared Commission region will be examined in the section "Handling Multi-Row SQL Queries".) The two items in the Enter Sale Info region are named P18_EMPNO and P18_SALE_AMOUNT. Item P18_EMPNO is a select list with values defined by the SQL query of Listing 7-6.

Listing 7-6. Source Query for the Salesman Select List

```
select EName, EmpNo
from EMP
where Job = 'SALESMAN'
order by EName
```

The items in the Commission Info region are named P18_PREV_COMMISSION, P18_SALE_COMMISSION, and P18_NEW_COMMISSION. Listing 7-7 contains the PL/SQL code that gets executed when the Submit button is clicked. This code illustrates several aspects of PL/SQL, which are described in the following subsections.

Listing 7-7. PL/SQL Code to Handle a Solo Commission

```
declare
    v_amount int := :P18_SALE_AMOUNT;
    v_saleCommission number(7,2);
    v_prevCommission number(7,2);
    v_newCommission  number(7,2);
begin
    -- Step 1: Calculate the new commission as 15% of the first $100
    -- and then 10% of the remaining sale price.
```

```
    if v_amount > 100 then
            v_amount := v_amount - 100;
            v_saleCommission := 15 + (v_amount * 0.1);
    else
            v_saleCommission := v_amount * 0.15;
    end if;

    -- Step 2: Retrieve the previous commission from EMP
    -- and calculate the new commission.

    select Comm
    into v_prevCommission
    from EMP
    where EmpNo = :P18_EMPNO;

    v_newCommission := v_prevCommission + v_saleCommission;

    -- Step 3: Update the employee's record.

    update EMP
    set Comm = v_newCommission
    where EmpNo = :P18_EMPNO;

    -- Step 4: Compute the item values.

    :P18_SALE_COMMISSION := v_saleCommission;
    :P18_PREV_COMMISSION := v_prevCommission;
    :P18_NEW_COMMISSION  := v_newCommission;
end;
```

Local Variables

A PL/SQL block can have a *variable declaration section* prior to the begin keyword. The declaration section starts with the keyword declare and is followed by a series of variable declarations. The code of Listing 7-7 declares four local variables: v_amount, v_saleCommission, v_prevCommission, and v_newCommission. The syntax for each declaration is similar to the syntax for declaring table columns in SQL, and the possible variable types are also the same. For example, the last three variables have the type number(7,2), which is the same type as the column Comm in the EMP table.

Local variables and item references can be used interchangeably in a PL/SQL block. The difference is that local variables are referenced as is, whereas an item reference requires a prepended colon. For example, note that the SQL update command in Step 3 references both the local variable v_newCommission and the item P18_EMPNO. Because items are referenced using bind variable syntax, they are easy to spot. However, local variable references in SQL commands are hard to distinguish from column names or function calls. To avoid confusion, you should always name local variables so that people know they are variables. A common convention, which is adopted here, is to begin each local variable name with v_.

Comments

As in SQL, PL/SQL denotes comments with two consecutive minus signs. All characters following the two minus signs are ignored until the end of the line.

Assignment Statements

Assignment statements in PL/SQL use := as the assignment operator. Assignment can also be used in the declare section to assign an initial value to a local variable.

Conditional Statements

PL/SQL supports several forms of a conditional statement; the form appearing in Listing 7-7 is good for general-purpose use. Note that the keywords act as section boundaries: the conditional expression appears between if and then, the statements to be executed when the condition is true appear between then and else, and the statements to be executed when the condition is false appear between else and end if. As usual, if there are no statements between the else and end if keywords, the else keyword can be omitted.

Handling Multi-Row SQL Queries

Now let's see how to build the Shared Commission region of Figure 7-6. Its Enter Sale region is essentially the same as in the Solo Commission region. Its item names are P18_EMPNO_SHARED and P18_SALE_AMOUNT_SHARED. The items in the Commission Info region are named P18_GROSS_COMMISSION, P18_COMMISSION_EACH, and P18_NEW_COMMISSIONS.

The select list P18_EMPNO_SHARED has the same definition as P18_EMPNO; the difference is that its Allow Multi Selection property is set to Yes, with a Height value of 4. Recall from Chapter 5 that the value of such an item is a string containing the result values separated by colons. For example in Figure 7-6, ALLEN and TURNER are chosen from the multi-valued select list P18_EMPNO_SHARED. Because their corresponding employee numbers are 7499 and 7844, the value of this item is the string "7499:7844".

It is not especially easy to extract the information you need from this string, so some fancy footwork is required. You will need to do two things: determine the number of selected employees, and extract their records from the EMP table.

To determine the number of selected employees, note that this number is one more than the number of colons in the string. To determine the number of colons, you can use the SQL replace function to create a new string in which the colons are replaced by the empty string (effectively removing the colons) and then compare the lengths of the two strings. That is, if P18_EMPNO_SHARED contains the string, the number of employees is given by this expression:

```
1 + length(:P18_EMPNO_SHARED) - length(replace(:P18_EMPNO_SHARED, ':', ''))
```

To extract the records for each selected employee, use the `instr` function, just as you did for the `Filter by Possible Department` page of Chapter 6 (refer to Figure 6-5). As in that page, the following query will retrieve the EMP-record of all selected employees:

```
select *
from EMP
where instr( ':'|| :P18_EMPNO_SHARED ||':',  ':'||EmpNo||':' ) > 0
```

With these issues taken care of, you can now write the process for the region's `Submit` button. The PL/SQL code appears in Listing 7-8.

Listing 7-8. PL/SQL Code to Handle Shared Commissions

```
declare
    v_saleCommission number(7,2);
    v_amount         int := :P18_SALE_AMOUNT_SHARED;
    v_empCount       int;
    v_commissionEach number(7,2);
    v_empInfo        varchar2(25);
    v_output         varchar2(250) := '';
begin
    -- Step 1: Calculate the new commission as 15% of the first $100
    -- and then 10% of the remaining sale price.
    if v_amount > 100 then
        v_amount := v_amount - 100;
        v_saleCommission := 15 + (v_amount * 0.1);
    else
        v_saleCommission := v_amount * 0.15;
    end if;

    -- Step 2: Determine the shared commission.
    v_empcount := 1 + length(:P18_EMPNO_SHARED)
                    - length(replace(:P18_EMPNO_SHARED, ':', '' ));
    v_commissionEach := v_saleCommission / v_empcount;

    -- Step 3: Update the EMP table.
    update EMP
    set Comm = Comm + v_commissionEach
    where instr( ':'||:P18_EMPNO_SHARED||':',  ':'||EmpNo||':' ) > 0;

    -- Step 4: Use a loop to collect employee info.
    for row in (
        select EName, Comm
        from EMP
        where instr( ':'||:P18_EMPNO_SHARED||':',  ':'||EmpNo||':' ) > 0 )
    loop
        v_empInfo := row.EName || ': ' || row.Comm || chr(13);
        v_output := v_output || v_empInfo;
    end loop;
```

173

```
     -- Step 5: Write the item values.
     :P18_GROSS_COMMISSION := v_saleCommission;
     :P18_COMMISSION_EACH  := v_commissionEach;
     :P18_NEW_COMMISSIONS  := v_output;
end;
```

Step 1, which calculates the commission on the sale, is the same as before. Step 2 calculates the prorated commission for each employee, which you get from dividing the commission by the employee count. Step 3 updates the table. Step 5 writes a value to each item in the Commission region.

The most interesting code appears in Step 4, in which you handle each selected employee. The issue is that the SQL query to retrieve the employee information returns multiple rows, so you cannot use the into-clause the way that you did earlier. Instead, the technique is to loop through the records in the query, processing one row each time through the loop.

The loop has the following basic structure:

```
for r in ( <SQL query> )
loop
     -- statements to process row r
end loop;
```

Variable r need not be declared. Each time through the loop, it will hold the next row of the query. If C is an output column of the query, the expression r.C will return the C-value of the current row. For example in Listing 7-8, the row variable is named row, and the two output columns of the query are EName and Comm. The loop code therefore makes reference to row.EName and row.Comm.

The body of the loop processes each selected employee. Its task is to construct the string that summarizes the new commission of that employee. The code creates the summary string by concatenating the employee's name with the new commission value. The expression chr(13) denotes a newline character.

Concurrent Database Updates

At any point in time, a web server such as APEX may be executing requests from multiple users concurrently. The users are not aware of this concurrency because APEX gives each user the illusion that the application is the only one running on the system. However, application developers must see beyond the illusion. Applications that are unaware of this illusion can unintentionally interfere with each other, with disastrous consequences. This section discusses these issues.

Lost Update Problem

One frequently encountered situation is called the *lost update problem*. It arises when two users update the same database record at approximately the same time, and the timing of the updates is such that the database system loses one of them. Here are two example scenarios.

First consider the Update Employee region of the Employee Data Entry page (refer to Figure 7-4). Assume that two users want to update Allen's record: user A wants to change the salary to 1800, and user B wants to change the job to ANALYST. If both users click the Get Info button at approximately the same time, they both retrieve the same record from the EMP table, which says that Allen is a salesman who has a salary of 1600. When user A changes the salary and clicks the Update button, that record will be replaced by one saying that Allen is a salesman who has a salary of 1800. User B, however, doesn't see the updated salary. When user B changes the job and clicks the Update button, the record will be replaced by one saying that Allen is an analyst making 1600.

This scenario is problematic, regardless of who writes first. If user A modifies first, user B will overwrite the new salary with its previous value; if user B modifies first, user A will overwrite the new job with its previous value. No matter what happens, the database system will lose one of the updates.

For a second example, consider the Solo Commission region of the Sales Commission page (refer to Figure 7-6). Suppose that Allen was involved in two sales, earning a $10 commission on one and $20 on the other. Users A and B concurrently enter one sale each. Suppose that the execution of their PL/SQL processes both hit Step 2 of Listing 7-7 at roughly the same time, meaning that both processes would see a current commission of $300. User A's process would then calculate a new commission of $310 in Step 3, and user B's process would calculate a new commission of $320. Whichever process updates last would overwrite the commission of the process updating first. The overwritten update would be lost.

In both of these scenarios, the occurrence of a lost update depended entirely on the timing of the user requests. For example in the first scenario, if user B happened to click the Get Info button after user A clicked the Update button, there would be no problem — user B would see the new salary, so user A's update would not be lost. Similarly in the second scenario, if user B hit the Submit button after user A completed processing the sale, then user B's process would have seen the updated commission.

This dependence on timing means that lost updates tend to occur at seemingly random times. For example, it is quite possible for an application to run for months (or years) without a lost update and then have several in short succession.

Lost updates are clearly a very bad thing. A lost update might not be detected until long after it occurred, at which point it might be too late. The application developer must ensure that they will not occur. Their unpredictable nature makes it hard to discover the problem via testing. Consequently, any PL/SQL process that updates the database must be written specifically to avoid lost updates. To do this, you need to understand how the database system handles concurrency.

Transactions

Database systems use the concept of a *transaction* to control the undesirable effects of concurrency. A transaction is a sequence of database actions that perform some meaningful activity independent of any other transaction. The database system guarantees that two transactions will not interfere with each other. In particular, it guarantees that an update made by one transaction will not be overwritten by a concurrent transaction.

In other words, if you can write your applications so that each user activity executes as a single transaction, you are guaranteed to have no lost updates. It is therefore important to know how APEX determines transaction boundaries.

The rule used by APEX is to commit the current transaction (and begin a new one) each time one of the following three events occurs: a page has finished rendering, a submit request has completed, or a process that modified the session state has completed. Roughly speaking, this means that if there is one associated process per button, each button click corresponds to a transaction.

With this in mind, let's return to the second scenario, in which two users concurrently update the Solo Commission region. Because each update occurs via a single button click, each corresponds to a single transaction. Therefore you are guaranteed that this lost update scenario cannot occur. Instead, the database system takes responsibility for detecting the conflict and resolving it. For example, Oracle automatically checks for potential conflicts when a transaction tries to commit, and aborts the transaction if it detects one. So in this scenario, Oracle would detect a conflict for the transaction that commits second, abort that transaction, and send an error message to the user.

Now let's consider the first scenario, in which two users concurrently update an employee record. Because the activity of updating a record requires two button clicks, it will be implemented via two transactions. So when user A clicks the Get Info button, that transaction reads the EMP record and commits. The database can now legitimately run other transactions before it runs the Update transaction from user A. In particular, suppose that it ran both of user B's transactions. When the Update transaction from user A is finally executed, the update from B will be lost.

Avoiding Lost Updates

The problem with the first scenario is that you need two button clicks to update an employee record. Because each button click is implemented as a separate transaction, the database system cannot detect any conflicts that might occur between the Get Info process and the Update process. The application, therefore, must be responsible for detecting these conflicts.

A common strategy is to have the Update process check to see whether someone else has already updated the record it is about to update. If so, the process must refuse to perform the update and ask the user to re-read the record.

The simplest way to implement this strategy is to have the Get Info process store a copy of each updatable value retrieved from the database. Before it performs the update, the Update process re-retrieves those values from the database and compares them with the stored copies. The process will perform the update only if the values are identical. Listing 7-9 shows a revision of the Get Info process of Listing 7-5 (bold lines are new). After retrieving the values for the specified employee, it saves them in the hidden items P17_ORIGINAL_JOB, P17_ORIGINAL_SAL, and P17_ORIGINAL_DEPT.

Listing 7-9. Revising the Get Info Code of Listing 7-5

```
begin
    -- First retrieve the data.
    select Job, Sal, DeptNo
    into :P17_UPDATE_JOB, :P17_UPDATE_SAL, :P17_UPDATE_DEPT
    from EMP
    where EmpNo = :P17_UPDATE_EMPNO;

    -- Then use hidden items to save a copy of the data.
    :P17_ORIGINAL_JOB  := :P17_UPDATE_JOB;
    :P17_ORIGINAL_SAL  := :P17_UPDATE_SAL;
    :P17_ORIGINAL_DEPT := :P17_UPDATE_DEPT;
end;
```

Listing 7-10 shows the corresponding revision of the Update process of Listing 7-4 (bold lines are new). It does so by re-reading the values from the database and comparing them against the original values in the hidden items. Because both the reading and writing of the database now occur in the same transaction, they are guaranteed to not lose updates.

Listing 7-10. Revising the Update Code of Listing 7-4

```
declare
    v_newjob  varchar2(9);
    v_newsal  number(7,2);
    v_newdept number(4,0);
begin
    -- First re-read the data.
    select Job, Sal, DeptNo
    into v_newjob, v_newsal, v_newdept
    from EMP
    where EmpNo = :P17_UPDATE_EMPNO;

    -- Then compare it with the original data.
    if :P17_ORIGINAL_JOB = v_newjob and
       :P17_ORIGINAL_SAL  = v_newsal and
       :P17_ORIGINAL_DEPT = v_newdept
    then
        -- The record hasn't changed, so update it.
        update EMP
        set Job    = :P17_UPDATE_JOB,
            Sal    = :P17_UPDATE_SAL,
            DeptNo = :P17_UPDATE_DEPT
        where EmpNo = :P17_UPDATE_EMPNO;
```

```
    else
        -- The record has changed, so abort.
        raise_application_error(-20000,
                        'The record is out of date. Get it again.');
    end if;
end;
```

The code to abort the process requires explanation. The `raise_application_error` function causes APEX to abort the process and display an error message on the page. The function takes two arguments: the first argument is the error code, which can be any number between –20,000 and –20,999; the second argument is the error message.

You can test this code by running the page from two different computers. In each browser window, select the same employee and click the Get Info button. Then do an update in each one and click the Update buttons. The second update operation will not work; instead, APEX will display the error message shown in Figure 7-7.

Figure 7-7. *Error message arising from an avoided lost update*

Using a Hash Function

Although this revised code works, the need to save and compare all the original values is tedious and will become more so as their number increases. An easier approach is to combine all the values into a single value; you can then save and compare that one value. The preferred technique is to use a *hash function*, which transforms a collection of values into a single, fixed-length value. A hash function also obfuscates its input, which makes it useful for encoding user passwords — as will be seen in Chapter 12.

APEX has a built-in hash function, named `apex_util.get_hash`. The input to this function is a collection that contains the values you want hashed. You should use the APEX built-in type `apex_t_varchar2` to hold this collection. For an illusrative example, consider the following code:

```
v_vals   apex_t_varchar2 := apex_t_varchar2('CLERK', 20);
v_result varchar2(1000)  := apex_util.get_hash(v_vals);
```

The first line of the code declares a variable `v_vals` of type `apex_t_varchar2`, and assigns it the collection that gets created by the type's constructor function (which is also called `apex_t_varchar2`). The arguments to the constructor function are the values `'CLERK'` and 20. The second line of the code declares a variable `v_result` of type `varchar2(1000)`, and assigns it the result of the `apex_util.get_hash` function. In other words, the variable `v_result` will contain the hash of the values {'CLERK', 20}.

You can use this hash function to revise the code for the Get Info process, so that the three updatable values are encoded into a single hash value. This hash value is then saved in the hidden item `P17_HASH`. This code appears in Listing 7-11 (bold lines are new).

Listing 7-11. Second Revision of the Get Info Code of Listing 7-5

```
declare
    v_valuesToHash apex_t_varchar2;
begin
    -- First retrieve the data.
    select Job, Sal, DeptNo
    into :P17_UPDATE_JOB,
         :P17_UPDATE_SALARY,
         :P17_UPDATE_DEPT
    from EMP
    where EmpNo = :P17_UPDATE_EMPNO;

    -- Then save the hash of these values.
    v_valuesToHash := apex_t_varchar2(:P17_UPDATE_JOB, :P17_UPDATE_SALARY,
                                      :P17_UPDATE_DEPT);
    :P17_HASH := apex_util.get_hash(v_valuesToHash);
end;
```

The code for the Update process should also be re-revised so that it re-reads the updatable values from the database, hashes them, and compares that has value with the saved hash value. The code appears in Listing 7-12 (bold lines are new).

Listing 7-12. Second Revision of the Update Code of Listing 7-4

```
declare
    v_valuesToHash apex_t_varchar2;
begin
    -- First re-read the data.
    select apex_t_varchar2(Job, Sal, DeptNo)
    into v_valuesToHash
    from EMP
    where EmpNo = :P17_UPDATE_EMPNO;

    -- Then compare it with the original data.
    if :P17_HASH = apex_util.get_hash(v_valuesToHash)
    then
        -- The record hasn't changed, so update it.
        update EMP
        set Job    = :P17_UPDATE_JOB,
            Sal    = :P17_UPDATE_SALARY,
            DeptNo = :P17_UPDATE_DEPT
        where EmpNo = :P17_UPDATE_EMPNO;
    else
        -- The record has changed, so abort.
        raise_application_error(-20000,
                    'The record is out of date. Get it again.');
    end if;
end;
```

179

Although this code does what you want, it is somewhat clunky. This code will be revisited at the end of Chapter 8, where you will see how to improve it using validations.

Success and Error Messages

A process that changes the database should display a message indicating what happened. Consider again the Employee Data Entry page. If the employee report contains only a few records, a user can verify that the update was successful by seeing how the report changed. However, if the report contained thousands of records, it would be far more difficult to determine what happened. It would be better if the deletion process displayed a success message such as Your record was deleted. APEX processes have the Success Message and Error Message properties for exactly this purpose. Figure 7-8 shows these property values for the Delete process.

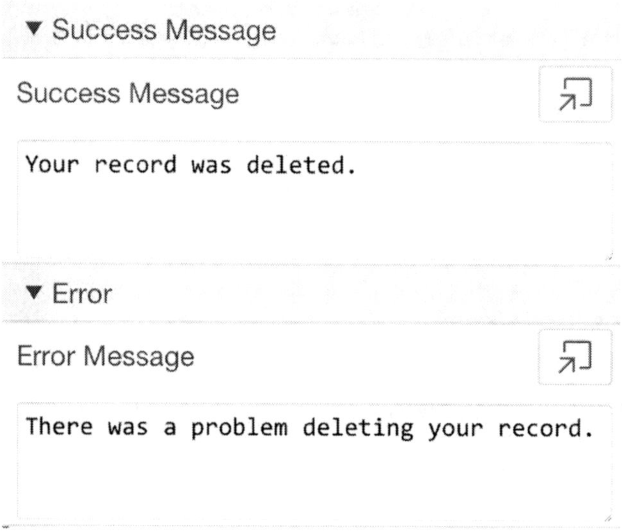

▼ Success Message

| Success Message | ⬈ |

> Your record was deleted.

▼ Error

| Error Message | ⬈ |

> There was a problem deleting your record.

Figure 7-8. *Success and error message properties*

Go to the property editor and add success and error messages to the processes in the Employee Data Entry and Sales Commission pages. Run a page and make some changes. Your specified success messages will be displayed when the page is re-rendered.

Success and error messages can contain HTML code and item references. For example, suppose that you want the success message for the Delete process to indicate the number of records affected, the way the SQL command window in the APEX SQL Workshop does. How do you get the number of affected records into the process' success message?

The solution is to use the built-in PL/SQL function SQL%RowCount. If you call this function after executing an SQL command, it will return the number of affected records. So for the Delete process, you can assign that value to a hidden item (call it P17_DELETE_COUNT) and then refer to that item within the message body. The revised PL/SQL code for the Delete process is shown in Listing 7-13 (the bold line is new).

Listing 7-13. Revising the Delete Process of Listing 7-2

```
begin
    delete from EMP
    where EmpNo = :P17_DELETE_EMPNO;

    :P17_DELETE_COUNT := SQL%RowCount;
end;
```

You can then change the text of the success message to this:

```
There were &P17_DELETE_COUNT. record(s) deleted.
```

Note that the reference to P17_DELETE_COUNT uses bind variable syntax in the PL/SQL process, but substitution string syntax in the HTML message.

Conditional Processes

So far, each process you have written has had an associated button, and you used its When Button Pressed property to specify the association between the process and its button. This is a natural and typical way to use processes, and usually all you need.

There are some situations in which the When Button Pressed property is not sufficient. One such situation is when a process can be executed by more than one button. For example, return to the Employee Data Entry page, and suppose that you want to log all changes made to the EMP table. To do so, first go to the SQL Workshop and create the table shown in Listing 7-14. This table will have a record for each change, which describes what change was made, who made it, and when.

Listing 7-14. SQL Code to Create the EMPLOG Table

```
create table EMPLOG(Request varchar2(20),
                    UserName varchar2(20),
                    RequestDate Date)
```

Then create a process for the Employee Data Entry page, called LogChanges, having the PL/SQL code of Listing 7-15.

Listing 7-15. PL/SQL Code for the LogChanges Process

```
begin
    insert into EMPLOG (Request, UserName, RequestDate)
    values (:REQUEST, :APP_USER, sysdate);
end;
```

This code refers to the built-in variables APP_USER and REQUEST. The variable APP_USER holds the name of the logged-in user, and the variable REQUEST holds the name of the button that was clicked. Thus, the LogChanges process inserts a record into the EMPLOG table containing the name of the button that was clicked, the user who did the clicking, and the date it occurred.

This process needs to execute each time the Insert, Delete, or Update button is clicked, but not when the Get Info button is clicked. Clearly, the When Button Pressed property is of no use here because it lets you choose only a single button.

The solution to this conundrum is to forego the When Button Pressed property and instead use the process' Type property (which is also in its Condition section). This property lets you specify additional conditions that must be true for the process to fire. The options are the same as for conditional rendering, as was described in Chapter 6. You should set the condition for the LogChanges process as shown in Figure 7-9: leave the When Button Pressed property blank, set the condition type to SQL Expression, and enter the following expression:

```
:REQUEST in ('Insert', 'Delete', 'Update')
```

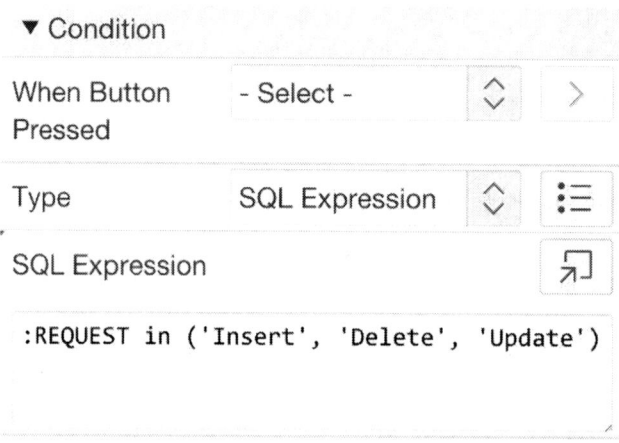

Figure 7-9. Condition section for the LogChanges process

This expression ensures that the process will fire only when a button named Insert, Delete, or Update is clicked. Because each of these buttons also has its own process, two processes will execute when one of them is clicked. The two processes will execute in order of their sequence number.

You might be thinking that you don't need a separate process to do the logging; instead, you could append the logging code to each of the button-specific processes for these buttons. This strategy works, but is not advisable. The problem is that doing so would duplicate the logging code, which means that if you want to change the way the logging works (such as by adding a new column to the EMPLOG table or changing the RequestDate column to hold the time as well as the date), you will need to update it in three places. Moreover, if you decide to add a new button to the page, you must remember to extract this logging code from an existing button and add it to the process for the new button. It is much more elegant and practical to have a separate process that can be called by multiple buttons.

Another situation in which a process needs an explicit condition is when it is associated with an item instead of a button. Recall that items of certain types (i.e., radio groups, select lists, text fields, and password fields) can be configured to perform a submit action. Such items should be able to have an associated process. The problem is that the When Button Pressed property doesn't give you the option of picking an item. You therefore must express the condition via the Type property.

For example, consider again the Employee Data Entry page. Suppose that you remove the Get Info button from the Update Employee region and instead configure the select list P17_UPDATE_EMPNO to submit when changed. For that submit action to execute the Get Info process, you need to set the process' condition to be the following SQL expression:

```
:REQUEST = 'P17_UPDATE_EMPNO'
```

Note the different uses of the two items in this expression: the left side of the equality refers to the value of item REQUEST (which is why it is prepended by a colon), whereas the right side refers to the name of the item P17_UPDATE_EMPNO (which is why it is in quotes). This is because the REQUEST variable holds the name of the object making the request, which is a string. In other words, there is no colon in front of P17_UPDATE_EMPNO because the expression is interested in the *name* of that item, not the *value* it holds.

Page Rendering Processes

So far, all of the processes in this chapter have executed during submit. The next topic is to consider processes that execute during page rendering. This situation often arises when a page uses redirection instead of submit, such as when linking from a record in a report.

For an example, let's build a page called Single Record View, which appears in Figure 7-10 and will be page 19 of the demo application.

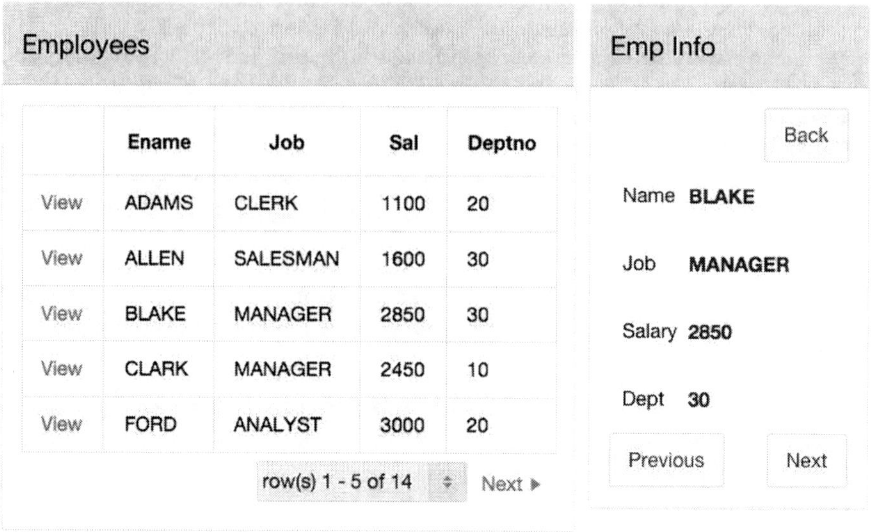

	Ename	Job	Sal	Deptno
View	ADAMS	CLERK	1100	20
View	ALLEN	SALESMAN	1600	30
View	BLAKE	MANAGER	2850	30
View	CLARK	MANAGER	2450	10
View	FORD	ANALYST	3000	20

Employees

row(s) 1 - 5 of 14 ⬍ Next ▶

Emp Info

Back

Name **BLAKE**

Job **MANAGER**

Salary **2850**

Dept **30**

Previous   Next

Figure 7-10. *Single Record View page*

The page contains two regions. The Employees region holds an employee report. A user can select a record by clicking the link in its first column; APEX responds by placing that record's values into the items of the Emp Info region. The items in Emp Info have the type Display Only to keep them from being modified. The Emp Info region has three buttons: the Previous and Next buttons select the previous or next record, and the Back button "unselects" the current record.

Although Figure 7-10 shows both the Employees and the Emp Info regions, they actually are never displayed together. The Employees region is displayed only when there is no selected record, and the Emp Info region is displayed only when there is a selected record.

In particular, a user begins by examining the employee information in report mode, which displays only the report region. Selecting a record causes the page to enter single-record mode, during which the report is hidden and the Emp Info region is displayed. The user can click the Next and Previous buttons to navigate through the records one at a time, or the user can click the Back button to hide the region and return to report mode. A similar feature is built into APEX interactive reports — clicking the pencil icon in an interactive report selects that record and puts you into single-record mode, and clicking the Cancel button from the single-record region brings you back to the report.

Several issues arise when you try to implement this page. How and when do the items in the Emp Info region get their values? How does the page know whether it is in single-record mode or report mode? How are the Previous and Next buttons implemented? These issues are discussed in the following sections.

Executing a Process Without a Submit

The source query of the employee report is:

```
select EmpNo, EName, Job, Sal, DeptNo
from EMP
order by EName
```

Note that the first column of the report is the employee number. This value is not displayed; instead, the report displays a link. Clicking the link sets a hidden item named P19_EMPNO to the selected employee number, and redirects to the same page. You specify this link the same way as in Chapter 6: Set the type of the column to Link; click the column's Target property to bring up the Link Builder wizard page; then fill out the page, setting the target to page 19, and setting the item P19_EMPNO to #EMPNO#.

Now that you have configured the link to set the value of P19_EMPNO to the chosen employee, you should create a process that retrieves the other values for that employee from the EMP table. Let's call this process FetchRecord. Its PL/SQL code appears in Listing 7-16.

Listing 7-16. PL/SQL Code for the FetchRecord Process

```
begin
    select EName, Job, Sal, DeptNo
    into :P19_ENAME, :P19_JOB, :P19_SALARY, :P19_DEPTNO
    from EMP
    where EmpNo = :P19_EMPNO;
end;
```

This code is similar to Listing 7-5, which is the code associated with the Get Info button on the Employee Data Entry page. That process executed on submit, conditional on its button. This process, however, cannot execute on submit because it is invoked by a link, and links perform a redirect. What you therefore need is for the process to execute after the redirection — that is, during page rendering.

Look again at the Rendering section of the page designer. There is a folder labeled Processes toward the bottom of the tree. The processes in this folder are executed during page rendering. You create these processes in the usual way, by right-clicking the folder and selecting the Create Process menu item. Figure 7-11 shows the contents of the Processes folder after creating the FetchRecord process.

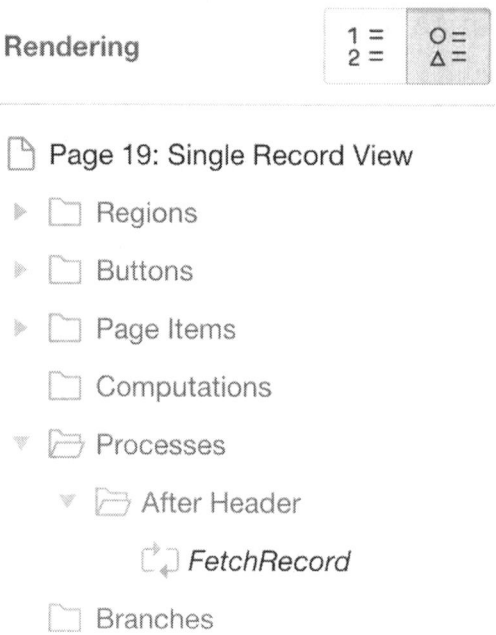

Figure 7-11. Rendering section of the page designer

Note that the process is placed in a subfolder labeled After Header, which corresponds to a specific point during page rendering: the time after the server generates the page's HTML header code, but before it generates the page contents. This is the default for executing a page rendering process. If you want finer control over when your processes execute, switch the page designer to the Group by Processing Order view (by clicking the button containing the 1 and 2). The rendering section will then be displayed as in Figure 7-12.

Rendering

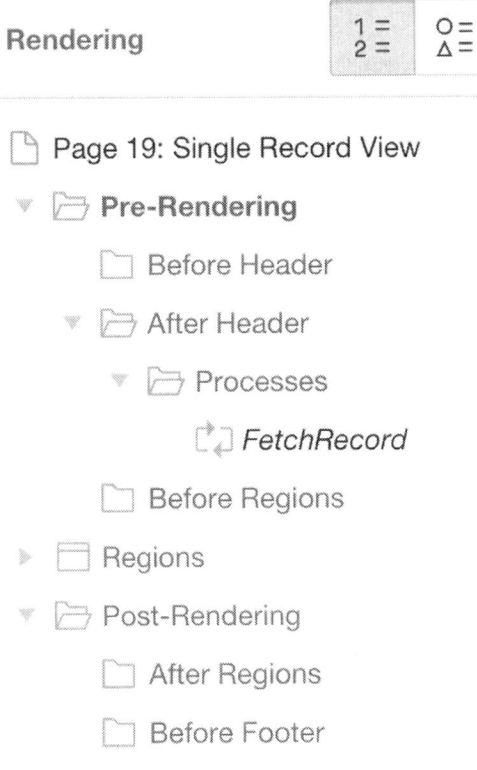

Figure 7-12. *Rendering section grouped by processing order*

Here you see all seven rendering stages: three *pre-rendering* stages; the stage where the regions are rendered; and three *post-rendering* stages. A process can be assigned to any of the six pre- or post-rendering stages. Note in this case that FetchRecord must execute during pre-rendering, because APEX will need to have the fetched values available when it renders the items. Since the three pre-rendering stages have little practical difference, you might as well use the default After Header stage.

Now that you have created FetchRecord as a page-rendering process, there is another question: how frequently should it execute? You certainly don't want the process to execute every time the page is rendered; instead, you want it to execute only when the user has selected a record. In other words, the process should be conditional on the following SQL expression:

```
:P19_EMPNO is not null
```

Report Mode vs. Single-Record Mode

A non-null value for P19_EMPNO identifies the selected record. Conversely, a null value for P19_EMPNO indicates that no record has been selected. Thus, the Back button should simply redirect to the same page, setting P19_EMPNO to null.

In other words, the value of P19_EMPNO determines whether the page is in report mode or single-record mode. The two regions can use the value of that item to determine their conditional rendering. In particular, the Employees region should render when the item value is null, and the Emp Info region should render when the value is not null. In this way, only one of them will be visible at any time.

Implementing Previous and Next Buttons

The Previous and Next buttons belong to the Emp Info region. Clicking them causes the region to display the previous (or next) record of the table. This section considers two different ways to implement this functionality. The first approach is easier to understand, but it has some limitations. The second approach is a bit harder to understand, but is much more elegant.

Approach 1: Different Processes for Previous and Next

Consider the Previous button, which needs to select the previous record. Assume for the moment that "previous record" means the record having the next-lowest employee number. The PL/SQL code in Listing 7-17 does the job.

Listing 7-17. Simplified Code for the Previous Button, Approach 1

```
declare
    v_prevEmp number(4,0);
begin
    select max(EmpNo)
    into v_prevEmp
    from EMP
    where EmpNo < :P19_EMPNO;

    if v_prevEmp is not null then
        :P19_EMPNO := v_prevEmp;
    end if;
end;
```

The if-statement is necessary to handle the case when you try to find the previous record of the first employee. In this case, the query would return a null value. Without the if-statement, the button would put that null into P19_EMPNO, effectively deselecting the record and returning to report mode. By using the if-statement, clicking the Previous button from the first record will have no effect.

Now suppose that you want to use a different column to determine the previous record. For example, suppose that you want the Single Record View page to use EName.

The preceding query does not extend easily to this case. Instead, you need to use the SQL analytic function lag, which finds the previous value based on a specified sort order. Listing 7-18 gives the resulting PL/SQL code.

Listing 7-18. PL/SQL Code for the Previous Button, Approach 1

```
declare
    v_prevEmp number(4,0);
begin
    select PrevEmp
    into v_prevEmp
    from (select EmpNo, lag(EmpNo) over (order by EName) as PrevEmp
          from EMP)
    where EmpNo = :P19_EMPNO;

    if v_prevEmp is not null then
        :P19_EMPNO := v_prevEmp;
    end if;
end;
```

The inner query creates a two-column table of employee numbers, in which each employee is paired with the employee appearing immediately before in the sort order. The outer query then selects the record from that table whose EmpNo value equals P19_EMPNO, and returns the PrevEmp value of that record.

In addition to the lag function, SQL also has the lead function that behaves the same way, except that it returns the next-highest value in the sort order. This function can be used in the implementation of the Next button, and its PL/SQL code is similar (and thus omitted).

Because the Previous and Next buttons each have their own process, you should set their actions to submit. You also need to configure each process to execute conditionally on its button. Although this is not the best solution to the problem, it works well and is worth implementing just to see it in action.

Approach 2: A Unified Previous/Next Process

Approach 1 suffers from the fact the Previous and Next buttons don't have any visible effect when they get to the first or last record; to the user, they seem to have stopped working. An alternative idea is to hide the buttons when they are not applicable. To do this, the page needs to "read ahead". That is, in addition to keeping track of the current employee number, the page also needs to keep track of the previous and next values. This way, you can hide the Previous button if the previous value is null (and similarly for the Next button).

Create the hidden items P19_PREV and P19_NEXT to hold the previous and next employee numbers. Then, whenever a record is selected, a process can "read ahead" and assign the appropriate values to these items. This process, called FindPreviousNext, appears in Listing 7-19.

Listing 7-19. PL/SQL Code to Find Previous and Next Values, Approach 2

```
begin
    select PrevEmp, NextEmp
    into :P19_PREV, :P19_NEXT
    from (select EmpNo, lag(EmpNo)  over (order by EName) as PrevEmp,
                        lead(EmpNo) over (order by EName) as NextEmp
          from EMP)
    where EmpNo = :P19_EMPNO;
end;
```

This code is similar to the code in Listing 7-18, but has two advantages. First, it no longer needs the if-statement, because you want P19_PREV or P19_NEXT to contain null values when the first or last record is encountered. Second, the code is not button-specific. It should get executed whenever a record gets selected, regardless of whether the selection is via a link from the report or via one of the Previous or Next buttons. Thus there is no longer a need for each button to have its own process, or in fact for either button to have a process. Instead, the FindPreviousNext process can execute during page rendering, just like the FetchRecord process. It is conditional on P19_EMPNO being non-null (also like the FetchRecord process).

As a consequence, the Previous and Next buttons can be configured much more simply. Consider the Previous button (the Next button is similar). Because the previous value has already been saved in the item P19_PREV, you can configure the button to redirect when clicked, placing the value of P19_PREV into P19_EMPNO. See Figure 7-13.

Link Builder - Target

▼ Target

Type	Page in this application

Page	19

▼ Set Items

Name		Value	
P19_EMPNO	∧	&P19_PREV.	∧

Figure 7-13. Configuring the action of the Previous button

To summarize, approach 2 implements previous/next functionality as follows. You first create hidden items P19_PREV and P19_NEXT. You then create the process FindPreviousNext, which calculates the value of these two items using the code of Listing 7-19. The process executes during page rendering and is conditional on this expression:

```
:P19_EMPNO is not null
```

Finally, you configure the Previous and Next buttons to redirect to the current page, assigning a value to P19_EMPNO. The Previous button uses the value of P19_PREV, and the Next button uses the value of P19_NEXT. Each button also uses conditional rendering, so that it displays only when its associated item value is not null.

As a result, the entire page consists of two relatively small processes: one that fetches the values of the selected record, and one that calculates the employee number of the previous and next records. A user will select a record by clicking either a link or a Previous/Next button. In each case, the page will determine the employee number of the selected record, save it to the item P19_EMPNO, and redirect. Everything works without any submit operations.

Report Data Entry

Another use for the report mode/single-record mode idea is to support data entry. To illustrate this idea, let's build the Report Data Entry page, which appears in Figure 7-14 and is page 20 of the demo application. The three regions of the page are shown together in the figure, but in actuality only one region is visible at a time. The page will be in report mode, update mode, or insert mode, depending on which region is visible.

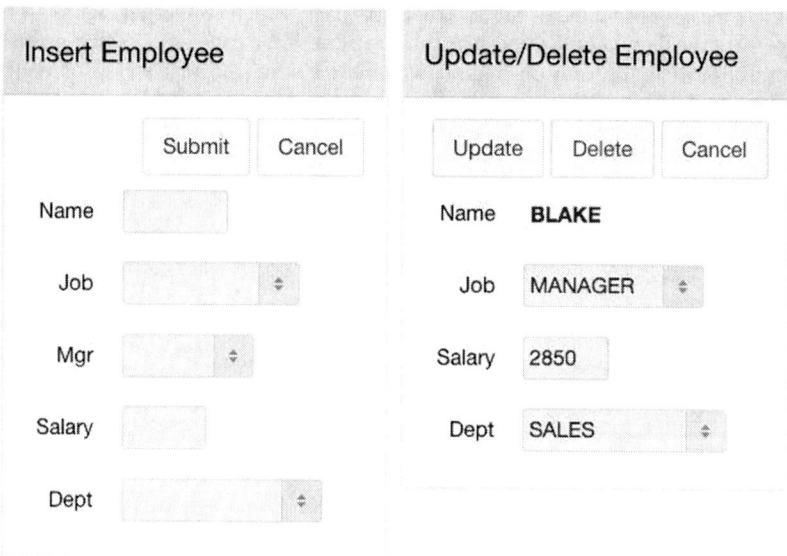

Figure 7-14. Report Data Entry demo page

Initially, the page displays the Employees region in report mode. From there, the user can click the Insert button to move to insert mode or click one of the Edit links to move to update mode.

The page displays the Insert Employee region when in insert mode. This region is essentially the same as the corresponding region in the Employee Data Entry page. Its Submit button creates a new EMP record having the specified values, and then clears the items in anticipation of another insertion. The Cancel button returns to report mode.

The page displays the Update/Delete Employee region when in update mode. The region's items are initially populated with the chosen employee's information. Clicking the Delete button deletes the chosen record and returns to report mode. Alternatively, the user can change item values in the region and click the Update button, which updates the database and returns to report mode. Clicking the Cancel button simply returns to report mode.

Now that you understand how the page works, you can turn to the problem of implementing it. The following sections examine the implementation of each region.

Implementing the Report Region

The implementation of the report is essentially the same as in the Single Record View page of Figure 7-10. One difference is that you will need a hidden item to distinguish between the three modes. Call this item P20_MODE. It will have the values Report, Insert, and Update, as appropriate, with a null value indicating report mode.

The EmpNo column is implemented as a link. The link redirects to the same page, and sets values for two items when it redirects: P20_EMPNO is set to the chosen employee number, and P20_MODE is set to Update. The Insert button also redirects, setting P20_MODE to Insert. The region is conditionally rendered according to this SQL expression:

```
:P20_MODE is null or :P20_MODE = 'Report'
```

Implementing the Insert Region

A new EMP record needs nine column values, but only five are specified by the user. The Insert Employee region has an item for each of these five values. The items are named P20_INSERT_ENAME, P20_INSERT_JOB, and so on. The region also has two buttons, named Submit and Clear. The region is conditionally rendered according to this SQL expression:

```
:P20_MODE = 'Insert'
```

The Submit button performs a submit operation. It has an associated process that does two things: it executes an SQL insert command, and it sets its items to null. Its code appears in Listing 7-20.

Listing 7-20. PL/SQL Code to Insert a New Employee Record

```
begin
    insert into EMP(EName, Job, Mgr, Sal, DeptNo, HireDate, Comm, Offsite)
    values (:P20_INSERT_ENAME,
            :P20_INSERT_JOB,
            :P20_INSERT_MANAGER,
            :P20_INSERT_SALARY,
            :P20_INSERT_DEPTNO,
            current_date,  0,  'N');
```

```
    -- Clear the region's visible items.
    :P20_INSERT_ENAME    := null;
    :P20_INSERT_JOB      := null;
    :P20_INSERT_MANAGER  := null;
    :P20_INSERT_SALARY   := null;
    :P20_INSERT_DEPTNO   := null;

    -- But do not change the mode.
end;
```

The Cancel button redirects, setting P20_MODE to Report.

Implementing the Update/Delete Region

The items in the Update/Delete Employee region get populated by a process named FetchRecordForUpdate, which executes during page rendering and is conditional on the SQL expression

```
:P20_MODE = 'Update'
```

The code for this process appears in Listing 7-21. The code is essentially the same as the FetchRecord process in Listing 7-16, except that it also deals with the lost update problem. (This issue was not relevant with the Single Record View page because that page performed no updates.) It deals with it by calculating the hash value of the three modifiable items and saving it in the hidden item P20_HASH.

Listing 7-21. PL/SQL Code for the FetchRecordForUpdate Process

```
declare
    v_valuesToHash apex_t_varchar2;
begin
    -- First, fetch the employee record and save its values.
    select EName, Job, Sal, DeptNo
    into :P20_UPDATE_ENAME,
        :P20_UPDATE_JOB,
        :P20_UPDATE_SALARY,
        :P20_UPDATE_DEPTNO
    from EMP
    where EmpNo = :P20_EMPNO;

    -- Then save the hash of the updatable values.
    v_valuesToHash := apex_t_varchar2(:P20_UPDATE_JOB, :P20_UPDATE_SALARY,
                                      :P20_UPDATE_DEPTNO);
    :P20_HASH := apex_util.get_hash(v_valuesToHash);
end;
```

The PL/SQL code for the region's Delete button executes an SQL delete command, similar to Listing 7-2, and then returns to report mode. Its code appears in Listing 7-22.

Listing 7-22. Code for the Delete Process

```
begin
    -- First, delete the record.
    delete from EMP
    where EmpNo = :P20_EMPNO;

    -- Then return to report mode.
    :P20_MODE := 'Report';
end;
```

At first glance, having the process return to report mode seems like a nice, user-friendly feature. But it also has an ulterior motive. It turns out that if you remove the statement, then deleting a record would generate an error. (Try it!) The problem is that the value of P20_EMPNO would refer to a non-existant record, which means that the FetchRecordForUpdate process would fail when it attempts to fetch it. Setting P20_MODE to Report solves the problem.

The code for the Update button executes an SQL update command after ensuring that there is no lost update. The code is essentially the same as the update code for the Employee Data Entry page (refer to Listing 7-10), additionally setting P20_MODE to Report. The code appears in Listing 7-23.

Listing 7-23. Code for the Update Process

```
declare
    v_valuesToHash apex_t_varchar2;
begin
    -- First re-read the data.
    select apex_t_varchar2(Job, Sal, DeptNo)
    into v_valuesToHash
    from EMP
    where EmpNo = :P20_EMPNO;

    -- Then compare it with the original data.
    if :P20_HASH = apex_util.get_hash(v_valuesToHash)
    then
        -- The record hasn't changed, so update it.
        update EMP
        set Job    = :P20_UPDATE_JOB,
            Sal    = :P20_UPDATE_SALARY,
            DeptNo = :P20_UPDATE_DEPTNO
        where EmpNo = :P20_EMPNO;

        -- And return to report mode.
        :P20_MODE := 'Report';
```

```
else
    -- The record has changed, so abort.
    raise_application_error(-20000,
                    'The record is out of date. Get it again.');
end if;
end;
```

APEX Built-In Processes

If you look back at the processes you have written so far, you will see that they make use of
certain basic tasks: retrieving the values of a record given its key; finding the key values of
the previous and next records given the current key value; updating the table by inserting,
deleting, or modifying a record; and clearing the session state for some items.

These tasks are common to many web applications. In fact, they are common enough
that APEX has provided built-in processes to perform them. This section examines
how to use these built-in processes, and the next section considers their strengths and
limitations. Knowing how and when to use the APEX built-in processes can relieve you of
the need to write PL/SQL code for the more common page development tasks.

To see these processes in action, let's build the Process Practice page shown in
Figure 7-15, which will be page 21 of the demo application. This page allows a user to
perform several operations on the EMP table. When the user chooses an employee from
the select list, the salary of that employee appears automatically in the Salary text box.
If the user modifies the contents of that text box and clicks the Update Salary button,
the change will be made in the EMP table. If the user clicks the Delete Employee button,
the chosen employee will be deleted from the table. Clicking the Clear button clears the
value of both the employee and salary items. And clicking the Previous Emp (or Next Emp)
button changes the chosen employee to the previous (or next) employee in the table.

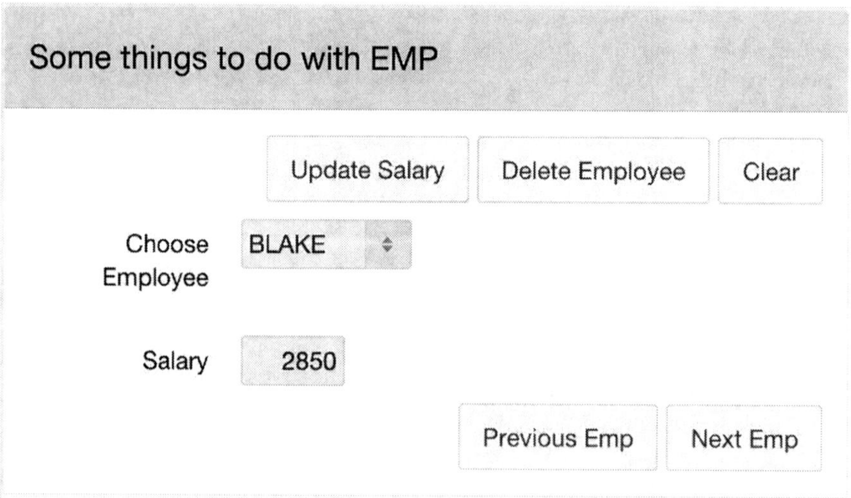

Figure 7-15. *Process Practice page*

The point of this page is that its functionality can be implemented entirely by APEX built-in processes. The following subsections describe the relevant process types and how they are used.

Automatic Row Fetch

An *automatic row fetch (ARF)* process is similar to the FetchRecord process of Listing 7-16. That is, its job is to fetch the record from the database having a specified key value, and place the values from that record into appropriate items of the page. For example, the Process Practice page has an ARF process that will automatically fetch the salary of the chosen employee and place it in the Salary text box. As with the FetchRecord process, the ARF process must be executed during page rendering because its job is to assign initial values to items.

To create an ARF process, go to the rendering tree for the page and create a new process. Give it a name and set its type to Automatic Row Fetch. The property editor will then display additional properties in the Settings section. You use those properties to specify the name of the table, the name of the key column, and the name of an item that will hold a key value. Figure 7-16 shows these properties for the Process Practice page.

▼ Identification

Name	Fetch EMP Records
Type	Automatic Row Fetch

▼ Settings

Table Name	EMP
Primary Key Column	EMPNO
Primary Key Item	P21_EMPNO

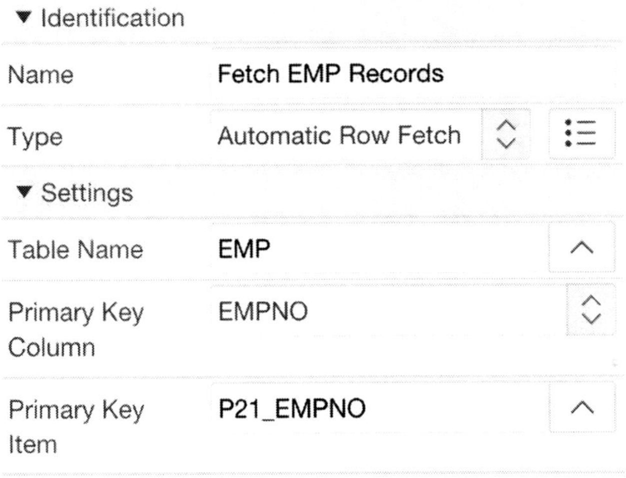

Figure 7-16. *Properties of an ARF process*

In addition to creating this ARF process, you need to create the items P21_EMPNO and P21_SALARY. Item P21_EMPNO is a select list whose values are defined by the query:

```
select EName, EmpNo
from EMP
order by EName
```

You can set the action of the select list to be Redirect and Set Value. There is no need for it to submit because the ARF process executes during page rendering.

The property values in Figure 7-16 specify that the ARF process should grab the value from the item P21_EMPNO, go to the EMP table, and retrieve the row whose EmpNo column has that value. However, it doesn't say what the process should do with the retrieved values. For example, how does it know to place the salary into P21_SALARY? For that, the process uses the source properties of the page items.

Chapter 5 introduced the source of an item, in particular the source types Static Assignment and SQL Query, and discussed how they specify an item's initial value. There is another source type, Database Column, whose purpose is to tell the ARF process where to place the retrieved row values. The ARF process will place a row value into every Database Column item on the page.

When you set the source type of an item to Database Column, the property editor will display the property Database Column in the Source section. Enter the name of the column in capital letters. Figure 7-17 shows the Source properties for the item P21_SALARY. This specification tells the ARF process to initialize the item with the retrieved value of the Sal column. Note that the Source Used property value is Always... because you want the ARF process to ignore the current item value when fetching a new one.

▼ Source			
Type	Database Column	◇	☰
Database Column	**SAL**		
Used	Always, replacing any existing value in session state	◇	

Figure 7-17. *Configuring an item to receive a value from the ARF process*

You should now be able to run the page and observe the ARF process in action. Choose various employees from the select list and watch their salaries appear in the number field.

Recall that when you wrote the FetchRecord process, you configured it to execute only when the key value was not null. The ARF process, on the other hand, deals with a null key value by setting the page's Database Column items to null; thus it does not need to be conditional.

An ARF process wants to assign a value to every Database Column item on the page. If it finds an item whose column name not in the table, it will abort with an error message. Consequently, it is impossible to have ARF processes for two different tables on the same page.

Automatic Row Processing

Another built-in process type is *automatic row processing (ARP)*. An ARP process is the complement to ARF — Instead of fetching values from the specified table into items, it is responsible for using item values to update the table.

An ARP process needs the same information as an ARF process, plus a little more. You specify a table, the key column of the table, and the item that holds the key value. You also must specify what combination of the three operations — Insert, Delete, and Update — you want the process to handle. Figure 7-18 shows the relevant ARP properties for the Process Practice page.

▼ Identification	
Name	**Process EMP Records**
Type	Automatic Row Processing (DML) ⌄
▼ Settings	
Table Name	**EMP**
Primary Key Column	EMPNO
Primary Key Item	P21_EMPNO
Return Key Into Item	
Supported Operations	☐ Insert ☑ Update ☑ Delete

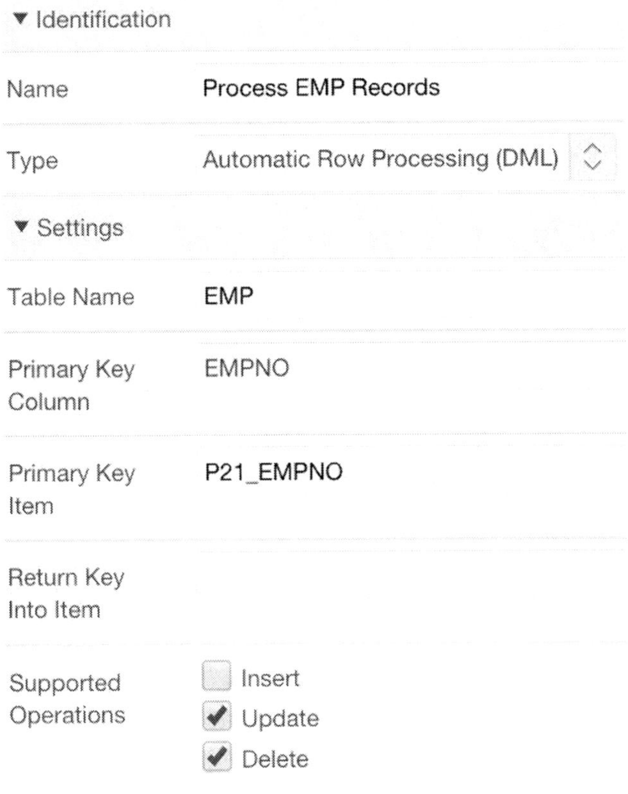

Figure 7-18. Properties of an ARP process

An ARP process should execute during submit and be conditional on its associated buttons. For example, the ARP process of the Process Practice page is associated with both the Update Salary and Delete Employee buttons. Assuming that these buttons have the names UpdateSalary and DeleteEmployee, the process' condition will be specified by the SQL expression:

```
:REQUEST in ('UpdateSalary', 'DeleteEmployee')
```

199

When one of these buttons performs a submit operation, the ARP process will execute one of its supported operations. But how does it know which of the operations to perform? For example, how does it know that the button named UpdateSalary wants to perform the Update operation, and DeleteEmployee wants to perform the Delete operation? There are two ways for a button to specify its intent. The first method is to set the Database Action property in the button's Behavior section. This property is blank by default, but can be set to SQL INSERT action, SQL DELETE action, or SQL UPDATE action.

Figure 7-19 shows the properties for the Update Salary button, showing that it wants the SQL UPDATE database action. The Delete Employee button is similarly set to the SQL DELETE database action.

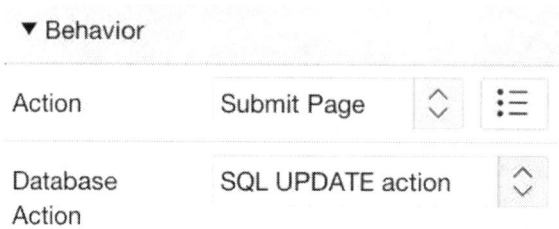

Figure 7-19. *Button's Behavior properties*

If a button does not have a specified value for Database Action, or if a non-button performs the submit, APEX uses the name of the request (which is the name of the item or button) to determine the operation. Figure 7-20 shows the naming convention, which can be found in the Help text for the Supported Operations property. The % character is a wildcard symbol that matches any string of characters, and the names are case-insensitive. For example, a button named SAVE (or Update, get_NEXT_emp, ChAnGe, etc.) will cause the ARP process to execute its SQL Update operation.

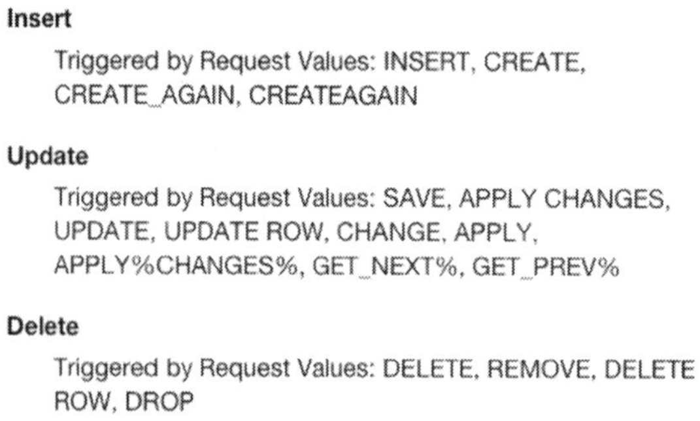

Insert
> Triggered by Request Values: INSERT, CREATE, CREATE_AGAIN, CREATEAGAIN

Update
> Triggered by Request Values: SAVE, APPLY CHANGES, UPDATE, UPDATE ROW, CHANGE, APPLY, APPLY%CHANGES%, GET_NEXT%, GET_PREV%

Delete
> Triggered by Request Values: DELETE, REMOVE, DELETE ROW, DROP

Figure 7-20. *Naming convention for ARP process requests*

After the ARP process determines the operation to execute, it uses the item values on the page to update the database. In particular, a Delete operation will delete the record having the specified key value, an Insert operation will insert a record having the values given by the items of type Database Column, and an Update operation will update the record having the specified key value with the values of the Database Column items.

After creating the ARP process on the Process Practice page, you should create the Update Salary and Delete Employee buttons. The action of each button should be Submit Page, and its Database Action should be SQL UPDATE or SQL DELETE, as appropriate. You now should be able to update a chosen employee by clicking the desired button on the Process Practice page. (However, you will not be able to delete until you create a Clear Session State process, as described in the next subsection.)

The ARF and ARP processes cooperate to guard against lost updates. You can verify this by opening the Process Practice page from two different machines and selecting the same employee on each; then update the salary of each. APEX will reject the second update because it is potentially in conflict with the first.

Because an ARP process encapsulates all behavior of the database operations, it cannot be customized. One problematic area concerns insertion. Recall that the earlier insertion processes (shown in Listing 7-3 and Listing 7-20) used default values for the columns HireDate, Comm, and Offsite. Such defaults are much more difficult to construct with an ARP process.

Clear Session State

When you write PL/SQL code for some task, it is easy enough to add statements to manipulate the session state. For example, recall the Report Data Entry page. The code for the Delete process in Listing 7-22 changes the value of P20_MODE after deleting the specified record. Similarly, the code for the Insert process in Listing 7-20 clears the items in its region in anticipation of another insertion operation. When you use an ARP process, however, such customization is not possible. The solution is to execute another process after the ARP process. The Clear Session State process type is often just what you need.

When you create a process of type Clear Session State, you are presented with several choices, as shown in Figure 7-21. The choice selected in the figure clears all items on the current page. Selecting the choice Clear Items brings up a wizard page in which you can specify one or more item names; executing the process will clear those items.

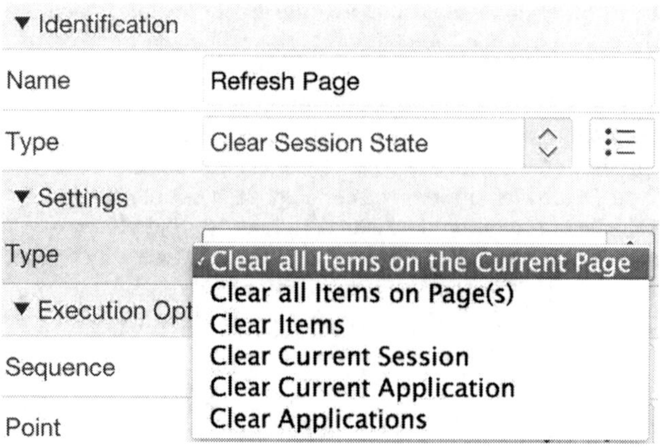

▼ Identification	
Name	Refresh Page
Type	Clear Session State

▼ Settings	
Type	

Clear all Items on the Current Page
Clear all Items on Page(s)
Clear Items
Clear Current Session
Clear Current Application
Clear Applications

▼ Execution Opt

Sequence

Point

Figure 7-21. Options for a Clear Session State process

A Clear Session State process typically executes during submit. The Process Practice page has one such process, which clears all items of the current page. Clearly, this process should execute when the Clear button is pressed. It should also execute when the Delete Employee button is pressed, in order to reset the value of P21_EMPNO (and thereby keep the ARF process from trying to fetch a non-existant record).

Form Pagination

When you built the Single Record View demo page, you wrote the PL/SQL process FindPreviousNext to compute the previous and next records of a chosen record; its code appeared in Listing 7-19. The APEX process type Form Pagination has similar functionality.

A process of type Form Pagination should be performed during page rendering. It requires you to specify the usual things: the name of the table, the name of the key column, and the item that holds the key value. In addition, you will need to specify the navigation order, the items holding the "read-ahead" previous and next values, and (optionally) an item that displays the record count. Figure 7-22 shows these properties for the Process Practice page.

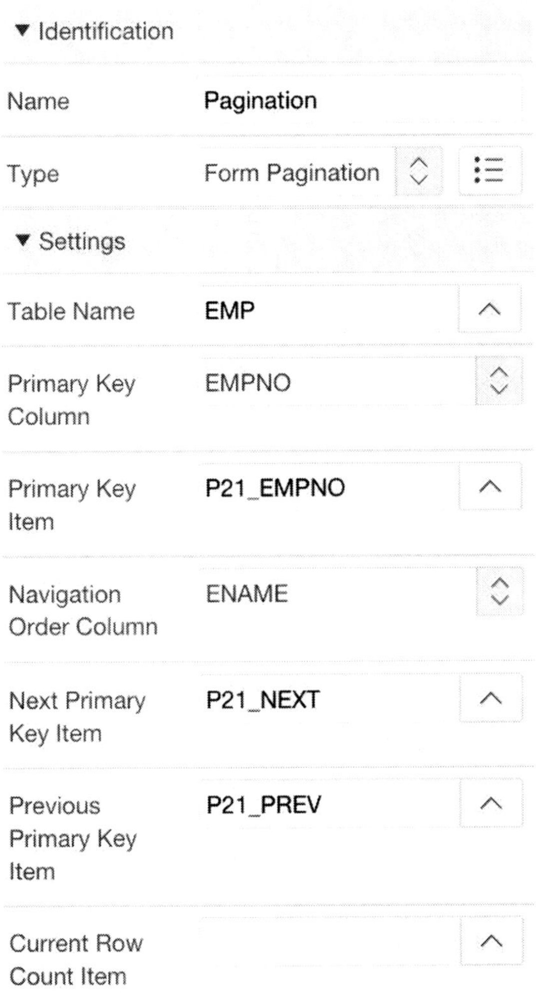

▼ Identification

Name	**Pagination**
Type	Form Pagination

▼ Settings

Table Name	**EMP**
Primary Key Column	EMPNO
Primary Key Item	**P21_EMPNO**
Navigation Order Column	ENAME
Next Primary Key Item	**P21_NEXT**
Previous Primary Key Item	**P21_PREV**
Current Row Count Item	

Figure 7-22. Properties for a Form Pagination process

The page-pagination process looks at the value of the primary key item, calculates the key values of the previous and next records in the specified navigation order, and places those values in the Previous Primary Key and Next Primary Key items. That is, its job is to calculate the key values of the previous and next records, but it does not change the current record. The responsibility for moving to the previous or next record lies with the buttons.

Recall that the Single Record View page already addressed this same issue. The Previous Record button simply needs to redirect, placing the value of the Previous Primary Key item into the Primary Key item. As before, use the Link Builder wizard to specify the details of the redirect. Figure 7-23 shows the configuration of the Previous Record button; the configuration of the Next Record button is similar.

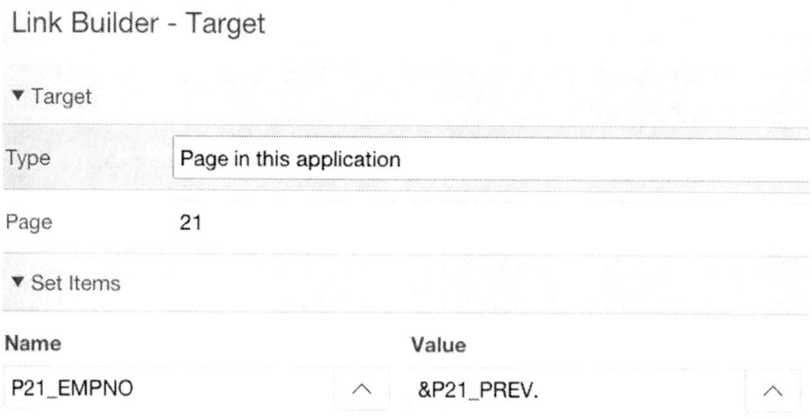

Link Builder - Target

▼ Target

Type	Page in this application
Page	21

▼ Set Items

Name		Value	
P21_EMPNO	∧	&P21_PREV.	∧

Figure 7-23. Configuring a Pagination Process button

Using the Built-In Processes

Now that you understand the functionality of the various built-in processes, let's try to apply them to a more realistic situation than the Process Practice page. This section examines the earlier pages you wrote, and considers the possibility of replacing any of their PL/SQL processes with built-in ones.

Employee Data Entry

This page, which was shown in Figure 7-4, does database retrieval and modification exclusively, and thus seems a perfect opportunity for using ARF and ARP processes. In particular, the ARF process ought to replace the process for the Get Current Info button, and the ARP process ought to replace the processes for the Delete, Insert, and Update buttons. The issue is that these latter operations are implemented in different regions, with each region having its own items. This duplication of items causes two problems.

The first problem concerns the duplicated key value. Note that the Delete Employee and Update Employee regions both have items for the column EmpNo. When you configure an ARP process, you tell it which page item holds the key value, and the process will always use that item when it needs to know the key value. Consequently, the ARP process will be able to reference just one of those items, and the other item will be useless.

The second problem concerns the duplicated values for Job, Salary, and Dept. The ARP process cannot handle two items assigned to the same column. When it performs an insert (or update) operation, it inserts (or updates) the value from every Database Column item on the page. If there are two items for the same column, it has no way of knowing which one to use.

The solution is to implement one region using the built-in processes, and implement the other regions using PL/SQL processes. Here, the implementation of the Delete Employee and Insert Employee regions is relatively simple, so a good strategy is to leave these regions alone and just modify the Update Employee region. Doing so requires the following tasks:

1. Delete the existing PL/SQL processes for the two buttons.

2. Set the source type of each item in the region to Database Column, having the appropriate column value.

3. Create an ARF process for the EMP table, specifying P17_UPDATE_EMPNO as its key-valued item. This process should execute on page rendering.

4. Create an ARP process for the EMP table, specifying P17_UPDATE_EMPNO as its key-valued item. Set its Supported Operations property to Update only by unchecking the boxes for the other two operations. This process should execute on submit, and be associated with the Update button.

5. Set the action of the GET CURRENT INFO button to submit. (Alternatively, get rid of the button and set the action of P17_UPDATE_EMPNO to Redirect and Set Value.)

6. Set the Database Action of the Update button to be SQL UPDATE.

Sales Commissions

This page, which was shown in Figure 7-6, has two processes that calculate employee commissions. These processes perform some database operations, but primarily perform numeric calculations. These processes do not correspond at all to the built-in processes.

Single Record View

This page, which was shown in Figure 7-10, consists of two regions that allow a user to switch between two ways of viewing the EMP table. The Employees region is a report of the entire table; and the Emp Info region shows a single record, with Previous and Next buttons to navigate through the table. The page displays only one region at a time, depending on whether it is in report mode or single-record mode.

The page has two processes, both executing during page rendering. The FetchRecord process fetches the record specified by hidden item P19_EMPNO, and the FindPreviousNext process calculates the key value of the previous and next records. These two processes are almost identical in function to the built-in ARF and form pagination processes. You can thus revise the page as follows:

1. Delete the two existing processes.

2. Create an ARF process for the EMP table, to execute during page rendering and using the existing hidden item P19_EMPNO as the key-valued item.

3. Create a Form Pagination process for the EMP table, to execute during page rendering and using P19_EMPNO as the key-valued item. Set the previous and next items to be the existing hidden items P19_PREV and P19_NEXT.

4. Set the source type of each visible item and the hidden P19_EMPNO item to Database Column, having the appropriate column value.

The replacement processes are so similar to the PL/SQL ones that nothing else needs to change. In particular, the definition of the column link and the behavior of the buttons remain the same. You can thus think of this page as a perfect example of the ARF and Form Pagination processes in action.

Report Data Entry

This page, which was shown in Figure 7-14, is a variation of the Employee Data Entry page. There is a region that displays a report on EMP, a region for the insert operation, and a region for the combined delete and update operations. The page is constructed so that only one of the regions is visible at a time, depending on whether the page is in report mode, insert mode, or update mode.

The page has four processes: a FetchRecordForUpdate process to fetch values of the current EMP record, and a process for each of the insert, delete, and update operations. You can replace these processes by one ARF and one ARP process, via the following tasks:

1. Delete the four existing processes.

2. Set the source type of each item to Database Column, having the appropriate column value.

3. Add an ARF process for the EMP table, to execute during page rendering and using the hidden item P20_EMPNO as the key-valued item.

4. Add an ARP process for the EMP table, to execute during page submit. Set its Supported Operations property to all three operations.

5. Set the Database Action of the Insert, Delete, and Update buttons to the appropriate SQL command.

6. Add a Clear Session State process to clear the items on the page, conditional on the Insert, Delete, and Modify buttons.

The Insert and Delete buttons use the session state process for different reasons. The Insert button needs to clear the value of its items in preparation for the next insert operation. The Delete button needs to clear the value of P20_EMPNO; otherwise, the ARF process will try unsuccessfully to fetch that deleted record when the page is re-rendered, and will abort ungracefully. In a more complicated example, it might be better to write a Clear Session State process for each button to clear just the necessary items, but here a single process that clears everything works just as well.

Note that the `Insert Employee` and `Update/Delete Employee` regions are never visible at the same time. When you built the page using PL/SQL processes, this was nothing more than a nice feature, based on the idea that hiding unneeded regions helps the user focus on the task at hand. However, this feature becomes essential if you implement the page using an ARP process. As mentioned earlier, an ARP process cannot handle multiple items of type `Database Column` for the same column, so the process would get confused if both regions were simultaneously visible. If the page design required that its three regions always be visible, you would be forced to use an ARP process for only one region and PL/SQL processes for the others.

APEX Built-in Form Pages

Although the APEX built-in processes save you time over having to write comparable PL/SQL processes, they still require you to develop the appropriate regions and items, configured so that the processes will work. To simplify things further, APEX provides wizards for creating prebuilt pages. You enter your information into the wizard, and it creates the necessary regions, items, buttons, and processes. Such wizards can be good shortcuts if you want what they produce.

To use one of these wizards, start at the `Create Page` wizard. On its first screen, select the `Form` icon (instead of the usual `Blank Page` icon). The application builder displays the screen shown in Figure 7-24.

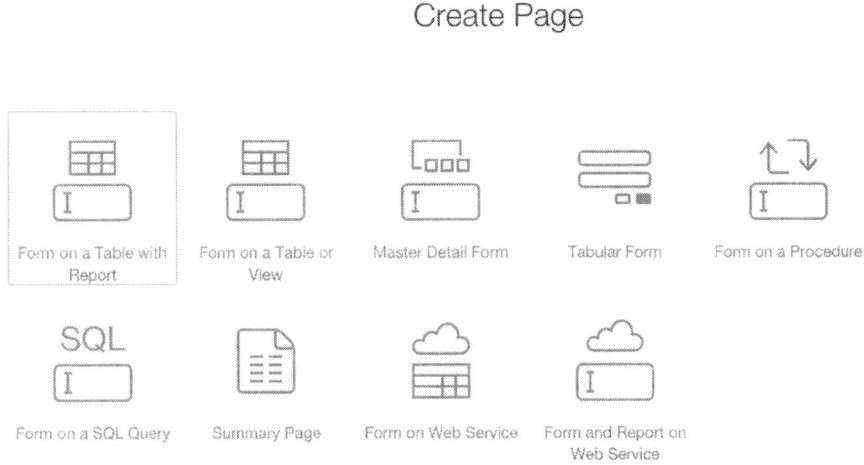

Figure 7-24. Possible APEX form pages

This section discusses three of these form pages: `Form on a Table or View`, `Form on a Table with Report`, and `Master Detail Form`.

Form on a Table or View

A Form on a Table or View page has a single region with items that correspond to the columns of a specified table (or view). Let's use the wizard to build a form page for the EMP table, called Simple Table Form. The page will be page 22 of the demo application and look like Figure 7-25.

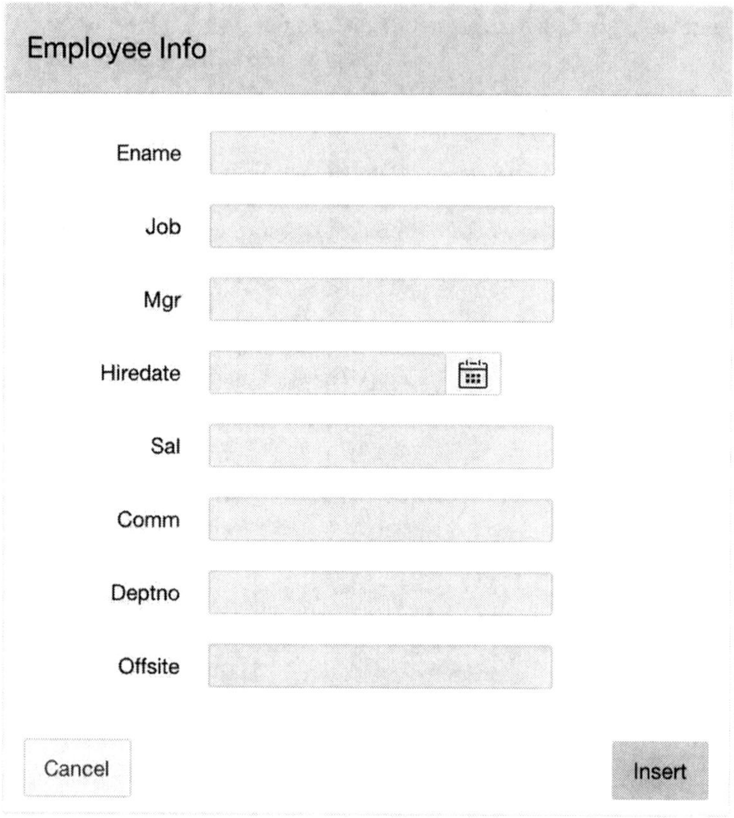

Figure 7-25. Automatically generated form on the EMP table

To create this page, select the Form on a Table or View icon (as shown in Figure 7-24). A wizard will lead you through the specification of the necessary information. It asks you for the standard page-creation information (such as page name, region title, and breadcrumb and navigation preferences), information about the table (table name, key column, and which columns to display) and the page functionality (the operations it should support and labels for buttons).

As part of the table information, the wizard will ask you to specify how a new key value is chosen. If you are using the EMP or DEPT table, choose Existing Trigger because those tables have triggers for exactly this purpose. Finally, the wizard will ask you where to branch after a button click. The examples so far have branched to the same page, which is also perfectly fine here. Chapter 9 will discuss the value of branching to other pages.

For consistency with the other pages in the demo, I chose to override the default button labels, so that the buttons are Insert, Delete, and Update.

It is useful to examine the components that were generated for this page, so you can understand what the wizard did. There are three processes: an ARF process executing during page rendering, an ARP process executing on submit, and a Clear Session State process to clear all page items on submit. The ARF and ARP processes use the hidden item P22_EMPNO to hold the key value. Each displayed column has an item of type Database Column and has a name derived from its column name. That is, the column Job has item P22_JOB, the column Mgr has item P22_MGR, and so on. Finally, there are buttons for Insert, Delete, Update, and Cancel.

The Insert and Update buttons both perform a submit action, having the respective database actions SQL Insert Action and SQL Update Action. Interestingly, the Delete button does not perform a submit, but instead redirects to the URL

```
javascript:apex.confirm(htmldb_delete_message,'DELETE');
```

The JavaScript confirm function displays a confirmation window; clicking Yes causes the page to submit using the request named DELETE. In other words, the Delete button actually does perform a submit, albeit indirectly through JavaScript. Moreover, because the request is named DELETE, the convention of Figure 7-20 tells the ARP process to use its delete operation.

Now let's examine how to use this page. Insertion is straightforward — simply enter values for the items and click the Insert button. The automatically generated ARP process will perform the insertion.

Deletion and updating are also possible, although it is not obvious how. The Delete and Update buttons are hidden until the P22_EMPNO item contains a value, at which time the Insert button takes its turn to become hidden. In other words, the region will be in either Insert mode or Delete/Update mode, depending on the value of P22_EMPNO.

The page assumes that a user will assign a value to P22_EMPNO via some other part of the application. When that occurs, the automatically generated ARF process will assign values to the displayed items, and the Update and Delete buttons will become visible. The user can then update those values or delete the record from the table, as desired. So for this page to be useful, there needs to be a way to assign values to P22_EMPNO.

It is important to realize that the page generated by the wizard is just a starting point. You are free to delete, modify, or create new components in any way that makes sense. For example, changing the types of some items to be list-based could help a lot. But make your changes carefully. For example, deleting or renaming the item containing the key value would break the entire page.

As an example, let's improve the Simple Table Form page. The first set of modifications is cosmetic: Change the type of P22_JOB and P22_MGR to be select lists; change the type of P22_DEPTNO and P22_OFFSITE to be radio groups; change the item labels; set the format mask of P22_HIREDATE; and organize the items into two columns. The second set of changes is functional: Change the type of P22_EMPNO from Hidden to Select List. Configure the select list so that it displays employee names, and has the action of redirect and set value. The resulting page is shown in Figure 7-26.

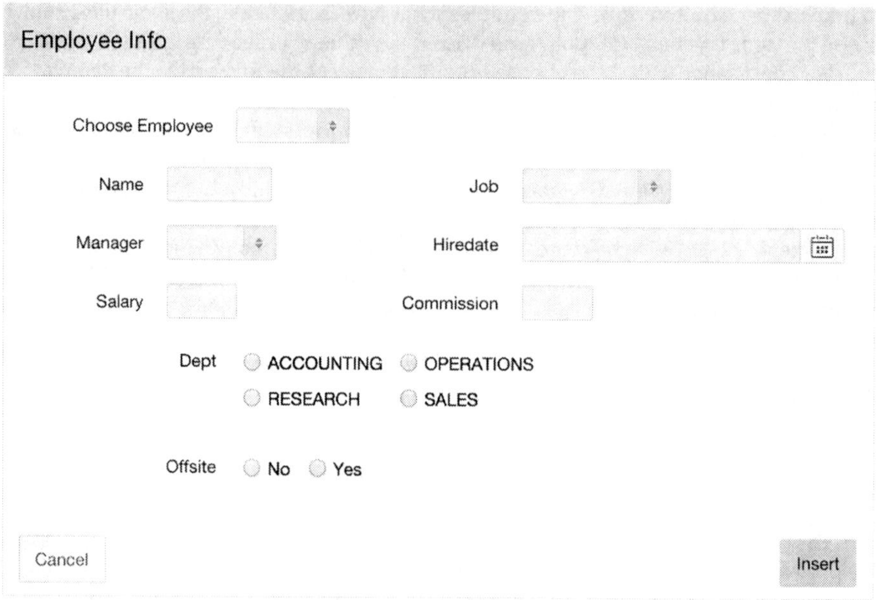

Figure 7-26. *Modifying the Simple Table Form page of Figure 7-25*

In addition to un-hiding P22_EMPNO, you will also need to change one of the properties in its Security section. The form wizard set the Session State Protection property to the value Checksum Required – Session Level. Checksums are important for avoiding malicious use, as you will see in Chapter 12. However, you don't need it here; in fact, it gets in the way. Change the property value to Unrestricted.

The result is that when a user chooses an employee name from the list, the corresponding employee number is saved in the session state. When the page redirects, the form's ARF process fills each item with the corresponding column value from that employee's EMP record, and the region enters update mode. For example, Figure 7-27 displays the resulting page after selecting employee ALLEN. Note that the Insert button is hidden and the Delete and Update buttons are now visible.

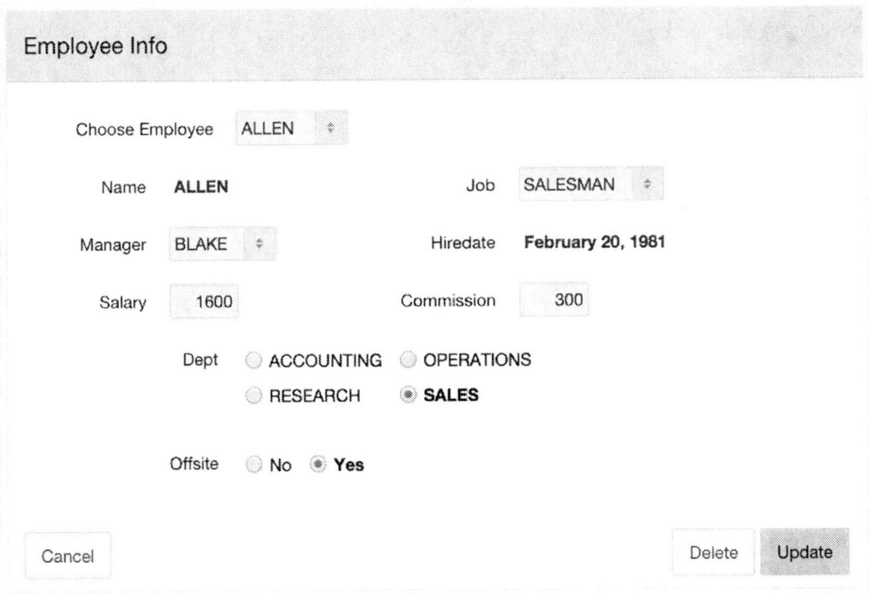

Figure 7-27. *Simple Table Form page in update mode*

A Form on Table or View page uses the same region for both insert mode and update mode. When P22_EMPNO is null, the page is in insert mode and displays the Insert button; and when that item is not null, it is in update mode and displays the Delete and Update buttons. Using the same region for both modes is economical, but it leads to this conundrum: how can you get different items to be displayed in different modes? For example in insert mode, you might want to display an item for every column of EMP, so that you can specify those values when inserting a new record. However in update mode, you might not want the user to be able to modify certain values (such as an employee's name or hire date). How do you handle these different requirements?

The solution is to display the items conditionally. Recall from Chapter 6 that each item has a Condition property section. You can hide an item during update mode by setting its condition to the SQL expression

```
:P22_EMPNO is null
```

Another option is to just disable the items instead of hiding them. Each item also has a Read Only property section. If its condition is satisfied, the item is displayed as if it were a Display Only item. Figure 7-28 shows the Read Only section for the item P22_ENAME. Its condition asserts that the item should be read-only when P22_EMPNO is not null (that is, when the form is in update mode).

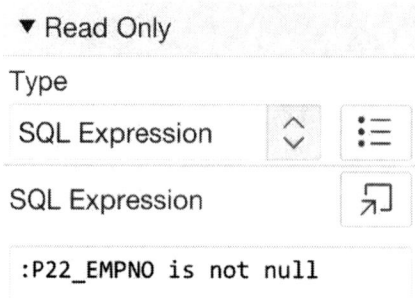

Figure 7-28. Item's Read Only section

One last customization for this page is to modify the behavior of the Cancel button. The wizard configures the button to simply redirect to the specified page, which means that clicking the button reverts unsubmitted changes of the form's items to their previously submitted values. Another possibility is to have the button clear all item values. To do this, click the button's Target property to enter the link builder, in which you can also set the Clear Cache property to clear page 22.

Form on Table with Report

A page created by the Form on a Table or View wizard cannot stand on its own; it needs a way for the user to select a desired record. The Simple Table Form page addressed this need by turning the EMPNO item into a visible select list. Another common technique is to pair the form with a report. This is the idea behind the built-in Form on Table with Report page.

Go to the Create Page wizard and select the Form on Table with Report icon. That wizard will generate two pages: a report page (which will be page 23) and a Form on Table or View page (which will be page 24). The wizard will ask you to specify information needed to generate the report (report type, table name, desired columns, and primary key) as well as the information needed to generate the form (which is the same as what it asked for before). The report page for the EMP table is shown in Figure 7-29, where I told the wizard to create an interactive report.

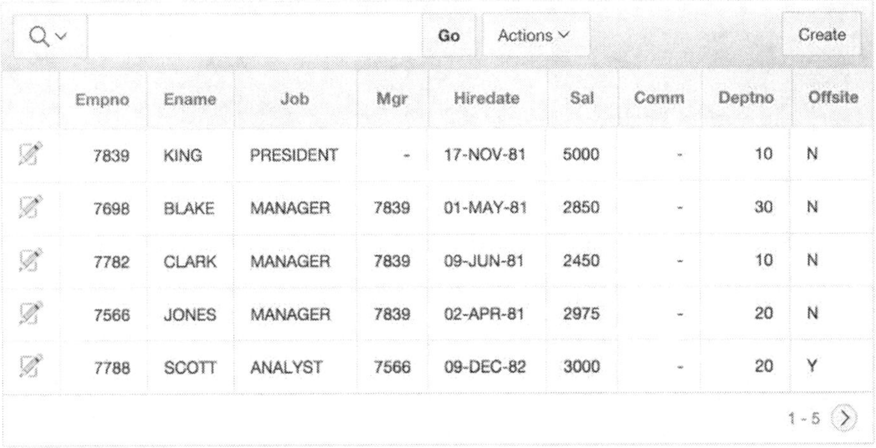

	Empno	Ename	Job	Mgr	Hiredate	Sal	Comm	Deptno	Offsite
✎	7839	KING	PRESIDENT	-	17-NOV-81	5000	-	10	N
✎	7698	BLAKE	MANAGER	7839	01-MAY-81	2850	-	30	N
✎	7782	CLARK	MANAGER	7839	09-JUN-81	2450	-	10	N
✎	7566	JONES	MANAGER	7839	02-APR-81	2975	-	20	N
✎	7788	SCOTT	ANALYST	7566	09-DEC-82	3000	-	20	Y

1 - 5 ⊙

Figure 7-29. *Report page of the Form on Table with Report wizard*

This report has a link for each row. Clicking one of the links redirects to the form page, setting the value of the hidden item P24_EMPNO to the chosen employee number. The form page thus enters update mode and behaves exactly as your Simple Table Form page does in update mode. The report also has a Create button. Clicking the button also redirects to the form page, but this time setting the value of the hidden item P24_EMPNO to null. The form page thus enters insert mode and behaves like the your Simple Table Form page does in insert mode.

In other words, the difference between the Form on Table or View wizard and the Form on Table with Report wizard is that the latter wizard creates a report page in addition to a form page. However, you built similar reports in Chapter 6 and have seen that doing so is relatively straightforward. So if you understand what you are doing, you can build the report of Figure 7-29 in about the same amount of time as using the wizard. Moreover, doing it yourself gives you considerably more design flexibility. For example, the Form on Table with Report wizard generates two pages, each containing a single region. Building the report yourself gives you the option of placing both regions on the same page.

Master-Detail Form

When a table contains a foreign-key constraint to another table, the two tables are said to have a *master-detail* relationship. For example in the sample database, DEPT is the master table and EMP is the detail table because every DEPT record has a set of associated EMP records. In Chapter 6 you built the Employees by Department demo page (refer to Figure 6-7), in which clicking a record of the master (DEPT) report brings up a report listing all the associated detail (EMP) records.

One can extend the notion of a master-detail report by associating a form region with each of the two reports. In this case you wind up with four regions: the master report, the detail report, a master record edit region, and a detail record edit region. The page type Master Detail Form implements this idea.

Run the Master Detail Form wizard on your demo application. The wizard asks you the standard set of questions (table name, primary key, which columns to display, etc.) for both the master and detail tables. Toward the end of the wizard, it will display a screen, part of which is shown in Figure 7-30.

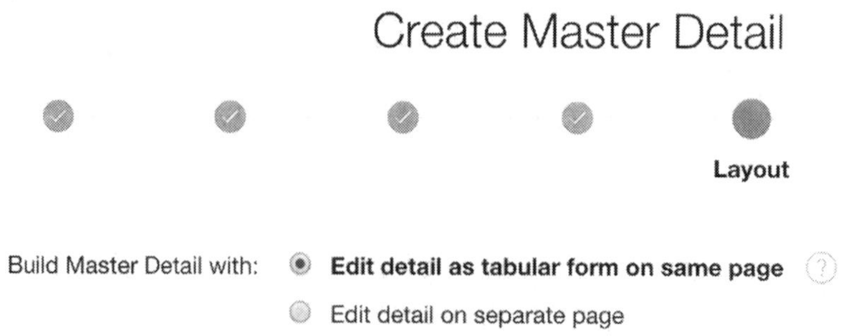

Create Master Detail

Layout

Build Master Detail with: ● **Edit detail as tabular form on same page** ?

○ Edit detail on separate page

Figure 7-30. Screen from the Master Detail Form wizard

If you select the option to place the edit detail on a separate page, the wizard will generate three pages: a page containing the master report; a page containing both the master edit region and the detail report; and a page containing the detail edit region. These pages will be pages 25 – 27 of the demo application, and are shown in Figures 7-31 through 7-33.

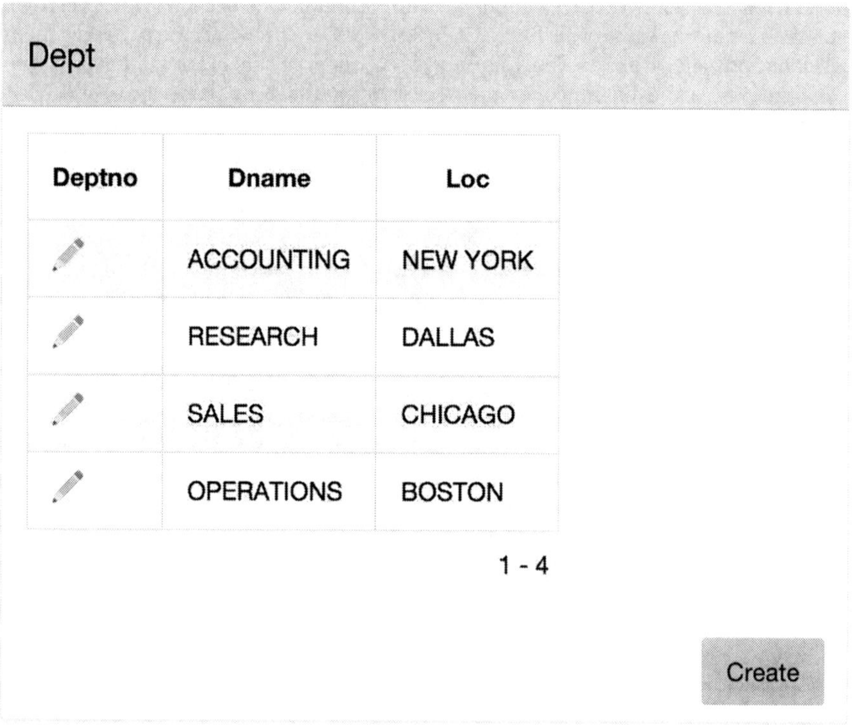

Dept

Deptno	Dname	Loc
🖉	ACCOUNTING	NEW YORK
🖉	RESEARCH	DALLAS
🖉	SALES	CHICAGO
🖉	OPERATIONS	BOSTON

1 - 4

Create

Figure 7-31. Master report page

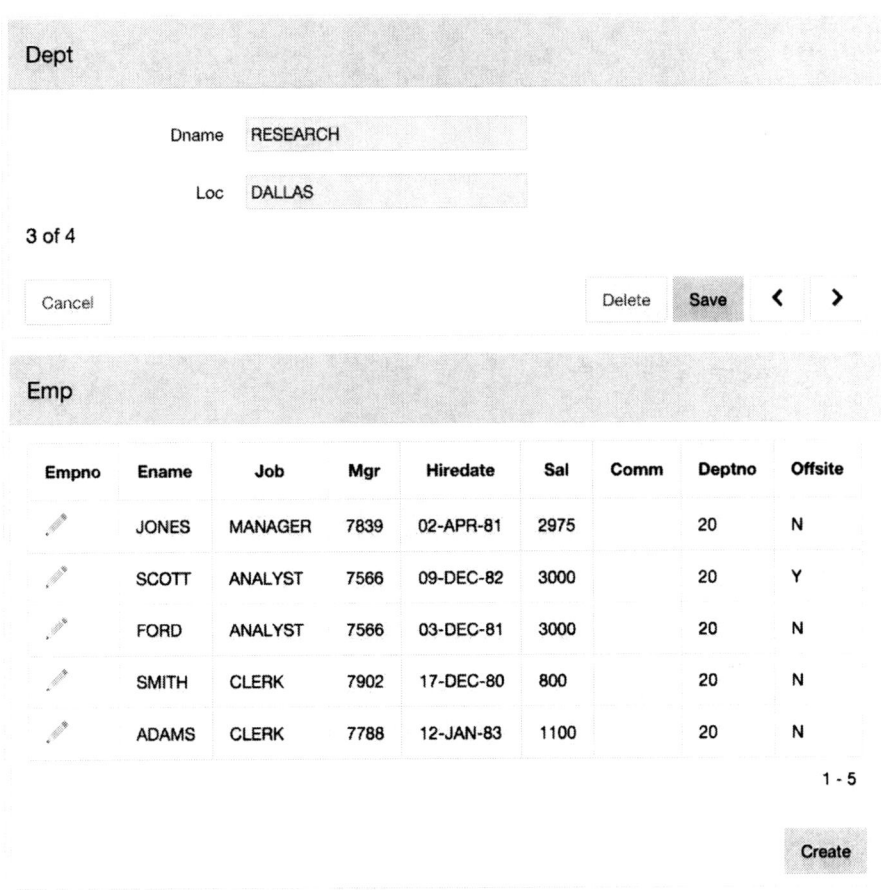

Figure 7-32. *Master edit and detail report page*

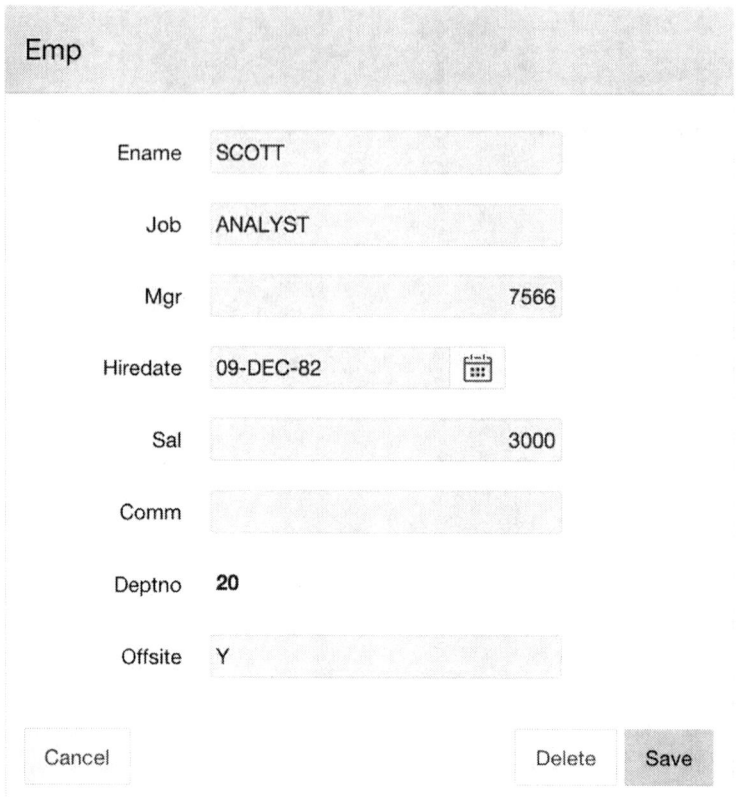

Figure 7-33. *Detail edit page*

Let's explore the implementation of these pages. Interestingly, there is nothing really new to see. The master report of Figure 7-31 and its detail report of Figure 7-32 both have the same structure as the Form with Report page of Figure 7-29. Their column links and Create buttons all redirect to the appropriate edit page. The column links set the appropriate key item (the DEPTNO item for the DEPT report and the EMPNO item for the EMP report) to the chosen record, and the Create buttons set that item to null. The detail edit region is also identical to the Form on Table or View region of Figure 7-26. The master edit region is nearly identical, but also has a Form Pagination process with the corresponding Next and Previous buttons.

If you had selected the tabular form option in Figure 7-29, the wizard would have merged the detail edit region into the detail report, as shown in Figure 7-34. This option requires only two pages instead of three, which in most situations is an asset. However, it raises the question of why the detail edit region of Figure 7-33 needs to be in its own page. Why not just make it another region of Figure 7-32? The answer is that each edit region has its own ARF and ARP processes, and two ARF (or ARP) processes cannot coexist on the same page. On the other hand, a tabular form uses different built-in process, which can coexist with ARF and ARP processes.

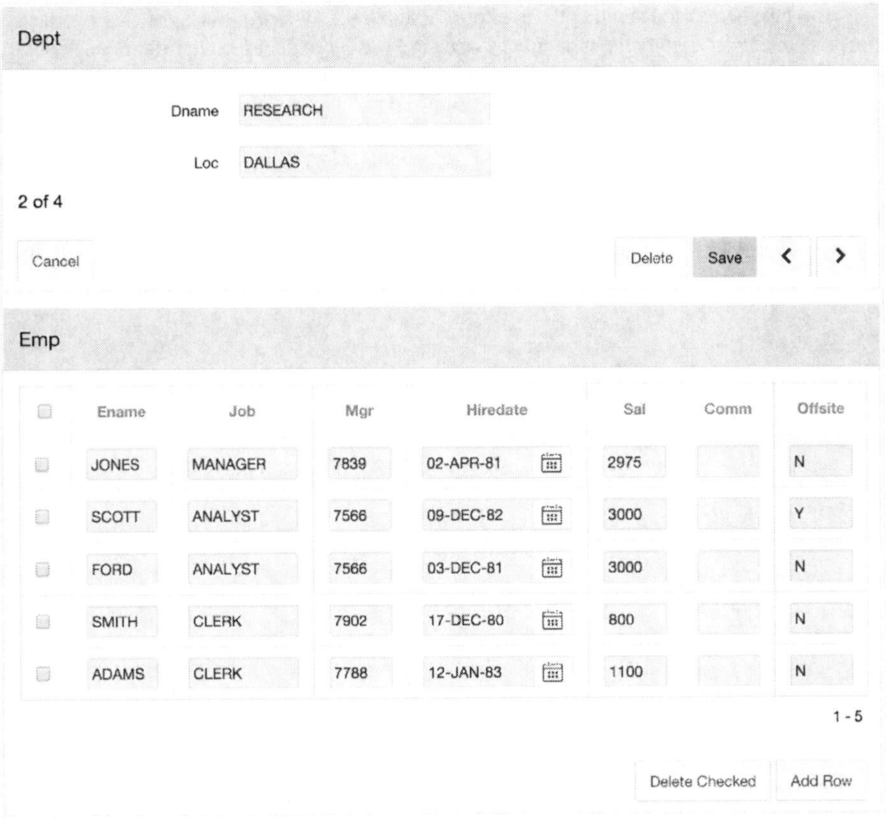

Figure 7-34. *Tabular form option*

Note that the report regions contain no processes, so it would be perfectly reasonable to place the master report region of Figure 7-31 on the same page as Figure 7-32. Although the Master Detail Form wizard does not do this, you can easily create the region yourself. In fact, it is quite possible to have all four regions on the same page, provided that you implement one of the edit regions using your own PL/SQL code instead of the built-in ARF and ARP processes.

Summary

A process is a page component that lets you access the database and perform calculations. This chapter examined the role that processes play in an application. For example, a button typically has an associated process that will execute when the button is clicked. A process can also be configured to execute during page rendering and calculate initial values for items.

You also examined several kinds of processes. A PL/SQL process is the most general purpose one. You specify its behavior by writing PL/SQL code. PL/SQL integrates SQL commands directly into the language, which makes it easy to write database-aware code. PL/SQL processes are very flexible — you can write a PL/SQL process to perform exactly the actions you wish.

The downside of using PL/SQL processes is that they require careful coding. You examined one common pitfall, known as the lost update problem. You learned how to recognize the problem and how to write the necessary PL/SQL code to avoid it.

APEX provides built-in processes for the more common tasks. You saw how to use these special-purpose processes, and learned about their advantages and limitations.

CHAPTER 8

■ ■ ■

Data Validation

When a process writes to the database, it typically takes its values from the session state. An application developer must therefore ensure that the session state values are *valid*, to ensure that the process was used appropriately and to preserve the integrity of the database. This chapter examines three aspects of a valid session state — constraint preservation, input validation, and process validation — and shows you how to implement them in an APEX application.

Constraint Preservation

The integrity of a database is important. The presence of an incorrect record not only reduces the value of any query involving that record but it also reduces the value of the entire database — because if one record is wrong, users will suspect that other records might also be wrong. Such databases can quickly become useless.

The primary mechanism that a database system uses to protect itself is the *constraint*. A database administrator typically specifies constraints when the tables are created. For example, the EMP table already has the following four constraints defined for it:

- *The column* EmpNo *is a key,* which ensures that no two employees have the same EmpNo value.

- *The column* DeptNo *is a foreign key of* DEPT, which ensures that every non-null value of DeptNo corresponds to an existing DEPT record.

- *The column* Mgr *is a foreign key of* EMP, which ensures that every non-null value of Mgr corresponds to an existing EMP record.

- *The column of* EmpNo *cannot be* null, which ensures that every employee has a number.

Let's add two more constraints to the database:

- An ENAME *value cannot be* null, which ensures that every employee has a name.

- A Sal *value must be at least 0*, which ensures against meaningless salaries.

You can define these constraints by separately executing the two SQL commands of Listing 8-1 from the APEX SQL workshop.

Listing 8-1. Two Additional Constraints for the EMP Table

```
alter table EMP
   add constraint ValidName
   check (EName is not null)

alter table EMP
   add constraint ValidSalary
   check (Sal > 0)
```

Whenever you write an APEX page that updates the database, you must be aware of its constraints. To investigate these issues, this chapter will use the Employee Data Entry page of Figure 7-4 in Chapter 7 as a running example.

Suppose that a user tries to insert a new employee into this page without specifying a name. Because that insertion would violate the null value constraint, the database will reject it, and APEX will display the error message shown in Figure 8-1.

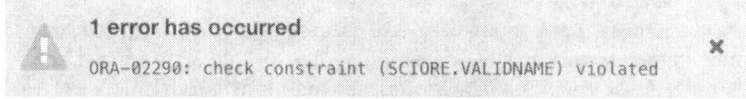

Figure 8-1. *Result of attempting to violate a constraint*

Although no harm is done, this method of handling the error is not satisfactory. One reason is that the error message is unhelpful, giving low-level details about the database that the user will know nothing about. Such details can also provide information that can help a hacker break into your system. (For example, the message of Figure 8-1 divulges that there is a schema named SCIORE, which means that there might be a corresponding username whose account could be targeted.) Another reason is that the page does not tell the user how to fix the mistake. Instead, it can give the impression that the problem is due to a bug in the system over which the user has no control.

Consequently, your APEX pages should always anticipate attempted constraint violations and handle them explicitly. There are features built into APEX that help you in this regard. Let's examine how to handle each of the above constraints.

A violation of the key constraint could occur if a user is able to choose the EmpNo value for a new employee. The best way to handle this constraint is to not give the user that choice. For example, the Employee Data Entry page does not have a place for a user to enter an employee number. Instead, the SQL insertion command obtains the new EmpNo value automatically from an insertion trigger, thereby guaranteeing that a unique value will be chosen.

A violation of a foreign key constraint could occur if a user is able to enter an incorrect value for DeptNo or Mgr. The solution adopted by the Employee Data Entry page was to use list-based items. The advantage of a list-based item is that you can populate it with exactly the values you want, which means that there is no way that the user can pick an incorrect one. (Caveat: this statement is true for a properly secured application. Chapter 12 discusses how a malicious user can select arbitrary values from an unsecured list-based item.)

A violation of a null value constraint on EName could occur if a user does not enter a value into the item P17_INSERT_ENAME. The solution to this problem is to use the item's Value Required property, which you can find in its Validation section. If you set the property to Yes, APEX will examine the item whenever a user submits the page. If its value is null, APEX will display an error message and redisplay the page without processing the request. This message is shown in Figure 8-2. Note that this error message is far better than the one in Figure 8-1.

Figure 8-2. *A better way to handle an attempted constraint violation*

Finally, consider the constraint on Sal. You can ensure that a user enters a non-negative salary by implementing the item P17_INSERT_SALARY as a number field instead of a text field. Number field items have the properties Minimum Value and Maximum Value, which are in its Settings section. Suppose that you set the minimum value to 0. If a user submits the page with a negative number, APEX will display the error message shown in Figure 8-3.

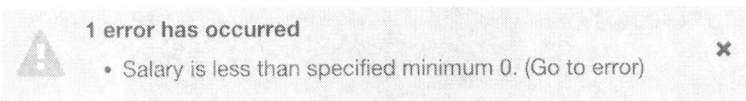

Figure 8-3. *Result of attempting to violate a numeric constraint*

Note that the application developer cannot specify these error messages. Instead, APEX uses a stock message that references the problematic item by its label. To specify your own error message, you can use a validation, as discussed in the next section.

In addition to these explicit constraints, a database also has implicit constraints that arise from the type of each field. For example, the column EName is of type varchar2(10), which means that a constraint violation would occur if a user tried to store a name containing more than ten characters. Figure 8-4 shows the error message that results from trying to insert a new employee having a 12-character name.

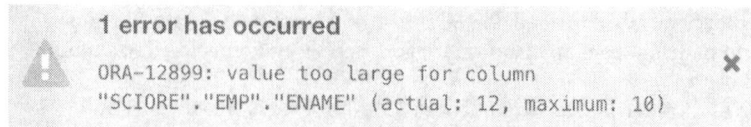

Figure 8-4. *Result of stuffing too many chars into a column value*

Again, such error messages are an unsatisfactory way to give feedback to the user. Hackers often try to generate constraint violations, not because they expect them to work, but because they are interested in the error message. The message in Figure 8-4 divulges that there is an EMP table having an ENAME column of type varchar2(10).

Fortunately, there is a simple way to avoid this problem. By setting the text field's Maximum Length property to 10, you guarantee that the text field cannot hold more than ten characters. If a user tries to enter too many characters into a text field, the extra characters will be ignored.

Similarly, a constraint violation would occur if a user tried to insert a non-numeric value for Sal or Comm. This problem can be avoided by implementing their items as number fields. If the number field contains a non-numeric value when the page is submitted, APEX will generate the error message instead of the database. Figures 8-5 and 8-6 show error messages that result from trying to insert a new record having a non-numeric salary. In Figure 8-5, the item P17_INSERT_SALARY is a text field, so the constraint error is caught by the database. In Figure 8-6, the item is a number field, which allows APEX to catch the error. Note that APEX generates a much better error message.

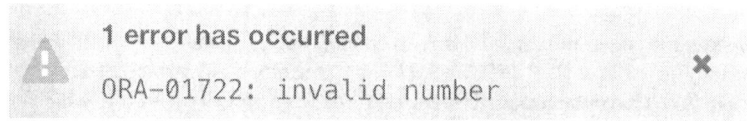

Figure 8-5. *Error message generated by the database for invalid numeric input*

Figure 8-6. *Error message generated by APEX for invalid numeric input*

Although a number field can check for non-numeric input, it cannot check for specific kinds of numbers. The reason is that SQL is very forgiving about inaccurate numeric input. For example, the SQL command of Listing 8-2 is completely legal.

Listing 8-2. Inappropriate but Legal SQL Command

```
insert into EMP (EmpNo, DeptNo, Sal,
                 EName, Job, Mgr, HireDate, Comm,  Offsite)
values (8090.4, 29.6, 130.678,
        'FRANK', 'SALES', 7839, current_date, 0, 'N')
```

The specified values for EmpNo, DeptNo, and Sal are problematic because the columns EmpNo and DeptNo are defined as integers, and Sal is defined to have at most two numbers to the right of the decimal point. However, when Oracle is asked to store a value into a numeric column that exceeds the column's precision, it automatically rounds the value to the nearest legal value before saving it. (Some database systems truncate the value instead.) The previous insertion command therefore creates a new employee having employee number 8090 in department 30, and having a salary of 130.68. Similarly in the Employee Data Entry page, if a user enters 130.678 as the salary value of a new record, APEX will process the input smoothly, without generating a constraint error.

Input Validation

Let's rethink the way APEX handles numeric input. Its behavior is technically correct, but rather misleading. It is likely that a user entering a salary with more than two numbers to the right of the decimal point has either made a typo (such as typing 130.678 instead of 1306.78) or doesn't understand the purpose of the field. In either case, it would be better if APEX informed the user of the problem instead of making a possibly incorrect assumption.

In general, you want APEX to stop users from entering inappropriate values, even if they are legal. Here are three more examples for the Employee Data Entry page:

- A user should not be able to delete or modify the record for an employee having the job PRESIDENT. (Assume that this functionality is performed some other way.)

- A user should not be able to enter a salary that is higher than the president's.

- Changes to the database should only be made between the hours of 9 AM to 5 PM.

APEX should reject a request that violates these conditions and inform the user why the request is inappropriate.

The way to enforce these validity checks is to create a *validation* in APEX. A validation is code that gets executed when the page is submitted. If a validation fails, submit processing stops, and the page is redisplayed with an error message for each failed validation. If all validations succeed, the submit processing continues normally.

To create a validation, go to the Processing section of the page designer, right-click the Validations folder, and select Create Validation. (If you configured the page designer to group components "by processing order," the folder is called Validating.) APEX will create a default validation named New, having the type PL/SQL Expression.

Figure 8-7 shows the possible validation types. Note that they are analogous to the conditional rendering types you examined in Chapter 6.

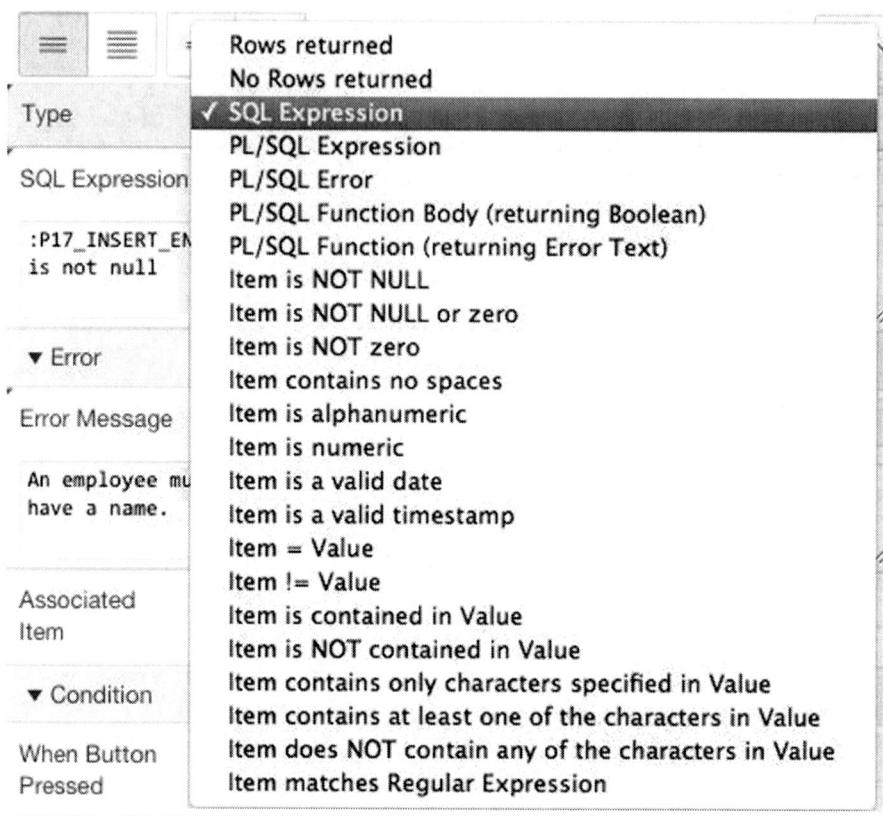

Figure 8-7. *Validation types*

A PL/SQL Expression validation succeeds if the specified PL/SQL expression returns true, and similarly for an SQL Expression validation. Two other useful validation types are Rows returned and No Rows returned. These validations are specified by an SQL query. A Rows returned validation succeeds if the query returns at least one row; a No Rows returned validation succeeds if the query returns no rows.

Whenever you select a validation type, the property editor will display the needed properties for specifying the validation. For example, the SQL Expression type has a corresponding text area for entering the expression, which can be partially seen in Figure 8-7. A Rows returned or No Rows returned validation has a text area for specifying the query.

A validation can execute conditionally, as determined by the properties in its Condition section. Typically, a validation is conditional on the button specified in its When Button Pressed property, but you can also specify an arbitrary condition by selecting the Type property.

224

You must specify an error message for each validation. The Error section contains the relevant properties. The Error Message property contains the text of the error message, which will be displayed in the notification. If you specify a value for the Associated Item property, the message will also be displayed next to that item.

To illustrate these concepts, let's write validations for each of the issues mentioned at the beginning of this section. Figure 8-8 displays the properties for a validation, named DontDeleteThePresident, that verifies that the president's record is not deleted. This validation has the type No Rows returned. Its query will return a record only if the chosen employee has the job PRESIDENT, which means that the validation will succeed if the chosen employee does not have the job PRESIDENT.

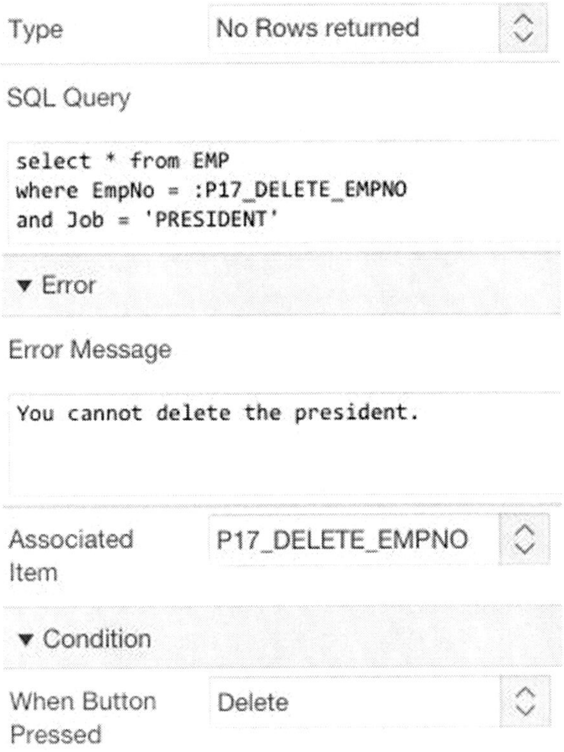

Type	No Rows returned ⌄

SQL Query

```
select * from EMP
where EmpNo = :P17_DELETE_EMPNO
and Job = 'PRESIDENT'
```

▼ Error

Error Message

```
You cannot delete the president.
```

Associated Item	P17_DELETE_EMPNO ⌄

▼ Condition

When Button Pressed	Delete ⌄

Figure 8-8. *DontDeleteThePresident validation*

Similarly, you can use the following No Rows returned query to write the validation SalaryNotTooLarge, which ensures that the value in P17_INSERT_SALARY is not larger than that of the president's:

```
select * from EMP
where Job = 'PRESIDENT' and :P17_INSERT_SALARY > Sal
```

The DontDeleteThePresident validation applies to the DELETE request, and SalaryNotTooLarge applies to the INSERT request. You also need to create two similar validations to validate the UPDATE request, although they are not shown here.

To verify that changes to the database occur only during standard working hours, you can create the validation WorkingHoursOnly, shown in Figure 8-9.

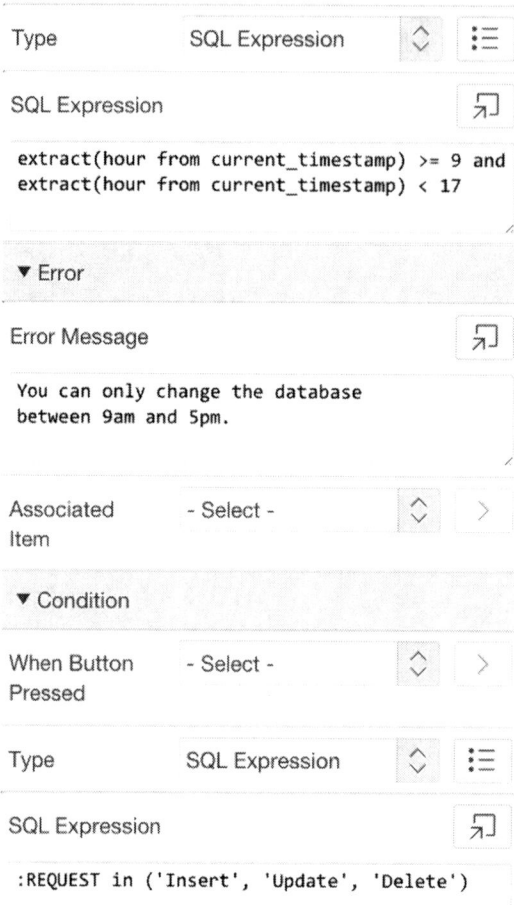

Figure 8-9. Validation to restrict the execution time of an operation

This validation uses an SQL expression to calculate the desired time interval — in particular, the function extract gets the current hour from the current timestamp. Note that this expression is independent of the session state, so the validation does not have a value for its Associated Item property. The validation is also conditional on the Insert, Delete, and Update buttons.

The final issue concerns how to enforce specific numeric formats. For example, the column Sal is defined as the type NUMERIC(7,2), which means that a salary value has no more than seven total digits, with no more than two digits to the right of the decimal place. The best way to verify this condition is to use a *regular expression*, which is a pattern that denotes a set of legal values. In this case, the following regular expression will work:

```
^\d{0,5}\.{0,1}\d{0,2}$
```

Without delving too deeply into regular expressions here, you should know that the character ^ matches the beginning of the string, \d matches any digit character, \. matches the decimal point, and $ matches the end of the string. The notation {m,n} matches at least *m* and at most *n* occurrences of the previous pattern. Therefore, the regular expression matches up to 5 digits, followed by 0 or 1 decimal point, followed by 0 to 2 more digits.

Oracle has the built-in function regexp_like, which returns true if a value matches a regular expression. The validation could therefore be defined by an SQL expression, as shown in Figure 8-10.

Type	SQL Expression	⌄	:≡
SQL Expression			⌐

```
regexp_like(:P17_INSERT_SALARY, '^\d{0,5}\.{0,1}\d{0,2}$')
```

Figure 8-10. *One way to express a regular expression validation*

APEX also has a regular expression validation type, which provides a place to enter the regular expression directly. Figure 8-11 shows its use.

Type	Item matches Regular Expression ⌄
Item	P17_INSERT_SALARY
Regular Expression	^\d{0,5}\.{0,1}\d{0,2}$

Figure 8-11. *Another way to express a regular expression validation*

Validations are also useful when the techniques of the previous section do not work. For example, the previous section discussed how to use an item's Value Required property to enforce a null value constraint. However, this technique will not work properly if the page contains multiple regions, each with its own submit button. The Employee Data Entry page is a case in point. If P17_INSERT_ENAME has a Value Required value of Yes, that restriction will be enforced even when the Delete or Update buttons are clicked. Consequently, you would not be able to delete or update a record without entering a dummy value into P17_INSERT_ENAME.

This problem can be fixed by using a validation to enforce the null value constraint. The validation will be conditional on the Insert button and have the following SQL expression:

```
:P17_INSERT_ENAME is not null
```

You can also use a validation to verify a foreign-key constraint. For example, the Employee Data Entry page uses a select list to restrict the possible departments of a new employee. Suppose instead that you want users to enter the department number into a number field. To enforce the foreign-key constraint, you simply have to ensure that the specified number is in the DEPT table. The solution is to create a validation having the following Rows returned query, conditional on the Insert button:

```
select * from DEPT
where DeptNo = :P17_INSERT_DEPT
```

Finally, you should use a validation whenever you want APEX to display a customized error message. For example, you saw in Figure 8-2 that APEX displays the stock error message Name must have some value when you attempt to insert a null value for EName. If you use a validation to test for the constraint, it can display any error message you want, such as An employee must have a name.

Process Validation

Chapter 7 examined the following algorithm for avoiding lost database updates: before an update operation changes the database, it first checks to see whether the relevant values have already changed; if so, the operation aborts. The code developed in that section aborted the operation by calling the function raise_application_error, which displayed the error message shown in Figure 7-7. Given that validations provide a cleaner way to handle error scenarios, it is natural to wonder whether a validation can be used in this situation as well. The answer is yes.

Recall the code for the Update button in Listing 7-12. That code can be divided into two parts: the first part re-reads the data and compares it with the original values; and the second part either performs the update or aborts, depending on the result of the comparison. The first part is essentially a validation. The update in the second part is a process that is conditional on the success of the validation.

Thus you can rewrite the code for the Update process so that the first part is moved to a validation. The code for the process becomes just a simple update, the way it was originally written in Listing 7-4:

```
begin
    update EMP
    set Job   = :P17_MODIFY_JOB,
        Sal   = :P17_MODIFY_SALARY,
        DeptNo = :P17_MODIFY_DEPT
    where EmpNo = :P17_MODIFY_EMPNO;
end;
```

You then create a validation to embody the first half of the code. Because the validation will need to execute PL/SQL code, its type needs to be PL/SQL Function Body (returning Boolean) — that is, PL/SQL code that returns either TRUE or FALSE. This code appears in Listing 8-3.

Listing 8-3. Validation Code for Detecting a Lost Update

```
declare
    v_valuesToHash apex_t_varchar2;
begin
    -- first re-read the data
    select apex_t_varchar2(Job, Sal, DeptNo)
    into v_valuesToHash
    from EMP
    where EmpNo = :P17_UPDATE_EMPNO;

    -- then compare it with the original data
    if :P17_HASH = apex_util.get_hash(v_valuesToHash) then
        return TRUE;
    else
        return FALSE;
    end if;
end;
```

The validation is conditional on the Update button, and its error message is The record is out of date. Please get it again. The result is that the Update process is executed only when the validation succeeds. If the validation fails, the error message will be displayed on the Employee Data Entry page.

Summary

In this chapter, you explored ways to stop users from inadvertently misusing a web application. You first considered database constraints. You saw how a properly chosen item type can avoid potential problems. For example, list-based item types can avoid foreign-key constraint violations. You also looked at item properties such as required values and min/max numeric values that can avoid or detect constraint violations.

You then considered the use of APEX validations. A validation is an APEX component whose purpose is to abort inappropriate submit operations. Validations provide a flexible, general-purpose way to handle constraints. They can display customized error messages for constraint violations and can be used to selectively check for constraint violations. They can also be used to check for inappropriate user activity, apart from constraint violations.

Finally, you reconsidered the Chapter 7 code to check for potential lost updates. You saw how to use validations to separate the code for lost-update testing from the code to update the database, which leads to a cleaner design with better error handling.

■ ■ ■

Branches

When the APEX server receives a submit request from a browser, it performs the validations and processes associated with that request. Its final task is to choose a target page to send to the browser. By default, APEX chooses the page that was submitted, but it is possible to specify another page by creating a *branch*.

You have been able to get this far through the book without needing to use branches because of the ease in which multiple regions can be created on a page and the way that these regions can be conditionally rendered to give the effect of multiple pages. But there are many situations in which an application will use multiple pages to implement a user activity. In this chapter, you investigate the use of branches to support these situations.

Separating Input from Output

A common application design technique is to use separate pages for input and output. A user enters input on a page and clicks a button; the application then branches to another page that displays the output.

As an example of this technique, consider the two pages shown in Figures 9-1 and 9-2. The pages have a single region each and work similarly to the single Filter by Job and Department page of Chapter 6. In particular, a user begins on the Filter and Branch page shown in Figure 9-1, choosing a job and department from the select lists and then clicking a button. The system then branches to the Filtered Employees page of Figure 9-2, which displays a report of employees who have that job and are in that department.

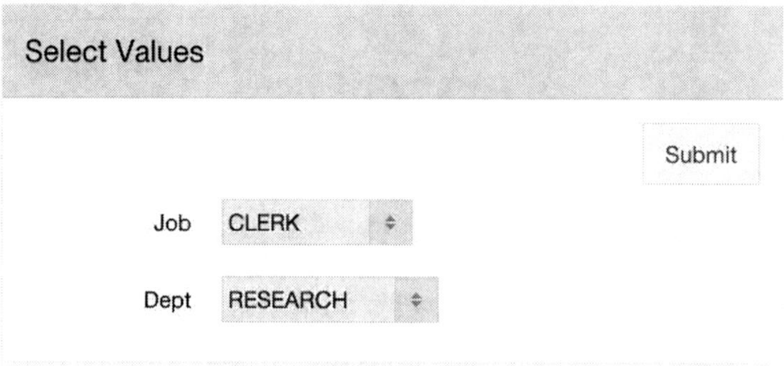

Select Values

Submit

Job   CLERK   ⇕

Dept   RESEARCH   ⇕

Figure 9-1. *Filter and Branch page*

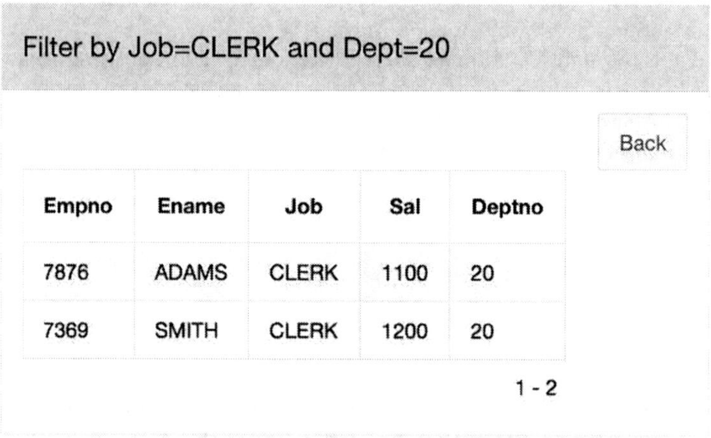

Filter by Job=CLERK and Dept=20

Back

Empno	Ename	Job	Sal	Deptno
7876	ADAMS	CLERK	1100	20
7369	SMITH	CLERK	1200	20

1 - 2

Figure 9-2. *Filtered Employees page*

Let's examine how to implement these pages. The Filter and Branch page will be page 28 of the demo application. Its region is titled Select Values and it has two select lists named P28_JOB and P28_DEPTNO. The values for these select lists are specified by the same SQL queries as in Chapter 6.

The Filtered Employees page is page 29 of the demo and its region is a classic report. Its source query, which is also similar to what you saw in Chapter 6, is the following:

```
select EmpNo, EName, Job, Sal, DeptNo
from EMP
where (:P28_JOB is null  or  Job = :P28_JOB)
and   (:P28_DEPTNO is null  or  DeptNo = :P28_DEPTNO)
order by EName
```

Each page has a button. The button on the Filter and Branch page will perform a submit action to save its two item values in the session state. The button on the Filtered Employees page can simply redirect back to page 28 because it has no need to submit.

Although the Filter and Branch page will have an entry in the navigation menu, the Filtered Employees page should not. A navigation entry is of no use for that page because a user should get to it only via the Filter and Branch page. This situation is true in general; when an interaction is broken up among several pages, usually only the first page of the interaction is accessible from the navigation menu.

There are two implementation issues that have not been discussed: how do you customize the region title of the Filtered Employee page, and how do you get page 28 to branch to page 29 upon submit? Each issue will be discussed in turn.

Consider the title bar of the Filtered Employees region. One downside of using a separate page for output is that the input is no longer visible. The design strategy from Figure 9-2 is to recapitulate the input within the region's title bar. Let's examine how to implement this feature.

Recall that a region's Title property is HTML code. Although HTML code cannot perform computation, it can reference the value of an item. Thus the technique is to write a process to compute the title of its output region and save it in a hidden item. Listing 9-1 gives the code for this process. This code considers the four cases in which the two items are empty or not, computes the region title appropriately, and saves it in the hidden item P29_REGION_TITLE.

Listing 9-1. Customizing the Title of the Filtered Employees Region

```
declare
    v_title varchar(100);
begin
    if :P28_JOB is not null and :P28_DEPTNO is not null
    then
        v_title := 'Job=' || :P28_JOB || ' and Dept=' || :P28_DEPTNO;
    elsif :P28_JOB is not null then
        v_title := 'Job=' || :P28_JOB;
    elsif :P28_DEPTNO is not null then
        v_title := 'Dept=' || :P28_DEPTNO;
    else
        v_title := 'All Employees';
    end if;
    :P29_REGION_TITLE := 'Filter by ' || v_title;
end;
```

This process belongs to page 28 and is conditional on the submit button. (You could also have placed the process in page 29 to execute during page rendering.) The HTML expression for the Filtered Employees region title then becomes a reference to that hidden item. In particular, the region title is the HTML expression "&P29_REGION_TITLE." Note that substitution string syntax is used to refer to the item.

Creating a Branch

In order to get page 28 to branch to page 29, you need to create a branch object. A `branch` object is similar to a process, in the sense that it performs an action in response to a submit. The difference is that a process executes code, whereas a branch redirects to a page. A branch typically executes after the relevant processes complete.

Creating a branch is similar to creating a process. Begin by going to the processing section of the page designer, as shown in Chapter 7 (refer to Figure 7-1). If you selected the icon to display the processing components by type (as shown in Figure 7-1), you will see a folder labeled `Branches`. If you have selected the icon to display the components by processing stage (as shown in Figure 7-2), you will see a folder labeled `After Processing`. In either case, right-click the folder and choose `Create Branch`. The page designer will create an unnamed branch that has the properties shown in Figure 9-3.

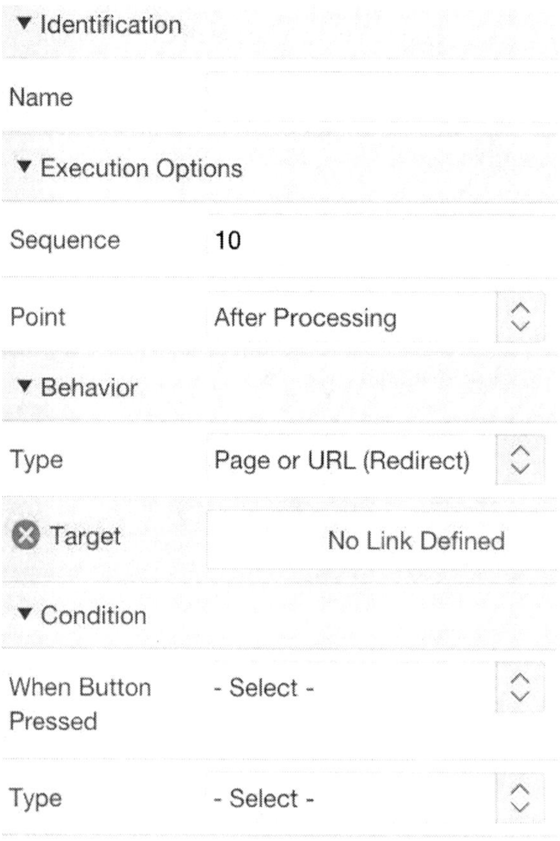

▼ Identification

Name

▼ Execution Options

Sequence   10

Point   After Processing   ◇

▼ Behavior

Type   Page or URL (Redirect)   ◇

❌ Target   No Link Defined

▼ Condition

When Button   - Select -   ◇
Pressed

Type   - Select -   ◇

Figure 9-3. *Properties of a newly created branch*

Clearly, you should give the branch a name. But what else do you need to do? Two important properties are Point and Type; their default values specify that the branch will execute after all processes and will redirect to a specified page or URL. These default values are almost always what you want, and you should leave them as is.

The other important property is Target. By default, this property shows an error, indicating that you need to specify the target of the branch. Clicking the property's link area brings up the Link Builder wizard (which you have seen several times before). Figure 9-4 shows the top part of the builder, configured to redirect to page 29.

Link Builder - Target

▼ Target	
Type	Page in this application
Page	29
▼ Set Items	

Name		Value	
	∧		∧

Figure 9-4. *Using the link builder to specify the branch target*

The branch's Condition section specifies when the branch should execute. As with processes, each branch typically has an associated button, and you specify that button in the When Button Pressed property. For example, the branch in the Filter and Branch demo page is associated with the submit button and has no other condition. The Type property allows you to specify additional conditions about when the branch should fire. The next section gives an example in which a branch will need an additional condition.

Conditional Branching

Chapter 7 discussed the pages Employee Data Input (refer to Figure 7-4) and Simple Table Form (refer to Figure 7-29). These pages have similar functionality — they both allow a user to insert, delete, and update the EMP table — but they use very different interfaces to do so. In particular, the Employee Data Input page is very expansive; it displays the entire EMP table and has a region for each operation below it. On the other hand, the Simple Table Form page is compact, displaying a single region that gets reconfigured for each operation.

Let's build a page that helps a user decide which page to use. This page, called Preference Chooser, is page 30 of the demo application and appears in Figure 9-5. The page has a single region that asks the user two questions. A user answers these questions and clicks the button; the button will then branch to page 17 (the Employee Data Input page) if either answer is Yes, or to page 22 (the Simple Table Form page) if both answers are No.

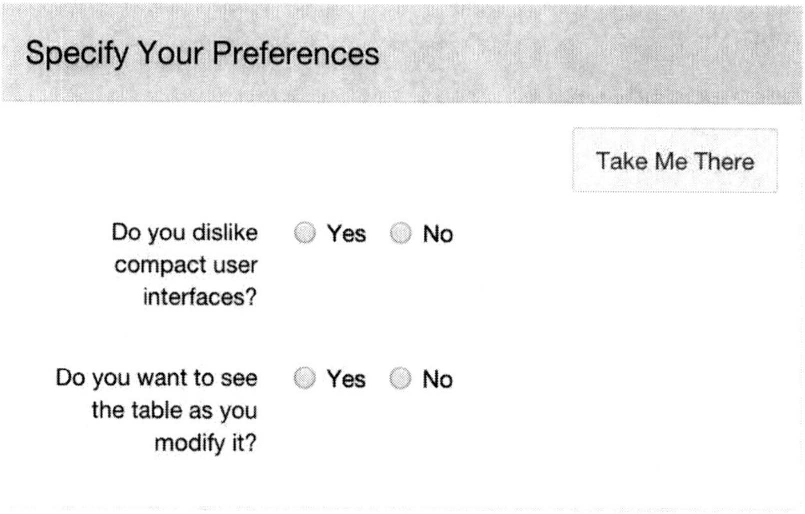

Figure 9-5. *Page with conditional branching*

You implement this page as follows. The two radio groups are named P30_NOT_COMPACT and P30_SEE_TABLE, and their values are both defined by this expression:

STATIC2:Yes,No

The button performs a submit operation. Intuitively, it is easy to imagine that the button makes the decision about which page to branch to. But that is not how it works; instead, you need to create two branch objects, each of which is conditional on the button. Each branch will also have an extra condition. The first branch object redirects to page 17 and has this condition:

:P30_NOT_COMPACT = 'Yes' or :P30_SEE_TABLE = 'Yes'

The second branch object redirects to page 22 and has this condition:

:P30_NOT_COMPACT = 'No' and :P30_SEE_TABLE = 'No'

When the button performs the submit, only one of these conditions will be satisfied. The branch having the satisfied condition will perform its redirection.

Wizard-Like Interfaces

The final example of branching is related to the problem of data entry. In each of the data entry pages of Chapter 7, a user creates a new record by entering the desired values into some items and then clicking an insert button. Such a design presupposes that the user has these values at hand. An alternative design is to create a series of pages that leads the user through the data entry process, much as a wizard does in APEX. The design will have four pages.

A user will begin on the Basic Info page (Figure 9-6) by entering the name, job, department, and salary of the new employee. The most common situation is for the employee to have been hired that day, so there is a check box for that case. The user then clicks the Continue button to submit the page.

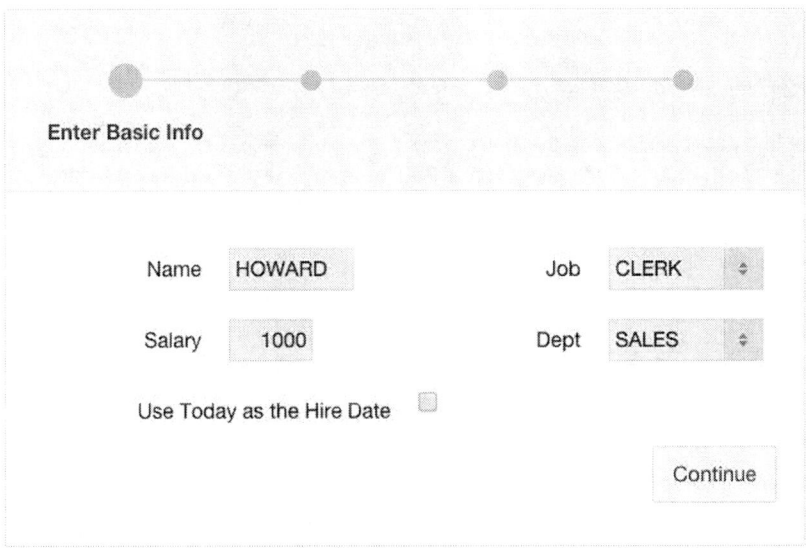

Figure 9-6. *Entering the basic info*

The next step is to determine the employee's manager. Assume that the company assigns managers to employees as follows: the president has no manager, employees with the job MANAGER report to the president, and other employees (except clerks) report to the manager of their department. The exceptions are clerks. In this company, any employee (except a clerk) can manage a clerk, so the manager of a new clerk must be specified explicitly.

If the new employee is a clerk, clicking the Continue button will branch to the Manager Info page (see Figure 9-7), in which the user can enter the employee's manager.

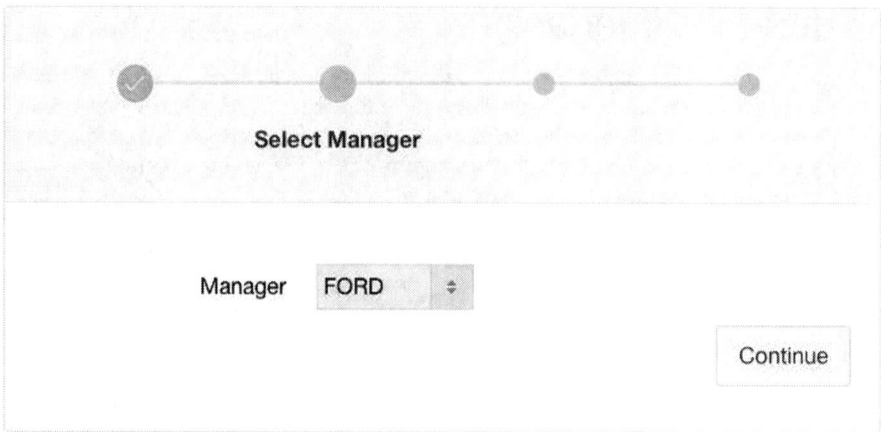

Figure 9-7. Selecting the manager

If the hire date checkbox on the Basic Info page is unselected, the application has to branch to the Hiredate Info page (Figure 9-8), in which the user can select a date. This branch will happen either from the Manager Info page or the Basic Info page, depending on whether the employee is a clerk.

Figure 9-8. Choosing the employee's hire date

The final page of the wizard is the Confirm Employee Info page (see Figure 9-9), which displays the selected values for the new employee. The wizard branches to this page when all the necessary values are known. This branch can occur from any of the three earlier wizard pages. The Basic Info page can branch directly to the confirmation page when the new employee is not a clerk and the hire date checkbox is selected; the Manager Info page can branch directly to the confirmation page when the checkbox is selected; and the Hiredate Info page always branches to the confirmation page.

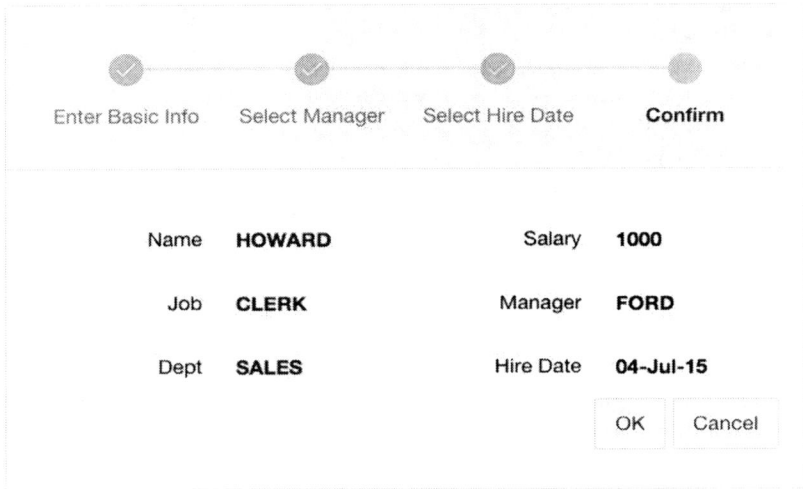

Figure 9-9. Confirming the employee's information

The Confirm Employee Info page has buttons labeled OK and Cancel. Clicking the Cancel button redirects to the Basic Info page and clears the session state of the wizard pages. Clicking the OK button inserts the new record into the EMP table and then branches to the Basic Info page.

Now that you understand the flow of control through the wizard, let's examine how to implement its pages. The following sections address the issues.

Implementing the Progress Bar

Each of the four wizard pages consists of two regions. One region displays a progress bar, and the other displays items and buttons. The progress bar regions are list regions, and the progress bar is the list that they display. So the first thing you need to do is create the list.

Create a list called New Employee Wizard by using the techniques you learned in Chapter 4. The list will have an entry for each of the four (not yet created) wizard pages, as shown in Figure 9-10.

	List Entry Label		Target Page ID or custom URL	
1	Enter Basic Info	⑦	31	∧
2	Select Manager	⑦	32	∧
3	Select Hire Date	⑦	33	∧
4	Confirm	⑦	34	∧

Figure 9-10. Entries for the New Employee Wizard list

You can now create the wizard pages. Start by creating four blank pages, numbered 31–34. Create a list region for each page, with the New Employee Wizard list as the source. Set the list's template (one of the properties in the region's Attributes component) to be Wizard Progress. Your pages should now display the progress bar region. You should observe that each page displays a different version of the progress bar, depending on the location of the page in the list.

Now create a region on each page to hold the items and buttons, using Figures 9-6 through 9-9 as models. The purpose is to get the basic structure in place; the following sections will discuss the actual implementation details. For example, Figure 9-11 shows the two regions for the Basic Info page.

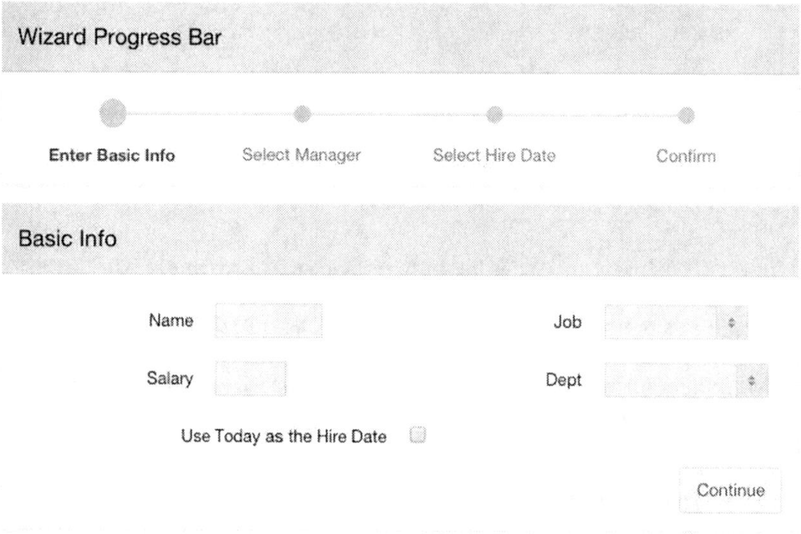

Figure 9-11. *Rough draft of the Basic Info wizard page*

Although this page layout is okay, the layout of Figure 9-6 is better. To create that layout, you simply have to adjust some region properties on each page:

- Set the template of the Wizard Progress Bar region to Wizard Container, and set the template of the Basic Info region to Blank with Attributes.

- Set Basic Info's parent to be Wizard Progress Bar. Doing so places the region within the progress bar region and makes the page look like it has only one region.

- Go back to the list template, which you just set to Wizard Progress. Click its template options and set the Label Display property to Current Step Only. (In Figure 9-9, the template option is All Steps to show the difference between the options.)

Basic Info Page

The Basic Info page has five items: P31_NAME is a text field, P31_SALARY is a number field, P31_JOB and P31_DEPTNO are select lists, and P31_HIRED_TODAY is a checkbox. The checkbox is defined by this static list:

STATIC:;Yes

This static expression asserts that the item has no display value and a result value of Yes when checked. As discussed in Chapter 4, the item has the value null when unchecked.

The Continue button performs a submit operation. During this submit, several things need to happen:

- If the new employee is not a clerk, the page needs to calculate the employee's manager.

- If the hire date box is checked, the page needs to set the employee's hire date to be today.

- The page needs to determine which of the other three wizard pages it should branch to.

The first bullet point requires that you write a process to calculate the manager of a non-clerk. Let's call this process ComputeManager. Its PL/SQL code appears in Listing 9-2.

Listing 9-2. PL/SQL Code for the ComputeManager Process

```
begin
    if :P31_JOB = 'PRESIDENT' then
            -- the president has no manager
            :P32_MANAGER := null;
    elsif :P31_JOB = 'MANAGER' then
            -- a manager's manager is the president
            select EmpNo into :P32_MANAGER
            from EMP
            where Job = 'PRESIDENT';
    else
            -- the employee's manager is the mgr of the dept
            select EmpNo into :P32_MANAGER
            from EMP
            where Job = 'MANAGER' and DeptNo = :P31_DEPTNO;
    end if;
end;
```

The ComputeManager process calculates its value in one of three ways, depending on the value of P31_JOB. In each case, it assigns the computed value to P32_MANAGER, which is the item on the Manager Info page. In other words, this process assigns a value to the item on the Manager Info page so that the user doesn't have to.

241

This process is associated with the Continue button and should execute only when the new employee is not a clerk. Thus it also has the following SQL expression as a condition:

```
:P31_JOB <> 'CLERK'
```

The second bullet point also requires you to write a process, which will be called ComputeHiredate. This process needs to calculate the current date and assign it to the item on the Hiredate Info page. Its PL/SQL code takes advantage of the built-in function sysdate and appears in Listing 9-3.

Listing 9-3. PL/SQL Code for the ComputeHiredate Process

```
begin
    :P33_HIREDATE := sysdate;
end;
```

The ComputeHiredate process is also associated with the Continue button. It should execute only when the P31_HIRED_TODAY box has been checked. That is, it is conditional on this SQL expression:

```
:P31_HIRED_TODAY = 'Yes'
```

The third bullet point requires you to create three branch objects, one for each possible target. Let's call these branches GoToPage32, GoToPage33, and GoToPage34. The target specification for each branch is straightforward: the targets are pages 32, 33, and 34, respectively. Each branch is also associated with the Continue button. The only difficult issue is to specify their respective conditions.

The GoToPage32 branch should fire when the user has to choose a manager, so its condition is this SQL expression:

```
:P31_JOB = 'CLERK'
```

The GoToPage33 branch should fire when the user does not need to choose a manager, but does need to choose the hire date; thus its condition is this SQL expression:

```
:P31_JOB <> 'CLERK' and :P31_HIRED_TODAY <> 'Yes'
```

Finally, the GoToPage34 branch should fire when neither the manager nor the hire date need to be chosen; thus its condition is this SQL expression:

```
:P31_JOB <> 'CLERK' and :P31_HIRED_TODAY = 'Yes'
```

Manager Info Page

Now consider the Manager Info page, which has the single item P32_MANAGER. This item is a select list with values that denote all employees who are allowed to manage clerks. Assuming that a clerk cannot manage another clerk, the item's list of values would be defined by the following query:

```
select EName, EmpNo
from EMP
where Job <> 'CLERK'
```

The page also has a Continue button whose action is submit. The page does not need to compute any values, so no processes are needed. But it does need to decide whether to branch to the Hiredate Info page or the confirmation page. Thus you need two branch objects, called GoToPage33 and GoToPage34. These branches are both associated with the Continue button.

The GoToPage33 branch should fire when P31_HIREDATE is not checked; thus its condition is this SQL expression:

```
:P31_HIRED_TODAY <> 'Yes'
```

Conversely, the GoToPage34 branch should fire when P31_HIREDATE is checked; thus its condition is this SQL expression:

```
:P31_HIRED_TODAY = 'Yes'
```

Hiredate Info Page

Now consider the Hiredate Info page. It has a single Date-Picker item named P33_HIREDATE to hold the hire date, a Continue button whose action is submit, and a branch to the Confirm Employee Info page that is conditional on the button. Submitting the page causes APEX to save the selected date in the session state and execute the branch.

Confirm Employee Info Page

Finally, consider the Confirm Employee Info page. Its six items are all of type Display Only, and their initial values are simply copied from the items on the other pages. For example, consider the employee's name, which is in the item P34_NAME. Its source type is SQL Expression and has the following value:

```
:P31_NAME
```

The source expressions for the items P34_SALARY, P34_JOB, and P34_HIREDATE are similar.

The source expressions for P34_MANAGER and P34_DEPTNO are different, however. Consider P34_MANAGER: if its source were the value of P32_MANAGER, the page would display the manager's employee number. Looking back at Figure 9-9, however, you

243

can see that the page displays the name of the manager, which is easier for a user to understand. Similarly, P34_DEPTNO displays the name of the department, even though the value of P31_DEPTNO is the department number.

To get P34_MANAGER to display the manager's name, set its source to be an SQL query instead of an SQL expression, as follows:

```
select EName
from EMP
where EmpNo = :P32_MANAGER
```

Similarly, the source of P34_DEPTNO is this SQL query:

```
select DName
from DEPT
where DeptNo = :P31_DEPTNO
```

The Confirm Employee Info page has two buttons. The Cancel button redirects to the Basic Info page and clears the cache of the four wizard pages. As discussed in Chapter 4, you use the link builder to specify the details of the redirection. Figure 9-12 shows the link builder values for the Cancel button. Recall that the Clear Cache property contains the page numbers of those pages whose item values should be cleared.

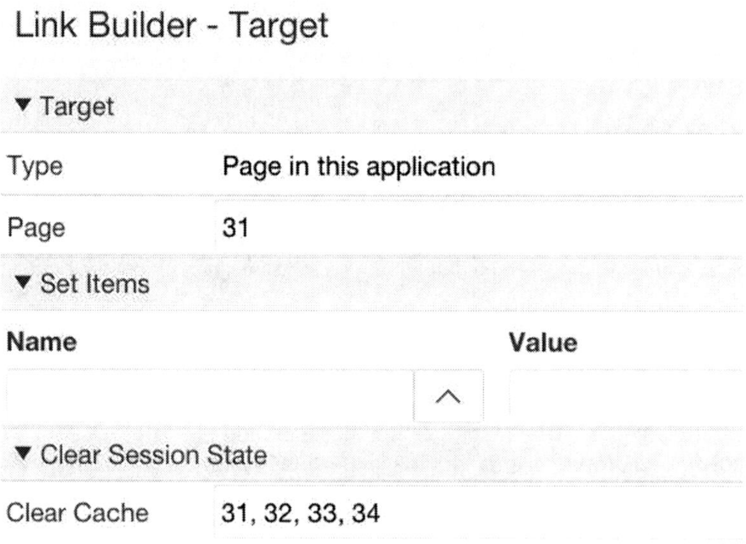

Link Builder - Target

▼ Target

Type	Page in this application
Page	31

▼ Set Items

Name		Value
	∧	

▼ Clear Session State

Clear Cache	31, 32, 33, 34

Figure 9-12. Link builder values for the Cancel button

The Continue button performs a submit action. The button has an associated process, called InsertRecord, which will insert the new employee record into the EMP table. The code for this process is similar to the code from Chapter 7 and appears in Listing 9-4.

Listing 9-4. PL/SQL Code for the InsertRecord Process

```
begin
    insert into EMP (EName, Job, Sal, DeptNo, Mgr, HireDate, Comm, Offsite)
    values (:P31_NAME, :P31_JOB, :P31_SALARY, :P31_DEPTNO, :P32_MANAGER,
            :P33_HIREDATE, 0, 'N');
end;
```

Recall that after the insertion occurs, the page should redirect to the first wizard page and clear the four wizard pages. To do so, create a branch object associated with the button. Use the link builder to specify the action of the branch, which will be exactly as in Figure 9-12.

Summary

This chapter looked at branch objects and gave some examples of their use. Branches execute during a submit operation after the validations and processes. A branch has two important components: its target and its condition.

The branch's target specifies the page (or URL) to redirect to. You specify the target using the link builder, just as you did when configuring a redirection for a button or link. Consequently, a branch can also assign values to items in the session state or clear item values on a page.

The branch's condition specifies when the branch is relevant. A page might have several target pages, depending on the value of the session state. You implement this situation by creating a branch for each target page and assigning a condition to each branch. The branch conditions should be non-overlapping so that one branch (at most) will be able to fire during any submit operation.

▩ ▩ ▩

Tabular Forms

Your use of reports has so far been read-only. Whenever you wanted to interact with a report, you had to do so indirectly. For example, consider the Report Data Entry page of Chapter 7 (refer to Figure 7-14). To use that page to modify a record of the employee report, you must perform the following three steps:

- Click the hyperlink of the desired record, which causes the FetchRecordForUpdate (or ARF) process to retrieve that employee's information from the database and store it in the appropriate items.

- Modify the content of those items.

- Click a button to perform the update.

The peculiar thing about these steps is that they don't use the contents of the employee report. In particular, consider the first step. Even if the employee report contains the information you want, you cannot access it; instead, you have to re-query the database.

A more desirable way to perform the first step would be to copy the values from the report into the items on the page as part of the redirect action. However, an even better way would be to make the changes directly on the report. APEX calls such a report a *tabular form*. In this chapter, you will examine the concepts and techniques needed to build and customize tabular forms. You will also look at the built-in tabular form processes and see how to use the *tabular form wizard* to create a ready-made tabular form page.

Creating a Tabular Form Region

In Chapter 3 you examined two report types: classic reports and interactive reports. A tabular form is a third report type. For the first example of a tabular form region, consider the page Tabular Form Practice, which is page 35 of the demo and is shown in Figure 10-1. This section examines how to build its Employees region; the next section examines the other two regions.

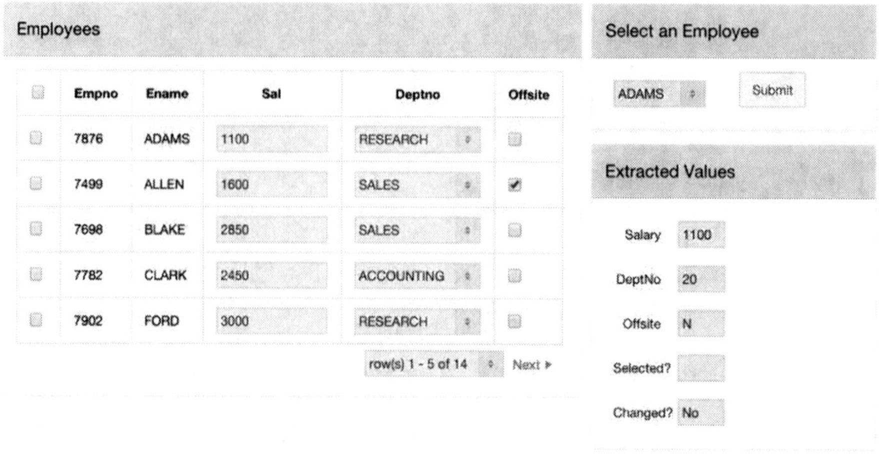

Figure 10-1. *Tabular Form Practice page*

To build the page, begin by creating a new region in a new page, as discussed in Chapter 3. Title the region Employees and choose Tabular Form as the region type. (A warning message will be displayed; ignore it. Its concerns will be discussed later, in the section "Tabular Form Wizard.")

You will be required to specify a source query, which should be the following:

```
select EmpNo, EName, Sal, DeptNo, Offsite
from EMP
order by EName
```

If you run the page, you will see what looks like a classic report. If you examine the property editor, you will see essentially no difference between the properties of a tabular form and those of a classic report. What makes tabular forms special?

The difference lies in the possible column types. A tabular form column has 18 possible types, as opposed to only 7 types for a classic report column. These types are shown in Figure 10-2.

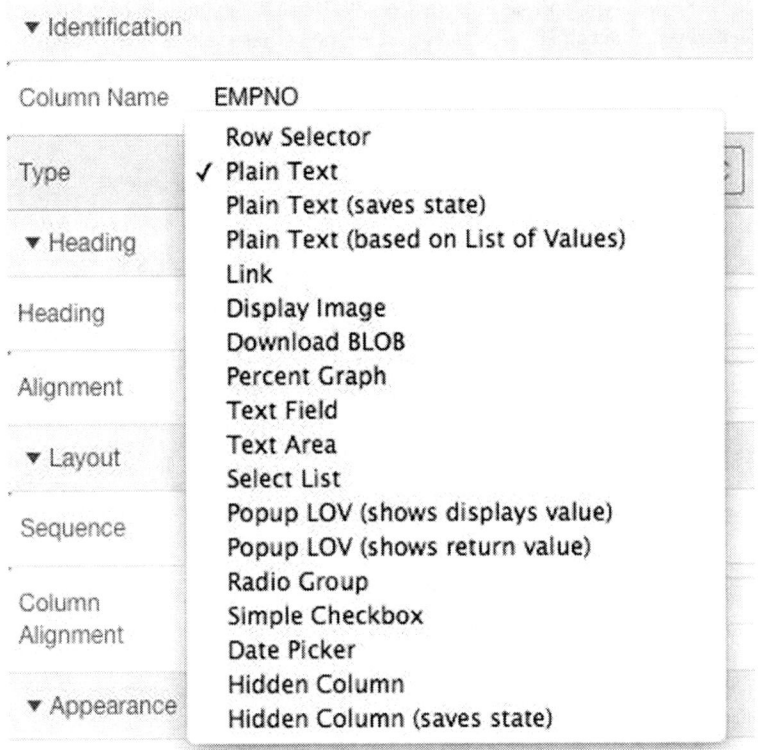

Figure 10-2. *Display types for a tabular form column*

Of the 11 new types, 9 are *modifiable*, meaning that a user can change their value directly in the report; the other two types are nonmodifiable. The default column type for a tabular form is Plain Text, which is a nonmodifiable type used in classic reports. The report shown in Figure 10-1 has three modifiable columns:

- Sal has the type Text Field
- DeptNo has the type Select List
- Offsite has the type Simple Checkbox

Modifiable columns have properties similar to their analogous item types. Text-based columns have a width that can be specified by the Width property in the Appearance section. List-based columns have a list-of-values query, which is specified in the List of Values section. For example, the query for the DeptNo list is this:

```
select DName, DeptNo
from DEPT
order by DName
```

The Simple Checkbox type corresponds to a Yes/No item. It can be used only for columns having two possible values, such as Offsite. One of these values corresponds to a checked box, and the other corresponds to an unchecked box. You specify these two values in the column's List of Values section via a comma-separated list; the value denoting a checked box is first in the list. For example, the definition for the Offsite column is simply this:

Y,N

The Employees region in Figure 10-1 has a column of checkboxes on its left. These checkboxes, which are called *row selectors*, provide a useful way for a user to select rows. You can create a row selector column by right-clicking the Columns folder in the rendering tree; Figure 10-3 shows the resulting menu. The row selector column will be named CHECK$01.

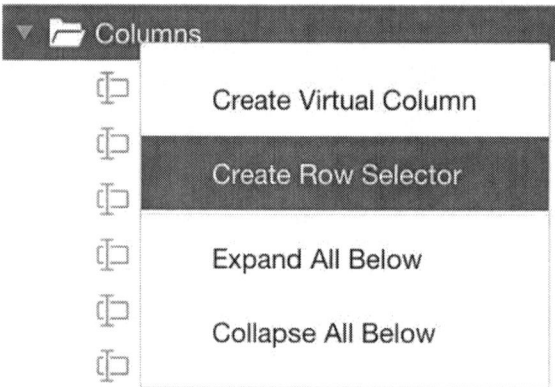

Figure 10-3. *Creating a row selector column*

After changing your tabular form to correspond to Figure 10-1, you should experiment with using other modifiable types for these columns, just to see their effect. And feel free to make random modifications to the column values — as soon as you reload the page, the tabular form will return to its original contents.

Accessing Values from a Tabular Form

Now consider the two right-hand regions of Figure 10-1. The item in the Select an Employee region is named P35_EMPNO. A user chooses an employee from that item and clicks the Submit button. A process associated with the button examines the tabular form; finds the row corresponding to the chosen employee; extracts the values of the Sal, DeptNo, and Offsite columns from that row; and places those values into the corresponding items of the Extracted Values region. In addition, the item labeled Selected? will contain an X if the row's selector box is checked and is blank otherwise; and the item Changed? will contain Yes if the user modified the column in the browser and No otherwise.

For a process to perform these tasks, the necessary column values must be in the session state. APEX therefore handles a tabular form as follows. When the page is submitted, the server saves the current contents of each displayed row in its session state. Well, it actually doesn't save the entire row; it saves only the values of the *state-saving* columns. Modifiable column types — which include the row selector — are always state saving. There also are two state-saving unmodifiable column types: Plain Text (saves state) and Hidden Column (saves state). These types were listed in Figure 10-2.

For an example, consider the Tabular Form Practice page of Figure 10-1. For the submit process to determine the row containing the chosen employee number, the EmpNo column must be state-saving. On the other hand, the EName column does not need to be state saving because the submit process does not need those values. You should therefore modify the properties of the Employees tabular form so that EmpNo has the type Plain Text (saves state), and EName has the type Plain Text. The tabular form will now have five state-saving columns: the row selector, EmpNo, Sal, DeptNo, and Offsite. When the page is submitted, the APEX server will save 25 values in the session state — 5 values for each of the 5 rows on the page. Note that the session state contains only the values of the currently displayed rows. If the user repaginates the tabular form, the existing values will be deleted from the session state and replaced by the values for the new page of records.

You are now ready to write the submit process, which is called ExtractValues. Typically, a process that acts on a tabular form loops through it, performing some action on each displayed row. For example, the ExtractValues process needs to examine the EmpNo value of each row; if it finds the value specified in P35_EMPNO, it should assign values from that row to the corresponding items in the Extracted Values region. Because this looping is so common, APEX performs it for you; the tabular form process only needs to contain code to handle a single row. Listing 10-1 displays the PL/SQL code for the ExtractValues process.

Listing 10-1. Code for the ExtractValues Process

```
begin
  if :P35_EMPNO = :EMPNO then
    :P35_SALARY := :SAL;
    :P35_DEPTNO := :DEPTNO;
    :P35_OFFSITE := :OFFSITE;
    :P35_IS_SELECTED := :APEX$ROW_SELECTOR;
    :P35_HAS_CHANGED := 'No';
  end if;
end;
```

The expressions :EMPNO, :SAL, :DEPTNO, and :OFFSITE refer to the column values of the row being processed. In general, if C is the name of a state-saving column, then :C is a bind-variable reference to that column's value in the current row moreover, the expression :APEX$ROW_SELECTOR refers to the row-selector value of the current row; its value is "X" if selected, and null otherwise.

When you create a process associated with a tabular form, you must be aware of two important properties. The first is the property Tabular Form, which appears in the Execution Options section; see Figure 10-4. Every process you wrote in Chapter 7 left this property blank. If you want the process to apply to a tabular form, you must assign the name of the tabular form to this property.

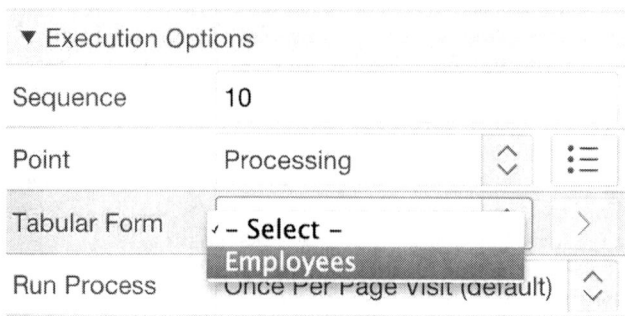

Figure 10-4. *Tabular Form property of a process*

The second important property is Execution Scope, which appears in the Condition section; see Figure 10-5. This property specifies how APEX should loop through the rows of the tabular form. The value All Submitted Rows says to consider all rows, and the value For Created and Modified Rows says to consider only the rows that have been changed. Figure 10-5 shows that the ExtractValues process loops through all rows.

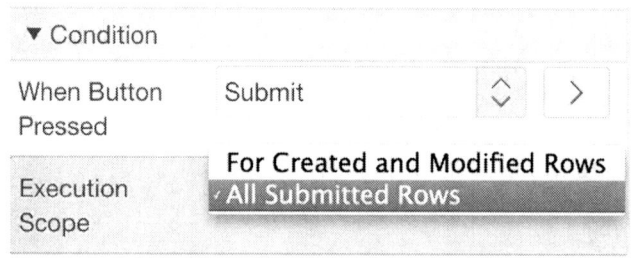

Figure 10-5. *Execution Scope property of a process*

The code for the ExtractValues process sets the item P35_HAS_CHANGED to the value No. This is only partially correct — if the user had modified the row prior to clicking the button, then the item should have the value Yes. APEX does keep track of which rows have changed, but your process cannot access this information directly. Instead, you determine the information indirectly, as follows.

Create a process called ExtractChanged that has the code of Listing 10-2. Configure this process to be associated with the tabular form, and have the execution scope For Created and Modified Rows. The code looks for the specified row and sets P35_HAS_ CHANGED to Yes when found. The point of the process is that it executes only for changed rows. Thus if the specified row has not changed, it will not be found during the loop, and the value of P35_HAS_CHANGED will continue to have the value No.

Listing 10-2. Code for the ExtractChanged process

```
begin
  if :P35_EMPNO = :EMPNO then
    :P35_HAS_CHANGED := 'Yes';
  end if;
end;
```

At this point, you should have a fully functional Tabular Form Practice page. Try it out: change the values of a row, choose the employee for that row from the select list, and click the submit button. You should discover that your changed values will appear in the Extracted Values region, but the tabular form will be re-rendered with its original values. This behavior should make sense to you. The modified values are still in the session state, but the tabular form recomputes its values from the database. If you want your changes to appear in the tabular form, you will need to update the database. This issue is covered in the next section.

Before you do so, however, let's make one more modification to the page. Suppose that you want the user to choose the desired employee by clicking a row selector check box instead of choosing from the select list. Listing 10-3 shows the revised code for the ExtractValues process. The primary difference is the if-condition, which now tests the value of the row selector instead of the select list. The assignment statements for P35_IS_SELECTED and P35_HAS_CHANGED have also changed because choosing the row selector automatically makes these values true (so you no longer need the ExtractChanged process). Note that if the user selects multiple rows, then row values will be extracted multiple times, which means that the Extracted Values region will contain the values of the last checked row. Also note that it does not matter whether you choose an execution scope of all records or only changed records. Clicking the row selector changes the record, so that record will be considered in either case.

Listing 10-3. Alternative Code for the ExtractValues Process

```
begin
  if :APEX$ROW_SELECTOR = 'X' then
    :P35_SALARY := :SAL;
    :P35_DEPTNO := :DEPTNO;
    :P35_OFFSITE := :OFFSITE;
    :P35_IS_SELECTED := 'X';
    :P35_HAS_CHANGED := 'Yes';
  end if;
end;
```

Updating the Database

Tabular forms are used primarily to modify the database. Consider for example the Tabular Form Update page shown in Figure 10-6, which is page 36 of the demo application. This page can be used to either delete or update rows. If a user wants to delete some rows, the user chooses the row selectors and then clicks the Delete Selected button. To update some rows, the user makes those updates directly in the form and then clicks the Update Changed button.

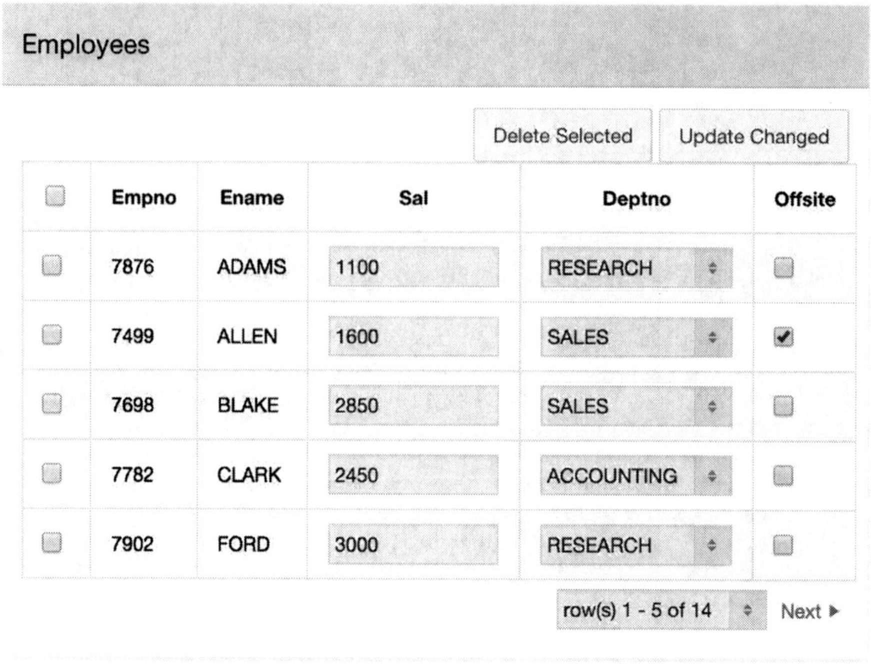

Figure 10-6. *Tabular Form Update page*

This page consists of a tabular form region titled Employees, and two buttons. You create the tabular form region exactly the same way as in the Tabular Form Practice page. You also need to create a process for each button. The process for the delete button is named DeleteSelected; its code appears in Listing 10-4. The code executes an SQL deletion statement for each selected record. Because selecting a record is considered a "change" to it, you can set the scope of the process to For Created and Modified Rows. (It would also be correct to set the scope to All Submitted Rows, but scanning the unselected rows would be somewhat pointless).

Listing 10-4. Code for the DeleteSelected Process

```
begin
  if :APEX$ROW_SELECTOR = 'X' then
      delete from EMP
      where EmpNo = :EMPNO;
  end if;
end;
```

The process for the update button is named UpdateChanged; its code appears in Listing 10-5. This code executes an SQL update statement for each row. If you set the process execution scope to For Created and Modified Rows, you guarantee that only the modified rows will be updated. Note that you could set the scope to All Submitted

Rows, but that would cause APEX to execute update statements for rows that had not changed, which is correct, of course, but also ridiculously inefficient.

Listing 10-5. Code for the UpdateChanged Process

```
begin
  update EMP
  set Sal=:SAL, DeptNo=:DEPTNO, Offsite=:OFFSITE
  where EmpNo = :EMPNO;
end;
```

Validations

Chapter 8 discussed the need to validate user input, and you saw how to use validations to check for inappropriate item values. The same concerns apply to tabular forms — you need to check their modifiable columns for inappropriate values.

A validation that applies to a tabular form works similarly to a process that applies to a tabular form. You specify the validation for a single row of the form, and APEX will loop through the displayed rows, applying the validation to each row. You can specify the execution scope of the validation to be For Created and Modified Rows or All Submitted Rows — the same as with a process.

For an example, let's create a validation that ensures that salaries are greater than zero. Go to the Tabular Form Update page and create a validation called ValidSalary. Its type can be SQL Expression, having this value:

```
:SAL > 0
```

Configure the validation to be associated with the tabular form Employees and set its execution scope to be For Created and Modified Rows. Then try it out. Change the salary of one or more employees to a negative number and click the Update Changed button. APEX will refuse to perform the update and will display your validation's error message together with the row numbers of the inappropriate values.

In Chapter 8, you saw how to use a validation to check for lost updates, and this issue is also relevant for tabular forms. When performing an update to the form, you need to ensure that the values to be modified have not changed since they were originally read in. The strategy is the same as in Chapter 8: for each row of the tabular form, you save the hash of its modifiable values. The easiest way to do so is to calculate the hash value in the tabular form's source query. That is, its source query should be the following:

```
select EmpNo, EName, Sal, DeptNo, Offsite,
       apex_util.get_hash(apex_t_varchar2(Sal, DeptNo, Offsite)) as HashVal
from EMP
order by EName
```

You don't want the hash value to be displayed in the report, but you need its value to be accessible. Thus you should set its column type to be Hidden (save state), which is state saving but not displayed. You can then create a validation that recomputes the hash value of the selected record from the database and compares it with the saved hash value. This validation code is most easily expressed as a Rows returned SQL query; see Listing 10-6.

Listing 10-6. Validation Code for the Tabular Form Update Page

```
select * from EMP
where EmpNo = :EMPNO
and apex_util.get_hash(apex_t_varchar2(Sal, DeptNo, Offsite)) = :HASHVAL
```

The execution scope of this validation should be For Created and Modified Rows. APEX will execute the validation query for each modified row. As the validation is of type Rows Returned, it will succeed for a row if the validation query returns at least one record. Because the query of Listing 10-6 returns a row if the current hash value for an employee is the same as the hash value originally computed for that employee, the validation will succeed exactly as when the row's modifiable values have not changed.

You can test your validation the same as you did in Chapter 8. Open the Tabular Form Update page on two different machines. On one machine, change some values of a row and click the Update Changed button. This update should succeed. Now change some values for the same row on the other machine and click the Update Changed button. This update will fail, displaying your validation's error message.

Built-in Tabular Form Processes

In the previous section you wrote two processes for the Tabular Form Update page: DeleteSelected and UpdateChanged. Although these processes were relatively easy to code, APEX makes it even easier by providing built-in processes for you. In particular, the built-in process type Tabular Form - Multi Row Delete corresponds to DeleteSelected, and Tabular Form - Multi Row Update corresponds to UpdateChanged.

To create a multi-row delete process, create a new process and set its type to Tabular Form - Multi Row Delete. You need to enter the table name and key column in the Settings section, as shown in Figure 10-7. Creating a multi-row update process is analogous.

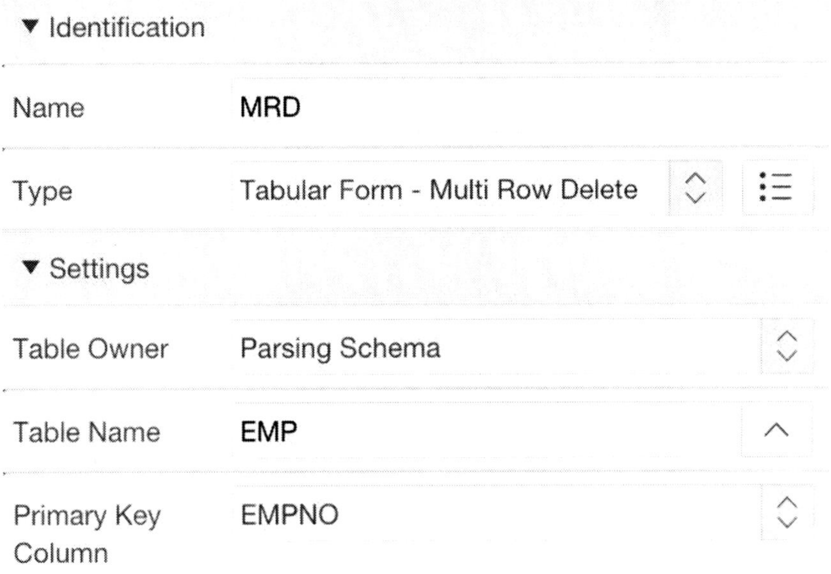

▼ Identification

Name	**MRD**
Type	Tabular Form - Multi Row Delete

▼ Settings

Table Owner	Parsing Schema
Table Name	**EMP**
Primary Key Column	**EMPNO**

Figure 10-7. *Configuring a multi-row delete process*

You can easily modify the Tabular Form Update page to replace the DeleteSelected process with a multi-row delete process. First, deactivate DeleteSelected by setting its condition type to Never (or you can simply delete the process). Then create a multi-row delete process. Configure this process the same as DeleteSelected: associate the process with the tabular form, connect it to the delete button, and set its execution scope. When you run the page, you should notice no difference in its behavior. That is, these two processes are functionally equivalent.

You can similarly create a multi-row update process to replace UpdateChanged. The nice thing about the multi-row update process is that it protects against lost updates. Consequently, you do not need to modify the form's source query to calculate a hash value and you can eliminate the lost update validation. (Note that you will need to remove the HashVal column from the source query, because the multi-row update process gets confused by state-saving computed columns.)

The one problem with automatic lost update detection is that you have no control over the validation error message. Figure 10-8 shows part of the automatically-generated lost update error message, which is not especially user-friendly.

1 error has occurred

- Current version of data in database has changed since user initiated update process. current row version identifier = "209864B9A03AC5B20896A473781C0CB330B7CB1ACF154324B4A3579EEC9225324F6A1FE2ECC6FBA158389470 application row version identifier = "A52E289876FD66A5B645B5254FED66DAB026C04D3BEB2145A01DDCE8261CC3291964A0D193DA7A038434E84 (Row 2)

Figure 10-8. *Lost update error message*

257

Tabular Form Wizard

When you create a tabular form region on a page, APEX displays the message shown in Figure 10-9. This message is a reminder that you are responsible for creating any necessary processes and validations on the tabular form. The message also invites you to use the *tabular form wizard*, which will create a page for you that contains the tabular form plus everything it needs.

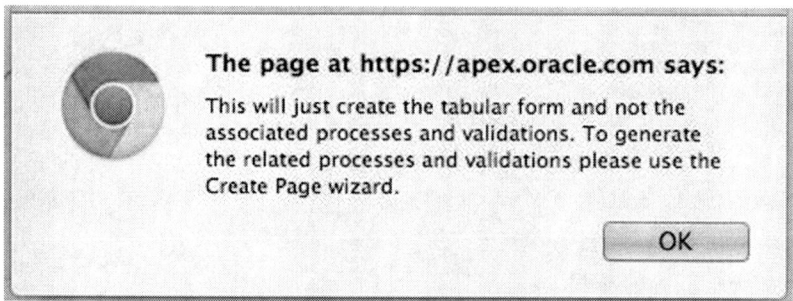

The page at https://apex.oracle.com says:

This will just create the tabular form and not the associated processes and validations. To generate the related processes and validations please use the Create Page wizard.

OK

Figure 10-9. *Invitation to use the tabular form wizard*

To get to the tabular form wizard, begin at the Create Page wizard: select Form as the page type and then choose Tabular Form. The tabular form wizard will ask you to supply the necessary data about the form, such as the following:

- Table name (choose EMP)

- Columns to display (choose EmpNo, EName, Sal, DeptNo, and Offsite)

- Primary key column (choose EmpNo)

- Means by which primary key values are determined (choose Existing Trigger)

- Modifiable columns (choose EName, Sal, DeptNo, and Offsite)

- Operations you want implemented (choose Update, Insert, and Delete) and the names of the corresponding buttons

The wizard will generate the page shown in Figure 10-10, which will be page 37 of the demo application. The wizard implements each modifiable column as a text field. You can easily customize the tabular form to look like Figure 10-6 by changing the type of the EName, DeptNo, and Offsite columns; setting the number of displayed rows to 5; and modifying the source query to order the rows by EName. You will also discover that the automatically generated source query is rather clunky; feel free to rewrite it.

Employees

	Empno	Ename	Sal	Deptno	Offsite
☐	7839	KING	5000	10	N
☐	7698	BLAKE	2850	30	N
☐	7782	CLARK	2450	10	N
☐	7566	JONES	2975	20	N
☐	7788	SCOTT	3000	20	Y
☐	7902	FORD	3000	20	N
☐	7369	SMITH	1200	20	N
☐	7499	ALLEN	1600	30	Y
☐	7654	MARTIN	1250	30	N
☐	7844	TURNER	1500	30	Y

row(s) 1 - 10 of 14 ⇕ Next ▶

Add Row

Cancel   Delete   Apply Changes

Figure 10-10. *Tabular form page*

The wizard also generates a multi-row delete process and a multi-row update process for the tabular form, as well as validations based on column type. For example, the tabular form in Figure 10-10 has validations to ensure that the Sal and DeptNo values are numeric. You are still responsible for creating the validations that enforce constraints, such as checking that salary values are positive.

The tabular form in Figure 10-10 has a feature that is missing from your earlier tabular forms: the ability to insert rows. Clicking the Add Row button causes the tabular form to display a new empty row; see Figure 10-11. This row is not yet in the database. (You can tell because the pagination item indicates that the table still has 14 records.) To insert the row, enter the desired column values and click the Apply Changes button. The tabular form is able use this button for both insert and update operations because the multi-row update process knows how to handle insertions as well as updates.

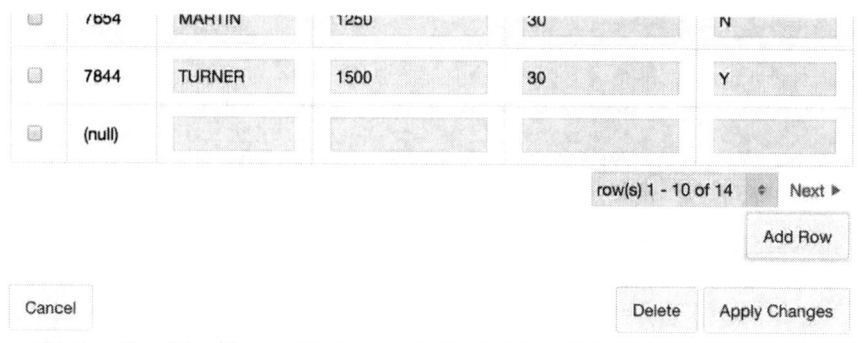

Figure 10-11. Adding a row to a tabular form

This ability to add a row to the tabular form is interesting. To discover how the Add Row button works, examine its Behavior properties. Figure 10-12 shows these properties; their values tell you that the button redirects to the JavaScript function addRow, which does all of the work.

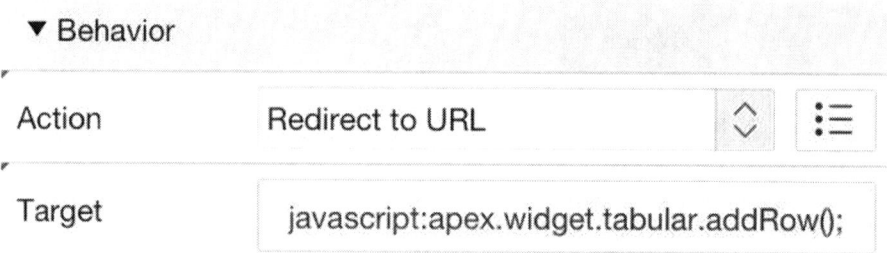

Figure 10-12. Behavior of the Add Row button

You can use this same target URL to add insertion functionality to your own tabular form regions. As an example, let's redo the Tabular Form Update page. You will need to make three changes:

- Create a new button labeled Add Row and give it the behavior shown in Figure 10-12.

- Change the type of the ENAME column to Text Field.

- Modify the UpdateChanged process to perform the insertion.

Figure 10-13 shows the revised page in action. The user has clicked Add Row and has filled in values for the modifiable columns. Clicking the Update Changed button will insert the new record into the EMP table.

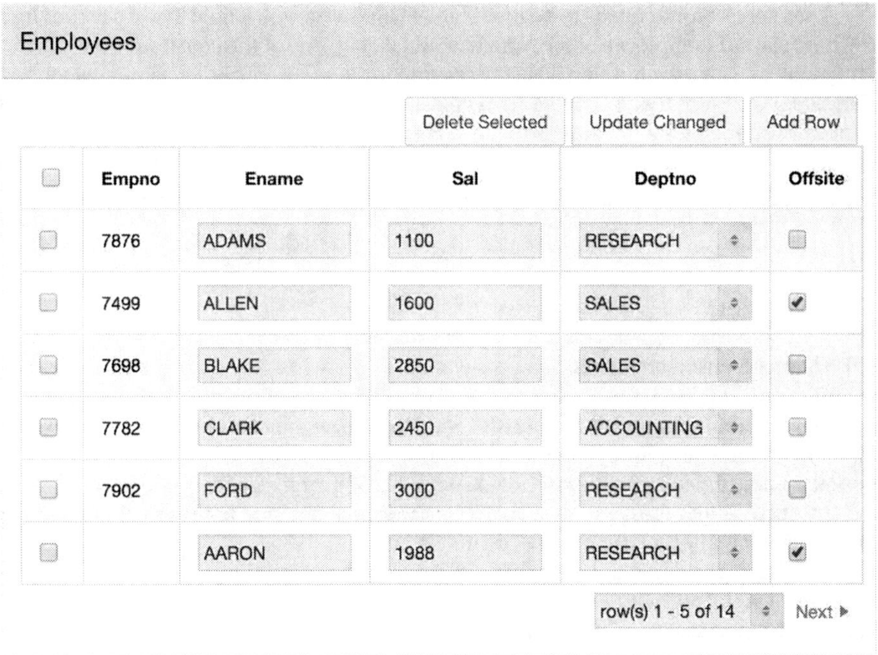

	Employees				
			Delete Selected	Update Changed	Add Row
☐	**Empno**	**Ename**	**Sal**	**Deptno**	**Offsite**
☐	7876	ADAMS	1100	RESEARCH ⇕	☐
☐	7499	ALLEN	1600	SALES ⇕	☑
☐	7698	BLAKE	2850	SALES ⇕	☐
☐	7782	CLARK	2450	ACCOUNTING ⇕	☐
☐	7902	FORD	3000	RESEARCH ⇕	☐
☐		AARON	1988	RESEARCH ⇕	☑

row(s) 1 - 5 of 14 ⇕   Next ▶

Figure 10-13. *RevisedTabular Form Update page*

A key part of the modification to UpdateChanged is how you determine whether to insert or update each changed row. The idea is to use a row's EMPNO value to decide — a null value means to insert, and a non-null value means to update. The revised code appears in Listing 10-7.

Listing 10-7. Revision of UpdateChanged to Support Insertion

```
begin
  if :EMPNO is null then
     insert into EMP (EName, Sal, DeptNo, Offsite)
     values (:ENAME, :SAL, :DEPTNO, :OFFSITE);
  else
     update EMP
     set Sal=:SAL, DeptNo=:DEPTNO, Offsite=:OFFSITE
     where EmpNo = :EMPNO;
  end if;
end;
```

261

The ENAME column needs to be modifiable. Otherwise, you would insert a record into EMP having a null employee name, which would violate one of the constraints on EMP. The problem with this situation is that users can now update employee names, which was something you were trying to avoid. This conundrum is an unavoidable consequence of performing updates and insertions in the same region. The solution taken in Listing 10-4 is to ignore any changes to the ENAME column during update, which admittedly is a poor user interface design. The only other solution is to perform insertions in a different region from the tabular form.

Summary

This chapter focused on tabular forms — what they are, what they can do, and how to build them. A tabular form is a report in which the values of specified columns are modifiable. Tabular forms are an effective way to perform data entry. You examined the different modifiable column types and their use, as well as the need for state-saving, nonmodifiable types. You also saw how to write PL/SQL processes that access the contents of a tabular form and save changes to the database, and how to write validations to ensure that inappropriate changes do not occur.

You then considered the ways that APEX supports the building of tabular forms. You first looked at the built-in multi-row delete and multi-row update processes; you saw how they can perform insert, delete, and update operations on the tabular form without the need for any PL/SQL code. You then looked at the tabular form wizard, which creates a tabular form on a new page. This wizard also creates the various buttons, processes, and validations that go with the tabular form, which makes it convenient to use. After the page has been created, you can use the techniques of this chapter to customize it to your particular needs.

■ ■ ■

Dynamic SQL

In this book, you have seen many examples of pages that are customized by session state values. For example, the SQL source query of a report is a good candidate for customization, as is an SQL statement in a process that accesses the database. A large portion of this customization comes from bound references in SQL statements.

However, there are limits to what can be customized. A reference to a session-state variable can replace a constant in the SQL query, but it is not allowed to replace a table name or a column name. In this chapter, you will examine a technique called *dynamic SQL*, which overcomes this limitation by using PL/SQL code to construct and execute an SQL statement at runtime. You will see how to use dynamic SQL as the source of a report or the contents of a process, and look at three examples that require dynamic SQL.

Dynamic Reports

Consider the Report Builder page shown in Figure 11-1, which will be page 38 of the demo application. The items in the top region allow a user to specify a report for a table. A user chooses the desired table, selects the columns to display, and then enters the text of the filtering condition. Clicking the submit button displays the specified report in the bottom region.

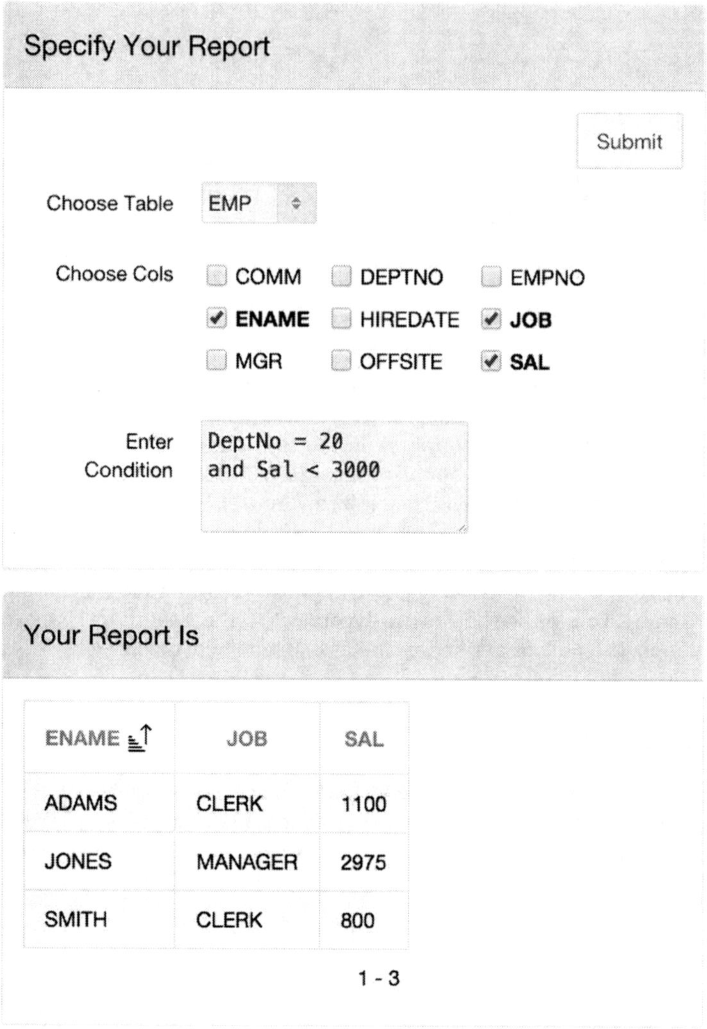

Specify Your Report

Submit

Choose Table   EMP ⬍

Choose Cols   ☐ COMM   ☐ DEPTNO   ☐ EMPNO
               ✔ **ENAME**   ☐ HIREDATE   ✔ **JOB**
               ☐ MGR   ☐ OFFSITE   ✔ **SAL**

Enter   DeptNo = 20
Condition   and Sal < 3000

Your Report Is

ENAME ⬆	JOB	SAL
ADAMS	CLERK	1100
JONES	MANAGER	2975
SMITH	CLERK	800

1 - 3

Figure 11-1. *Report Builder page*

What does it take to implement these two regions? The Specify Your Report region is relatively straightforward. The region has three items. The select list P38_TABLE displays the names of relevant tables. One way to specify its values is to use a static expression such as this:

```
STATIC:EMP,DEPT
```

Another way to specify its values is to use a query, which would make use of Oracle's User_Tables table, as follows:

```
select Table_Name as DisplayVal, Table_Name as ResultVal
from User_Tables
order by DisplayVal
```

The P38_COLS item displays a checkbox for each column of the selected table. It uses the cascading lists technique of Chapter 6, with P38_TABLE as its cascading LOV parent item. Its values are defined by the following query, which makes use of Oracle's User_Tab_Cols table:

```
select Column_Name as DisplayVal, Column_Name as ResultVal
from User_Tab_Cols
where Table_Name = :P38_TABLE
order by DisplayVal
```

The item P38_WHERE is a text area in which the user enters the filtering condition. This condition will be used as the where clause of the report's source query.

The Your Report Is region displays a report that is customized according to the values of these items. This region is not so straightforward to implement. Suppose that you tried to create the region as a classic report: its source query would need to look something like this:

```
select :P38_COLS
from   :P38_TABLE
where  :P38_WHERE
```

The problem is that such a query is syntactically illegal. The rule is that a bind variable can be used only to reference a constant, and this query is trying to reference columns, tables, and SQL code. To solve this problem, APEX provides the region type Classic Report (based on Function). The source of this region is a PL/SQL function that computes the desired SQL query as a string. Figure 11-2 depicts the Identification and Source properties for the region.

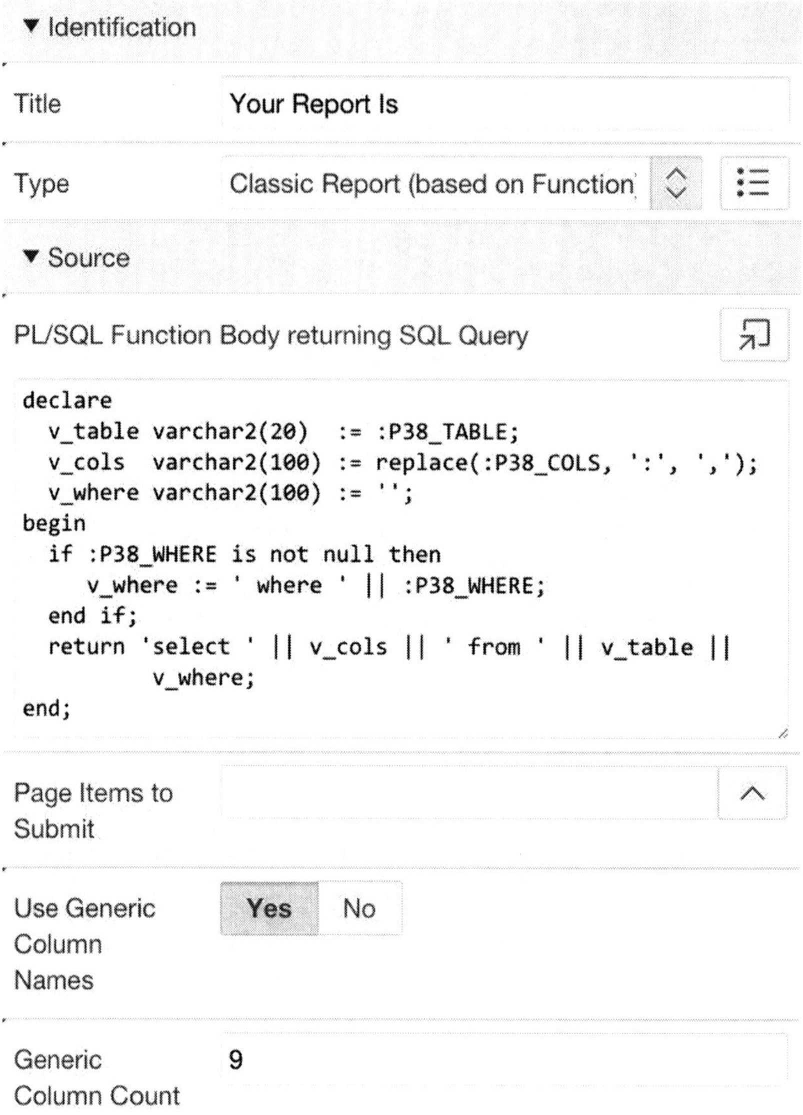

▼ Identification

Title	Your Report Is
Type	Classic Report (based on Function ⇕ ☰

▼ Source

PL/SQL Function Body returning SQL Query ⬏

```
declare
  v_table varchar2(20)   := :P38_TABLE;
  v_cols  varchar2(100) := replace(:P38_COLS, ':', ',');
  v_where varchar2(100) := '';
begin
  if :P38_WHERE is not null then
     v_where := ' where ' || :P38_WHERE;
  end if;
  return 'select ' || v_cols || ' from ' || v_table ||
         v_where;
end;
```

Page Items to Submit	⌃

Use Generic Column Names	**Yes** No

Generic Column Count	9

Figure 11-2. Implementing the Report Builder report region

The PL/SQL code constructs the desired SQL query string piece by piece. The construction of the column list is perhaps the only non-obvious part. Recall that P38_COLS is a multivalue list item, which means that its value will be a string containing the selected column names separated by colons. However, the column names need to be separated by commas in the query. Thus, all you need to do is use the replace function to replace each colon by a comma and then assign that string to the variable v_cols.

The technique of using code to construct the source query is called *dynamic SQL* because the query is computed dynamically at runtime. Dynamic SQL is appropriate whenever the source query can vary in ways that go beyond simple customization by constants.

One of the consequences of using dynamic SQL is that the columns of the report may not be known until runtime. In this case, you must tell APEX to define *generic* column names for the report. You do so via the property Use Generic Column Names, which can be seen at the bottom of Figure 11-2. When that property is set to Yes, the property Generic Column Count also appears, so that you can specify how many generic columns to create.

Figure 11-2 specified a count of 9, which means that APEX will generate 9 columns for the report. The names of these columns will be COL01, COL02, and up to COL09. This specified count is a maximum; if the report happens to use fewer columns (as shown in Figure 11-1), the others will be ignored.

When dealing with generic columns, you also need to specify the column headers of the report; otherwise, the column headers will be the generic column names, which is not user friendly. The relevant properties are in the report's Heading section, which appears in the Attributes component of its rendering tree. Figure 11-3 shows the five heading types. The default type is Custom Headings, which lets you specify the heading of each column individually. The two Column Names types use the column name as its heading and ignore any customization.

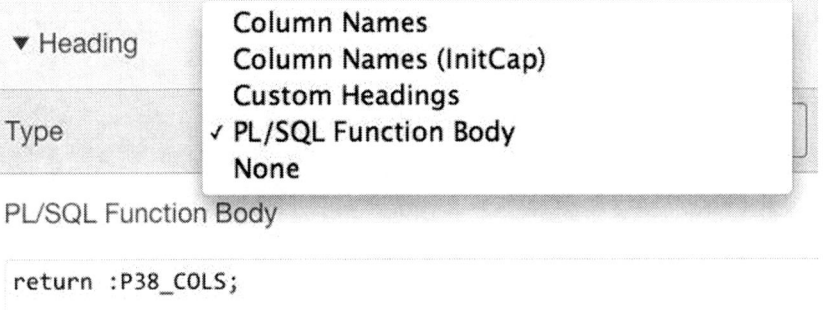

Figure 11-3. *Specifying headings for generic columns*

The heading type PL/SQL Function Body is the best choice for handling generic columns. Selecting it causes APEX to display a text area for entering PL/SQL code; that code should return a string containing a colon-separated list of columns. In this example, the check box group P38_COLS contains exactly what you need, so your code can simply return its value, as shown at the bottom of Figure 11-3. In more complex situations, you can write a PL/SQL block to compute the desired string.

When you run your page, you will notice that the report will display the following error message until you choose at least one column:

```
failed to parse SQL query: ORA-00936: missing expression
```

The reason is that when P38_COLS is empty, the SQL string generated in Figure 11-2 begins "select from ...", which is not legal SQL. A good way to avoid this unpleasantness is to render the report region conditionally. In particular, set its Condition Type property to P38_COLS is not null.

Dynamic Processes

Chapter 7 discussed how to use an SQL statement within a PL/SQL block: place the statement directly within the block and parameterize it using bind variables. However, this syntax is not sufficient for dynamic SQL. This section explores the issues and their solution.

For an example, let's build the Count and Delete page shown in Figure 11-4, which is page 39 of the demo application.

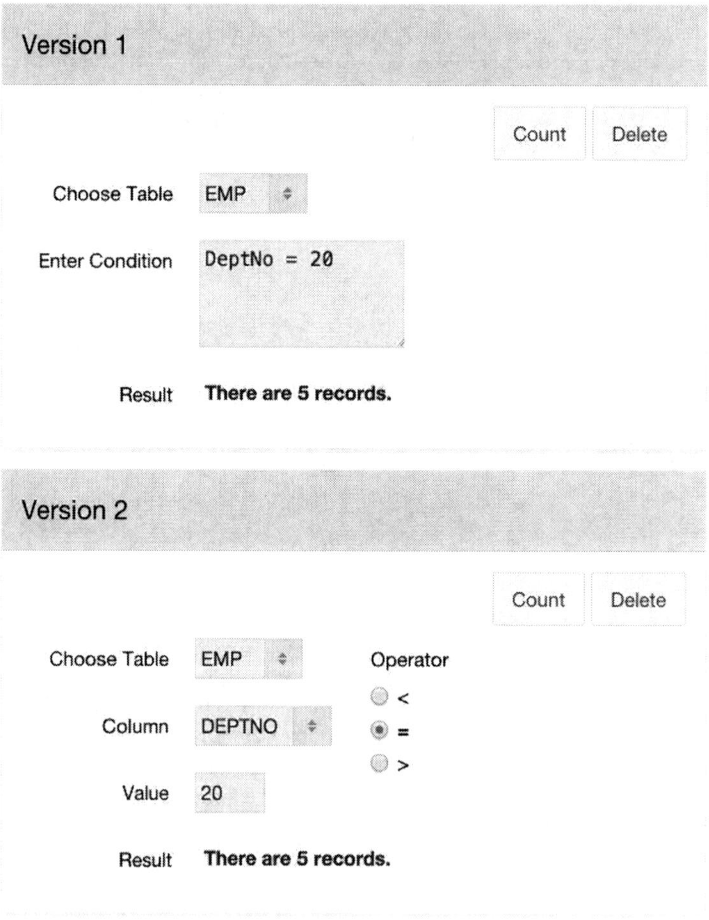

Figure 11-4. Count and Delete page

This page contains two regions that have essentially the same functionality. In each case, a user chooses a table and specifies a filtering condition on it. Each region has the same two buttons: the Count button displays a message giving the number of records satisfying the condition, and the Delete button deletes those records from the table. Figure 11-4 shows the result of clicking the Count button in both regions.

Both regions in Figure 11-4 display the same condition: the employees in department 20. The difference between the two regions is how the user specifies the filtering condition. In the Version 1 region, the user can enter an arbitrary condition, similar to the Report Builder page. In the Version 2 region, the user composes the condition by choosing a specific column, operator, and value. Note that this second way of specifying the condition doesn't require knowledge of SQL syntax and is perhaps more user-friendly, but it limits the kinds of conditions that can be expressed.

The creation of the items and buttons on this page is straightforward. The Version 1 region has three items: item P39_TABLE1 is a select list whose values are defined as STATIC2:EMP,DEPT, item P39_WHERE1 is a text area, and P39_RESULT1 is a display-only item.

The Version 2 region has five items. The item P39_TABLE2 is defined the same way as P39_TABLE1. The item P39_COLUMN2 is a select list having P39_TABLE2 as its cascading parent; its values are defined by this SQL query:

```
select Column_Name as DisplayVal, Column_Name as ResultVal
from User_Tab_Cols
where Table_Name = :P39_TABLE2
order by DisplayVal
```

The item P39_VALUE2 is a text field, and P39_RESULT2 is a display-only item. Finally, item P39_OPERATOR2 is a radio group with values defined as STATIC2:<,=,>. Note that the label appears above the group, which results from setting the item's Template property to Optional-Above.

The most interesting aspect of the page is the question of how to write the processes for the four buttons. Each process performs the same three tasks:

- It constructs a string containing the appropriate SQL command.

- It executes that string.

- It uses the result of the execution to formulate the output message.

Note that the source code for a dynamic report needs to perform only the first task because APEX executes the query string when it renders the report. A process, on the other hand, does not have this luxury, and it has to explicitly execute the SQL string.

The PL/SQL command to execute an SQL string is called *execute immediate*. This command is somewhat intricate to use — in fact, each of the four button processes uses it slightly differently. Let's examine each process in turn.

First, consider the process for the Version 1 Delete button. This process must execute an SQL deletion command, but because it doesn't know the table and its where-clause until runtime, the process needs to use dynamic SQL. The code appears in Listing 11-1.

Listing 11-1. Delete Process for Version 1 of Figure 11-4

```
declare
  v_cmd varchar2(100);
begin
  v_cmd := 'delete from ' || :P39_TABLE1 || ' where ' || :P39_WHERE1;

  execute immediate v_cmd;

  :P39_RESULT1 := SQL%rowcount || ' records were deleted.';
end;
```

The first statement constructs the SQL deletion command as a string using the chosen table and specified condition. The second statement uses the execute immediate command in its most basic form: you simply pass the SQL string to it. The third statement assigns a value to the result item by using the SQL%rowcount function (which was discussed in Chapter 7).

Now consider the process for the Version 1 Count button. This process needs to execute a query that will calculate the record count, saving the retrieved value in a variable. In Chapter 7, you saw how to use the SQL into-clause for that purpose. For example if you did not have to use dynamic SQL, you could write the query corresponding to Figure 11-4 like this:

```
select count(*) into v_count
from EMP
where DeptNo = 20
```

However, dynamic SQL requires that you associate the into-clause with the execute immediate command instead of with the SQL query. Listing 11-2 shows the proper code.

Listing 11-2. Count Process for Version 1 of Figure 11-4

```
declare
  v_query varchar2(100);
  v_count integer;
begin
  v_query := 'select count(*) from ' || :P39_TABLE1 ||
             ' where ' || :P39_WHERE1;

  execute immediate v_query
  into v_count;

  :P39_RESULT1 := 'There are ' || v_count || ' records.';
end;
```

Now consider the process for the Version 2 Delete button. Listing 11-3 and Listing 11-4 give two plausible ways to write the code, both of which are incorrect.

Listing 11-3. Constructed Query Does Not Handle String Values Correctly

```
declare
  v_cmd varchar2(100);
begin
  v_cmd := 'delete from ' || :P39_TABLE2 ||
            ' where ' || :P39_COLUMN2 || :P39_OPERATOR2 || :P39_VALUE2;
  execute immediate v_cmd;
end;
```

Listing 11-4. Constructed Query Is Illegal in Dynamic SQL

```
declare
  v_cmd varchar2(100);
begin
  v_cmd := 'delete from ' || :P39_TABLE2 ||
            ' where ' || :P39_COLUMN2 || :P39_OPERATOR2 || ':P39_VALUE2';
  execute immediate v_cmd;
end;
```

The issue is how to handle the constant in P39_VALUE2. The code in Listing 11-3 adds that value directly into the constructed string. For example, the string corresponding to Figure 11-4 is this:

```
delete from EMP where DeptNo=20
```

This string happens to be correct SQL. However, suppose that the user selected Job as the column and CLERK as the value. The deletion command would be this:

```
delete from EMP where Job=CLERK
```

This command is incorrect because string values need quotes around them. You could fix the code of Listing 11-3 by having it retrieve the type of the column and then add quotes to the string if warranted, but doing so is awkward and there is a better solution.

The code in Listing 11-4 attempts to get around this issue by generating a bind reference to the value. For example, the deletion command generated by Figure 11-4 would be this:

```
delete from EMP where DeptNo=:P39_VALUE2
```

Although this is exactly what you would use in a non-dynamic SQL process, it is not allowed in dynamic SQL because all bind variable references must be placed in the execute immediate command. In particular, execute immediate has a using-clause especially for this purpose. Listing 11-5 gives the correct code for the Version 2 Delete button.

Listing 11-5. Correct Code for the Version 2 Delete Process

```
declare
  v_cmd varchar2(100);
begin
  v_cmd := 'delete from ' || :P39_TABLE2 ||
            ' where ' || :P39_COLUMN2 || :P39_OPERATOR2 || ' :1';

  execute immediate v_cmd
  using :P39_VALUE2;

  :P39_RESULT2 := SQL%rowcount || ' records were deleted.';
end;
```

This code demonstrates how to handle parameterized SQL statements in dynamic SQL. All bind variable references go in the using-clause of the execute immediate command, separated by commas if there are more than one. Placeholder variables mark the locations in the SQL string where the bind variables would have gone.

In Listing 11-5, there is only one placeholder, namely :1. A placeholder has the same function as the formal parameter of a procedure. In effect, the execute immediate statement "calls" the SQL statement, passing it the value of each bind variable reference. The names of the placeholders are irrelevant. APEX will assign the values from the using-clause to the placeholders in the order in which the placeholders appear in the SQL statement.

Finally, consider the Version 2 Count button. The code for this process appears in Listing 11-6. Note that the constructed string is parameterized and a query; thus the execute immediate command will use both the into- and using-clauses.

Listing 11-6. Code for the Version 2 Count Process

```
declare
  v_query varchar2(100);
  v_count int;
begin
  v_query := 'select count(*) from ' || :P39_TABLE2 ||
              ' where ' || :P39_COLUMN2 || :P39_OPERATOR2 || ' :1';

  execute immediate v_query
  into v_count
  using :P39_VALUE2;

  :P39_RESULT2 := 'There are ' || v_count || ' records.';
end;
```

Combining Dynamic Reports and Processes

For a final example, let's reconsider the Single Record View demo page from Chapter 7 (refer to Figure 7-10). Recall that this page displays a report of all employees, sorted by EName. When a user selects an employee, the page turns into single-record mode, displaying the data of the selected record and providing buttons to navigate to the previous and next record in sorted order.

The task is to modify the page so that a user can dynamically change the sort order of the records. Figure 11-5 illustrates the new page, called Sortable Single Record View, which is page 40 of the demo application. The page is identical to the earlier one, except that it also has a select list for specifying the desired sort field. Selecting a sort field will cause the report to be redisplayed in that sort order; in addition, clicking the Previous or Next button will use that sort order to determine the new current row.

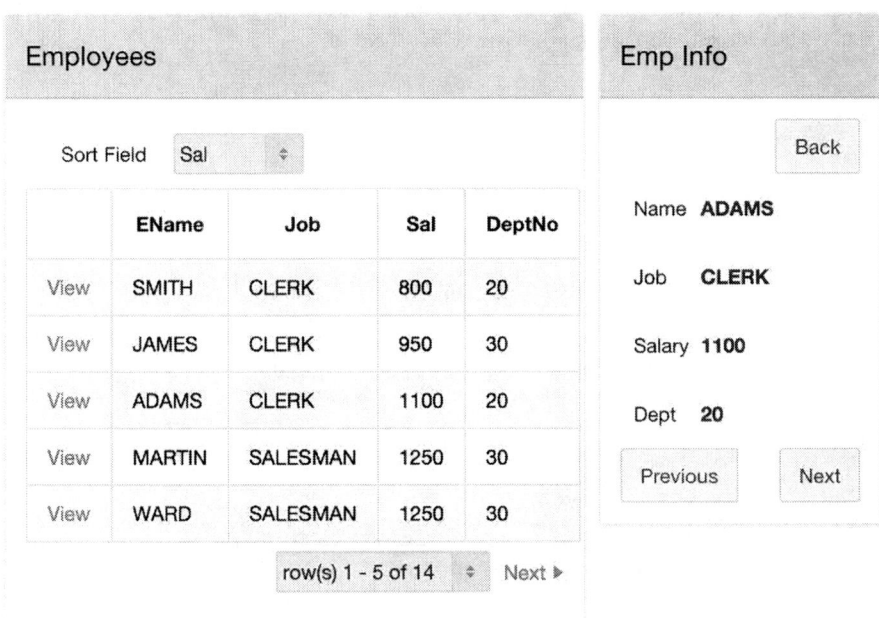

Figure 11-5. *Sortable Single Record View page*

As with Figure 7-10, Figure 11-5 shows both the Employees and Emp Info regions, even though only one of them is displayed at a time.

The easiest way to create this page is to copy the earlier page. To do so, go to the page designer for any page, click the + icon near the top, and select Page as Copy (see Figure 11-6). This choice will initiate the Page Copy wizard.

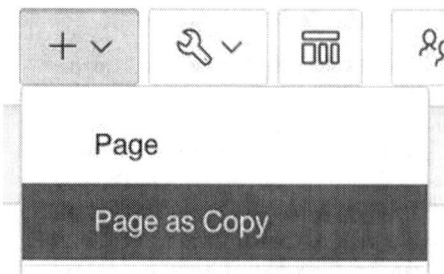

Figure 11-6. *Initiating the Page Copy wizard*

The first wizard screen asks for the destination application, which in this case is Page in this application. The second screen is where you specify the copying. Figure 11-7 displays this screen, with the appropriate values filled in.

Page to Copy

Application: **87059** ?

* Copy From Page   19. Single Record View   ⌄ ?

* Copy To New Page Number   40   ?

* New Page Name   Sortable Single Record View

* User Interface   ◉ **Desktop** ?

Figure 11-7. *Second screen of the Page Copy wizard*

The third screen allows you to change the names of the buttons and items, which you can leave as is. The fourth screen is for specifying the navigation menu entry, which you should fill in the same as for any new page.

One concern with copying a page is to ensure that its various item references are updated. It turns out that item references within the PL/SQL code do get updated, but references within the link builder do not. Thus, the targets of the column link and the three buttons need to be updated from page 19 to page 40, as do the variables set during the redirect.

After you have successfully copied the page, you can modify it. The first modification is to add a select list to the Employees region so users can choose the sort field. This select list is named P40_SORTFIELD. Its values are defined by this static expression:

```
STATIC2:EName,Job,Sal,DeptNo
```

The presence of a changeable sort field affects two parts of the page: the source query for the report and the FindPreviousNext process, which computes the next/ previous records in single-record mode. In both cases, you need to use dynamic SQL. The report's source query is generated by the PL/SQL code of Listing 11-7.

Listing 11-7. Dynamic SQL code for the employees report

```
declare
  v_sort varchar2(20);
begin
  if :P40_SORTFIELD is null then
    v_sort := 'EName';
  else
    v_sort := :P40_SORTFIELD;
  end if;
  return 'select EmpNo, EName, Job, Sal, DeptNo ' ||
         'from EMP ' ||
         'order by ' || v_sort;
end;
```

This query uses dynamic SQL to construct the appropriate query, based on the selected sort field. If no sort field has been selected, EName is the default. Because you are using dynamic SQL, you have to set the Use Generic Column Names property to Yes and specify a column count of 5. APEX will consequently create five columns, named COL01 through COL05. Because the column headers will be the same regardless of the sort field, you can hardcode them into the PL/SQL column-header property, as follows:

```
return ':EName:Job:Sal:DeptNo';
```

The column-header string begins with a colon because the header of the first column is empty.

You also need to specify the link for the first column. Even though the column is named COL01, not EMPNO, you can still set its properties as you did in Chapter 7. In particular, select COL01 from the rendering tree and set its type to Link. Set its Link Text property to View and then click its Target property to bring up the Link Builder wizard. Here you need to set the target to page 40; you also need to set P40_EMPNO to the value of the first column. Because that column is named COL01, its value is #COL01#. See Figure 11-8.

Link Builder - Target

▼ Target

Type	Page in this application
Page	40

▼ Set Items

Name		Value	
P40_EMPNO	∧	#COL01#	∧

Figure 11-8. *Specifying the behavior of the column link*

You also need to configure the sortability of the report's columns. Recall from Chapter 3 that each column in a classic report has a property named Sortable — the value Yes means that users can choose the sort order at runtime by clicking the column header, and No turns off that feature. In a classic report using non-dynamic SQL, these values default to No when the source query has an order by-clause (in fact, you cannot set them to Yes). However, generic columns have a default sortability of Yes, so if the source query has an order by-clause, you must set the Sortable value of each column to No. (If you fail to do this, APEX will display an error message when it tries to render the report.)

You should now have a working sortable report. Test it out. Selecting a sort field should cause the report to re-render with the new sort order, and clicking the link for a row should display the Emp Info region for the selected row.

The only problem is that the Previous and Next buttons still use EName as the sort field. You need to modify the process that underlies those buttons so that it refers to P40_SORTFIELD instead of EName. This process was called FindPreviousNext in Chapter 7, and its code appeared in Listing 7-19. For reference, Listing 11-8 reprints that code.

Listing 11-8. Original Code for the FindPreviousNext Process

```
begin
  select PrevEmp, NextEmp
  into :P19_PREV, :P19_NEXT
  from (select EmpNo, lag(EmpNo)  over (order by EName) as PrevEmp,
                      lead(EmpNo) over (order by EName) as NextEmp
        from EMP)
  where EmpNo = :P19_EMPNO;
end;
```

The revised code appears in Listing 11-9. Although this code seems complex, it is essentially the original code broken into pieces and translated into dynamic SQL. The initial if-statement handles the case in which no sort field has been chosen.

Listing 11-9. Revised Code for the FindPreviousNext Process

```
declare
  v_subquery varchar2(200);
  v_query    varchar2(250);
  v_sort     varchar2(20);
begin
  if :P40_SORTFIELD is null then
    v_sort := 'EName';
  else
    v_sort := :P40_SORTFIELD;
  end if;

  v_subquery :=
    'select EmpNo, ' ||
          'lag(EmpNo)  over (order by ' || v_sort || ') as PrevEmp, ' ||
          'lead(EmpNo) over (order by ' || v_sort || ') as NextEmp ' ||
    'from EMP';

  v_query := 'select PrevEmp, NextEmp ' ||
              'from (' || v_subquery || ') ' ||
              'where EmpNo = :1';

  execute immediate v_query
  into :P40_PREV, :P40_NEXT
  using :P40_EMPNO;
end;
```

Summary

This chapter examined some situations in which it was necessary to customize the table names and column names in an SQL query. You saw how handle such situations by using dynamic SQL to construct and execute an SQL query string at runtime. In the case of customizing a report, you learned how to use the APEX report type Classic Report (based on a Function), which exists precisely for this purpose. In the case of customizing a PL/SQL process, you learned how to use its execute immediate command.

Dynamic SQL forces APEX to validate and process the query string at runtime; this additional overhead increases the time it takes to process the page. Moreover, in the next chapter you shall see that dynamic SQL can open a window for potential security breaches. Consequently, dynamic SQL should be used only of necessity. Such situations occur rarely, but it is good to know how to handle them when they do occur.

CHAPTER 12

■ ■ ■

Security

Your demo application allows everyone to have complete access to every page, which is very unusual for a web application. This chapter examines the APEX facilities for restricting access. These facilities can be divided into *authentication*, which identifies the legal users, and *authorization*, which specifies what information each legal user is allowed to see. You will also consider the issue of how to protect the data from malicious users.

Authentication

Authentication is the ability to identify the current user of the application. APEX users identify themselves by providing a username and password. APEX supports several possible *authentication schemes*, which maintain the user/password list in different ways and at different organizational levels.

Here are four common authentication schemes, in order from the most general to least general:

- *LDAP Directory scheme*: The user/password list is maintained within an organization's LDAP directory. This scheme allows an organization to assign a single account to each person to be used for all systems that it maintains. The resulting ease of administration often makes LDAP the authentication scheme of choice for many organizations.

- *Database Accounts scheme*: The user/password list is maintained within the Oracle database system. This scheme allows a user to have a single account for multiple Oracle-based systems (including APEX applications). The downside of this scheme is that users will also have direct access to the Oracle database, which might not be desirable.

- *Application Express Accounts scheme*: The user/password list is maintained within the application's workspace. The APEX administrator for a workspace manages the list for that workspace. If a person needs to access applications from different workspaces, the person needs an account for each workspace.

- *Custom scheme*: The owner of the application maintains the user/
  password list. A person will need a separate account for each such
  application. Custom schemes are often used by applications that
  allow people to create and manage their own accounts.

This book has been assuming that your demo application does not perform any
authentication. APEX considers this to be a *No Authentication* authentication scheme.

Managing Authentication Schemes

An APEX application can contain multiple authentication schemes, but only one scheme
can be current at a time. To create a scheme, go to the home page for the application, click
the Shared Components button, look for the Security section, and select Authentication
Schemes.

You are taken to a screen that lists the authentication schemes that have been
created for your application. You should have one scheme listed, which is the scheme
that you selected when you created the application (see Figure 12-1).

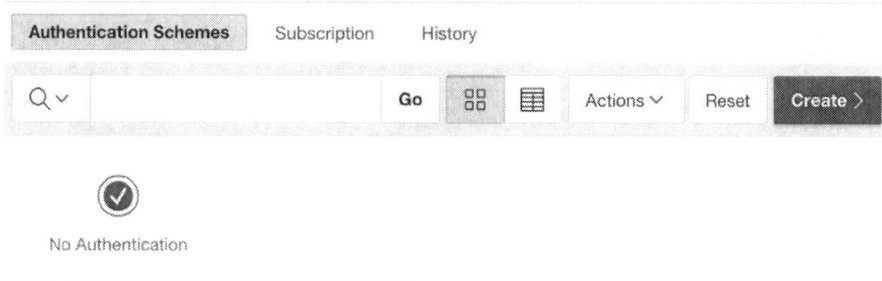

Figure 12-1. *Authentication Schemes screen*

To create other schemes, click the Create button. Select the option Based on a
pre-configured scheme from the gallery. Then give your new scheme a name,
choose a scheme type, fill in the appropriate information, and click the Create
Authentication Scheme button.

Each time you create a new authentication scheme, APEX makes it the current
scheme. If you want to switch to a different scheme, go back to the list of schemes, click
the icon corresponding to the scheme, and then click the Make Current Scheme button.
If you want to delete a scheme, make sure that it is not current, click its icon, and then
click the Delete button.

For fun, create an Application Express Accounts scheme and make it current.
When you run your application, you will be taken to a Login page (which will be
automatically created if it doesn't already exist). Entering your APEX username and
password should work, and entering random values should not work. If you are an
administrator of the workspace, you could also try creating new usernames and logging
in with them.

If you have an Oracle database account, create a `Database Accounts` scheme, make it current, and log in that way.

If you have access to an LDAP server, you can try creating an `LDAP Directory` scheme. You will need to enter the necessary configuration information into the creation screen, such as the hostname of the LDAP server and the distinguished name string. Note, however, that LDAP servers are often inside firewalls. If the APEX server runs in a different domain from the LDAP server, you might encounter firewall issues that make this scheme unworkable.

Finally, create a `Custom` authentication scheme. The creation screen will display the properties shown in Figure 12-2.

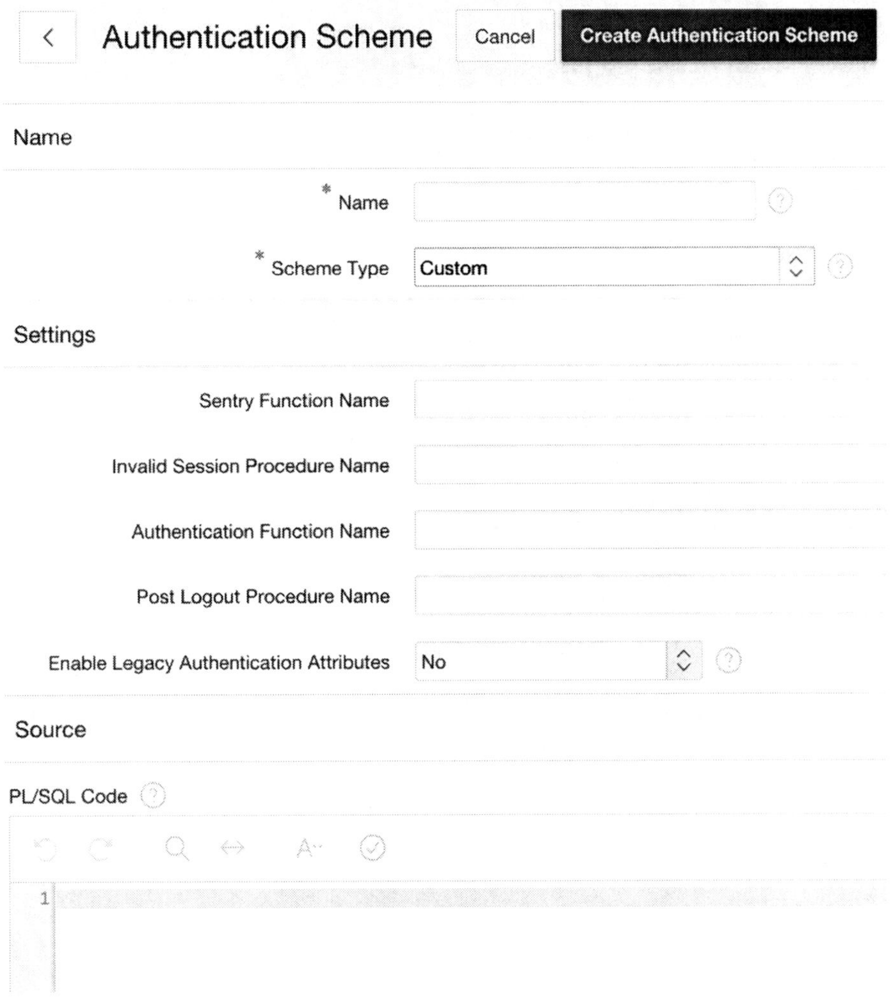

Figure 12-2. *Properties for a Custom authentication scheme*

The Settings section allows you to specify four functions, but only the Authentication Function Name property is typically used. The authentication function is called each time a login is attempted. Its return value will be true or false, indicating whether the login should succeed or not. The Settings section asks only for the name of the function; APEX expects that the function will be defined elsewhere. Typically, the function will be defined as a stored procedure in the database, but if not, the Source section provides a place for you to enter the desired code. The authentication function must have parameters named p_username and p_password. When a user submits the Login page, APEX calls the authentication function, assigning the specified username and password to those parameters.

Listing 12-1 gives the code for a simple authentication function that always returns true.

Listing 12-1. alwaysTrue Authentication Function

```
function alwaysTrue(p_username in varchar2,
                    p_password in varchar2) return boolean
is begin
  return true;
end;
```

Place this code in the Source section, set the value of the property Authentication Function Name to alwaysTrue, and finish creating the authentication scheme. When you run the application, the Login page will ask you for a username and password, but will accept anything you enter.

Writing an Authentication Function

Now that you understand how custom authentication works, it is time to implement a more useful authentication function. The following sections address three important issues: how to store the username and password information, how to manage user accounts, and how to authenticate a user.

Storing Username/Password Information

The standard way to store username/password information is to create a table; let's call this table USERS. The USERS table will have three columns: UserName, Password, and IsAdministrator. This third column indicates whether the user has administrative privileges. In addition, you should create two "built-in" users: a user ADMIN, who is an administrator with the password 1234; and a user GUEST, who is not an administrator and has a null password. These tasks can all be performed in the SQL command tool. Listing 12-2 gives the corresponding SQL statements, which should be executed individually.

Listing 12-2. SQL Statements for the USERS Table

```
create table USERS (UserName varchar2(12), Password varchar2(1000),
                    IsAdministrator char(1));

insert into USERS (UserName, Password, IsAdministrator)
values ('ADMIN',
        apex_util.get_hash(apex_t_varchar2('ADMIN','1234'), null),
        'Y');

insert into USERS (UserName, Password, IsAdministrator)
values ('GUEST',
        apex_util.get_hash(apex_t_varchar2('GUEST',null), null),
        'N');
```

The treatment of passwords requires some explanation. For security, passwords should always be stored in an encoded form, not in plaintext. Listing 12-2 uses the function apex_util.get_hash to perform the encoding. (This function was introduced in Chapter 7 and used for lost update detection.) Recall that the function takes a collection of values as input and produces a string as output. The constructor function apex_t_varchar2 creates the collection of values from its arguments. For example, the encoded password for ADMIN is the output of the hash function, given the collection {'ADMIN','1234'} as input.

The reason to use a hash function for password encoding is that it obfuscates its input value — given the output of the function, there is no practical way for someone to determine its input. So you can feel safe knowing that even if the database system were compromised (for example, if the hard drive were stolen), the intruder could not make use of the encoded password information.

Note that the hashed passwords in Listing 12-2 include the username as part of the hash value. This technique increases safety somewhat by thwarting the following attack: An intruder creates an account and then creates a sequence of passwords for it, noting the hash value of each one. The intruder can then compare these hashed passwords with the passwords stolen from the USERS table. Suppose that a match is detected. If the username is not part of the hash value, the intruder has most likely discovered a user's password. However, if the username is part of the hash value, detecting a match tells the intruder nothing.

The apex_util.get_hash function has two arguments: the first is the collection of values to be hashed, and the second argument is a Boolean value. The second argument in Listing 12-2 is null, which is treated as false. In Chapter 7, the function was called with only one argument, which implied a second argument value of true.

The second argument indicates whether the function should add the session ID to the input values. The hash value will be more secure if it includes the session ID, but it then will be of use only within the scope of that session. Because lost update detection occurs within a single session, it is reasonable to use a second argument of true, which is what occurred in Chapter 7. However, password encoding spans sessions, and a second argument of false (or null) is mandatory.

Adding User Accounts

Your demo application needs a way to add other rows to the USERS table. Figure 12-3 shows a page called Manage Users that serves this purpose; it will be page 41 of the demo application. The page has two regions: the All Users region lists the records from USERS, and the New User region lets you add a user to that table. (Note that the screenshot cuts off the password values in the All Users region to save space.)

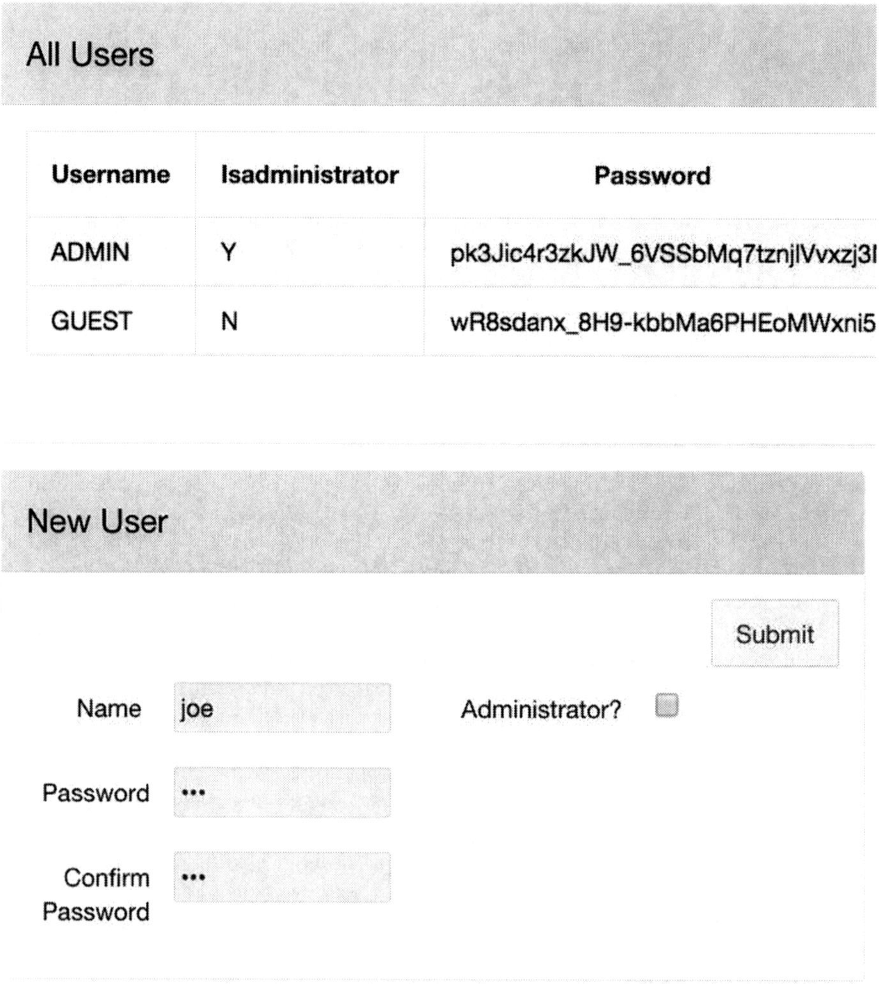

Username	Isadministrator	Password
ADMIN	Y	pk3Jic4r3zkJW_6VSSbMq7tznjlVvxzj3l
GUEST	N	wR8sdanx_8H9-kbbMa6PHEoMWxni5

All Users

New User

Submit

Name: joe   Administrator? ☐

Password: •••

Confirm Password: •••

Figure 12-3. Manage Users page of the demo application

The All Users report displays the encoded password for each user. These passwords appear in the report for demonstration purposes only. In a real application, encoded passwords should not be displayed — the values serve no useful administrative purpose, and displaying them increases the probability of their being cracked.

Figure 12-3 shows the contents of this page just prior to adding a non-administrator user named JOE having the password "joe". Although this username was entered in lowercase, it will get saved in the table in uppercase to ensure that usernames are case insensitive. And, of course, the password will be saved as an encoded string using the hash function.

When the submit button is clicked to create the new user, two validations and a process will be executed. One validation ensures that the chosen username does not already appear in the USERS table. This validation has the type is No Rows returned, and is defined by the following query:

```
select * from USERS
where Username = upper(:P41_NAME)
```

The other validation ensures that the two passwords are identical. This validation has the type SQL Expression, and is defined by the following code:

```
(:P41_PASSWORD = :P41_CONFIRM) or
(:P41_PASSWORD is null and :P41_CONFIRM is null)
```

The second line of the validation accounts for the possibility that the password can be null.

The process converts the username to uppercase, hashes the password, converts the checkbox value to Y or N, and inserts a record into the USERS table. Its code appears in Listing 12-3.

Listing 12-3. Code to Create a New User

```
declare
    v_isAdmin       char(1);
    v_username      varchar2(20) := upper(:P41_NAME);
    v_valuesToHash apex_t_varchar2 :=
                           apex_t_varchar2(v_username, :P41_PASSWORD);
begin
    if :P41_ADMIN is null then
        v_isAdmin := 'N';
    else
        v_isAdmin := 'Y';
    end if;

    insert into USERS (UserName, Password, IsAdministrator)
    values (v_username,
            apex_util.get_hash(v_valuesToHash, null),
            v_isAdmin);
end;
```

Authenticating Users

Now that you have a way to create users, you have to create a scheme to authenticate them. Return to the Authentication Schemes screen and create a new Custom scheme. The authentication function you need appears in Listing 12-4.

Listing 12-4. Custom Authentication Function

```
function custom_authentication (p_username in varchar2,
                                p_password in varchar2) return boolean
is
    v_userName      varchar2(20) := upper(p_username);
    v_valuesToHash apex_t_varchar2 :=
                                apex_t_varchar2(v_username, p_password);
    v_userCount     int;
begin
    select count(*) into v_userCount
    from USERS
    where UserName = v_userName
    and    Password = apex_util.get_hash(v_valuesToHash, null);

    return v_userCount = 1;
end;
```

The authentication function converts the provided username to uppercase to ensure that usernames are case insensitive. It then executes a query that sees whether there is a record in the USERS table having that username and encoded password. If so, it returns true.

Public Pages

Consider an application whose authentication scheme is something other than No Authentication. When an unauthenticated user attempts to access any page of the application, that user will be directed to the Login page and will not be allowed to proceed until authenticated.

An application often contains public pages that require no authentication as well as private pages that do. Each page has the property Authentication that allows you to specify whether it is public.

For example, suppose that you want the home page of the demo application to be public. Go to the property editor for the page and scroll down until you find the Security section. Its Authentication property has two values: Page Requires Authentication (the default) and Page is Public. Change the value to Page is Public and save. To test the change, log out of the application. You will find that APEX enables you to visit the application's home page, but if you try to access any other page, you will be requested to log in.

Authorization

An authentication scheme specifies which users are allowed to access the non-public pages of an application. It is a good start, but often is not sufficient. A web application can have several types of users, with certain pages (or parts of pages) appropriate only for certain types. So you need a way to specify which users can access what information. This aspect of security is called *authorization*.

APEX implements authorization by allowing each page or page component to have an associated *authorization scheme*, which specifies a set of users. If a page (or component) has an authorization scheme, it will be visible only to the users specified by that scheme.

Creating an Authorization Scheme

Recall that the built-in variable APP_USER holds the username of the current user. An APEX authorization scheme is defined by a Boolean expression, typically involving the value of APP_USER — a user is authorized when the expression returns true.

Authorization expressions are similar to validation expressions, and their types are similar. For example, the Exists SQL Query type denotes true if the query returns at least one record. The type PL/SQL function returning Boolean is PL/SQL code that explicitly returns true or false.

As an example, let's create three authorization schemes for the demo application: Administrators, which returns true if the current user is an administrator; Guests, which returns true if the current username is GUEST; and Built-in Users, which returns true for the user GUEST or ADMIN.

The Administrators scheme can be defined by the following exists query:

```
select *
from USERS
where Username = :APP_USER and IsAdministrator = 'Y'
```

The Guests scheme can be defined by the following PL/SQL function:

```
return :APP_USER = 'GUEST';
```

The Built-in Users scheme can be defined by the following PL/SQL function:

```
return :APP_USER = 'GUEST' or :APP_USER = 'ADMIN';
```

To create an authorization scheme, go to the home page for the application, click the Shared Components button, and then select Authorization Schemes from the Security section. You are taken to a screen that lists the authorization schemes that have been created for your application, which is probably empty at this point. Clicking the Create button brings up the authorization scheme wizard.

On the first wizard screen, specify that you want to create the scheme "from scratch". On the second screen, give the scheme a name, select its type, and enter the specification in the appropriate box; Figure 12-4 shows these specifications for the Administrators scheme.

Application: **87059 Employee Demo** (?)

* Name   Administrators

* Scheme Type   Exists SQL Query

* SQL Query   select *
            from USERS
            where UserName = :APP_USER and IsAdministrator = 'Y'

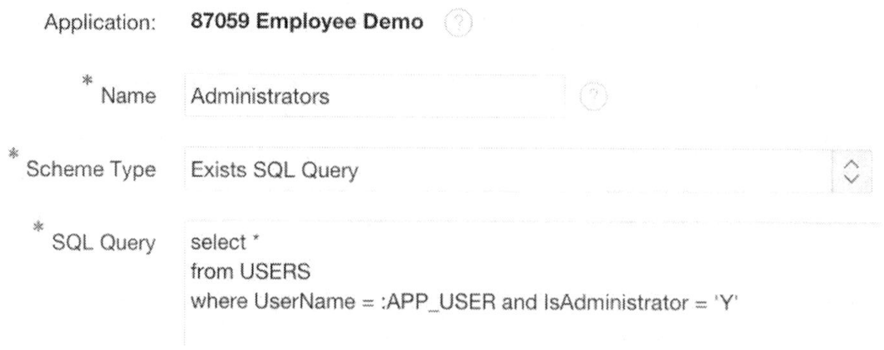

Figure 12-4. *Specifying an authorization scheme*

The second wizard screen will ask you to provide an error message (such as **Only administrators are allowed to view this page**) and to specify how often the authorization scheme should be validated. Two common choices are Once per session and Once per page view. Evaluating the scheme once per session is far more efficient and is the default. You would choose to evaluate once per page view only if the authorization condition is likely to change within the session.

For example, consider the authorization scheme defined by the following PL/SQL function:

```
return :APP_USER = 'ADMIN'
        and extract(hour from systimestamp) >= 9
        and extract(hour from systimestamp) < 17;
```

This scheme returns true only for the ADMIN user, and only between the hours of 9 am and 5 pm. If the purpose of the authorization scheme is to restrict access to those times, its evaluation point needs to be Once per page view.

Component Authorization

Every page component has a property Authorization Scheme, which appears in its Security section. You assign an authorization scheme to the component by choosing from a select list. Figure 12-5 depicts this select list for the demo application.

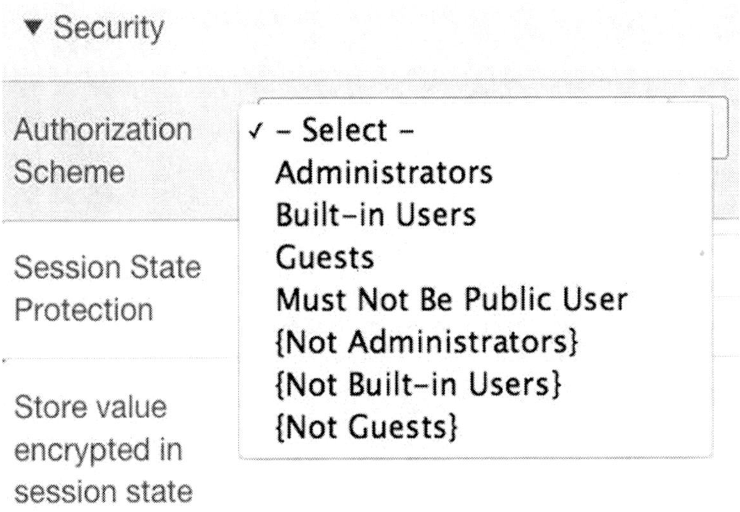

▼ Security

Authorization Scheme	✓ – Select – **Administrators** **Built–in Users** **Guests** **Must Not Be Public User** **{Not Administrators}** **{Not Built–in Users}** **{Not Guests}**
Session State Protection	
Store value encrypted in session state	

Figure 12-5. *Assigning an authorization scheme to a component*

The first option is –Select–, which denotes that no authorization is required. The next three options are the three authorization schemes you created. The last three options are the negations of these, which are automatically generated by APEX. The Must Not Be Public User scheme is built in to APEX and will be discussed later.

For an example, consider the Employee Data Entry page from Chapter 7 (refer to Figure 7-4). That page had a region to display a report of the EMP table, as well as regions to delete, insert, and update table rows. Assume that anyone can view the employee report, but guests are not allowed to modify it. In this case, you would assign the authorization scheme Not Guests to the delete, insert, and update regions; and assign –Select– to the report region. The result is that users authenticated as GUEST will see only the report region; the other three regions will be hidden from them.

For a second example, consider the Manage Users page of Figure 12-3. If you want the two regions on the page to be accessible only to administrators, assign the authorization scheme Administrators to each of them. As a result, administrators will see the page as shown in the figure; non-administrators will see a page having a navigation bar and menu, but no content.

Because displaying an essentially blank page to a user is awkward, the page ought to display something to the non-administrators. One solution is to create a region that displays the message This page is for administrators only and assign the authorization scheme Not Administrators to it. Another solution is to assign an authorization scheme to the entire page, as discussed later.

Assigning an authorization scheme to a component causes that component to be displayed or hidden, depending on the current user. This behavior is very similar to the conditional rendering that you examined in Chapter 6. So the question is this: why use component authorization at all — why not do everything using conditional rendering?

The answer is that yes, it is possible to use conditional rendering to perform authorization. If you create a condition having the same definition as the authorization scheme, the region will behave exactly the same. However, using explicit authorization is better for three reasons:

- A single authorization scheme can be used for several components.

- Each authorization scheme has a name, which makes it easier for the application developer to understand the effect of the authorization condition.

- Authorization and conditional rendering have entirely different purposes in an application, and it is clearer if they are kept separate.

Page Authorization

Instead of assigning an authorization scheme to the components of a page, you can assign it to the page itself. Each page has the property Authorization Scheme in its Security section, with the same options as in Figure 12-5.

For an example, let's build a page named Change Password, which will allow users to change their own password. This page is shown in Figure 12-6, and will be page 42 of the demo application.

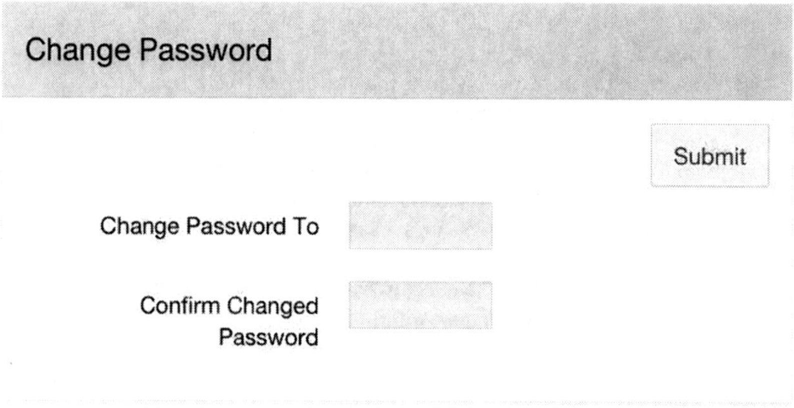

Figure 12-6. *Change Password page*

This page consists of a single region having two items of type Password: P42_PASSWORD and P42_CONFIRM. Clicking the submit button invokes a validation and a process. The validation ensures that the two entered passwords are identical, via this SQL expression:

:P42_PASSWORD = :P42_CONFIRM

The process updates the USERS table via the following PL/SQL code:

```
declare
  v_valuesToHash apex_t_varchar2 :=
                         apex_t_varchar2(:APP_USER, :P42_PASSWORD);
begin
  update USERS
  set Password = apex_util.get_hash(v_valuesToHash, null)
  where UserName = :APP_USER;
end;
```

How should this page be authorized? Assume that everyone should be allowed to change their own password except for the built-in users GUEST and ADMIN. The authorization scheme for the page should be Not Built-In Users.

Assigning an authorization scheme to a page makes it inaccessible to unauthorized users. In particular, if an unauthorized user attempts to render the page, APEX instead displays an error message. Figure 12-7 shows the error message that results when a built-in user tries to access the Change Password page. Clicking the OK button on the message returns the user to the previous page.

Not a built-in user.

Access denied by Page security check

Figure 12-7. *Result of unauthorized page access*

This error message does the job, but not very well. The error message is somewhat harsh. (In fact, the message is backward — APEX uses the error message defined for the Built-in Users scheme because the negated scheme, being automatically generated, has no error message.) A much more user-friendly approach is to simply hide the page from an unauthorized user. In the case of the Change Password page, this amounts to not displaying its navigation menu entry to an unauthorized user. Fortunately, this is easy to do because each list entry has an Authorization Scheme property.

To find the property, start at the application's Shared Components screen and navigate to the List Entry screen for the desired list entry — in this case, you want the Change Password entry of the Desktop Navigation Menu list. The property you want is in the Authorization section. Choose the Not Built-in Users authorization scheme; then log in as ADMIN or GUEST, and note that the entry for the Change Password page is missing from the navigation menu.

A good rule of thumb is this: if a page has an authorization scheme, its associated navigation menu entry should have the same authorization scheme.

Not Public User Scheme

The authorization scheme Not Public User is built into APEX. It returns true for any logged-in user and false if the user has not logged in. Its primary use is to selectively hide components on public pages.

For example, suppose that your application's home page is a public page. However, suppose that not all the page should be public; in particular, the Quick Link region should be visible only to logged-in users. This situation can be handled by setting the authorization for that region to Not Public User.

Avoiding Malicious Use

A web application's authentication and authorization schemes form a detailed specification of who is allowed to access what components of which pages. Each authenticated user has a well-defined, limited interface to the data — provided, of course, that the user accesses the pages in the intended manner.

The problem is that there are various ways for a user to subvert the intended functionality of a web application. This section focuses on three such techniques: SQL injection, cross-site scripting, and URL modification. With *SQL injection*, a user submits an SQL code fragment that masquerades as input data, and which alters the query that is processing this pretend "data." With *cross-site scripting*, a user saves a malicious JavaScript code fragment as part of a table's data value; when another user subsequently displays that value, the JavaScript code also executes. With *URL modification*, a user sends a URL to the server in a form that the server expects; however, the action requested by that URL is something that no legitimate page would ask for.

APEX has several properties to help you guard against malicious use. In fact, it is relatively straightforward to use these properties to build a tamper-proof application. To take advantage of them, however, you need to understand what the threats are and how APEX can guard against them.

SQL Injection

Recall the Report Builder demo page from Chapter 11 (refer to Figure 11-1). The intent of this page is to display a subset of either the EMP or DEPT table by entering a simple condition in the Enter Condition text area. However, it is possible for a malicious user to enter a condition that causes the page to display data from other tables in quite unintended ways. For example, Figure 12-8 shows a condition that displays the contents of the USERS table.

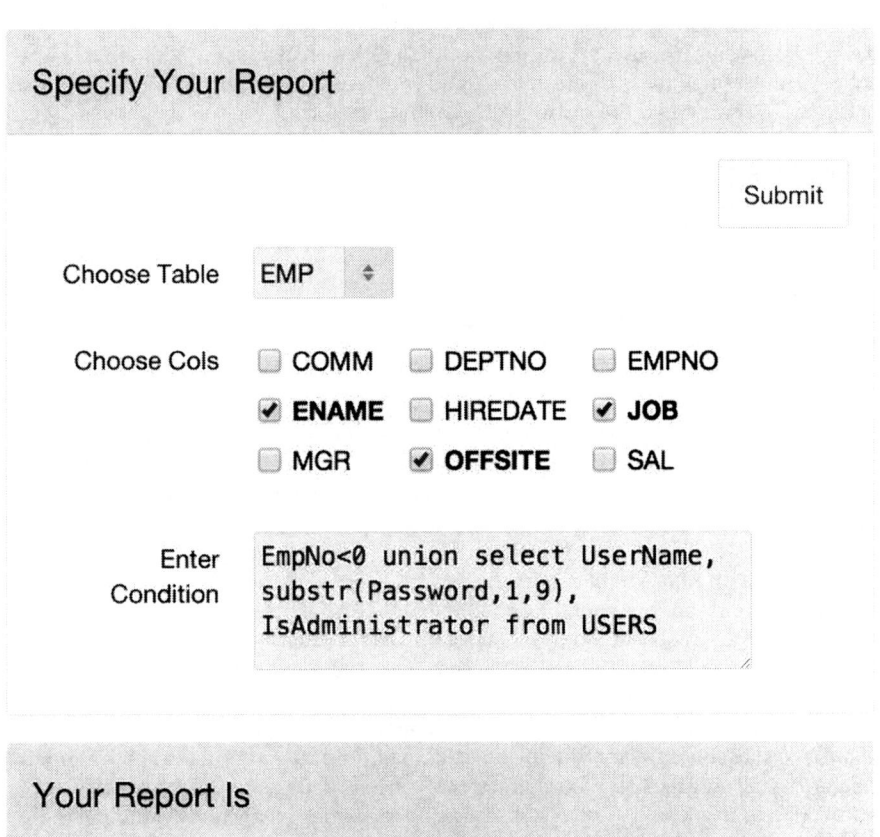

Figure 12-8. *Unintended use of the Report Builder page*

Note that the string typed into the `Enter Condition` item is not a legal SQL condition. Instead, it consists of a legal condition, `EmpNo<0`, plus some additional SQL code. To understand the purpose of the input, you have to know how the PL/SQL function of Figure 11-2 constructs the report's source query. Recall that the code generates the beginning of a query for `EMP` and then appends the specified condition to the end of it. The source query generated for Figure 12-8 becomes the following:

```
select EName, Job, Offsite
from EMP where EmpNo < 0
union
select UserName, substr(Password,1,9), IsAdministrator
from USERS
```

Note that the user has taken advantage of the `union` keyword to broaden the scope of the query. The intended query on the `EMP` table is now just a subquery of the overall query. Moreover, the condition `Emp<0` causes that subquery to return no output records, which means that the output of the overall query comes entirely from the second subquery.

This second subquery can be arbitrary, subject only to the restriction that it must have the same number of columns as the first subquery, and each output value must match the type of the corresponding column of the first subquery. This restriction explains why the second subquery extracts only the first nine characters of the password. Because the `Job` column is defined as `varchar2(9)`, attempting to select additional characters would generate an SQL error.

A malicious user might use this exploit to obtain the encoded passwords of users, in order to subsequently crack them and gain unauthorized access to the application. Of course, having only the first nine characters of the encoded passwords is not sufficient. The malicious user could, however, discover the remaining characters by running the exploit several more times, each time grabbing the next nine characters of the password.

This technique is called *SQL injection*. SQL injection occurs when a malicious user enters SQL into a text-based item to change a query from its intended purpose. The preceding example shows that SQL injection can have serious consequences. Thus, application developers must be aware of the possibility of SQL injection and avoid it at all costs.

In a sense, the `Report Builder` page was asking for trouble because the `Enter Condition` item expected SQL code. The real perniciousness of SQL injection is that it can succeed even when an item expects a value. For example, let's build a page titled `SQL Injection`, which will be page 43 of the demo application. Figure 12-9 shows an intended use of this page.

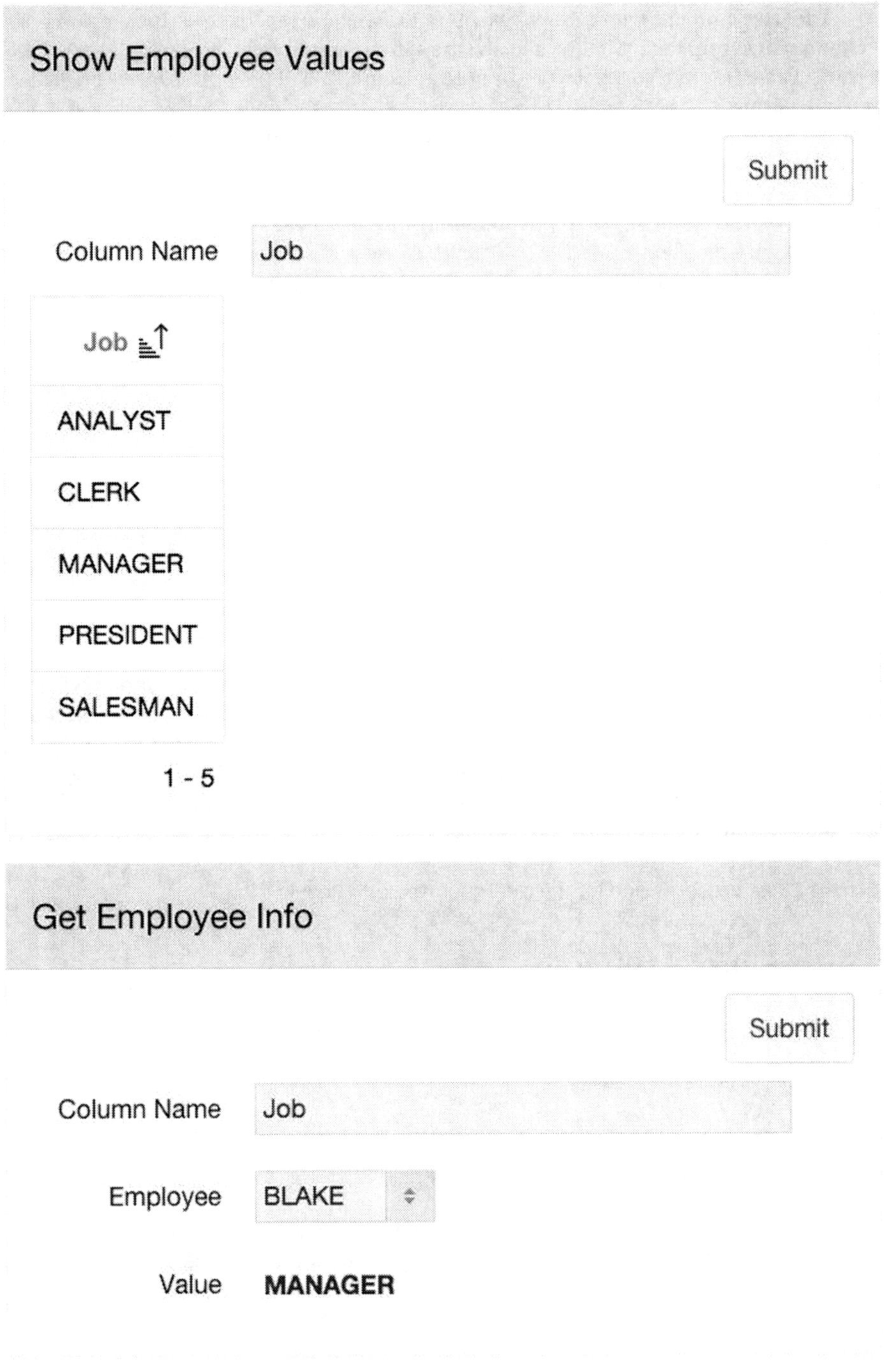

Show Employee Values

Submit

Column Name Job

Job ⬚↑
ANALYST
CLERK
MANAGER
PRESIDENT
SALESMAN

1 - 5

Get Employee Info

Submit

Column Name Job

Employee BLAKE ⬍

Value **MANAGER**

Figure 12-9. Intended use of the SQL Injection page

The page contains two regions. The input to the Show Employee Values region is a column name from the EMP table; clicking the submit button then displays a report of the distinct values for that column. For example in Figure 12-9, the report displays the five jobs appearing in the EMP table. The Get Employee Info region is similar: its input is a column name and employee number; clicking the submit button displays the value of that column for the selected employee. For example in Figure 12-9, the region tells you that Blake is a manager.

Let's first consider how to implement the Show Employee Values region. It will have a single item: a text field named P43_COLUMN1. Clearly, the region type must be a report of some sort; and because the report needs to be customized based on a column name, the type must be Classic Report (based on Function). Listing 12-5 gives the PL/SQL code for the report's source.

Listing 12-5. PL/SQL Code for the Show Employee Values Report

```
return ' select distinct ' || :P43_COLUMN1 || ' from EMP';
```

You also need to enable generic column names. Specify a column count of 1, and set the column heading type to PL/SQL Function Body having this expression:

```
return :P43_COLUMN1;
```

Now let's consider how to implement the Get Employee Info region. It has three items: P43_COLUMN2 is a text field, P43_EMPNO2 is a select list that displays employee names and returns employee numbers, and P43_VALUE2 is a display-only item. The region has a process associated with the submit button; the code for this process appears in Listing 12-6. The code first constructs a query string to retrieve the value of the specified employee; it then uses execute immediate to retrieve the specified value for the employee P43_EMPNO2 and place it in the display-only item P43_VALUE2.

Listing 12-6. Process Code for the Get Employee Info Region

```
declare
  v_query varchar2(100);
begin
  v_query := 'select' || :P43_COLUMN2 || ' from EMP where EmpNo = :1';

  execute immediate v_query
  into  :P43_VALUE2
  using :P43_EMPNO2;
end;
```

Although the regions on this page seem innocuous enough, they are vulnerable to SQL injection. Figure 12-10 shows how either region of the page can be used to display the entire encoded password of the ADMIN user. (The screenshot cuts off the encoded passwords to save space.)

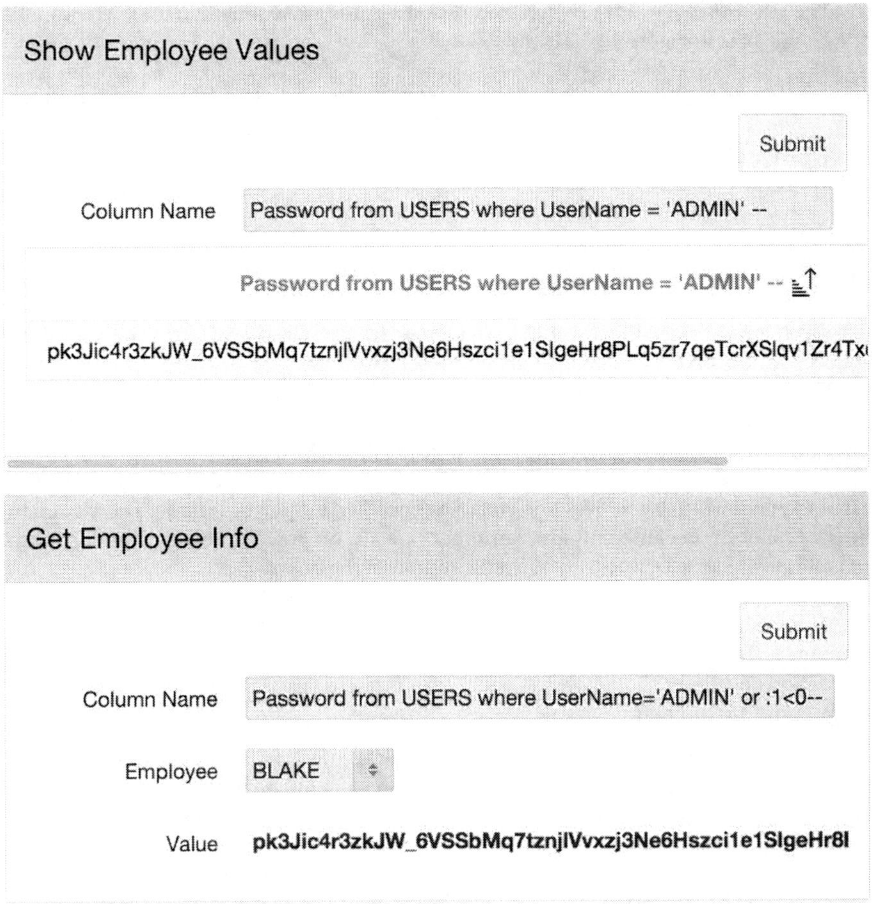

Show Employee Values

Submit

Column Name   Password from USERS where UserName = 'ADMIN' --

Password from USERS where UserName = 'ADMIN' -- ↥

pk3Jic4r3zkJW_6VSSbMq7tznjlVvxzj3Ne6Hszci1e1SlgeHr8PLq5zr7qeTcrXSlqv1Zr4Tx

Get Employee Info

Submit

Column Name   Password from USERS where UserName='ADMIN' or :1<0--

Employee   BLAKE   ⇕

Value   **pk3Jic4r3zkJW_6VSSbMq7tznjlVvxzj3Ne6Hszci1e1SlgeHr8l**

Figure 12-10. Malicious use of the SQL Injection page

The value for P43_COLUMN1 in Figure 12-10 is this:

```
Password from USERS where UserName = 'ADMIN' --
```

When APEX uses this string to construct the source of the report, it gets the following SQL query:

```
select distinct Password from USERS where UserName = 'ADMIN' -- from EMP
```

Recall that the character "`--`" denotes a comment in PL/SQL. Thus the from EMP part of the SQL code is totally ignored. In other words, the SQL injection transformed a query on the EMP table into a query on the USERS table.

The Get Employee Info region uses essentially the same injection trick. The value for P43_COLUMN2 in Figure 12-10 is the following:

```
Password from USERS where UserName = 'ADMIN' or :1 < 0 --
```

When APEX uses this string to construct the source of the report, it gets the following SQL query:

```
select Password from USERS
where UserName = 'ADMIN' or :1 < 0 --from EMP where EmpNo = :1
```

Again, everything after the comment characters is ignored, so the injection winds up creating a query on the USERS table instead of the EMP table.

Note that the malicious user must carefully craft the injected code so that the resulting SQL string is legal. Consider the Get Employee Info example. The execute immediate statement passes an employee number to the SQL query; although the malicious query will not use this value, it still needs to have a formal parameter to receive it. The expression :1<0 achieves this goal. The specified employee number is assigned to the parameter :1. Because employee numbers are always positive, this expression always evaluates to false, so it does not affect the output of the query.

In general, SQL injection is possible whenever a query string is constructed from raw, unchecked user input. In such cases, a malicious user might be able to enter a code fragment as input that changes the purpose of the constructed query. Therefore, an application developer should always check user input to ensure that it is in the intended format. Here are three strategies.

- *Avoid text-based input.* Note that the SQL injection technique of Figure 12-10 would not work if the user were forced to choose a column from a list. (Although the URL modification technique could circumvent this strategy, as you will see later.)

- *Write an APEX validation for the input that detects possible code fragments.* For example in Figure 12-10, you might refuse to accept column names that contain spaces or comment characters.

- *Translate the input into a "cleansed" form.* That is, write a function to transform a user value into an acceptable one. In Figure 12-10, the function might remove all spaces from the input or it might convert each space into the escaped HTML character .

For another example, let's see how these strategies can be used to improve the Report Builder page shown in Figure 12-8. The issue, of course, is that the text-based item Enter Condition requires the user to enter SQL code. The first strategy suggests that you try a non–text-based way to specify the condition. The Version 2 region of the Count and Delete demo page (refer to Figure 11-4 in Chapter 11) showed how this could be done, at least for simple conditions. The APEX query builder provides a more complex solution. The second strategy suggests you write a validation that rejects conditions that contain the keywords union or select, which seems particularly apropos in this case.

■ **Note** If you have never used the query builder, you should try it. Starting from the APEX SQL Workshop, click Utilities and then Query Builder. Click a table name to include it in the query, and explore.

Cross-Site Scripting

In the *cross-site scripting* technique, a malicious user saves some JavaScript code as part of a database value. The code acts like a booby-trap: when another user displays a page containing that value, the user's browser executes the JavaScript code without the user's knowledge. The JavaScript code might do things like emailing the user's session information to the attacker (thereby letting the attacker pretend to be the user) or having the APEX server execute a specified function.

What makes cross-site scripting so evil is that the victim executes the JavaScript code *with the victim's level of authorization.* So if an administrator falls prey to a cross-site scripting attack, for example, the attacker would be able to obtain administrator-level access to the database.

A successful cross-site scripting attack has three requirements: First, some table must have a column of type varchar2(n), where n is large enough to hold the JavaScript code; second, some page of the application must have a text-based item used for data entry into this field; and third, some page of the application must be configured to display the tainted value in "raw" unescaped form.

As it stands, your demo application is not susceptible to cross-site scripting because neither EMP nor DEPT have a sufficiently large column. So for the purpose of this example, you should alter the DEPT table by expanding the column Loc to varchar2(80). The required SQL is this:

```
alter table DEPT
modify Loc varchar2(80)
```

Now you can build a page to demonstrate cross-site scripting attacks. The Cross-Site Scripting page is page 44 of the demo application and is shown in Figure 12-11.

Deptno	Dname	Loc
10	ACCOUNTING	**NEW YORK**
40	OPERATIONS	**BOSTON**
20	RESEARCH	**DALLAS**
30	SALES	**CHICAGO**

1 - 4

Figure 12-11. Cross-Site Scripting page

This page has two regions. The Departments region is a classic report on the DEPT table, and the Update Location region lets a user change the location of a chosen department by using the techniques of Chapter 7. When a user selects a department from the select list P44_DEPTNO, an ARF process fetches that record from the table and places its Loc value into the item P44_LOC. The user can modify this value and click the Submit Changes button, at which point an ARP process will update the selected record.

Note that the values in the Loc column are formatted in bold. One way to format the column is to use the HTML Expression property, as discussed in Chapter 3. In particular, the value of that property for the LOC column could be this:

```
<b>#LOC#</b>
```

Another way to format the column is to generate the HTML tags from within the report's source query. In particular, you should set the source of the report to this:

```
select DeptNo, DName, '<b>' || Loc || '</b>' as Loc
from DEPT
order by DName
```

Note that the query wraps HTML tags around the department name. Although it seems to work, it doesn't (yet). If you run the page, these tags appear in the report, as shown in Figure 12-12.

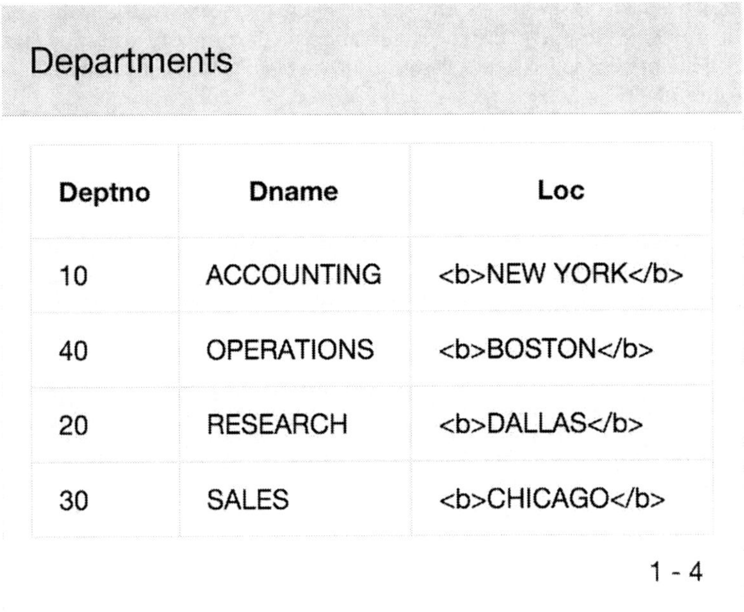

Departments

Deptno	Dname	Loc
10	ACCOUNTING	NEW YORK
40	OPERATIONS	BOSTON
20	RESEARCH	DALLAS
30	SALES	CHICAGO

1 - 4

Figure 12-12. *Report displays the HTML tags*

If you think about it, this result makes some sense — after all, the report simply displays the output of the query. However, the situation is actually more complex than that. Consider how APEX renders a report: it generates an HTML table and places the output values within it. So, for example, the HTML code to display the first row of the report would look like this:

```
<tr><td>10</td>
    <td>ACCOUNTING</td>
    <td><b>NEW YORK</b></td></tr>
```

Although the <b> and </b> tags were entered into the table as data, the browser will wind up treating them as HTML. In order for APEX to display the tags in the report, it must do extra work. In particular, it transforms the < and > characters into different characters that happen to display the same. This transformation is called *escaping the special characters*. In particular, the character < is replaced by < and the character > is replaced by >.

Each report column has the property Escape special characters in its Security section. By default, it is set to Yes, which is why APEX does all that work to display the HTML tags in Figure 12-12. Now go to the Loc column and set the property to No. The tags in the Loc values will not be escaped, and will thus be treated as HTML. The report will now look like Figure 12-11.

This ability to format data within the SQL source query is quite powerful and lets you do things that are not possible via the HTML Expression property. For example, you can choose to format certain values in a column as text, and other values as a link or an image. This power, however, comes with a price. As soon as you set a column's Escape special characters property to No, you open yourself up to a cross-site scripting attack. The help screen for this property is particularly vehement on this point; see Figure 12-13.

Escape special characters

To prevent Cross-Site Scripting (XSS) attacks, always set this attribute to **Yes**. If you need to render HTML tags stored in the page item or in the entries of a list of values, you can set this flag to **No**. In such cases, you should take additional precautions to ensure any user input to such fields are properly escaped when entered and before saving.

Figure 12-13. Help text for the Escape special characters property

To demonstrate, let's see how easy it is to use this page to compromise the application. From the Update Location region, choose any department, such as OPERATIONS. The Location field should show the current value, which is BOSTON. Change that value to this:

```
BOSTON<script>alert('Your application has been compromised')</script>
```

This new value is a string consisting of the location, followed by a script that calls the JavaScript function `alert`. When a browser renders this string, it will display "BOSTON" and then call the script. In other words, the update will have no visible effect on the report. However, the script will run each time someone renders the page.

Click the `Submit Changes` button. Before the page reloads, your browser will display an alert similar to Figure 12-14. Now navigate to a different page and come back to this one — the alert will again be displayed. It is a bit chilling to realize that without this alert, you would have had no idea that your application was already seriously compromised.

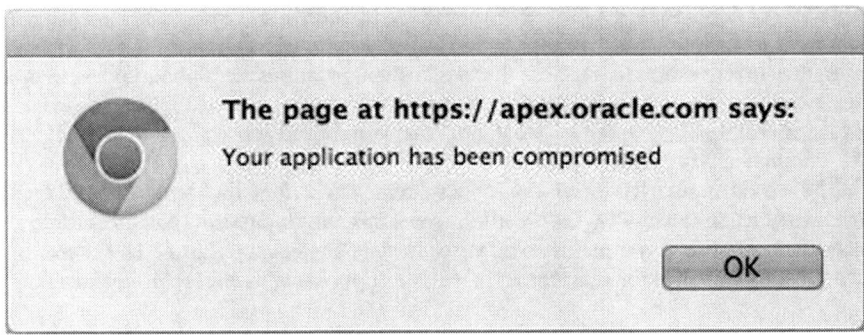

Figure 12-14. *Cross-site scripting attack succeeded*

The JavaScript code you wrote is not malicious. The `alert` function just displays an alert window in the user's browser, and functions as a wake-up call. A malicious JavaScript string will almost certainly not throw an alert and will do something far more sophisticated and nasty. In all likelihood, you will not discover the problem until it is too late. It is therefore up to you to ensure that this cannot happen.

The only way for an application to eliminate cross-site scripting is to ensure that a page does not display unescaped data. Three approaches are possible, which will be considered in turn:

- Reject inappropriate data

- Escape the data before saving it in the database

- Escape the data before it is displayed

Reject Inappropriate Data

In any data entry page, it is good practice to keep inappropriate data from being entered into the database. This is what database constraints and APEX validations are all about. The act of checking input data for unexpected HTML follows the same principle. There are two approaches you can take.

The first approach is to use the property `Restricted Characters`, found in an item's `Security` section. This property lets you specify which characters are allowed in the input. Figure 12-15 shows the possible choices. You can require that the input be only alphanumeric or you can restrict the use of certain special characters.

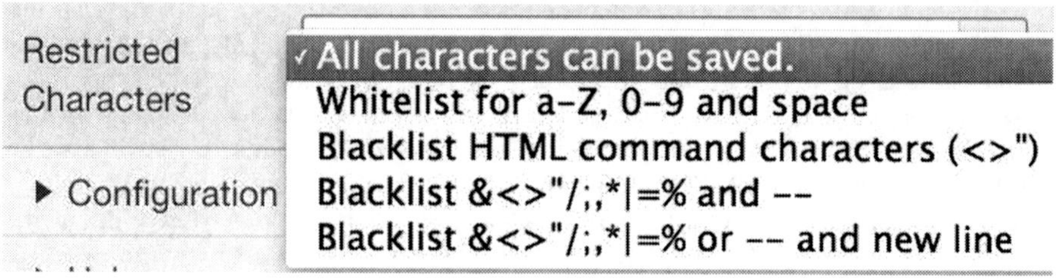

Restricted Characters

Configuration

✓ All characters can be saved.
Whitelist for a–Z, 0–9 and space
Blacklist HTML command characters (<>")
Blacklist &<>"/;,*|=% and --
Blacklist &<>"/;,*|=% or -- and new line

Figure 12-15. *Choices for the Restricted Characters property*

In the current example, suppose that department locations are alphanumeric; in that case, it would make sense to set the Restricted Characters property for P44_LOC to be Whitelist for a–Z, 0–9, and space. If not, then you should at least set it to Blacklist HTML command characters.

The second approach is to write an APEX validation to perform the restriction. APEX provides a function called APEX_ESCAPE.HTML, which takes any input string and turns it into a visibly identical string that contains no HTML characters. For example, Listing 12-7 shows the PL/SQL code for a validation that returns false if the input contains any HTML characters.

Listing 12-7. Validation to Guard Against Unwanted HTML Input

```
declare
  v_LocEscaped varchar2(100);
begin
  v_LocEscaped := APEX_ESCAPE.HTML(:P44_LOC);
  if :P44_LOC = v_LocEscaped then
    return true;
  else
    return false;
  end if;
end;
```

Escape Data Before Saving It

Instead of rejecting HTML-based input, you can instead transform it to a version without HTML characters. The APEX_ESCAPE.HTML function is useful here as well. For example, you could replace the existing process in the Update Location region by a PL/SQL process that first escapes the values before saving. The code for this process appears in Listing 12-8.

Listing 12-8. Escaping Unwanted HTML Input

```
begin
  update DEPT
  set Loc = APEX_ESCAPE.HTML(:P44_LOC)
  where DeptNo = :P44_DEPTNO;
end;
```

Escape Data Before Displaying It

An application might not be able to guarantee that the database does not contain any HTML code, because users might have other ways to enter data. So to ensure against cross-site scripting, it is a good idea to always escape the data before displaying it on a page. That is what the Escape special characters property is all about (refer to Figure 12-13). If every column in your report has this property set to Yes, your report is immune to cross-site scripting attacks.

However, if a column of your report needs this property to be No, you must escape the necessary characters. Again, the APEX_ESCAPE.HTML function is very useful. For example, Listing 12-9 gives the original source for the example report.

Listing 12-9. Original Source Query

```
select DeptNo, DName, '<b>' || Loc || '</b>' as Loc
from DEPT
order by Dname
```

Listing 12-10 shows a revised version in which the data has been escaped.

Listing 12-10. Revised Source Query

```
select DeptNo, DName, '<b>' || APEX_ESCAPE.HTML(Loc) || '</b>' as Loc
from DEPT
order by DName
```

URL Modification

To understand the third type of malicious attack, you need to consider how web applications get used. In a typical scenario, a user types the URL for the application's home page into a browser. From there, URLs are largely irrelevant; the user clicks tabs, links, and buttons to navigate to the other pages.

This scenario corresponds to the intended use of the application. The navigational links on a page are usually designed to help the user decide what pages to examine next. In fact, one criterion for measuring the quality of an application is the extent to which navigational aids contribute to a coherent user experience.

Of course, a user need not follow this scenario. If a user can figure out the URL structure of an application, the user could access an arbitrary page of the application by simply constructing a valid URL to it. This possibility presents several difficulties for APEX developers. The following sub-sections examine these difficulties and their solutions.

APEX URL Structure

APEX URLs have a specific structure. For example, the URL for my demo application's home page is apex.oracle.com/pls/apex/f?p=87059:1.

All applications on the apex.oracle.com server have the same URL prefix, up through f?p=. Following that, the URL consists of a colon-separated set of arguments. As discussed in Chapter 2, the first argument is the application's ID on that server, and the second is the page number. Other chapters introduced some of the other arguments.

An APEX URL supports nine arguments; if the value of an argument is missing, a default value is used. For an example of these arguments, consider the Employees by Department page of Chapter 6, which appears again in Figure 12-16.

Departments

Dname	Loc	Empcount	Deptno
ACCOUNTING	NEW YORK	3	Click for details
OPERATIONS	BOSTON	0	Click for details
RESEARCH	DALLAS	5	Click for details
SALES	CHICAGO	6	Click for details

1 - 4

Employee Details: RESEARCH department

Empno	Ename	Job	Sal
7876	ADAMS	CLERK	1100
7902	FORD	ANALYST	3000
7566	JONES	MANAGER	2975
7788	SCOTT	ANALYST	3000
7369	SMITH	CLERK	800

1 - 5

Figure 12-16. Employees by Department page

Recall that when you click a Click for Details link, a redirect occurs, and the page is re-rendered. Listing 12-11 shows the resulting URL from clicking the link for RESEARCH (the common prefix is omitted to save space).

Listing 12-11. URL for Employees by Department Page

```
f?p=87059:12:106255251576904::NO:RP:P12_DEPTNO,P12_DNAME:20,RESEARCH
```

The third argument of the URL is the session identifier for the request. The next three arguments are not especially relevant for you (one is blank, NO means not to enter debug mode, and RP means to reset report pagination). The seventh and eighth arguments, however, are very relevant. The seventh argument specifies a comma-separated list of item names (here, P12_DEPTNO and P12_DNAME), and the eighth specifies a list of corresponding values (here, 20 and RESEARCH).

GET vs. POST

Requests that a browser makes to a web server can be of different types. The two most common types are GET and POST, which differ in how they pass information to the server. A POST request places the information in a specific area within the request packet. A GET request, on the other hand, passes information to the server via its URL.

In APEX, POST requests are made by submit operations. To process a submit, the browser extracts the values of the page items, packages them into the POST request, and sends it to the server. The server then uses these values to change the session state. If you want to verify this, go to any page with a submit button. When you click the submit button, notice that the URL does not change. That is, the input to the computation is not reflected in the page URL, which also means that you cannot bookmark the result of a submit operation.

On the other hand, redirect operations in APEX make GET requests. Redirection can be performed by several kinds of components, such as buttons, list-based items, column links, and branches. As part of the redirection, APEX lets you assign values to specified items in the session state. For example, in the Employees by Department page, the Click for Details column link sets P12_DEPTNO and P12_DNAME to the department number and name of the current record, respectively. The browser sends this information to the server by encoding it within the URL, as shown in Listing 12-11.

Because the structure of an APEX URL is well known, it is possible for an authenticated user to construct a URL that accesses the application in a way the application developer did not intend. The following sections consider two techniques.

Page Scanning

The first technique is called *page scanning*. A user constructs a sequence of URLs to access every possible page, just to see what page (if any) shows up. The possibility of page scanning means that you cannot make a page inaccessible just by hiding it. For example, consider the Change Password page from Figure 12-6. In that section, you saw how to hide the page by assigning an authorization scheme to its navigation menu entry. Although it is a good design strategy, it doesn't make the page inaccessible because any user could access the page via this URL: apex.oracle.com/pls/apex/f?p=87059:42.

Because there is no good way to eliminate page scanning, a developer's only recourse is to use authorization to limit accessibility. In other words, the fact that page scanning is possible means that it is absolutely essential to define an authorization scheme for each page, regardless of its visibility from the navigation menu.

Item Modification

The second technique, *item modification*, can be used to attack pages that set item values via a URL. A user takes an existing legitimate URL for that page, modifies the assigned values, and submits the modified URL.

As an example, consider the Simple Table Form page from Chapter 7, which is shown again in Figure 12-17. Recall that the Choose Employee item is a select list named P22_EMPNO that performs a redirect and set value action. When employee Blake is chosen in the application, the URL for the redirect looks something like this: f?p=87059:22:106255251576904::NO::P22_EMPNO:7698.

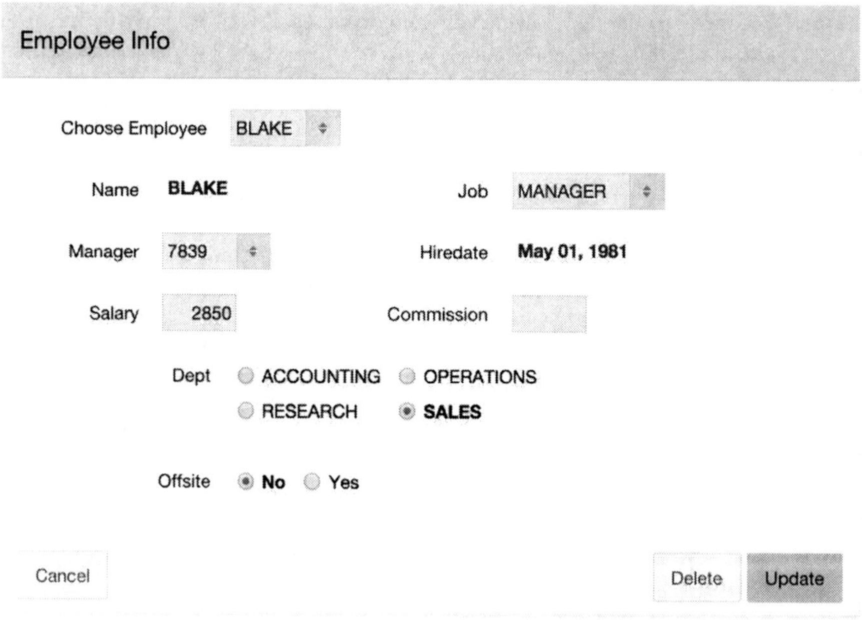

Figure 12-17. Simple Table Form page

The URL's last two arguments tell APEX that prior to rendering the page, it should set the session state value for P22_EMPNO to be 7698. During page rendering, an ARF process will use that value to retrieve an employee record from the database and assign values to the remaining items on the page.

Once I realize this, it becomes easy to modify this URL to retrieve the information for any employee. For example, if I enter the same URL into my browser, changing the last four characters to 7782, I will see the information for employee Clark.

At first glance, item modification seems like no big deal. After all, why should I go out of my way to type a value into the URL when I can use the select list to do it for me instead? The real point of this technique is that it works regardless of how the item is implemented on the page.

In Figure 12-17, P22_EMPNO is a select list that displays all employees. But suppose instead that it displays only the employees in the sales department, because the application developer wants users to see information for only those employees. It doesn't matter, because a user can bypass the select list by entering any employee number directly into the URL. Moreover, item modification will work even if the item is hidden, as in the original page generated by the form wizard (refer to Figure 7-25).

For another example of item modification, consider again the Employees by Department page. Listing 12-11 showed the URL that results from selecting the Click for details link for the research department. The situation is essentially the same as before. You can modify this URL by replacing the values 20 and RESEARCH to the values for any department, not just the departments listed in the master report.

Item modification can also be applied to pages that use submit instead of redirect. That is, you can use item modification to change the value of items that are passed via POST and don't even appear in the URL. Consider the Filter by Job and Department page of Chapter 6, which is shown again in Figure 12-18. Suppose that you choose Job and Dept values (say, CLERK and RESEARCH) from the select lists and then submit. The URL will look something like this: f?p=87059:9:106255251576904::NO:::.

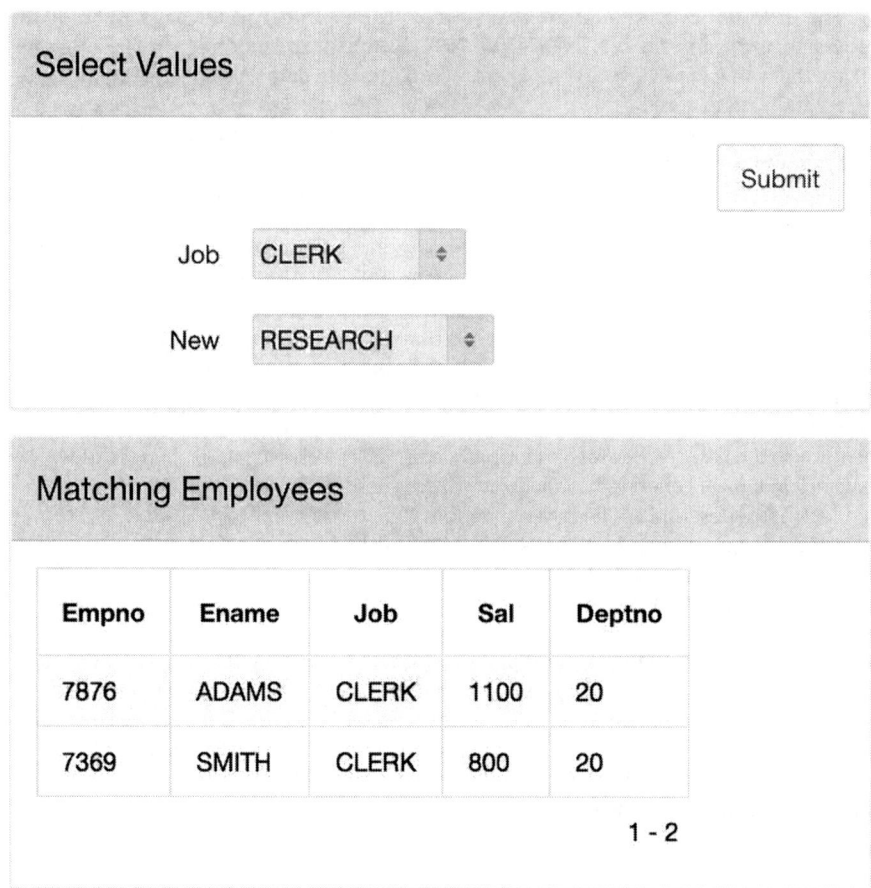

Figure 12-18. *Filter by Job and Department page*

This URL indicates that the input is being sent via a POST request. Suppose now that I modify the URL by adding item names and values to the last two arguments, as follows: f?p=87059:9:106255251576904::NO::P9_JOB,P9_DEPTNO:MANAGER,10.

APEX executes the request as follows. It first performs the submit by copying the item values from the browser to the session state; it then copies the specified values from the URL to the two specified items and renders the page. Thus, the values of P9_JOB and P9_DEPTNO that were chosen on the page will be overwritten by the values from the URL — that is, the resulting report will list the manager of the accounting department. Note again that this technique works for any valid input values, regardless of the values displayed in the select lists.

The possibility of item modification means that you cannot depend on list-based items to enforce any kind of restriction on input data. This has ramifications for SQL injection and cross-site scripting. Recall that the discussion of those techniques noted that an attacker needs a sufficiently-long text-based item for data entry, so the use of list-based items was preferred. However, an attacker can use item modification to enter the attack code directly into the URL. Thus the use of list-based items cannot provide security (and, in fact, give a false sense of security) unless there is a way to prohibit item modification.

Guarding Against Item Modification

APEX has a functionality called *page access protection*, whose sole purpose is to prevent item modification attacks. There are several levels of protection. This section will discuss only the most general-purpose one: Arguments Must Have Checksum. It works as follows.

Suppose that a page is protected at this level. If a URL for that page assigns item values, that URL must also contain a checksum for those values. When the APEX server receives a request, it extracts the argument values, computes their checksum, and compares it with the checksum within the URL; if they differ, the request is rejected.

The idea is that the checksum function is known only to APEX. When APEX generates the URL for a redirect operation, it calculates the checksum and adds it to the URL. If the user modifies the item values in any way, the existing checksum will no longer be correct; moreover, the user will have no way of knowing how to compute the correct value. Similarly, a user cannot create an item-saving URL from scratch because there is no way for the user to determine its checksum. Thus, item modification is impossible.

There are two steps to enabling page access protection for a page. The first step is to enable the application's Session State Protection property. Starting from the application's home screen, click the Edit Application Properties button and then click the Security tab. The property is in the Session State Protection section. Most likely, the property is already enabled; if not, select Enabled. The second step is to go to the page properties for the page. The Page Access Protection property is in the Security section; select the option Arguments Must Have Checksum.

As a test, set up page access protection for the Employees by Department page. Then go to the page and click the link for the research department. You should see a URL similar to this: f?p=87059:12:106255251576904::NO:RP:P12_DEPTNO,P12_DNAME:20, RESEARCH&cs=1OFzVgvoxRFQBVRnEe9Ww2QSzoVM

Note that this URL is the same as in Listing 12-11, except for the checksum information at the end. Now try to perform item modification on this URL (with or without changing the checksum value). APEX detects the modification, returning the error message shown in Figure 12-19.

Session state protection violation:
This may be caused by manual
alteration of a URL containing a
checksum or by using a link with
an incorrect or missing checksum.
If you are unsure what caused this
error, please contact the
application administrator for
assistance.

Contact your application administrator.

Figure 12-19. Detecting an attempted item modification

There is one additional complication: if you want page access protection, you will
need to enable it for every page of your application because a URL for one page can set
the items for another. For example, suppose that the Employees by Department page
(page 12) has been protected. Now consider the home page of the application, which is
page 1. Because it does not have any items, you might assume that there is no need to
require a checksum. But a clever user could issue this URL request: f?p=87059:1:106255
251576904::::P12_DEPTNO,P12_DNAME:10,ACCOUNTING.

This request sets the session state value for P12_DEPTNO and P12_DNAME before
loading the home page. The user can then navigate normally from the home page to the
Employees by Department page. If those items get their source from the current session
state value, the page will be rendered with the user-specified values. In other words, the
user will have successfully performed item modification despite your good intentions.

Summary

This chapter focused on the question of how to ensure the security of an application. It discussed how to configure the application so that each user can do only what that user should be able to do — no more and no less. There are three aspects to the security issue: authentication, authorization, and establishing safeguards.

Authentication ensures that an application knows the identity of its users. Users identify themselves by supplying a username and password; the application's authentication scheme is responsible for matching the username/password against a master list. APEX supports several authentication schemes, depending on which part of the organization manages the user/password list. You saw how to build a custom authentication scheme, in which the application itself is responsible for the list.

Authorization specifies what each identified user can do. The fundamental authorization mechanism is the authorization scheme, and each authorization scheme specifies a set of users. By associating an authorization scheme with a page (or page component), you restrict access to that page (or component) to the users specified by its authorization scheme.

Safeguards are necessary to keep users from doing things they are not authorized to do. This chapter covered three well-known techniques: SQL injection, cross-site scripting, and URL modification. In SQL injection, a user submits an SQL code fragment as "data" in a way that causes the underlying process to execute the wrong query. In cross-site scripting, a user saves a malicious JavaScript code fragment as "data"; the malicious code then executes when another user attempts to display that data. With URL modification, a user sends a URL to the APEX server in a form that the server expects; however, the action requested by that URL is something that no legitimate page would ask for. You examined ways to guard against each of these techniques. The bottom line is that if you are aware of the risks, it is relatively straightforward to ensure the complete security of your application.

Index

▒ T

▒ U, V

⟨**IOUG**⟩ *For the Complete Technology & Database Professional*
independent oracle users group

IOUG represents the **voice of Oracle technology and database professionals** - empowering you to be **more productive** in your business and career by delivering education, sharing **best practices** and providing technology direction and networking opportunities.

Context, Not Just Content

IOUG is dedicated to helping our members become an #IOUGenius by staying on the cutting-edge of Oracle technologies and industry issues through practical content, user-focused education, and invaluable networking and leadership opportunities:

- *SELECT Journal* is our quarterly publication that provides in-depth, peer-reviewed articles on industry news and best practices in Oracle technology

- Our #IOUGenius blog highlights a featured weekly topic and provides content driven by Oracle professionals and the IOUG community

- Special Interest Groups provide you the chance to collaborate with peers on the specific issues that matter to you and even take on leadership roles outside of your organization

- COLLABORATE is our once-a-year opportunity to connect with the members of not one, but three, Oracle users groups (IOUG, OAUG and Quest) as well as with the top names and faces in the Oracle community.

Who we are...

... **more than 20,000** database professionals, developers, application and infrastructure architects, business intelligence specialists and IT managers

... **a community of users** that share experiences and knowledge on issues and technologies that matter to you and your organization

Interested? Join IOUG's community of Oracle technology and database professionals at www.ioug.org/Join.

Independent Oracle Users Group | phone: (312) 245-1579 | email: membership@ioug.org
330 N. Wabash Ave., Suite 2000, Chicago, IL 60611

CPSIA information can be obtained
at www.ICGtesting.com
Printed in the USA
LVOW12s1726310716

498510LV00002B/6/P

9 781484 209905